PLANNING S
FOR
WORLD EVANGELIZATION

PLANNING STRATEGIES FOR WORLD EVANGELIZATION

By
EDWARD R. DAYTON
and
DAVID A. FRASER

WILLIAM B. EERDMANS PUBLISHING COMPANY
GRAND RAPIDS, MICHIGAN

Library of Congress Cataloging in Publication Data:

Dayton, Edward R.
  Planning strategies for world evangelization.

  Bibliography: p. 497.
  Includes indexes.
    1. Missions. 2. Evangelistic work.
  I. Fraser, David Allen, 1943– joint author.
  II. Title.
BV2061.D35   266   79-27014
ISBN 0-8028-1832-3

*To the men and women of the
Missions Advanced Research and Communication Center
without whom this book would not be possible*

CONTENTS

xvi   *Contents*

FIGURES

PREFACE

*T*his is a book about the process of evangelization, what it is and how to go about it. More specifically, it is a book about cross-cultural evangelization. One might immediately question the need for another book on this topic. Are there not enough? Should we not get to work applying what we already know? Why *this* book?

For the past fourteen years, the Missions Advanced Research and Communication Center (MARC) has been seeking to put in better focus the task of world evangelization. The founding of the Center coincided with the first modern conference on world evangelization held at Berlin in 1966. In many ways Berlin was a new beginning for evangelization. Berlin put down the biblical roots needed to regenerate the process. Since that time there has been a growing recognition of both the magnitude and the possibility of the task on the part of world Christian leaders as well as a growing number of young people. The founding of the Institute of Church Growth and its successor, the Fuller School of World Mission, by Donald McGavran opened the door to new understanding of what God was doing in his world and what he would have his Church do. The last twenty years have seen hundreds of books on the theology of mission, mission and communication theory, sociological and anthropological insights, as well as a host of specific case studies. After a period of almost forty years, during which little mission research was attempted, the academic input needed to give a balanced view of the what and the how and the why has once again found its place.

But there have been few books written on mission strategy, and none that we are aware of on how to analyze and plan a specific mission endeavor. And this is precisely what this book is all about: planning mission strategies. It is an attempt to place the entire mission enterprise within a framework that will allow both the individual and the organization to approach their task with an overall understanding. It presents a ten-step planning model that we believe can be applied to thoughts and plans for any effort of cross-cultural evangelization.

The outline of the book follows this ten-step model. At the beginning of each of these major sections are some statements which will serve as the theses of the chapters that follow. We have called these *Considerations*. In many cases they are purposely provocative. At the end of each section you will find a list of questions. We believe that questions are often more important than answers. There are already too many standard solutions and pat answers. Every situation we face is unique, and thus the answer to every situation is unique. The questions we will ask have a commonality about them; indeed, one could describe our planning model as nothing more than a series of questions that we believe should be asked at each of the ten different stages in the total process. The balance of the book could be seen as an attempt to demonstrate why those questions are important and useful.

This book is written from a Western perspective to Westerners. We do not believe that the day of Western missions is past. We do not agree that the best strategy for the church in the West is to withdraw from the world scene and first get its own house in order. Rather, we believe that part of the necessary corrective for the Western church is to capture a sense of what God wants done to see his Kingdom established, to recognize the magnitude of the task, to accept the sacrifice needed to be a part of that task, and to get on with the task in a way that honors the millions of people throughout the world who have never heard that God loves them. We believe the principles we describe are universally applicable *for planning strategies,* but since we believe that each people group needs to be respected and communicated to within the context of its culture, we speak as Westerners to Westerners.

A great deal of what we have to say is built upon the work of others. What we have tried to do is to put their thousands of hours of research and experience into a comprehensive model. Where we have failed to give them adequate credit, we apologize. Much of our work has been done within the larger fellowship of MARC. The concepts, models, surveys, studies, and publications which we have used have been discussed, dissected, and debated within that organization for over twelve years. We knew that one day the very premise on which MARC was founded—understanding God's strategy and becoming a part of it—would demand that we attempt a more exhaustive formulation. We owe much to both the staff and the Fellows of MARC.

Neither MARC nor this book would have ever been possible if it were not for the confidence and encouragement of the leadership of MARC's parent organization, World Vision International. We express our deep appreciation to World Vision's President, Stan Mooneyham, and to Executive Vice-President Ted Engstrom.

Monrovia, California
Nashville, Tennessee
July, 1979

Edward R. Dayton
David A. Fraser

INTRODUCTION

Beginnings

Perspective

Strategy

Management

Management for Mission

CHAPTER 1

Beginnings

*T*hese are great days for the Church and world Christianity. When we compare our situation with the world that William Carey faced in 1790, we have much cause to rejoice. In his beautifully descriptive book, *An Enquiry Into the Obligation of Christians to Use Means for the Conversion of the Heathen*, Carey estimated that fewer than one-third of the countries of the world had any gospel witness. Today we can confidently state that there are few if any countries in the world where there is not at least a handful of believers. Christianity has truly become the world's first universal religion. To many this has signaled an end to the Great Era of Missions and has called for a pulling back of our mission effort, particularly missions from Western nations such as North America and Great Britain.

In many countries of the world the Church has certainly come of age, and some churches now have the strength and the will to carry out the evangelization of their respective countries. In fact, the Church is growing so rapidly in some countries that outside assistance is needed from teachers and enablers, rather than leaders and initiators. It is easy to conclude that the future missionary must adopt a different stance from the pioneer of a hundred years ago. If, as we passionately believe, there is a need for men and women from one country to serve the church in another country, certainly a new type of servant attitude is required.

But an analysis which sees the world as evangelized because there is a Christian witness within every national boundary is at best faulty. First, within many of these countries there are pockets of unreached people whose culture is so different from that of the Christians living within the same country that there is little human possibility of Christians reaching those unreached without becoming cross-cultural missionaries. Second, there are still countries which have very few Christians. Conservative estimates indicate that 80 to 85 percent of the non-Christians in the world can be reached only by cross-cultural evangelism.

To understand what that means, imagine the world is a circle representing four billion people as in Figure 1-1. Now divide that circle into

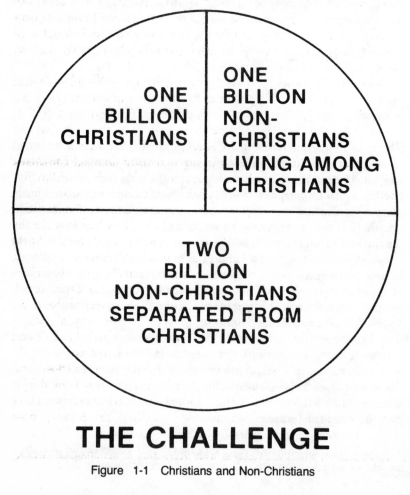

THE CHALLENGE

Figure 1-1   Christians and Non-Christians

four quarters—a billion each. One billion of those people name Jesus as Lord and declare themselves to be Christians. In two of our four quadrants there is a reasonable mixture of Christians and non-Christians. We can assume that there are enough churches in the countries or areas represented to carry out the evangelization of these non-Christians with what we call near-neighbor evangelism. If this is true, then it seems logical and appropriate that the missionaries from other countries serving in these areas should relate themselves to the churches in that country.

But the other two quadrants indicate that there are two billion more people who do not know Christ. (Two billion was the approximate population of the world in 1900.) In these countries and areas the Christians number 2 percent or less of the population. From a human viewpoint it does not appear that the few Christians and churches in these areas have the potential to reach the two billion by themselves. They need the rest of the Church to help.

During the 1970s we have been greatly helped by some missiological notations which attempt to describe the varying difficulty of the evangelistic task and our response to it. Using the notations E-0, E-1, E-2, and E-3,[1] we are better able to communicate the task that lies before us. Some members of local churches do not have a personal relationship with Jesus Christ. Insuring that these nominal Christians truly understand the evangelical message is the task of those within that church. This has been called E-0. Evangelism carried out within one's own culture, within one's own people group requires minimum training. In this setting the spontaneous witness of Christians is often the most effective evangelistic tool. Evangelism within one's own cultural group has been designated as E-1. But once one crosses a cultural boundary—a boundary of language, a boundary of class, or a boundary of ethnic difference—then the task becomes much more complicated. Here the evangelist must first understand *the people* to whom he or she is called. There are varying degrees of difficulty in cross-cultural evangelism. Situations of minimum difficulty have been designated as E-2, and situations of the greatest difficulty have been designated as E-3.

In Figure 1-1, the first quadrant may have many nominal Christians. These people require E-0 evangelism. In the second quadrant are people who are living among and sharing the same culture as Christians. These people require E-1 evangelism. But the remaining two billion, those

1. This notation, which has received wide acceptance in missiological circles, was first suggested by Dr. Ralph Winter.

with whom we are immediately concerned in this book, require E-2 through E-3 evangelism. They need to be reached across cultural barriers.

What is happening to the size of the two billion? If church membership remains the same, if by the year 2000 Christians still number 25 percent of the world's population, that two billion outside of Christ will have risen to 5.25 billion, a number greater than the total population of the world in 1980. Worse, conservative estimates indicate that no more than 10 percent, and perhaps as few as 5 percent, of all cross-cultural missionaries are attempting to reach these unreached peoples where there is no existing church. It is certainly time to rethink missions, but not in the direction of fewer pioneer or church planting missionaries, but more.

"But," some will reply, "should these missionaries be *North Americans?* Won't missionaries from the Third World countries do a much better job?" Perhaps. But there are many areas of the world where the North American will be more acceptable than someone from another Third World country or ethnic group. Also, few Third World missionaries have the resources for extensive cross-cultural evangelism.

This means three things: First, there is a need for some old and new mission agencies to *work through new strategies* to reach the two billion. Second, there is a need for some hard planning in *the area of missionary preparation.* Third, we will have to start our planning with an understanding of the *people to be reached* and focus our attention on strategies that attempt to reach them within the context of their need, rather than on the basis of preconceived means and methods. This book is based on the profound belief that God has given his Church some new insights into how to think about reaching unreached people.

WHAT DO WE MEAN BY A PEOPLE GROUP?

We tend to think of the world as made up of 220 nation-states, as defined by the United Nations. From a political viewpoint, this is very acceptable. But from the viewpoint of world evangelization, thinking of the world in these terms greatly clouds the issue. For the world is made up of thousands of groups within these national borders. It has been estimated that there are over fifteen thousand different *ethnic* groups. In addition to ethnic groups, there are occupational groups, such as taxi drivers in Seoul, Korea and whalers off the coast of South Africa. There are class and caste groups, such as the four hundred scheduled castes of India. There are people who share common situations, such as the refugees from Vietnam. And the list can go on and on.

Each of these groups has a particular need, and the gospel message needs to be communicated in a way that meets that particular need. Rather than think about 220 nations we need to think about twenty to thirty thousand groups of unreached people.

At first glance this may make the task seem almost insurmountable. But as we will discuss in chapter 5, the great advantage of thinking of the world as people groups is the notion that each group has the ability to evangelize itself. Once the gospel has taken hold, once a church is planted within this group, the potential for the gospel spreading through the whole group lies within the group. If, for example, there are twenty-five thousand people groups in the world that need a gospel witness, and if four cross-cultural missionaries from outside the group are needed to reach them, then only 100,000 missionaries are needed. The task no longer appears overwhelming. The number of people who must come to know Christ in order to put the *process* of evangelization in motion is much smaller than the three billion who do not now acknowledge Christ as Lord.

A COMPREHENSIVE APPROACH IS NEEDED

It is the thesis of this book that in the same way that every individual is unique before God, so every people group is unique before God. This uniqueness indicates that there are no universal *means and methods* of evangelism. Each group must be seen in a special context, with its special needs and special abilities. If this thesis is accepted, it then follows that the only place to begin the evangelization of any people is with the people themselves. This is the basis of our strategy for evangelism. Followed to its logical conclusion, it gives the cross-cultural missionary in a field situation a comprehensive way to approach any unreached people. We will maintain that the approach described in this book is universally adaptable regardless of the culture of the missionary or the culture of the people being reached.

Over and over we will have to restate that this is an *approach to thinking*, rather than doing. When people think about strategies, they naturally think about means and methods. We would like to take a step back from means and methods and begin to view these unreached people as people whom God loves, a people worthy of all of our time and energy.

This approach, which we have called "planning strategies for evangelism," has grown out of the work of the Missions Advanced Research and Communications Center since its inception in 1966. It has been extensively tested in different field situations since 1973. It was first formalized in a report to the Lausanne Consultation on World Evangelization in 1974. Since then the field workbook, *Planning Strategies for Evangelism* (Dayton, 1978a), has been extensively revised and has been both linguistically and culturally translated. It has become a basic working document of the Strategy Working Group of the Lausanne Committee for World Evangelization.[2]

In its simplest sense, this present book intends to undergird *Planning Strategies for Evangelism,* to give the cross-cultural missionary the understanding needed to discover, describe, and reach an unreached people, and to see Christ's Church planted among them. It is both a working text and a reference book. It attempts to lead the reader through steps to *planning* and evaluating what has been done.

At the same time this book is an attempt to bring the task of cross-cultural mission into a comprehensive whole. It is the confluence of a number of different streams. There is the stream of church growth promulgated by Dr. Donald McGavran and the School of World Mission of Fuller Theological Seminary since the mid-1960s. There is the stream of communication theory from places such as the Wheaton Graduate School. There is the stream of social anthropology exemplified by the "Willowbank Report" of 1978. There is the stream of evangelical consultations on evangelism that have been held worldwide, and the biblical foundations that were laid in Berlin in 1966 and built upon in Lausanne in 1974. There is the stream of the work of MARC, which has been attempting to classify and identify people groups since its founding in 1966. Finally there is the stream of modern systems analysis and the adaptation of new psychological and sociological insights into the management of the human enterprise.

The day of the Western missionary is not fading from the scene, nor is the need for well-trained, culturally sensitive men and women who are willing to share the Good News of salvation in a foreign culture. If we are to give the same attention to the two billion as we do to the one billion, we need seventy-two thousand more cross-cultural missionaries in 1980.

God calls us to contemplate the kind of world that he desires for the future and to follow the precepts of his Word and the leading of his Spirit into that future. Let us begin.

---

2. At this writing *Planning Strategies for Evangelism* was in its sixth edition, and the seventh edition was being planned.

CHAPTER 2

Perspective

*T*he experience of the last fifteen years has taught us that there is a great deal of resistance to the idea of *planning* strategies for evangelism. Many people find it difficult to believe that the insights of the so-called secular world are applicable to the missionary task of the Church. Evidently this concern for what appears to many to be humanistic attempts to carry out God's business is rather cyclical. Most of us have forgotten the huge amount of research and planning that typified the missionary enterprise in the late nineteenth and early twentieth centuries. Indeed, the research that was gathered for the Edinburgh Conference in 1910 was so vast that at last report it was still uncollated in the Missionary Research Library of the Union Theological Seminary in New York. Few people today are aware of the level of research that typified the missionary enterprise from 1890 to the early 1920s. We tend to believe that statistical summaries, analyses of population mix, studies on how to reach particular ethnic groups, and extensive mapping of the missionary enterprise are either new discoveries or applications of secular methodology. One has only to browse through the research section of a missions library to discover that we have yet to equal the depth of inquiry that typified this thirty-year period.[1] One can

1. An excellent example of this is the American edition of the World Survey (Interchurch World Movement, 1920). One finds in the Table of Contents that

9

trace the demise of the interest in research and planning from its peak in 1910 to the issuance of the last missionary atlas in 1924. It has taken almost twenty years since Donald McGavran's early attempts to make the social sciences respectable within the Christian community to a day when many agencies are discovering that it is only in thinking about the future that they can follow God's will.

In order to put this book in proper perspective, we need to look first at the whole idea of the future and how we think about it. To some readers this may seem like a diversion. If you are comfortable with the idea of *planning* for mission, move on to chapter 3.

THE FUTURE LIES IN THE FUTURE

Although a wise person once observed that "there is nothing new under the sun," there is a growing realization that the future of our planet is going to be radically different from the past. The idea of the future and what it will be like is an important concept.

History is a summation of significant events. Time is marked off by a series of events such as the rising of the sun.[2] The amount of history that is being compressed into time is rising significantly. Obviously there is an increase in the number of people. There is also an increase in our technological capacity, and our ability to communicate is rising rapidly. As more events occur and become important to us, they in turn create new events and new history.

While all of this is happening, our thoughts about the future are based upon our perceptions of the past. For centuries humanity has forecast the future on the basis of past experience. Most of us are fairly confident that the sun will rise tomorrow morning as it has risen every morning since the dawn of creation. In former history it was easy to believe that *all* of life was governed by the past.

But with the compression of history by an increasing number of events in a shorter period of time, it has become more and more difficult to predict the future on the basis of the past. Or, to put it another way, we have less and less time in which to make decisions about the future.

---

thought had been given to all kinds of means and methods. Statistics on the entire Christian movement within the United States had been plotted. Analysis has been made of all types of people groups including new Americans, Negroes, Spanish-speaking Americans, Native Americans, and a number of others.
2. For an interesting and thorough discussion on the whole concept of time, see *The Future of Time* (Yaker, et al., 1971).

The impact of this increasingly complex future has been termed "future shock,"[3] and people respond to it in various ways. Some respond by not thinking about the future at all, and they do no planning. Such a response implies a theology weighted toward the sovereignty of God. After all, if God knows everything that is going to happen, there is no sense in our worrying about it, for there is nothing we can do to change it.

Others respond to this increasingly complex future by doing some planning. "We'll plan as far as we can, then leave the rest to God." This approach implies a dichotomous view of the man/God relationship. It makes no attempt to acknowledge the paradox of God's sovereignty and man's freedom.

A third response is to plan a complete future. "All of the future lies in our hands. We are completely responsible for it." Such a view can be either a denial of the sovereignty of God or a mature acceptance of the paradox, as we will see below.

Another approach is one of planning little things. "We'll leave the big ones up to God." This implies a limited view of the impact we can make as individuals.

Finally there is the response that might be called planning in paradox. Here Christians take thought about (plan) everything, yet at the same time assume that God is at work in everything. How one thinks about the future has a great deal to do with how one thinks about evangelization.

A THEOLOGY OF THE FUTURE

Christians have a straight-line view of history. We believe that there is a culmination, a blessed hope that lies ahead. We do believe that God holds us responsible for the future in terms of our individual lives and our response toward others. When Paul deals with ethics in the twelfth chapter of Romans, he is talking not about how we should live our lives in the past, but about how we should live our lives in the future. The Bible holds us responsible for how we will act in the society of which we are a part.

3. Alvin Toffler (1970) was probably the prophet of future shock in the early 1970s with his book by the same name. Other futurists, such as Herman Kahn, had a profound impact on the future just because they discussed it. Kahn and Wiener's book, *The Year 2000* (1967) was credited with having a major impact on the policy of the government of Brazil because of the predictions it made about that country.

The Bible also describes how God continually renews the individual. Past errors are forgotten and forgiven: "as far as the east is from the west, so far has he separated our iniquities from us" (Ps. 103:12). To us this implies that in "God-thinking" only the positives are considered for the future. Yet even while affirming how God makes all things new, the Bible paradoxically describes how both the good and bad results of the past will be present in the future. There are "laws" at work. We understand, also, that God's grace sometimes interferes with these laws, and that humans plan and act within the environment of God's grace and God's sovereignty. Therefore any statement about what will happen in the future is a *statement of faith.* A goal is a statement of faith, and plans are statements of faith.

We are called upon to make such statements of faith—to set goals, and to predict tomorrow's outcomes. Our goals and plans (statements of faith) should be based upon what we believe God is saying through his word about the future. They should be based upon our biblical understanding of the kind of world God desires, and upon what we believe we should do corporately to respond to God's will for the future. To make no statements about tomorrow is to exhibit no faith.

Since all statements about tomorrow are statements of faith, a Christian response to the future ought to begin with what we imagine is the kind of future God desires for mankind. (We will say more about this in detail below.) Once we understand what God desires for the future of mankind, then we are responsible for taking both individual and corporate action that will move mankind toward that future. This should cause us to make individual statements (or goals and plans) about what we, in faith, believe the future should be like, and what we and others should do about it. And even as we make these statements, we need to be ready to modify them as we acquire new understanding. As the writer of Proverbs says, "A man's mind plans his way, but the Lord directs his steps" (Prov. 16:9). All of this requires us to live in the tension of paradox: God is sovereign; mankind is free and responsible.

We can no longer survive as mankind, nor can we make biblical responses to the will of God, by extrapolating the past to predict the future and our responses within it. We do not reject the lessons of the past nor the continuing revelation of God to his Church. We stand in continuity with it.[4] But history has become so compressed that we no

---

4. Robert E. Webber, in his book *Common Roots* (1978), has done an excellent job of describing what happens when as evangelicals we detach ourselves from history.

longer have an adequate historical base for projection. Meanwhile our organizational stability works against us, rather than for us. As organizations settle down into "the way we do things," they too get trapped into functional obsolescence.

We have moved from an era of little or no change into an era of rapid change, and now we are moving into an era of accelerated change. If we can learn to think about the world and world evangelization in terms of what we believe the future should be, it will reduce the degree of future shock. At the same time, if we can have a better understanding of each other's plans, we can feel more comfortable about fitting into them.

In short, we need to manage the present in terms of the future. The only decisions we can really make are decisions about the present, and since all decisions about the present are the building blocks of the future, they are more likely to be correct if they are made in light of a desirable future. This forces us in effect to attempt to write future history. So we say with the apostle Paul, "forgetting what lies behind, we press on to the goal of the upward call in Christ Jesus" (Phil. 3:14).

THE IMPORTANCE OF THE FUTURE

The idea of the future is not only important for our personal application and our own view of our mission, but it is also important for those we are trying to reach. Traditional societies have a very large history or past, a very short present, and usually no concept of the future. It is assumed that tomorrow will be like yesterday. Any ideas of the future are seen as an extrapolation of the past. The tools needed to cope with the future are already learned and at hand. One can observe one's father and mother, as well as the society in which one lives, and confidently find all that is needed to live an effective life.

Modern societies operate from an entirely different perspective. Inherent in the idea of modernization is the idea of change. Things will be better, and therefore different, tomorrow. The impact of technology and its accompanying modernization has been well documented (Ellul, 1964).

The idea of the future is ingrained in the Western mind from birth. People in the West know that they must plan for tomorrow. They carry a diary or datebook. They plan to meet a person on the twentieth of the following month at 2:00 p.m., and in all probability they will meet this person. Husbands and wives plan for their children. But as Peter Berger points out in *The Homeless Mind* (1974), planning for one's children is a new idea in history.[5] One hundred years ago most children in Western families died. Today most children live. Two hundred years ago most children grew up to have the same vocation as their mother or father.

Today we in the West plan for our retirement, and our everyday church life is full of future plans. Even if we have not identified the process that we go through, almost every Westerner sets goals for the future and modifies his or her life in light of those goals. In addition, the Westerner is less and less surprised by the future because the marvels of technology have become commonplace. The future is no longer a question of "if" but rather a question of "when?"

The impact of this change and its gathering momentum completely bewilder members of traditional societies. The old methods of coping are no longer adequate, and quite surprisingly (for the Western mind) the idea that one can imagine one's future and plan for it is foreign to emerging and developing peoples. Time and time again when we have presented this idea of setting goals and making plans within Third World countries, people have responded, "Why didn't anyone tell us about this before? Of course, this is the way to handle the future. Have you been keeping this a secret from us?"

As we move ahead in this book and lay out the whole idea of attempting to imagine God's desirable future and designing plans to bring about that future, this idea of our future lying in the future will become more and more significant.

5. For a recent discussion on the impact of modernization on American culture, see Lasch, *Culture of Narcissism* (1979). See also the works of Peter Berger, such as *Pyramids of Sacrifice* (1974), and Peter Berger and others in *The Homeless Mind* (1973).

CHAPTER 3

Strategy

*W*e have said that this book is about strategies, strategies for evangelism. It is designed to help Christians at all levels discover God's strategy for them personally, for their organization, and for the work to which God has called them. More specifically it is a book which attempts to help us develop strategies for reaching unreached people around the world.

But what do we mean by "strategy"?

> Strategy differs from tactics. One has to do with the general plan of a campaign and the principles on which it is based; the other deals with the carrying out of the plan in its details, the various instrumentalities, agencies, and methods which are thought necessary to arrive at the aim which has been chosen. Tactics must be the constant study of those responsible for the conduct of the missionary enterprise. It is indispensable, but quite different from the study of the principles on which the world mission is built, the rationale of the enterprise as a whole. (Soper, 1943, p. 235)

In one sense everyone and every organization has a strategy or strategies, a way of approaching a problem or achieving a goal. Most organizations do this quite unconsciously, others have developed their strategies into almost standard approaches. The apostle Paul had a

15

strategy. We read in Acts 17:2 that on the Sabbath Paul went into the synagogue *as was his custom*. Paul's strategy was to move to a major city, visit the synagogue if there was one, proclaim Jesus, and then let events take their natural course.

A strategy is an overall approach, plan, or way of describing how we will go about reaching our goal or solving our problem. It is not concerned with details. Paul's ultimate goal was that Christ should be preached throughout the world. His day-to-day plans would differ, but at least in the beginning of his missionary journeys, his strategy remained the same.

Unfortunately, strategy means different things to different people. It was originally used as a military term meaning an overall approach unlike the detailed approach of "tactics." In a military sense, both strategy and tactics mean "how one goes about things" rather than the idea of plans. This should not surprise us since the military strategist always has to assume that there is another military strategist trying to imagine his opponent's strategy. In other words, the military strategist has to take into account the many possible moves of his opponent. Thus his strategy has to include many options. However, although strategy can include a wide range of "means and methods," "contingency plans," and various "operations," it can also exclude a wide range of options. It has a great deal to say about what will *not* be done.

Strategy is a way to reach an objective, a time and place when things will be different than they are now. For the military it might be capturing a key town or city. For the businessperson it might mean achieving a desired volume in a particular market. For a Christian organization it may mean everything from deciding what country to serve in to the overall approach to reaching a particular group of people.

Strategy, then, has a much broader scope than long-range or major plans.

WHY HAVE A STRATEGY?

As Christians, a strategy forces us to seek the mind of God and the will of the Holy Spirit. What does God desire? How can we conform to the future that he desires?

Strategy is an attempt to anticipate the future. Strategy, like plans and goals, is our *statement of faith* as to what we believe the future should be like and how we should go about reaching that future.

Strategy is a way of communicating our intention to others. It helps us to communicate with one another within our own organization as well as with other Christians, organizations, and churches.

Strategy gives us an overall sense of direction and cohesiveness. It also helps us in deciding what we will *not* do, for it excludes certain ways of doing things. For example, on a world-wide basis, we might decide to work primarily with people who are very receptive. This excludes for the moment all non-receptive people.

TYPES OF STRATEGIES

There are many different approaches to strategies. We will discuss four: The Standard Solution Strategy, The Being-in-the-Way Strategy, The Plan-So-Far Strategy, and The Unique Solution Strategy.

The Standard Solution Strategy works out a particular way of doing things, then uses this same approach in every situation. An example would be the approach of World Literature Crusade (also known as the Every Home Crusade) which attempts to put a piece of Christian literature in the hands of people in every home in every city in the world. Members of this crusade assume that everyone can read, and that everyone can make a decision for Christ if they are exposed to the right kind of literature.

The use of the "Four Spiritual Laws" is another example of a standard strategy at one level, while Campus Crusade's "Here's Life . . . " campaign in different cities around the world during the 1970s is an example of the larger standardized strategy. Again the assumption is made that what will be effective at one place will be effective in another.

Evangelism-In-Depth, which was first begun in Latin America, is an example of a standard country-wide strategy which was used in a number of different countries in Latin America. It was eventually adapted for Africa as New Life for All.

The problem with the Standard Solution Strategy is, first, that there is a tendency not to take into account what others are doing. Because this strategy has a standard solution, it assumes that the problems are standard. Second, a standard strategy usually assumes that everyone will participate and understand what the strategy is. Obviously this does not always work. Third, a standard strategy usually grows out of one culture and has more and more difficulty as it moves into new contexts.

The Being-in-the-Way Strategy at first appears to be no strategy at all. People who adopt this strategy believe that it is not necessary to plan. They have no specific intentions about the future. They assume that

God will lead. The implications of this strategy are that long-range planning is not very important because this is God's job. This strategy also eliminates failure because that is God's problem. Many times it labels everything it accomplishes as "success." It also runs into the problem of consensus; if two or more people or organizations are each using a Being-in-the-Way Strategy, they may be in *each other's* way. This strategy is usually adopted when emphasis is placed on the basic need for a deeper personal spirituality. It is assumed that if this deeper spirituality occurs, evangelism will take care of itself.

There is much to be said for this strategy. One could point to the evangelist Philip in the book of Acts who was certainly led by the Lord into new situations. In the early days of the faith missions, particularly the inland missions, such as the China Inland Mission, the Africa Inland Mission, and the Sudan Interior Mission, missionaries courageously took the gospel into unknown continents. They knew that they had a goal. They often did not know what they were going to encounter. Often it was disease and death. We need to honor these earlier missionaries who laid the foundations for modern-day missionary journeys.

A third strategy is the Plan-So-Far Strategy. This assumes that we will plan to begin the work, and God will do the rest. This strategy does not focus on outcomes, but on beginnings. It assumes that "once we're there," God will do the rest. An example would be the agency that after negotiations with a local government received permission to begin a craft industry in a country. However, the agency made no specific plans as to how it would relate to the Christian churches that were already in the country, churches that in their view were a mixture of Christianity and animism. .

At first glance it would appear that the Plan-So-Far Strategy, as well as the Being-in-the-Way Strategy, requires greater faith. Deeper reflection will reveal, however, that it takes considerably more faith to understand what God wants to happen in a particular situation and to make a commitment to bring about what one believes God intends.

The Unique Solution Strategy assumes that every situation we face is different, that each one requires its own special strategy. It assumes that we can find a way, that there is an answer. It assumes that we should make statements of faith (set goals) about the future. It assumes that standard solutions probably will not work. This book is about how one discovers Unique Solution Strategies. We believe that there are some approaches that can be used to discover God's strategy for each unique situation.

THE CHRISTIAN ADVANTAGE

As Christians we have a tremendous advantage in considering strategy. Because we have the word of God, a source of ultimate values and absolutes, we can most appropriately develop grand strategies. God has ordained the means as well as those who will be saved. We can rest in the confidence that God's will will be done. Our role is to cooperate with him in bringing his Kingdom to fruition.

IS OUR STRATEGY "WESTERN"?

If you are new to this idea of strategy, you may logically ask the question, "Isn't all this just a Western technological approach? Aren't we trying to use modern human methods to do God's work?" This is a valid question. It is one that needs to be asked about *any* approach that one takes. We are continually torn between those ideas which come from our human wisdom and those which come from "the wisdom from above."

The first answer to our question is that the use of strategies is not a modern invention. Strategies are as old as the one that Joshua employed in his capture of the city of Ai. Almost every time we have an ultimate goal in mind, whether it be the capture of a city or the conversion of a people, we consciously or subconsciously have a strategy in mind.

And yet in the more refined sense of an overall approach (which we advocate in this book), strategies are the result of Western thinking and the technological age. The Western or Judeo-Christian way of thinking is different from that of many other societies. As we stated before, Christians have a straight-line view of history. Because we are a literate society, we think linearly, one concept after another. The ten-step approach we will recommend for developing a strategy is a product of linear thinking. (Again, we remind you that we are talking about a way of *thinking* rather than acting.) Implicit in our approach is the idea of long-range planning, which we will discuss below. Such attempts to predict and, to some degree, control the future are indeed the products of today's society. But this is the society in which God has placed us. The Bible is *written* revelation, "line upon line, precept upon precept." We in the West are biased toward Western ways of thinking. Such thinking is useful to other societies only to the extent that it can be translated into the culture of that society.

ARE STRATEGIES PERMANENT?

To a large degree we have already answered this question in our discussion above about the Standard Solution Strategy. But, as we will explain later, we think no strategy is permanent. Strategies, like plans, are roadmaps toward the future. They can be revised as we gain new experience or better understand the will of God. They are nothing more than tools that God can use to make us more effective servants.

WHAT HAPPENS WHEN THERE IS NO STRATEGY?

All over the world we have visited missionaries who seem to be in the business of doing, rather than getting things done. They appear not to have any strategy as to why they are there and what God intends to do because they are there. When asked for their goals and purposes, they give answers which sound fine, such as "to bring the Word to this people." One mission executive expressed his goal as "laying Japan at the feet of Christ." These are noble sentiments. But time and time again we found that these sentiments were not supported by well-thought-through ideas as to *how* this was to be accomplished or *when* it was to be accomplished.

Others have shared our same experience. Gordon MacDonald, a pastor on the East Coast, wrote a paper to his missionary friends after returning from one visit to a mission field, and we think he makes several excellent points.[1]

It is absolutely essential that each field have a strategy statement which covers both its long- and short-range plan of attack. Failure to develop such a statement leaves the home board, the director, the supporters, and most of all, the missionaries in doubt as to the objectives of their tasks and use of time.

1. A strategy statement enables a board to evaluate the thrust of the mission's work periodically and determine the quality of work being accomplished.

2. A strategy statement enables the board to make intelligent evaluations of requests and activity changes which various personnel endeavor to make.

3. A strategy statement enables the board to be of assistance in terms of recruiting further personnel and financial support.

1. This paper was first published by MARC with the title "Reflections on Mission Strategy" (1974).

4. A strategy statement enables the board to answer responsibly to the constituency as to the progress of the work on any given field.

5. A strategy statement makes clear to any potential candidate the type of work being done, where he can fit into the picture, and the route he must follow to qualify as a senior missionary.

6. A strategy statement enables the missionary to know just how he fits into the overall picture of the field's objectives.

7. A strategy statement enables the missionary to follow a pre-planned series of actions and activities over a number of years on the field. He or she is never without understanding as to how his or her work should be done.

8. A strategy statement brings the entire field conference together as a team. It helps avoid personality conflicts and the dominance of certain personalities when various activities are brought up for review. Like a constitution, the strategy becomes a final court of appeal for each activity a missionary hopes to engage in.

9. A strategy statement gives the conference a sense of meaning and purpose. It identifies each missionary according to his or her worth to the conference and his or her place in the overall structure.

A strategy statement is a plan for the evangelization of a given area. It defines the activity to be done, the area in which it is to be accomplished, and the methods to be employed. Beyond that, it defines the lines of authority and the relationships between the field conference and the home board. The statement ought to be in the hands of every board member, the director of missionaries, every missionary, and every potential recruit for the particular field. In detail, a strategy statement ought to include the following items.

1. The definition of the field in terms of its geographical, cultural, and linguistic identity. Thus a field might be defined geographically in terms of the country and specific provinces. Second, the field ought to be defined in terms of special cultural groups (specific classes of people, specific racial identities, tribes, etc.). Finally, the field ought to be defined in terms of languages and dialects.

2. A clear-cut statement of the objectives of the mission in the defined area. Is the mission in the field as a service agency or as an actual people-ministering agency? These objectives ought to be so clearly stated that they will serve as a fence, defining exactly what a missionary ought to be doing, and what he or she ought to be staying away from.

3. A list of specific activities which meet the requirements of the objectives. The list may be quite long. It ought to include a second list of things the field conference, in conjunction with the home board, has decided to stay away from. The conference may elect to have a literature-distribution program, for example, but it may wish to inform all interested parties that it is not in the bookstore business. This list of activities will be also helpful to prospective missionary candidates who are confused as to what missionaries do.

4. A game plan which states the accepted form in which each zone or area of the field will be attacked. It is essential that this game plan not be laid out according to time periods, but that it be a schedule of phases or events. In actual practice, the phases may at certain points be flowing into one another. But by the use of such a plan, a missionary and the board ought to know in what phase he finds himself at any given point on the field. (Phase one, for example, may include that time spent in orientation on the field, to whom the junior missionary is accountable, how he is to train, and what he is to learn. Phase two may be his settling into an area and the activities of getting acquainted with the populace and building his own quarters. Phase three may be a specific evangelistic activity which includes visitation, literature distribution, open-air meetings, and market-day evangelism. Phase four may be the founding of a church while phase five defines the training of Christians for personal work. Each of these phases ought to be broken down in definitive statements as to what can be attempted and what past success and failure has been.)

5. A statement of authority lines. What is the relationship of the field conference to the home board? How much autonomy and on what matters of decision does the conference have jurisdiction without consultation? What is the governmental structure of the conference? How often are there elections? Who is qualified to run? To what extent can the home board control elections? How does a junior missionary get full voting and administrative rights?

It seems to me that a good understanding here will include a sliding scale of authority given over to the conference from the board in proportion to the size of the field in terms of personnel. A field conference numbering three couples, for example, is much too small to have a high degree of autonomy. There is the problem of a dominant personality ruling the other two; there is also the temptation to politics and conflicts due to one always trying to get another couple to see things his or her way. Once a conference goes beyond the size of seven couples, its authority ought to increase.

6. A statement in regard to relationship to national personnel. To whom are they answerable, and who evaluates the worth of their work? At what juncture does a national worker take over completely from the missionary the responsibility for a work and its facilities?

7. A schedule of the reports to be made by field directors, secretaries, and individual missionaries; what the report ought to include, to whom it should be sent, and the absolute deadline for such reports.

In general terms, there ought to be a strategy statement for the whole mission following the same guidelines set forth here. Then there ought to be a strategy statement for each individual field. Finally, each missionary ought to have his own strategy statement which fits the form and order of the field statement. In other words, his statement ought to be a demonstration of how he plans to fit into the overall field strategy.

The strategy statement ought to be reviewed annually by the board at home, the field conference, and the director in personal consultation with each furloughed missionary. It will guarantee the highest degree of communication between the home office and the field.

The strategy should be revised only when a visit has been made to the field by the home director, who is able to see firsthand the proposals by the field conference and can recommend such changes to the home board. Ultimately the strategy is changeable only by majority vote of both the conference and the home board in concurrence with the director.

The strategy statement also ought to include the following items:

1. A map of the field showing all communities, roads, and significant geographical facts (mountains, bodies of water, capital of provinces, etc.).

2. A definition of the commerce and culture of the field.

3. A brief history of the area and how the mission came into the area.

4. A zonal breakdown with identifying symbols for use in the statement.

5. A list of the number and types of personnel (both national and American) needed in each zone.

6. A position description for each type of personnel defining what his objective is and how he accomplishes it.

7. An appeal to interested parties who might be interested in coming to the field.

8. A financial statement of how monies are invested. A list of needed projects to which interested benefactors might refer.

Such a completed statement should be mass produced attractively so that any person who is interested in either joining the field staff or supporting the work can be fully informed as to the steps to be taken.

A prospective missionary will be interested in knowing:

a. Language requirements and how long he will need to study.
b. Living situations, locations, and types of housing.
c. Climate requirements.
d. Financial support principles.
e. His schedule of activities commencing from the time he arrives on the field as junior missionary to the point of senior status.

STRATEGY AND THE IDEA OF THE FUTURE

If we are going to get on with the business of world evangelization we need to have a way of thinking about the future. Since we cannot predict it in any detail, we can only consider the future and our actions in it in broad terms. But think of them we must. The way we describe our approach to the future is our strategy.

CHAPTER 4

Management

*I*t would be an interesting, if not stimulating, exercise to choose at random ten mission agencies in the United States and to analyze the success or failure of their new endeavors during the past five years. As we read much of the missionary literature, particularly the house organs of Western mission agencies, we are struck by the absence of any discussion on the *root* cause of major failures. What we usually read are such phrases as "the renewed opposition," or "hardening of people's hearts," or "a changed attitude on the part of the government." All of these may be accurate statements. What we suspect, however, is that many of these failures were the result of weak or no management on the part of mission leadership.

Some years ago one mission agency discovered that the government of a small, predominantly Islamic country was willing to accept certain missionaries. This was startling news. At the annual field mission conference one of the leaders spoke in impassioned terms about the need to reach this particular group of people now that the door was open. A number of missionaries responded to the challenge. They left their work and went to this new country. No apparent thought or discussion was given as to why the government had changed its attitude or why the government might be likely to change its attitude again. No thinking was done as to the particular type of missionaries that would be required, and who would be acceptable to the government. As a result, "a change in government policy" three years later forced all of the missionaries to leave the country and seek ministry elsewhere. We contend that the major cause for this seeming debacle was the absence of good management.

WHAT DO WE MEAN BY MANAGEMENT?

Thus far we have talked about such things as goals, plans, and strategies. These terms ought to be familiar to anyone conversant in modern management literature. We are, in fact, talking about applying management methods to the work of world mission. Management, like strategy, is a much misunderstood term. To many it connotes manipulation. One well-worn definition of management is "the art or science of getting things done through and with other people." To some this smacks of Machiavellianism.

In his book *Professional Management: New Concepts and Proven Practices* (1973), Louis A. Allen points out that there are different kinds of work: *technical* work and *management* work. Most of us are familiar with technical work. When we conduct an evangelistic crusade, we are doing what Allen would call technical work. When we are flying a mission aircraft, we are doing technical work. When we prepare a sermon, we are doing technical work. Allen sets the phrase "technical work" over and against the phrase "management work." Allen wants us to realize that management is work. Like many other management theorists, Allen breaks management work down into four functions: planning, organizing, leading, and controlling. The management work of planning is, to a large degree, what this book is all about.

Planning is setting a desirable objective, imagining all of the different ways of reaching that objective, and then laying out step-by-step programs for reaching the objective. Planning includes not only the means and methods that will be used, but also considers who will do the task, how much it will cost, and when it will be done.

Organizing is arranging the work that needs to be done in a way that is most likely to bring about the desired result. Organizing looks at the plans that have been made and asks such questions as, "What would be the most effective way to relate people one to another to carry out this task?" Organizing deals with the relationships between individuals. It is the type of thing that Paul talks about in the twelfth chapter of Corinthians when he describes the ideal church as a human body. Organizing takes energy and effort, as do all the other functions of management.

Leading describes the work of a manager: selecting and training people, delegating the necessary authority to carry out tasks, insuring that communication exists within the organization, and motivating members of the organization toward the goal.

Controlling is a word which at first may sound quite ominous to Christians. The important thing to recognize here is that it is a matter of controlling the work, not necessarily the people. Good plans must have good measurement. If no one is assigned the task of measuring progress, it is very easy for any organization to lose its way in the highways and byways of the future.

The work of management, then, involves planning, organizing, leading, and controlling. But, as Allen also points out, if given a choice between doing technical work or doing management work, most people will decide to do technical work. There are a number of reasons for this. First, management work involves thinking. Thinking is not easy; in fact, it is very hard. Second, most management work is not directly measurable. After someone has built a bridge, the result is immediately obvious. However, for the manager the completion of the bridge may be months and years in the future, and he or she may get very little credit for it.

Bad management is very noticeable. Some indicators are low organizational morale, financial shortages, ineffective efforts, and a general feeling of confusion. Good management, on the other hand, is quiet and more difficult to recognize. Management is like one's health—it is easier to describe by its absence than by its presence. Management is a learned skill. There are natural or born leaders. There are no born managers.[1]

The complexity of the management task rises exponentially with the size of the organization. Most organizations begin with a natural leader, often one who has a strong charismatic personality, and an ability to inspire others with his or her vision of what God would have accomplished. This type of leadership is effective as long as the leader has the time and energy to oversee the entire operation. But as soon as an organization multiplies to the point where the natural leader cannot give day-to-day guidance, management skills are needed. Sometimes a natural leader can become a management leader. More often the natural leader has to be replaced by someone who understands that planning, organizing, leading, and controlling an organization are essential if the organization is to prosper.

1. For further discussion we recommend Ted W. Engstrom's book, *The Making of a Christian Leader* (1976), as well as Edward R. Dayton and Ted W. Engstrom, *The Christian Executive* (1979).

NEHEMIAH WAS A MANAGER

Management is a modern term, but the skills that it encompasses are as old as the Old Testament. A good illustration is the post-exile leader Nehemiah. We know little about Nehemiah prior to his introduction as the cupbearer to the king, but we know a great deal about how he set about carrying out the task to which God called him.

From the time that Nehemiah first heard the report of the disgrace of the unrepaired walls and burned gates of Jerusalem (1:3) and wept, fasted, and prayed in his response (1:4), until the time he disclosed his plans to the king and queen (2:3–8), four months elapsed. It is obvious that during this time Nehemiah did a great deal of *planning*. He thought about what material would be needed (2:8). He recognized that he had a long-term task, and he planned for his own dwelling (2:8). He knew that he would need considerable supplies as well as moral and physical assistance (2:9, 10). In other words, he did long-range planning.

When Nehemiah arrived in Jerusalem (2:11), he immediately conducted a survey in order to do some short-range planning (2:12), and after thinking about how to organize the work (3:1–32), he exercised his leadership by motivating the people of Jerusalem and the countryside to do the work (2:17, 18).

Nehemiah's enterprise, like most grand enterprises that attempt to glorify God, met with all kinds of obstacles. The least of these was the actual building of the wall. There were enemies inside (4:1f) as well as outside (6:10–14). There was internal dissension (5:1f) as some Jews sought to lord it over their brothers. It was necessary to change plans to meet the new attacks of the enemy (4:10–14, 21–23). There were also communication problems. The workers were spread out and attack could come from any direction, so Nehemiah appointed someone to sound the alarm, a man who was constantly by his side (4:18). When the wall was completed, Nehemiah moved on to the next phase and gave new assignments (11:1, 2).

Though management may be a fairly recent word, the practice of management—"the art or science of getting things done through and with other people"—has always been with us.

THE ROLE OF THE HOLY SPIRIT

Some years ago a missionary friend in Japan wrote to one of us, "With all of our well-oiled machinery and our well-laid plans, are we not in danger of attempting to do the work of the Holy Spirit?" Our response was a resounding, "Yes!" With power there always comes the danger of using the power with the wrong means or toward the wrong ends. There is power in being literate, and in being able to plan and organize. There is power that comes with the resources of the West. There is the individual power that comes with position in any organization. This power can either be a tool used in the hands of God under the direction of the Holy Spirit, or it can be turned inward to bring glory to the ones who wield it. Power brings with it a responsibility, and the greater the responsibility, the greater the danger.

Some might conclude from this that the safest thing to do is to adopt the Being-in-the-Way Strategy (pp. 17, 18). After all, if we generate none of our own plans, but attempt to follow the Spirit's leading day by day, we are less likely to exercise power in the wrong direction. We, however, would argue that the *absence* of planning is more likely to dampen the work of the Spirit than extensive planning. Why is this so?

When we plan, when we attempt to think into the future, we are communicating to one another how we believe God is leading us. If our plans are, as we believe they should be, statements of faith, then we are telling one another, "This is what I believe we should do. This is the direction we should go." Since these are still plans rather than actions, the possibility exists that others who are closer to the mind of the Spirit may have an opportunity to work with us. In other words, in order for a body to operate, all of the members must work and fit together. We can only work and fit together if we have a common understanding as to what it is we are to do. As the prophet Amos observed, "Can two walk together unless they be agreed?" (Amos 3:3).

THE CREATIVE TENSION

The Bible is very clear about our responsibility to carry out the work of the Kingdom in obedience to God. At the same time the Bible is clear about God's sovereignty. There is no intellectual way to merge the ideas of human freedom and God's sovereignty. Similarly, there is no way to merge human responsibility with the leading of God's Spirit.

Evidently God intends that we should make statements about the future, to set goals and objectives. At the same time we are to trust him. Nehemiah's example is a good one. His immediate response upon hearing of the need was prayer (1:4). When he made new plans, he prayed: "And we prayed to our God and set a guard as a protection against them day and night" (4:9). When he uncovered the enemies' plans he gave God the credit (4:15). When he passed judgment he did that which he believed God would have him do (5:9).

RESULTS OF GOOD MANAGEMENT

Many mission agencies are profiting from good management. We think of one group that made a twenty-five-year-plan for evangelizing Indonesia. In light of what they thought God wanted accomplished, they began to establish specific goals for different key cities within Indonesia. They worked with the local churches so they could participate in the detailed planning. They provided adequate resources based upon their projections as to what would be needed for the next five years. During the first phase of their effort they saw new churches appearing all over Indonesia. Such results are not uncommon. One can find many agencies that have reaped the benefits of good management.

Good management, however, does not guarantee success. Again and again we must deny any suggestion that we believe the future is controllable. One can be the best of managers and still be overcome by natural disasters. One can be the best of managers and not be doing the will of God. We believe that poor management can hinder the Spirit and produce failure in situations that might otherwise have been successful.

THE DETAILS OF MANAGEMENT

We will have much more to say about applying management to the missionary task. The entire approach of this book is to attempt to illustrate how one goes about that task.

Setting goals will be discussed at length in chapter 31. Here we will describe in detail how to discover and set goals for the mission enterprise and why goals are the foundation of it.

Planning will be described in detail in chapter 32. We will cover both long-range and short-range planning and attempt to lead the reader through the entire process.

Organizing and the problem of bringing about change within the organization is covered in depth in chapter 30.

Leading is discussed under the heading of "Taking Action" in chapter 33.

Controlling is discussed under the heading of "Evaluation" in chapter 34.

RECAPTURING THE BIBLICAL BALANCE

We need to recapture the biblical balance between thinking and acting. Paul railed against the worldly-wise in his first letter to the Corinthians because there was no relationship between what they knew intellectually and their actions (1 Cor. 1:20f). As James writes so eloquently, the wisdom from above is a wisdom that *acts* (Jas. 3:17). Thinking that does not result in acting is sub-biblical. Acting without thinking is no less so.

Perhaps what we are saying is summed up best in the familiar verse from Proverbs: "A man's mind plans his way, but the Lord directs his steps" (16:9).

CHAPTER 5

Management for Mission

*I*f we accept the idea of the previous chapter that management is not only permissible, but that God gifts certain individuals to carry out the role of management in his mission, how do we apply the idea of management to world evangelization? What can we say about management for mission?

AN OVERVIEW OF THE TASK BEFORE US

The Lord Jesus Christ has commanded his Church to make disciples of every nation. This task has been given to his Church, his Body. Every Christian in every local church and in every country of the world is called upon to be a witness to the saving power of Jesus Christ. No matter who we are and where we are, if we claim Jesus as Lord, God wants us to proclaim our faith by what we say and how we live.

The witness of the Church is multiplying around the world. On every continent, in cities, towns, and villages, men and women are sharing the gospel with their friends and neighbors. However, in addition to these local witnesses, God has set apart certain men and women to go forth from where they live to reach those cities, towns, and villages where there is no witness. And if the world is to be evangelized, if every person in the world is to have an opportunity to know Jesus Christ as Lord and Savior, then cross-cultural missionaries need to understand the people to whom they are called, to uncover God's strategy and plans for reaching these people, and to sense that God is setting them aside to be about his business in a particular part of the world.

Let us begin with some definitions. What do we mean by world evangelization?[1]

We have divided the definition of world evangelization into *nature, purpose,* and *goal* so as to build a bridge between God's intention and our response.

The *nature* of evangelization is the communication of the Good News.

The *purpose* of evangelization is to give individuals and groups a valid opportunity to accept or reject Jesus Christ as Lord and Savior.

> The purpose of the world mission is primarily that of making known the gospel of God's love to men in Jesus Christ. That is the meaning of evangelism in its broadest sense. (Soper, 1943, pp. 234f)

> The solidarity of the missionary enterprise in its multiform activities lies in the fact that there is but one ultimate aim to be achieved through them all. Whether it be the task of evangelizing through direct preaching and other forms of pastoral work, or education, or medical work or agriculture, the purpose which runs through them all is to make known the full meaning of the revelation of God in Jesus Christ and to make it possible for all to enter intelligently into the new life which the acceptance of the gospel opens to them. (Soper, 1943, pp. 242f)

If this purpose is to be carried out in any meaningful way, we need a measurable *goal.* The *goal* of world evangelization and the only biblical goal that we can actually observe, is that men and women should come not only to accept Jesus Christ as Lord and Savior but that they should come to serve him in the fellowship of his Church. This is our statement of faith.

We believe every man and woman in the world should have a valid opportunity to know Christ. *Every man and woman in the world.* The task seems so enormous. Few people today talk about *world* evangelization. Somehow that seems like too big a dream in a world that every

---

1. Much of what follows is drawn from *That Everyone May Hear* by Edward R. Dayton (1979).

day grows more complex; a world torn by disasters, political upheaval, and starving people. Where do we begin? We might begin with population.

When we look at today's world population (Figure 5-1), we are surprised at what has happened in such a few years. Between the time of Jesus' birth, when the population of the world was estimated at 250 million, and Martin Luther's dramatic challenge at Wittenberg, the population only doubled. In 1500 years the population of the world increased from 250 million to 500 million people. In 1793 William

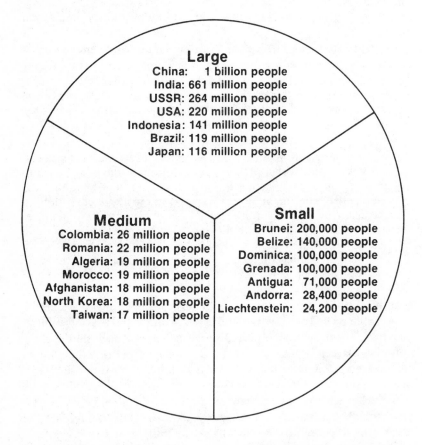

THE WORLD: 220 COUNTRIES

Figure   5-1   Countries by Size

Carey, the so-called "father of modern missions," set sail for India. In a little over 250 years the population had doubled again. It now totaled one billion. By the time of the Edinburgh Missionary Conference in 1910, the population once again doubled, and stood at two billion. In the brief years since that time the population has more than doubled, and if the same rate continues, the population will be somewhere between six and seven billion people by the year 2000.

How does one even begin to *think* about a world like that? One way to think about it is in terms of the world's countries. While these are sometimes called nation-states, we are not really talking about the nations that the Bible describes; rather, we are talking about geographical territories or political entities.

The 220 countries of the world listed by the United Nations in 1979 vary in size, from the estimated one billion people in China to the mere 24,200 people in Liechtenstein (Figure 5-1). This tremendous variation shows how difficult it is to talk about world evangelization in terms of countries. It is one thing to evangelize Liechtenstein. It is quite another to evangelize the 141 million people of the many-islanded country of Indonesia.

Another way to think about the world is in terms of its religions (Figure 5-2; see p. 36 below). Christians—those who acknowledge Jesus Christ as Lord—number approximately one billion people (in 1979). The second largest religion in the world is Islam, with an estimated 700 million Muslims. Six hundred million Hindus are found all over the world, with the majority in India. Marxism and what we might call "secular religions"—beliefs to which men and women have given their hearts—include approximately 800 million people. It is estimated that there are 500 million traditional Chinese. There are 250 million Buddhists in the world and 275 million traditional religionists ("Animists")—those who worship nature and the spirit world. Traditional Japanese, fifteen million Jews, and all of the other religions of the world make up the balance.

The accuracy of these numbers is not important. What is important is that they indicate that approximately 75 percent of the people in the world do not recognize the name of Jesus Christ. Although this breakdown helps us, it still does not give us a workable strategy for reaching the world. The problem is much more complex.

Referring to Figure 1-1 on page 4, we can see that of the three billion people who are not Christian, only one third or one billion people are living among culturally similar Christians who know Jesus and share his love. In other words, no matter how earnestly all of the local churches

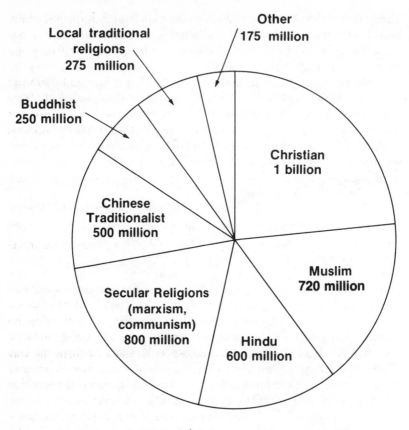

THE WORLD: ITS RELIGIONS

Figure 5-2   World's Religions

in the world reached out to their neighbors, only one-third of the non-Christians in the world could be reached by Christians who speak their language and understand their culture.

So how *do* you evangelize such a world? *Not one country at a time,* because countries vary so much. India, with its 1979 population of 623 million people, has seventeen official languages and 400 scheduled castes. Certainly evangelizing India is quite a different task from evangelizing Andorra with its 29,200 people.

Not one person at a time. As we have already tried to show, the ability of individuals who are already Christians to reach the rest of the world without some cross-cultural training and understanding is inadequate. *The way to evangelize the world is by taking one people at a time.*

What do we mean by a "people?" In 1977, the Lausanne Strategy Working Group gave this definition: "A people is a significantly large sociological grouping of individuals who perceive themselves to have a common affinity for one another. This common affinity can be based on language, religion, ethnicity, residence, occupation, class or caste, situation, or combinations of any of these." For example:

— Urdu-speaking Muslim farmers of the Punjab

— Cantonese-speaking Chinese refugees from Vietnam in France

— Welsh working-class miners

— Tamil-speaking Indian workers on Malaysian rubber plantations

— White swinging singles in North American apartments

The definition may seem rather filled with scientific jargon when one first reads it. Before examining the definition we need to state what we do *not* mean. By a people we do not necessarily mean a tribal group. By a people we do not necessarily mean all the people living within a country. When we think of a people we try to think of them the way God sees them, or to put it another way, to understand them *in terms of reaching them with the gospel*. We are attempting to define the world *in terms of world evangelization*.

By "significantly large," we mean a group large enough to be called a group. By "sociological grouping of individuals," we mean people who are relating to one another in a particular situation. "Who perceive themselves" needs some further defining. People who live in a high-rise apartment in New York City may know one another as a group of strangers, as individuals. Yet in their individuality and their statements about themselves, they see themselves as part of a group, which, from the view of world evangelization, has a commonness about it. There is "a common affinity for one another."

Now this sociological grouping, this common affinity can be based on a lot of things: language, religion, ethnic background, place of residence, business or occupation, class or caste, the situation they are in, or a combination of these.

Notice the boundaries that the above examples place around a particular people:

Not just *Urdu-speaking,* or just Urdu-speaking *Muslims.* Rather, Urdu-speaking Muslim *farmers* who happen to live in the Punjab.

There are many *Cantonese-speaking* Chinese. Some of them are *refugees.* The people we are describing are Cantonese-speaking refugees *from Vietnam* who are now *living in France.*

To speak of evangelizing *Wales* is one thing. To speak of evangelizing the *working class* of Wales narrows it down. But to speak of evangelizing the Welsh working-class *miners* is even more specific.

What is an *unreached* people? The Strategy Working Group defines it as follows: "An unreached people is a group that is less than 20 percent *practicing* Christians."

What do we mean by *"practicing* Christians?" How Christians will work out their religion in different places of the world will differ tremendously. The gospel has a marvelous ability to impregnate a culture and modify its Christian expression. Committed Christians within a particular group will know quite easily who are the practicing Christians and who are not.

Why 20 percent? Why not 50 percent or 3 percent? The answer lies in our understanding of the diffusion of new ideas within a group. Because the group we are describing has internal consistency, it can be assumed that once an idea has taken hold in a major portion of the group, the group has the ability to diffuse the idea within itself.[2] Observation and research has shown that when approximately 10 or 20 percent of the people within a group have accepted an idea or a new religion, they have the ability to evangelize the rest of the group. When there are no Christians within a group, someone from the outside—a missionary— must enter the group with the Good News. Initially the number of outsiders will increase, but as the group grows, the number of outsiders should decrease. When the number of practicing Christians reaches 20 percent, these outsiders are no longer needed to reach the group. We have tried to depict this idea in Figure 5-3.

The world that we are concerned with is the world of unreached people. Some of these groups are large and some are small. The point is that we need to *discover God's strategies,* his best way for reaching these people. Certainly if the God of the universe is capable of being concerned with *each individual* in the world, he is just as concerned for the *peoples* of the world.

2. For further information, see such works as *The Diffusion of Innovation* (Rogers, 1962).

Why 20 Percent?

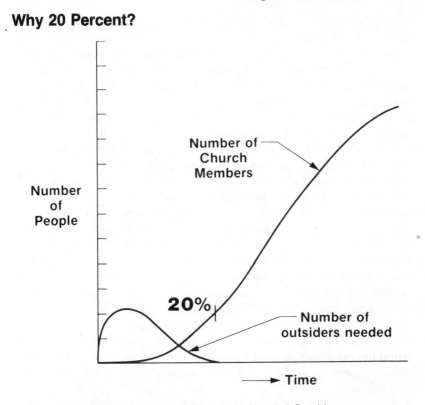

Figure 5-3 Church Growth vs. Needed Outsiders

THE UNIQUENESS OF THE TASK

Every situation that we face is unique. Never before in history has this combination of individuals and events come together to form this particular period of history. Why is this important to us? Human beings in general, and Westerners in particular, are enamoured with techniques and methods. Western society is oriented toward technological solutions. It tacitly assumes that there is not only a solution to each problem, but that the solution can become a standard approach to the problem the next time it appears.

Few of us stop to think that this is rather a new idea in history. It started during the Industrial Revolution and the resulting novel concept of interchangeable parts. There was a time in history when very few man-made parts were interchangeable. True, arrows all had to fit the same bow, and cannonballs had to roll down the barrel of the cannon. Uniforms looked alike, but they were not all standard sizes. But today's technological world assumes quite the opposite. If a light bulb fails or a tire blows out, they can be easily replaced. Coin-operated machines have a standard method of operation—a 25-cent piece. New automobiles have a standard fuel—unleaded gasoline.

The Industrial Revolution also introduced the idea that organizations could be constructed around work centers, and the corollary idea that *people* were interchangeable soon followed. The plethora of how-to-do-it books witnesses to our Western preoccupation with standard solutions. From sex to singing and psychology to swimming, from preaching to painting and conversation to conservation, we push forward the idea that there is a best way, often an *only* way of doing something.

Slowly, all too slowly, we are learning that there is a difference between inanimate things and human beings. We are leaving behind the notion that the electronic computer might be a model of the human mind. Rather than a maze of fixed wires and electronic components, the amazingly fertile mind can best be pictured as an underwater motion picture of the ocean's bed, with the various flora and fauna and sea life intermingled, now touching, now apart—ever varying. Such a mind has limitless capacity for new concepts, new combinations, and new relationships.

Every individual in the world is unique—in some small way a reflection of the Creator. The same is true for groups of people. The more we look at large social systems, the more we understand how little we know about the function of societies. Indeed, we now see that when we attempt to extrapolate our understanding of small social groups to large systems, our intuition is more often wrong than right. We even have a name for it: "counter-intuitive thinking."[3]

How slow the Church is to learn what the world has learned! "Oh," some reply, "we don't want to follow the world." That is right. But we are! The trouble is that instead of moving ahead, we are following at a distance. Christians, more than anyone else, should acknowledge the

---

3. The idea of counter-intuitive thinking came out of the studies that were done at MIT under the direction of Jay Forrester (1969) on future possibilities for the control of the world's resources. Computer models indicated that the results that one might expect were seldom realized when projections for such things as food, population, pollution, and water studies were combined. For further reading in this area see the report prepared for the Club of Rome (Meadows, 1974).

uniqueness of the human personality and the magnificent varieties of the manifestations of God's Spirit in the world. One would think we would learn just by observing the beautiful multiplicity of the local expression of the Church. Our God is infinitely adaptable and very willing to let us be ourselves in our worship, fellowship, caring, and witness. Some prefer applause while others are given to quiet meditation. Some emphasize one gift or spiritual manifestation more than another. One group feels closest to God in the cool serenity of a Gothic cathedral. Others sense his presence in the noisy warmth of a cottage meeting.[4]

And yet we who are concerned for evangelism categorize, classify, and duplicate our evangelistic methods as though each new discovery was *the* final answer. We invent solutions and then look for problems on which to try them out. We observe an individual or a group and consciously or unconsciously search our box of evangelistic tools for just the right ones to use. We ask, "What would work here? What solution can we rely on to carry out successful evangelism?"

Since this book deals with evangelization, one might quickly assume that we are opposed to any and all evangelistic methods, and that we will offer no alternatives except to allow the Spirit to move where he will. But this is not the case.

There *are* evangelistic methods that work. Furthermore, we need men and women who are called to perfect and use the evangelistic tools that God has provided. One does not suddenly build a radio station. It takes knowledge, dedication, and a willingness to learn through mistakes so we can pass on to others what God has taught us. Evangelistic methods are like the mechanic's tools. Some are simple while others are complex. Each needs to be used at the right time in the right place.

To refuse to learn from both the profane and holy lessons of history is foolish. But to fail to see the uniqueness of every individual and every group of individuals, is to fail to read correctly God's given revelations. We glibly tell people, "God has a wonderful plan for your life," and then act as though his plan was identical for everyone. *There is no general method or methods of evangelism.* Every time the miracle of new birth occurs it is the result of a unique event. Does not our own individual spiritual history teach us the same lesson? There may be

4. Robert E. Webber, in his book *Common Roots* (1978), has done us an excellent service by differentiating between faith and formulation. All evangelical Christians acknowledge a common faith. We need to allow ourselves to see the diversity as this faith is formulated in different ways and in different cultures.

many of us who were led to a personal confrontation with Jesus Christ at an evangelistic meeting, and yet closer examination will uncover a multitude of different events that led us to our decision for Christ.

So we reject standard solutions, but affirm that there is a large range of useful evangelistic tools. To put it another way, in a farmer's tool shed there are a wide variety of tools. Which tool the farmer selects will depend on the need of the moment and the farmer's understanding of the task.

Having affirmed the uniqueness of each situation, we would also like to affirm that there is a universal approach to *thinking* about the process of evangelization.

THE BASIC APPROACH

Management for mission is best thought of in terms of a process. In its shortest version this process might be defined as:

1. Define the mission in terms of need.
2. Plan the mission in the spirit of prayer.
3. Attempt the mission in the power of the Spirit.
4. Evaluate the mission with the mind of the Spirit.

Since we believe that each situation will be unique, we strongly believe that one must start with the situation or the need at hand, and let that define not only the means and methods that will be used, but also the specific members of the force for evangelism. We believe that planning—"casting a net into the future," attempting to make statements of faith about how God would have us carry out his mission—is the way to move forward. We recognize that there will always be the tension between human planning and God's leading. This is why we feel it is so important that such planning be done in a spirit of prayer.

With the need in mind and our understanding of how that need should be met defined in terms of plans, we believe we should move forward courageously, trusting God not only for the end result, but also for the power to carry out the means and methods that we have selected.[5]

5. A good illustration of this would be Paul's attempt to evangelize the eastern end of present-day Turkey. "When they came opposite Mysia, they attempted to go into Bithynia, but the Spirit of Jesus did not allow them to go; so, passing by Mysia, they went down to Troas. And a vision appeared to Paul in the night: A man of Macedonia was standing beseeching him and saying, 'Come over to Macedonia and help us.' And when he had seen the vision, immediately we sought to go into Macedonia, concluding that God had called us to preach the gospel to them" (Acts 16:7-10).

After we have attempted each part of the mission we need to evaluate our progress because we need to understand what the Spirit is saying to us. What have we learned? Do we have a better understanding of the mission? What is God leading us to do now? This is a circular model. Evaluation leads to a new definition of mission.

A CIRCULAR MODEL

We have found it useful to expand these four steps into ten more detailed steps in a circular model shown in Figure 5-4. The division of the rest of this book is based on the steps in this model.

To illustrate the usefulness of this model, we will apply it to an area that is familiar to most of us—the area of farming.

God has called us to be sowers of the seeds of the gospel. We are told that the Good News will eventually be proclaimed to all nations. God has also called us to be reapers of the harvest. Jesus has told us to look out on the fields that are ready for harvest (Jn. 4:35). He has also told us to go into all the world and to bring in the harvest by making disciples (Mt. 28:18, 19). In addition, God has called us to watch the harvest multiply "thirty-fold, sixty-fold, one-hundred fold." Seed is to produce more seed.

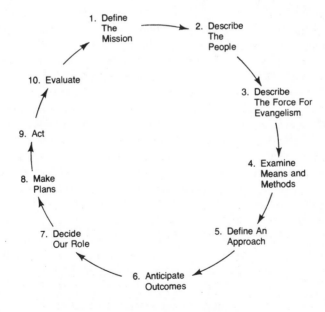

Figure 5-4 The Planning Model

God can use the story of the farmer and his crops to help us understand how to prepare, sow, cultivate, reap, and multiply a harvest for him.

1. Define the mission

Those of us who are not farmers do not understand the overall situation faced by a farmer. If a farmer owns land, and that is where all the farming is to take place, then he or she does not have to face the question of where to plant the crops. However, the farmer is faced with questions of *what* crop to plant in which of the fields, which crop will have the most benefit not only for the farmer's family but also for the village or country. This may not be a simple procedure. There is a cost involved in seed, soil preparation, sowing, irrigating, cultivating, and reaping.

Like the farmer, the evangelist needs to consider his or her mission. In some cases the field will be determined, and the mission will be easily decided. In other cases we will be like a farmer with many fields, and we will need to wait for God's direction through such circumstances as the availability of the field, workers, tools, and resources.

2. Describe the people

Our "field" is not merely a geographical territory. In actuality, it is people. Every field is made up of the soil of *people*. Different fields will have different soils. What causes this difference in soil? Interestingly, some crops draw nutrition from the soil at a very high rate while others do not. So, too, we discover that if the Muslim religion has permeated the field, the soil will be quite different than if animism has permeated the field.

Some fields are full of rocks that need to be cleared away. These can be rocks of misunderstanding about Christianity or rocks of cultural practices. Other fields will be overgrown because no one has worked the field in many years.

As the farmer needs to understand the field before going forth to cultivate it, so we need to understand the people to whom God has called us. We need to understand their culture, economy, religions, and working situations. We need to attempt to understand these people as God understands them.

3. Describe the force for evangelism

Who is to work the field? There is much to be done: clearing, tilling, fertilizing, sowing, cultivating, irrigating, reaping, processing, storing, distributing the results of our labor. Who will work beside the farmer? Field hands? Neighbors? Are there special agencies that can provide information about new crops or new ways of treating the soil?

Again like the farmer, the evangelist needs to look to other Christians to help bring in the harvest. Are there those who have worked with this kind of people before, who have insight and experience? Are there others working in the same field? How do we relate to them? Who has done research on this people or people like them? Who has special skills in preparing literature, doing broadcasts, teaching, planting churches, doing follow-up and consolidation, and a myriad of other things?

How can all these Christians relate to one another? They can relate to one another because of an allegiance to a common Savior. Christians are all part of his body, the Church. Every Christian is called to be a laborer. Some are called to one field, and some are called to another.

4. Examine means and methods

Like the tools of farming, the tools of evangelism can be very simple or very complex. In a certain field a farmer may be able to do all that is necessary with only a hoe. As the field grows larger, a wooden plow pulled by oxen will be needed. Perhaps there will come a day when a tractor-drawn harrow will be the appropriate tool. Or consider the means of irrigating the field. One farmer may depend only on the seasonal rains. Another may develop a simple method of flooding the field from a nearby stream. In a modernized society, a complex system of pipes and sprinklers may be used.

Look at the parallel to the education part of evangelism: One approach to evangelism may be to give a New Testament to each person and then to wait for the Holy Spirit to convict the people to read it. Another method might be to hold inquirers' classes. In a more modern society, correspondence courses could be broadcast over the radio.

Both the farmer and the evangelist need to think through what "tools"—means and methods—will be used at each stage.

5. Define an approach

We have been looking at the different things a farmer must consider: the crop desired, the soil available, and the laborers, tools, and methods needed. To achieve results, whether farming for a physical crop or a spiritual crop, these considerations must be seen in the context of an approach or a strategy.

Part of this strategy is deciding what will *not* be done. For example, if the ground is to be prepared by an ox-pulled plow and cultivated by hand, tractors or mechanical cultivators will not be needed. Similarly, if we have decided to have a four-person group of cross-cultural missionaries live in a community and establish relationships of friendship, we will not need to use outside radio broadcasts.

6. *Anticipate outcomes*

Every farmer has a crop in mind when a field is sown with seed. But beyond that some decisions will have been made about how the crop is to be used. Part of the crop will be stored as seed for next year's planting. Part will be used as food by the farmer. Hopefully there will be an excess to be bartered or sold to others.

So, too, the evangelist needs to anticipate outcomes. If the seed of the gospel takes root, and young Christians are brought into Christ's Kingdom, then one needs to anticipate the establishment of a church community, a community that not only cares for itself, but reaches out to others.

Just as the farmer anticipates the size of the harvest and trusts God to provide the increase, so we too need to believe that God has a specific harvest for us. If we do not, we will not be prepared to train young Christians as to what it means to be part of Christ's body in their community.

7. *Decide our role*

Some farmers *do* all the farming by themselves. They buy seed, and prepare, plant, cultivate, and irrigate the soil. The farmer with a larger farm may do one or more of these things, and he may give some tasks to others depending on their skills. Then there are those people who have a great interest in farming but do not farm themselves. For example, a person may be vitally concerned with developing a new type of seed that will produce a better crop. This seed researcher might make a very poor farmer.

So, too, the evangelism researcher may be called only to one role. We need to know what God has gifted us to be and do, and we also need to know where we fit in with others he has called to reach the same people. Christians need one another.

8. *Make plans*

Only a foolish farmer decides what needs to be done but never makes plans to do it. There is a series of things that must happen, each in its proper time. For a one-person farm, plans will be simple and will develop quite naturally and routinely. Every farmer knows seed must be saved for next year. But when a number of people are involved, plans will be more complex: How and when will the seed be obtained? How and when will the ground be prepared? How and when will the seed be planted? How and when will it be watered? How and when will it be cultivated? How and when will it be harvested? How and when will the crop be stored and preserved? How and when will the crop be distributed? And most importantly: Who will be responsible for each of these phases of the plan?

Plans that are to be used by many people need to be communicated, usually in writing because they permit us to evaluate whether what we want to do can, in fact, be done. Jesus reminded us that one does not sit down to build a tower without counting the cost. In order to count the cost we need to plan.

9. Act

Plans help the farmer know what resources will be needed so they can be provided when needed: Seed must be stored. Tools must be cleaned and sharpened. New ones may need to be purchased. Means for providing water must be arranged and—most importantly—there must be an agreement with the people who are going to do the work.

So we see that resources include:

— People
— Tools
— Money
— Supplies

All of these need to be brought together to begin the process.

How foolish to make preparations and then never to act. Often it takes courage to act. It certainly takes faith! To act is to commit ourselves to the future. Once the seed is in the ground it cannot be retrieved. Once it is allowed to grow, it must be harvested.

10. Evaluate

The farmer is evaluating all the time. He evaluates last year's harvest, its quality and quantity. The means and methods used last year and in previous years are examined and carefully weighed. How neighbors did on their farms is evaluated. All of this evaluation is used in planning for the next crop.

The farmer also plans to evaluate as he goes along. The soil is tested, growth is measured. The moisture in the soil is tested. Insects or disease that might damage the crop is monitored, and insecticides are obtained as a result of this analysis. The crop and the weather are carefully followed, and the planned harvest date is changed as needed.

So, too, Christians need to evaluate what God has done and is doing in the world. No one can predict the future. We can only make statements of faith and set goals for what we believe God wants done.

AN ITERATIVE MODEL

These ten steps appear quite neat and orderly on paper. They follow what might be called linear logic. They appear to say, "Do this. Now do this. Follow that by doing this." But Steps 1 through 8 are all part of a thinking process. The human mind is too broad and comprehensive to be shut up to this type of step-by-step thinking. What actually happens is that even as we are thinking about Step 1, our mind is rushing ahead to think about Steps 2, 3, 4, 5, and 6. It is, in fact, an iterative process. In order to make a decision about Step 1 we track ahead five or six steps. When we get to Step 2 we not only track ahead, but we look back at Step 1. Unfortunately, writing things down on paper forces us to think linearly. Since we have to write one thought after another, our mind soon becomes trained to think in these categories. (See Figure 16-2 on p. 224 below for a better understanding.)

When we cannot explain in such a step-by-step description how we arrived at a conclusion, we fall back on such words as "intuition" to describe what happened. As we noted earlier in this chapter, our minds refuse to submit to mechanistic descriptions. Often non-literate societies will arrive at conclusions or solutions without going through the "logical" process of the literate person.

By using a diagram that indicates the circular nature of our thinking process, we are, to some degree, freed from the limitations of the written (linearly produced) word.

We will have more to say about this in chapter 16. What is important here is to realize that the ten-step model is nothing more than a model, a way of thinking and discussing the overall task.

CONCLUSION

There are no standard means and methods. Each situation is unique. However, there is an *approach* that one can take to any mission. Part of the solution to the need always includes thinking about the need. As Western Christians, we are sometimes criticized by our Eastern brothers and sisters for our seeming lack of time spent in contemplation and meditation. We are activists. We like to get things done. The idea of management in mission will help us to learn to contemplate before we act. We call this contemplation "planning." When we plan, the Holy Spirit can move and act to help us be more conformed to his will.

One final word before we plunge into applying this model to the task of cross-cultural evangelism: what first appears to be quite technological and Western is our best defense against mechanized man-made solutions. Our approach begins by assuming that we do *not* know God's strategy for a particular people, that we do not have the answers. It assumes that by beginning where the people are in their own context, we can discover how the Good News can best reach them. Our emphasis is on *people* rather than on methods.

STEP 1

DEFINING
THE MISSION

CONSIDERATIONS

1. Mission has its source in the triune God. The mission of the Church is the mission of God.

2. Only if the Church is understood as missionary, is it understood at all. The intrinsic nature of the Church is missionary because it is sent out by God.

3. Only a theology of the Kingdom can overcome the polarization that has developed between the conciliar and evangelical Protestants. The error of both has been to eliminate the tension between the Kingdom as present and the Kingdom as coming.

4. The debate that pits social action against evangelization is meaningless.

5. No abstract statement of the priorities of the Church is possible. Priorities are always related to specific contexts. The road to Jericho sets its own agenda.

6. Christian development always has the goal of evangelization, because it offers the only true basis for effective human relationships without which development cannot be fully achieved.

7. Mission is a broader reality than evangelization. Yet the Church ceases to participate in mission when it no longer engages in evangelization.

8. Jesus Christ is the permanent norm for evangelization as both the evangelist *par excellence* and as the content of the gospel.

9. While all Christians are called to be involved in evangelism, not all are called to be evangelists.

10. The Good News can never be fully or finally expressed in a single statement or creed. It is a message with a unifying center in Jesus Christ

which has innumerably diverse expressions. In actuality, the only way the gospel can be preserved in all its purity and authenticity is by rephrasing and changing it to show how it is a word for all seasons and situations of human experience and culture.

11. Evangelization should be seen as a process to be enhanced, not a goal to be achieved.

12. Mission definition is people specification. Until we know who we are to evangelize, we have no evangelistic mission.

13. When we realize that there are over fifteen thousand people groups that have no contact with practicing Christians, we realize both the enormity of what needs to be done and the possibility that it can be done. There are 300,000 churches in America. This works out to one people group for every twenty churches to reach. When we add the thousands of Third World churches, we have a task that is no larger than the resources of the sacrificial body of Christ.

CHAPTER 6

Mission and the Church

*T*here is no such thing as farming "in general." A farmer engages in wheat farming in Oregon, sugar cane sharecropping in Mississippi, wet rice farming in the Philippines, and orange growing in Israel. There are similarities between all types of farming: plants are cultivated, animals are raised, and the common factors of soil, nutrients, seed, water, light, diseases, pests, tools, and the market are dealt with. Yet farming can be radically different depending upon the crop being grown and the type of technology being used.

In a similar fashion, we do not engage in evangelism "in general." Only a clear idea of the mission and purpose of an evangelistic endeavor makes plans, priorities, strategies, and work assignments possible. To do the task of evangelism we need to know what our purpose is.

This may seem to be a simple matter. After all, evangelism is evangelism, not poaching eggs, producing hoe handles, or preparing theological extension courses. Actually, an answer to the question of what we are about when we are doing evangelism is far from simple, and many of the obvious answers leave us without very much help in deciding whether this or that activity is an important, or even legitimate part of evangelism. There is often no simple consensus as to what "good" evangelism really is.

When we set out to engage in evangelism, one of the most important elements in defining our business is the question of who our ultimate "customer" is: what specific group of people are we attempting to evangelize? To define our mission we need to know what evangelization involves and who it is we are going to evangelize. Just as we cannot farm in the abstract, so we cannot evangelize in the abstract. We always are evangelizing *someone*. Who that someone is makes a great deal of difference in the plans, strategies, and priorities we follow. Evangelization is always in a specific context. Deciding what that context will be is a crucial part of defining what our mission is.

In this first section we will deal with three basic questions that serve as the foundation for all the remaining steps: First, *what is the mission of the Church?* Second, *what is evangelism?* What are the distinguishing characteristics that define an act or process as *evangelism* and set it off from a variety of other good and essential things we might also be involved in doing? Third, *whom are we to evangelize?* How do we decide the specific limits of evangelization as we carry out the specific mission that we believe God has given us? What factors are involved in selecting a people group to evangelize?

MISSION AND THE CHURCH

If there ever was an era when a consensus existed as to the mission of the Church, it has long since passed. One recent article documents five alternative perspectives within the supposedly monolithic Roman Catholic Church (Ponsi, 1978). Likewise, a number of publications take note of the polarization of concepts within the Protestant Churches (Beyerhaus, 1971, 1972; McGavran, 1977; Stott, 1975; Krass, 1974; Braaten, 1977; Costas, 1977, 1974; Anderson, 1961; Verkuyl, 1978). To develop a theology of evangelization or even the mission of the Church cannot be done simply by appealing to the consensus of the scholars or even the practitioners of evangelization. A very demonstrable diversity exists and must be acknowledged from the outset, even if it is not possible to give fair or in-depth treatment of the range of options.

The following pages deal with the theology of the mission of the Church only briefly—not because it is not worthy of more extensive discussion, but because it cannot be expanded without changing the basic purpose of this book. Others have dealt with the question in more depth (Stott, 1965; McGavran, 1977; Krass, 1978; Peters, 1972; Braaten, 1977; Soper, 1943; Kraemer, 1938; Hahn, 1965; DeRidder,

1971). But we need at least to outline our perspective, which influences all the other parts of this book.

MODELS OF THE CHURCH

The Church has been given numerous commands and models to reveal what it ought to be and do. Paul Minear (1960) has catalogued no less than ninety-six analogies which are used in the New Testament to express the nature and relationship of the Church as a reality God has brought about in the world. It is not difficult to catalogue a large number of specific commands given to the early Christians and their churches, commands to engage in caring, nurturing, witnessing, worshipping, studying, and giving. All these ministries were ignited with enthusiasm by the early Christians as they began to see themselves as part of the movement of the Spirit of God. Somehow in the midst of all these words and portraits the modern Church must seek its essential identity and dynamic for carrying out its business in the twentieth century.

Undoubtedly the question of the mission of the Church can and is being answered in a number of mutually complementary ways. Some of the images of the Church are, however, more important than others in determining the priorities and ethos of mission. For example, Minear considers the notions of the Church as a people of God, a fellowship in faith, a new creation of the Spirit, and the body of Christ to be the integrating and dominant images of the Church in the New Testament. When Hans Küng wrote his study, *The Church* (1967), he emphasized three images as descriptive of the fundamental structure of the Church: the people of God, the creation of the Spirit, and the body of Christ.

These basic images must be made foundational for any theology of the mission of the Church. They have profound implications not only for the way in which evangelization is carried out by the Church, but also for the nature and quality of the inner life of the community of the children of God.

But these dominant images do not exhaust the various portraits of what the Church ought to be and do in our world. There are more: The Church ought to be a good Samaritan, binding up the wounded and caring for their needs. It ought to be a good shepherd, searching high and low for wandering sheep and warding off marauding wolves. It ought to be a faithful manager, carefully using and preserving the resources of this world for future generations. It ought to be an angry prophet, denouncing injustice and declaring the judgment of God on the oppressors of this day. It ought to be a gentle and compassionate rabbi, calling the children of the world, and blessing and teaching them. It ought to be a community so alive with love and enthusiasm that the Lord can daily add new members to its number. It ought to be a unified body that cares about all of its members.

Think of all the metaphors and images found in the New Testament that reveal the nature and mission of the Church: light, salt, leaven, a pillar holding up the truth, an ambassador for God, a farmer sowing seed, a temple of worship, a servant carrying a cross. The list goes on and on!

There are so many important and necessary things that the Church is to be and do that the center about which they all revolve can be lost if one aspect or facet is considered apart from the others. In the end all these images and commands are rooted in the reality that the Church is a result of and a participant in the mission of God. God is acting in history to bring about his redemption and reign over a creation in rebellion. God has miraculously revealed himself by acting in history in the person of Jesus Christ and through his people. The Church is both a result of and a copartner with God in the process of effecting the Kingdom of God here on earth.

Paul Minear expresses this centering of mission upon the reality of God's activity in this fashion:

> through all the analogies the New Testament writers were speaking of a single reality, a single realm of activity, a single magnitude.... Image after image points beyond itself to a realm in which God and Jesus Christ and the Spirit are at work. It was of that work and of that realm that the New Testament writer was thinking as he spoke of Kingdom or temple or body ... the reality of the church is everywhere anchored in the reality of God, the Holy Spirit, Jesus Christ. (1960, pp. 222–223)

To express and define the essence of the mission of the Church is to delineate the *Missio Dei* (Vicedom, 1965). *The Church's mission is its participation in and cooperation with what God is graciously doing redemptively here on the earth.* It is to be a sign of the presence of the Kingdom in word and deed. It is to be a partial answer to the prayer, "Thy Kingdom come, thy will be done, on earth as it is in heaven." It is to understand the Church in its reality as the new creation of God, the body of Christ, the temple of the Spirit. The mission of the Church must be understood and defined in terms of the triune God whose creation and agent in the world is the Church of Jesus Christ. Wilhelm Andersen is right when he states: "The basic and decisive recognition for a theology of missions consists in this: *Mission has its source in the Triune God*" (1961, p. 301).

However mission is imaged, it must be rooted and centered in the reality and power of a loving, gracious God who so loved the world that he sent his unique Son to liberate and open us to the life of his kingly rule in the company of his people. The movement outward to seek and save the lost, to deliver those who live in the fear of death, to feed the hungry and to clothe the naked, to set at liberty those that are oppressed, is rooted in the movement of God in sending the Son and the Spirit. "As the Father sent me, so send I you" (Jn. 20:21). "The overall task of the missionary Church is to interpret and translate, in its preaching, teaching and works of love, the will of God to salvation, as it is revealed in the eternal mission, the Father's sending of the Son" (Sundkler, 1965, p. 56).

THE MISSIONARY NATURE OF THE CHURCH

Because its center is a self-giving, self-revealing God who sends, the Church is inherently missionary. Having been liberated by the power of the Spirit, the Church cannot help but make this same liberation available to all the peoples of the earth. It is "outward bound," centered on the triune God and motivated to share his love and compassion for all peoples in all ages. Unless the missionary nature of the Church is understood, the meaning and significance of the Church is completely obscured. That the Church has often not manifested this nature is only an indication that it is always in the process of becoming what it ought to be.

This is a central motif and constitutive quality of the Church. Without its living dynamic, the Church becomes only another human association, an appendix of social and cultural interests which offers no more than another human answer to the current age's malaise. Many writers have seen mission at the heart of the life of the Church; none, however, more graphically than Emil Brunner: "The Church exists by mission as fire exists by burning."[1]

1. This conclusion about the Church has been expressed in a variety of ways. Some recent statements: "The very being of the church is shaped by its missionary calling to go into the uttermost parts of the world. This missionary structure of the church derives from its apostolic origin. . . . The church is sent by the

Because we are dealing with a central biblical motif as well as a crucial element of the identity of the Church, it is not easy to provide a simple, abstract statement of what that mission is without reducing it to something far less than what it is in reality. It has historical as well as cosmic and spiritual dimensions. It is dynamic as it is reshaped and reformed in a variety of radically different socio-economic contexts. It is multi-faceted, embodying a wide array of functions and activities that are held in tension only so long as mission is focused on the person of Jesus Christ as Lord and Liberator. That different parts of the Church seize upon certain strands of mission and attempt to make them the dominating and exclusive motifs of mission is evidence of this polymorphous quality.

The whole Church, in facing the whole world in the totality of its historical, social, and spiritual development, must embody all of the meanings connected with mission. Certain parts of the Church will specialize and engage in only one facet of mission, and the Church must be careful that these specializations do not limit the mission of the Church. As the body of Christ encompasses sight, hearing, walking, and touch, so also the Church should encompass all facets of mission.

The purpose of this book is to focus on that part of mission that

---

Spirit; the Spirit is sent by the Son, and the Son is sent by the Father. Because church and mission belong together from the beginning, a church without mission or a mission without the church are both contradictions" (Braaten, 1977, p. 55). "Thus the Church, in its ministry, is carrying out God's will that all creation should know His once-secret plan: that all people in this life should be freed and should come to mature fellowship in union with God and that in eternity they should share his glory (Col. 1:27). This is the goal of God's action, in Christ and in the ministry and mission of the Church. . . . The Church is not an end in itself. The Church exists only for mission. The Church *is* mission" (Krass, 1974, pp. 6, 11). "Mission is not a special function of a part of the church. It is the whole church in action. It is the body of Christ expressing Christ's concern for the whole world" (Miller, 1957, p. 69). ". . . it has increasingly been seen that the essence of the Church cannot be thought of apart from that peculiar movement towards the outside, the world. The distinction between the Church and the world can never signify that there is a separation such that, fundamentally, the Church and the world have nothing to do with each other. Rather, there is a centrifugal motive in the Church's existence" (Berkouwer, 1976, p. 391). ". . . the church is basically a missionary community, i.e., her fundamental character can only be understood from the perspective of God's mission to the world. There is an intrinsic, inseparable relation between the church as such and her calling. In other words, the church is a miraculous redemptive community. Not only is she the product of God's redemptive action in the world, but from the beginning she has been called to be the Spirit's instrument in the activity out of which she herself was born" (Costas, 1974, p. 8).

traditionally has been labeled "evangelization." Current debates over the mission of the Church have led to polarization between the ecumenical and evangelical wings of the Protestant churches. We want to consider a number of issues concerning mission and evangelization in the light of that polarization.

THE DEBATE OVER EVANGELIZATION

From the outset we want to make clear that we consider the extremes in both camps of the contemporary debate to be unfortunate and a needless divorcing of elements of the mission of the Church from one another. There are a host of issues that are successfully mediated within the life of the Church only when they are kept in tension and not allowed to become exclusive preoccupations. One thinks of such issues as personal vs. social gospel, the Kingdom present vs. the Kingdom to come, the inward journey of discipleship vs. the outward journey of evangelism, word vs. deed, and so on. In this connection we empathize with Carl Braaten's words:

> We refuse to take sides in the polarization between evangelical-minded and ecumenical-minded theologians who needlessly restrict the gospel either to its vertical dimension of personal salvation through faith in Jesus Christ or its horizontal dimension of human liberation through the creation of a just social order. It is painful to hear leading evangelicals sneer at the concerns of the ecumenical people who connect mission to liberation, revolution, humanization, dialogue, secularization, socialization, and the like. For the deepest human longings and profoundest social needs are gathered up and reflected in such slogans. To dismiss them to a place of secondary importance is to pass by on the other side while modern man lies in the ditch bleeding to death. It is equally disturbing when ecumenical voices fail to find the language to underscore the permanent relevance of gospel proclamation in sermon and sacraments, in words of witness as well as deeds which lead to personal conversion and the spread of Christianity. In stressing now the social dimensions of the gospel we do not diminish one bit its depth dimension in personal life and the *koinonia* of faith and worship. A theology of the gospel includes both forgiveness and freedom, both faith and food. (1977, pp. 3–4)

The current polarization is an expression of deep differences over a number of crucial questions. On the one hand, there are those who advocate a new understanding of mission and evangelization in the light of all that has been discovered about other religions and the principles articulated in modern theology (Hocking, 1932, 1940; Tillich, 1963; Schlette, 1963). They have stressed a more this-worldly interpretation of Christianity with emphasis on the servant role of the Church in relating to the dire social and political needs of millions of people. Salvation is seen as essentially the humanization of humanity and its world. J. C. Hoekendijk is a representative of this trend. He interprets salvation by the Old Testament idea of "shalom" (an order of peace, integrity, justice, community, and harmony). Evangelism is *not* the planting of churches or the use of confessional propaganda to convince people to believe what Christians have confessed down through the centuries. Salvation is the liberation of oppressed peoples from structures and institutions that dehumanize.

Christ is seen as already present in all the religions as well as the regional and ethnic histories of humanity. People can find salvation without direct contact with or belief in the distinctive Christian gospel. Traditional religions are the "ordinary ways of salvation," whereas explicit commitment to Christian faith is God's "extraordinary way of salvation." In some cases this is joined with the idea that the crucifixion and resurrection of Jesus Christ brought about the reconciliation of all people so that all are born again irrespective of their knowledge or attitude toward the historical saving activity of God in the particular people of Israel or his Messiah, Jesus of Nazareth. Evangelization is the announcement of this fact and the "conscientization" of people in regard to their real social situation so as to bring about the shalom which God desires on this earth. The traditional views and practice of mission are rejected as inadequate, as masks for the ideology and extension of influence of ecclesiastical institutions. Traditional evangelism in these terms is seen as "often little else than a call to restore 'Christendom,' the *Corpus Christianum,* as a solid, well-integrated cultural complex, directed and dominated by the church" (Hoekendijk, 1950, pp. 42–43).

On the other hand, there are those who take a more traditional approach to the nature and task of evangelization. An example is the Frankfurt Declaration of 1970 where several German theological professors and missiologists registered their affirmation of traditional understandings of mission and their rejection of the developing new approaches.

Christian mission discovers its foundation, goals, tasks, and the content of its proclamation solely in the commission of the resurrected Lord Jesus Christ and His saving acts as they are reported by the witness of the apostles and early Christianity in the New Testament. Mission is grounded in the nature of the gospel. . . .

The first and supreme goal of mission is the *glorification* of the name of the one *God* throughout the entire world and the proclamation of the Lordship of Jesus Christ, His Son.

We therefore oppose the assertion that mission today is no longer so concerned with the disclosure of God as the manifestation of a new man and the extension of a new humanity into all social realms. *Humanization* is not the primary goal of mission. It is rather a product of our new birth through God's saving activity in Christ within us, or an indirect result of the Christian proclamation in its power to perform a leavening activity in the course of world history. . . .

Jesus Christ our Savior, true God and true man, as the Bible proclaims him in His personal mystery and His saving work, is the basis, content, and authority of our mission. It is the goal of this mission to make known to all people in all walks of life the Gift of His salvation.

We therefore challenge all non-Christians, who belong to God on the basis of creation, to believe in Him and to be baptized in His name, for in Him alone is eternal salvation promised to them. . . .

Mission is the witness and presentation of eternal salvation performed in the name of Jesus Christ by His Church and fully authorized messengers by means of preaching, the sacraments, and service. This salvation is due to the sacrificial crucifixion of Jesus Christ, which occurred once for all and for all mankind.

The appropriation of this salvation to individuals takes place first, however, through proclamation, which calls for decision, and through baptism, which places the believer in the service of love. Just as belief leads through repentance and baptism to eternal life, so unbelief leads through its rejection of the offer of salvation to damnation. . . .

The primary visible task of mission is *to call out the messianic, saved community* from among all people.

Missionary proclamation should lead everywhere to the establishment of the Church of Jesus Christ, which exhibits a new, defined reality as salt and light in its social environment. . . .

The offer of salvation in Christ is directed without exception to all men who are not yet bound to him in conscious faith. The adherents to the non-Christian religions and world views can receive this salvation only through participation in faith. They must let themselves be freed from their former ties and false hopes in order to be admitted by belief and baptism into the Body of Christ. . . .

The Christian world mission is the decisive, continuous saving activity of God among men between the time of the Resurrection and the Second Coming of Jesus Christ. Through the proclamation of the gospel, new nations and people will progressively be called to decision for or against Jesus Christ. . . .

We do, however, affirm the determined advocacy of justice and peace by all churches, and we affirm that 'assistance in development' is a timely realization of the divine demand for mercy and justice as well as of the command of Jesus: 'Love thy neighbor.'

We see therein an important accompaniment and verification of mission. We also affirm the humanizing results of conversion as signs of the coming Messianic peace. (Beyerhaus, 1971, pp. 113–120)

Both sides have some areas of agreement. Both argue that a more humane and non-oppressive social order and a more just distribution of resources are important concerns of the Church. Both want to see discipleship have its expression in concrete, this-worldly concerns that result in the extension of God's Kingdom into spheres where humanity is oppressed and exploited. But there is disagreement over the priority of the various elements involved in carrying out mission, over what is means and what is end, over the very understanding of the concepts of the Bible as they are utilized to build the foundation for a theology and practice of mission. These differences clearly lead to different prescriptions for the kinds of actions and allocation of resources in mission.

THE KINGDOM OF GOD AND MISSION

We are convinced that only a theology of the Kingdom of God can bring coherence and order to the debate (Bright, 1953; Ladd, 1964, 1974). Jesus' proclamation of the good news of the Kingdom of God is the basis and content of mission. God is bringing about the extension of his rule over an unruly world. The *Missio Dei* is the Kingdom of God and the integrating aim of mission.

The problems that exist within the new as well as the traditional understanding of mission lie in the degree to which they truncate or lose contact with this dynamic reality. Those who have come to stress humanization as the encompassing image of mission have tended to eliminate the tension between the Kingdom as present and the Kingdom as coming. The have been prone to separate the gospel deed from its necessary proclamation in word, to confuse human political action with the acts of God in establishing his Kingdom, to erase the line between the Church as the community of the subjects of that Kingdom and the world as those being called to enter the Kingdom, to neglect the importance of the call to explicit discipleship in a personal sense. The degree to which the political and social dimensions of that Kingdom are stressed to the exclusion of the other equally important dimensions is the measure to which humanization as an ideal narrows the nature of the Kingdom and makes it less than what Jesus proclaimed.

The traditionalists have also often narrowed the scope of the Kingdom. They too have tended to eliminate the tension between the Kingdom present and the Kingdom coming, only in the other direction. They have been prone to eliminate the political and social implications of the gospel, to stress the word over the deed, to offer a discipleship that is only personal and individualistic, to break the connection between the Church as participant in the Kingdom of God and God's action in the world, and to identify the mission of the Church only with proclamation. The degree to which they have stressed a personal-spiritual salvation to the exclusion of the political-social dimensions of the Kingdom is the measure to which they have narrowed the nature of the Kingdom and made it less than what Jesus proclaimed.

Johannes Verkuyl is right in the way in which he sketches the various elements of mission as implicated in the Kingdom of God:

> The kingdom to which the Bible testifies involves a proclamation and a realization of a total salvation, one which covers the whole range of human needs and destroys every pocket of evil and grief affecting mankind. Kingdom in the New Testament has a breadth and scope which is unsurpassed; it embraces heaven as well as earth, world history as well as the whole cosmos. (pp. 197–198)

Thus mission involves confronting people with the urgency and importance of responding to that Kingdom. They are addressed by Jesus to repent and enter through the forgiveness of sins and the accepting love of a heavenly Father. Conversion is imperative if they are to leave the kingdom of darkness and enter into the eternal life and light offered by God. It is a personal, though not an individualistic, call to discipleship: to take up one's own cross and follow Jesus the Messiah. Mission is all this and more. It is the process by which a community of the people of God is formed from all the peoples of the earth. Conversion is not an end in itself but leads to the participation in a people of God with a mission. In the support and nurture of that worshipping community, the Christian finds himself or herself called to participate in the struggle against every form of human ill and evil. The whole of human life falls under the Lordship of Christ, and the mission of the Church finds its wholeness in that comprehensive Lordship.

For years we have debated "social action or evangelism?" Social action dealt with mankind's human needs, while evangelism dealt with spiritual needs. We thus neatly carved people into physical and spiritual beings. Try as we might, we could not bring these two together, nor could we abandon one for the other. The Bible was clear in demanding that we do both. The pendulum often swung back and forth. At times the mission of the Church to non-Christians was confined to doing good to people in need without "interfering" with their values. For others, a people's "ultimate destiny" was the key concern, for what good would it do to help people in this life if they were left "outside Christ" in the next?

As is often the case, the two sides often talk past one another. They fail to see that "social action or evangelism?" is a non-question. It has meaning only when put into context: "Social action or evangelism where? When?" Christian social action and evangelism are actions carried out by Christians. Social action that is not anchored in a biblical theology or a Christian value system is adrift. To speak of liberation apart from the Liberator, of peace but not the Prince of Peace, is to offer something that is sub-Christian. Likewise an evangelism that does not hold men and women accountable for their actions toward one another announces a truncated gospel. The gospel Jesus preached calls people to be more human, to become more what God wants them to be, not only in the hereafter, but in the here and now. It is necessary "for the church to incarnate in *works* of liberation the *gospel* of liberation which, as a *liberated community,* it proclaims" (Krass, 1978, p. 107).

MISSION, EVANGELISM, AND DEVELOPMENT

In this generation, with more mission agencies and churches becoming explicitly involved in various development projects, it is important to address the nature of that expression of mission and its relationship to evangelism. Development is the process of forging new values and enabling a community to have a part in determining its own destiny. *Christian* development makes a statement about what those values should be. It sees value in two dimensions: people interacting with people, and people finding ultimate meaning and value in the person of Jesus Christ. Christian development believes that men and women can be free only when they find freedom in Christ. Christian development always has the *intention* of evangelization, because it offers the only true basis of effective human relationships without which development cannot be fully achieved.

When we enter a situation, our intention may be simply to proclaim the Good News. We may go to an unreached people as evangelists with the intention of being communicators, seeing our calling and gifts as being related to announcing God's word of reconciliation. But once we find ourselves in the community, the demands of the very gospel we proclaim may force us to take other actions. The road to Jericho sets its own agenda.

> Bishop James M. Thoburn of India would on occasion tell of his own experience. He went to India passionately in earnest to "preach the gospel to the heathen," but he had not been there long before he found himself inevitably doing many things which he had never thought of as involved in his original purpose. There was a famine and as a result he found hundreds of homeless children on his hands. What could he do but care for them? The next step was their education, and so he found himself a schoolmaster, and later his school work had to be carried to the point where men could be trained for Christian work. So it went until there were higher schools and hospitals and other forms of work—all in addition to what he thought he had been called to do, "preach the gospel to the heathen." He had discovered that in order to make Christ known and to let men see what the love of God meant it was as necessary to care for men's bodies and see that they had at least the rudiments of education as it was to preach and baptize. (Soper, 1943, p. 243)

Biblical evangelism starts at the point of need of a people. Christian love demands that we reach out to all the needs of a people in compassionate service. Development is not a sub-Christian response that acts as a substitute for the real task of evangelism. It is part of the Christian's commitment to communicate the gospel in word and deed. By its very nature it is limited in scope. Who has the resources to carry out effective development in every poor community of a country? Christian development models what the local church should be, a community of people helping one another, able to love because they are loved by the Maker of the universe.

Christian development therefore has large potential to establish a church that has the capacity to carry the gospel to the edge of its cultural boundaries. One can imagine what a vital force such a church can become! A church that sees Christianity not just as a system of belief with a creedal religious practice, but rather as a joyous desire to share its life in every dimension will quickly become a missionary church. It also will become a community that sees all of life under the Lordship of Christ and continually seeks ways to relate the Kingdom of God in its midst to all the needs of humanity.

Christian development has a number of components. First, it is carried out by Christians, people who have had their own personal encounter with the person of Jesus Christ, people who know that there *is* something more to life than bread. The gospel contains more than the content of the message. If the receptor does not see any evidence of a desirable transformation in the life of the one who offers the gospel, why should he or she be attracted to it?

Second, Christian development attempts to integrate into the process a new world view that results from knowing Christ in such a way that it is seen as part of all that is being offered, that it has a wholeness that encompasses all of life. At the same time, Christian development seeks to avoid the charge that it creates "rice Christians" by its integral and unconditional concern for all of life.

Third, Christian development adopts a stance of learner as well as teacher. Christians engaging in development are themselves undergoing the same process. They are moving toward a more human existence and will learn new dimensions of it from every community they help. This is not to suggest that the Christian becomes a missionary to find a better religion, but rather that he or she expects that the Holy Spirit will have something unique to say when the gospel penetrates a new culture or subculture. Christians discover a beauty and dignity in the pre-Christian culture which also serves as an example of authentic humanness. Christians come as enablers, enablers of other people who have an equal potential to be Spirit-filled, God-led leaders of their own communities.

Fourth, Christian development plans to give the knowledge of the gospel and the outward opportunity to the community so that the community can confront Jesus Christ and who he claims to be. Whether this event should happen is not at question. When and how it will happen are the questions. To enable a community to see how its life is lived in reference to its Maker and Redeemer is not an easy task. It means helping it to realize the immediate relationship between physical, social, cultural, and spiritual dimensions as it confronts Christ.

Fifth, Christian development is just as concerned with measuring a community's movement toward the Savior as it is in measuring progress in food production and health care. In measuring the "quality of life," it includes the spiritual dimension. It is not necessary to be limited only to measuring "decisions for Christ" or church membership.

If the goal of biblical evangelism is to make disciples who will communicate Christ's love to others, Christian development can be a powerful means of evangelism. It crystallizes the dimensions of the Kingdom of God as they infiltrate the life of a particular community. Whether through health care, clean water (more than a cup of it!), agricultural improvement, education, training for income production, or the creation of new social structures, people come to discover that the Christian faith is an incarnated and embodied faith.

Abraham Maslow (1972) pointed out that people have a hierarchy of needs: food, safety, social interaction, esteem, and what he called "self-actualization." These are the dimensions of human life. As Christians, we understand that each must be satisfied if life is to be as full as God intended it to be. To love a people is to respond to their need. All the levels described by Maslow's hierarchy are valid human needs. Christian love demands that we do everything within our power to go to another people, not with set solutions as to what we imagine may be their need, but rather with minds and hearts open to what *they* perceive to be their need.[2]

To those with few material needs we offer not only more satisfying interpersonal relationships and feelings of self-worth, but we point them to the One in whom can be found true "self-actualization," a self-actualization experienced by the indwelling of the Holy Spirit and centered upon a suffering Savior. To those in material need we offer what we can, not because it is their ultimate need, but because Christian love demands it. We cannot call people to a "new life in Christ" unless we are willing to demonstrate that new life.

We may not always be able to do that. We may be called to live and proclaim Christ among a people whose needs overwhelm us. Our vial of oil and our purse may be quickly emptied. To cease to announce the possibility of reconciliation with God, to refuse to meet the need for a new allegiance or a new set of values just because we cannot meet all the needs of hunger and safety and self-esteem is sub-Christian. But to refuse to give what we are able to give is just as sub-Christian.

2. James Engel elaborates on this in *Contemporary Christian Communications, Its Theory and Practice* (1979).

CHAPTER 7

Evangelization

E vangelism is part of the mission of the Church. The Church is in the world as the agent and sign of the Kingdom of God. As such the Church is sent into the world to serve all peoples of the earth, and to have the compassion of God for all human needs. Whenever the Church touches the world through caring service, sensitive evangelization, prophetic opposition to injustice, and an identification with the sufferings of others, it is engaged in mission. Mission as participation in the *Missio Dei* is a broader reality than evangelism. Evangelism is indeed an indispensable and central component of mission and the Church. The Church ceases to participate in the mission of God when it no longer engages in evangelism. But evangelism does not exhaust the purposes for which God sends it into the world as he sent his Son (Jn. 20:21).

THE MEANING OF THE WORD
IN THE NEW TESTAMENT

Our word for "evangelism" or "evangelization" is derived from a Greek word: *euangelion*. Actually there are four forms of the basic word: two verbs meaning "to proclaim good news," and two nouns, one meaning "evangelist" and the other meaning the "good news"

70

brought by the evangelist (Friedrich, 1964; Becker, 1976). In order to discover the meaning of evangelism as part of the mandate of the Church in mission, we must begin with the perspective and authority of the New Testament.

The overwhelming emphasis of the New Testament is on the saving events surrounding the incarnation, life, teachings, miracles, death, and triumphant resurrection of Jesus Christ (Stott, 1975, pp. 44–54). Whether it be the Gospels of Matthew, Mark, Luke, and John, or the letters of Paul, Peter, James, and John, the focus of concern is the meaning of Jesus Christ, the Messiah and Lord of all. God has entered human history and provided salvation for all who carry the burden of guilt and live in the fear of death. Nothing can ever be the same because Jesus Christ has remade all of human history by his power and permanent presence. God's love has been manifested so completely that all who put their trust in Jesus of Nazareth are promised eternal life and the gift of God's Spirit. God has made his rule available and present through Jesus Christ, and all who turn from their idols in repentance can enter that Kingdom and become citizens of the commonwealth of heaven.

There is not a single page or paragraph of the New Testament that does not find its center in this flaming reality (Braaten, 1977). It is significant that although the books of Matthew, Mark, Luke, and John are not called gospels in the New Testament, they soon acquired that name in the early Church. There was the realization that they described, each in its own unique way, the very heart of the Good News which the Church was to proclaim. The Good News was the story of Jesus of Nazareth who was the Lord of the universe.

These *euangelion* words are focused on *a message to be communicated.* It is interesting to note that these four words are derived from the Greek word *angelos,* which means "angel" or "messenger" of God. The message of good tidings from God is to be shared with all peoples. Jesus Christ himself announced this gospel: "The right time has come . . . and the Kingdom of God is near! Turn away from your sins and believe the Good News!" (Mk. 1:15). "Jesus went all over Galilee, teaching in the synagogues, preaching the Good News about the Kingdom. . ." (Mt. 4:23). Jesus is the first evangelist of the New Testament, continuing and fulfilling the ministry of John the Baptist. Evangelism has its origin, pattern, and basis in the activity of the evangelist Jesus Christ. We proclaim the Kingdom of God which he proclaimed and manifested.

According to Jesus, the Kingdom of God which was promised in the Old Testament is now dynamically present to overcome evil, to deliver humans from the power of sin and death, and to usher people into the blessings of the reign of God himself. The fulfillment of the promises of God no longer await the apocalyptic events of the end of time, but are already being anticipated by his own ministry and miracles. Those who are present are fortunate and blessed because their "eyes see and ... ears hear" (Mt. 13:16). Although it is inaugurated by Jesus, that Kingdom will not reach its fulfillment until the coming of the Son of Man on the clouds with the angels (Mt. 24:30, 31). Still, God is no longer waiting for the initiative of humans to submit to his reign but is invading history in a new and unexpected way. His Kingdom is invisible except to those who have the eyes of faith. We cannot control or manipulate it. We can only submit to it.

Jesus commits the message of the Kingdom to his apostles and tells them to carry it to all peoples: "This Good News about the Kingdom will be preached through all the world for a witness to all mankind; and then the end will come" (Mt. 24:14). "Go throughout the whole world and preach the gospel to all mankind. Whoever believes and is baptized will be saved; whoever does not believe will be condemned" (Mk. 16:15). "This is what is written: the Messiah must suffer and must rise from death three days later, and in his name the message about repentance and the forgiveness of sins must be preached to all nations, beginning in Jerusalem. You are witness of these things" (Lk. 24:46–48).

This message is so charged with the power of God that when it is accepted it brings God's salvation, and when it is rejected it brings God's condemnation (Jn. 3:16–21). It produces peace and reconciles enemies such as the Jews and Gentiles. To evangelize in the New Testament perspective is to declare the salvation made available in Jesus Christ. But it involves more than a single, simple form of communication. Whereas we have tended to restrict proclamation to preaching from a pulpit, to mass evangelism, or to quiet personal witness (each in its own way an authentic form for declaring the Good News), the New Testament ransacks the Greek vocabulary to emphasize all the ways in which the message of the presence of God's Kingdom can be proclaimed.

The Good News is to be *proclaimed (kērussō)* like a herald declaring a victory. It is a word that can be *declared with enthusiasm (apophthengesthai), spoken freely and openly (parrēsiadzesthai),* even *called out in a loud voice (krazō).* Or it can be a matter of everyday simple *speaking (legō, laleō)* or *conversing (homileō)* with another. It can be *discussed (dialegesthai),* explained or *interpreted (diermēneuō), transmitted (paradidomai),* or simply *announced (angellō).* The evangelist who relates this message acts not as one dispassionately relaying one message among others or a message that does not concern his or her own deepest being. It is a message that is *confessed (homologeō)*, a reality to which the evangelist gives *witness (matureō)* as one who personally knows the power and dynamic of the Good News. This word from God can be *described (diēgeisthai, ekdiēgeisthai, exēgeisthai)*. It can be expressed with such conviction that its recipients are *entreated (parakaleō)*, *admonished (elenchō)*, seriously *warned (epitimaō)*, and *persuaded (peithō)*. It is declared not only to those who have never heard of the Kingdom in Jesus Christ but also to Christians. They are *taught (didaskō)* the Good News, and it is *revealed (gnōrizō)* to them (Friedrich, 1965, pp. 683–718, particularly p. 703).

In sum, the New Testament declares an important message which needs to be communicated. This message comes from God in the person of Jesus Christ. He is both the evangelist *par excellence* and the one who embodied the Good News in dynamic works of power, signs, and authoritative teachings which he gave to his disciples. This message is of such importance that it has the power to convey the abundant life of the Kingdom of God to those who are willing to receive it.

EVANGELISTS OF THE KINGDOM

The word for evangelist, unlike the other Greek terms dealing with evangelizing and evangel, is found infrequently (only three times). It refers to Philip (Acts 21:8), Timothy (II Tim. 4:5), and evangelists as gifts to the Church (Eph. 4:11). It might seem strange in the early Church where so much evangelization took place that so few were given this designation. In these three passages, the evangelist is distinguished from the apostle. Some have suggested that the word may denote a *function* rather than an office in the early Church. It is apparent that all the apostles were also evangelists, but not all evangelists were also apostles. Those who were evangelists were subordinate to the apostles in that they carried on the work of the apostles with their authorization. The second-century church considered the evangelists to be successors of the apostles. It should be noted that the custom of calling the writers of the gospels "evangelists" arose only after their writings became known as "gospels."

The reticence of the New Testament in using this designation is the result of two things. First, the whole Church was seen as engaging in the task of proclaiming the gospel. Through casual contacts, preaching in the marketplaces, and acts of charity and love, all the members of the body were involved in declaring the reality of the gospel. As time progressed, some believers may have been recognized as being especially called and gifted to communicate the gospel. All three of the biblical references to individuals as evangelists come relatively late in the history of the apostolic Church. It signals a growing awareness that:

> although evangelism is a prime responsibility of the whole Church and to that extent all Christians are to be involved in evangel*ism*, not all Christians are called to be evangel*ists*. All Christians belong to the Church, which is inescapably involved in evangelism, but many Christians will find their primary sphere of service *within* the Body of Christ. (Watson, 1976, p. 35)

Second, it may be that the focus of attention is so strongly on the proclamation of the message that other concerns such as properly designating people in terms of office or function are overshadowed. New Testament documents show relatively little concern for matters of ecclesiastical order and prove difficult to appeal to to settle many of our modern disputes about this or that way of organizing the offices of the church. We know there were those with a special calling and gift for evangelism by the third or fourth decade of the birth of the Church. We also know that the message was carried by all members of the Church even when they were not formally designated as evangelists. Their new life motivated them to share it naturally and continuously throughout the Roman world (Green, 1970).

The concern of the early Church was not to sort out the relationships of offices and organizations followed by various parts of the Church so much as it was to facilitate the spread of the gospel and to help Christians understand the radical ways in which their lives and relationships were to change because of their new participation in the presence of the Kingdom. The emphasis was on clarifying and applying the meaning of the Good News, not on spelling out a set of job descriptions and organizational slots for evangelists and other functionaries to fill. Consequently, there are few references to specific individuals who had a special ability and devotion to evangelization.

Yet we do not want to forget that the apostles were considered evangelists *par excellence,* worthy of imitation. They gave witness to the resurrected Christ who had personally commissioned them. It is their primary witness and proclamation which is preserved in the New Testament and serves as a model for proclaiming the Good News. Modern-day evangelists witness to the gospel of the apostles who served as the first link in the chain of tradition that passed on the proclamation of the Kingdom of God that began with Jesus of Nazareth.

WHAT IS THE GOSPEL?

Paul describes the Good News as a sacred trust (II Tim. 4:17) which has been committed to him by God and which he must proclaim at every opportunity. His basic attitude is that those without knowledge of the Good News have a right to hear. We are obligated to share it (Rom. 1:13–15): "I want to win converts among you also, as I have among other Gentiles. For I have an obligation to all peoples, to the civilized and to the savage, to the educated and to the ignorant. So then, I am eager to preach the Good News to you also who live in Rome." Again in his letter to the Corinthians (I Cor. 9:16) he describes this conviction: "I have no right to boast just because I preach the gospel. After all, I am under orders to do so. And how terrible it would be for me if I did not preach the gospel!"

The shape and content of this message is so definite that Paul describes it as a "pattern of sound words" (II Tim. 1:13) which he urges Timothy to hold firmly in a spirit of faith and love. To evangelize means to make *this* message known in the power of the Holy Spirit. There are substitute gospels that might claim to be the word from God but, in actuality, are only products of human creation which have the potential of invalidating the true gospel (Gal. 1:6–9). Yet it is equally clear that the gospel can be expressed in a variety of ways. A study of the speeches of Acts, the declarations of Jesus, and the indirect statements of the gospel in the apostolic letters reveals this.

There was a unity to the proclamation of the early Church that was found in the common witness to Jesus Christ. It was, however, "varied in its presentation of his relevance to the varied needs of the listeners, urgent in its demand for decision" (Green, 1970, p. 66). The "pattern of sound words" was not a straitjacket, rigidly restricting the expression of the gospel to but one formula or form. Yet it was substantive enough to gauge the faithfulness of the varied expressions. If there was a diversity of expression, there was also a unifying center that found its limits in the reality of the crucified and risen Lord Jesus Christ (Dunn, 1977). What is the nature and content of this message which the evangelist proclaims? If we are to understand evangelization, we must understand it in terms of the evangel which motivates its activity and serves as the content, the basis, the form, and the emphasis of evangelism.

There are a variety of ways to approach this question. One might ask, what is the irreducible minimum one must know and believe in order to be saved? Or one might ask, given the diversity of contexts in which the gospel is being proclaimed, what is the shared commonness in all these contexts that makes each a faithful witness to the gospel? Or, it might be approached from a theological perspective: what is the core of the proclamation of the early Church against which all other proclamation must be measured if it is to be judged a valid expression of the Good News? In each case the answer might be somewhat different, or at least phrased in a different fashion.

Many attempts to encapsulate the gospel have been made. Many point to Paul's words in I Corinthians 15:1–5 as the first attempt:

> And now I want to remind you, my brothers, of the Good News which I preached to you, which you received, and on which your faith stands firm. That is the gospel, the message that I preached to you. You are saved by the gospel if you hold firmly to it—unless it was for nothing that you believed.
>
> I passed on to you what I received, which is of the greatest importance: that Christ died for our sins, as written in the Scriptures; that he was buried and that he was raised to life three days later, as written in the Scriptures; that he appeared to Peter and then to all the apostles.

Here we have an early and brief statement of the essential content of the Good News: Jesus Christ died for our sins and was raised to new life. Whatever the gospel is about, it centers in the person and actions of Jesus Christ. God has intervened to make available the salvation of all humans. This salvation which is declared in the gospel is found in Jesus Christ, a carpenter from Nazareth.

Other attempts to state the essential content of the gospel have been made. An examination of these statements shows the degree to which they all agree that Jesus Christ is the essence of the gospel. It should be noted here that we are talking about the irreducible *minimum* or starting point of the gospel, not the destination of understanding which would be desirable for all disciples of Christ. We are seeking the center of the gospel, not its circumference.

Following are some statements which express the heart of the evangel:

> To evangelize is to spread the good news that Jesus Christ died for our sins and was raised from the dead according to the Scrip-

tures, and that as the reigning Lord he now offers the forgiveness of sins and the liberating gift of the Spirit to all who repent and believe. (Douglas, 1974, p. 4)

Thus in spite of the development of thought exhibited in them, the three major witnesses [Jesus, Paul, John] of the theology of the New Testament are in agreement in the twofold message, that God has caused his salvation promised for the end of the world to begin in Jesus Christ, and that in this Christ event God has encountered us and intends to encounter us as the Father who seeks to rescue us from imprisonment in the world and to make us free for active love. (Kümmel, 1975, p. 332)

Evangelization will also always contain—as the foundation, center, and at the same time summit of its dynamism—a clear proclamation that in Jesus Christ, the Son of God made man, who died and rose from the dead, salvation is offered to all men as a gift of God's grace and mercy. And not an immanent salvation, meeting material or even spiritual needs, restricted to the framework of temporal existence and completely identified with temporal desires, hopes, affairs and struggles, but a salvation which exceeds all these limits in order to reach fulfillment in a communion with the one and only divine Absolute: a transcendent and eschatological salvation, which indeed has its beginning in this life but which is fulfilled in eternity. (Pope Paul VI, 1976, p. 21)

The whole content of [Paul's] preaching can be summarized as the proclamation and explication of the eschatological time of salvation inaugurated with Christ's advent, death, and resurrection. (Ridderbos, 1975, p. 44)

The heart of the apostolic kerygma is the proclamation of the Lordship of Jesus (II Cor. 4:5). Christians are those who have received Christ Jesus as Lord. (Ladd, 1974, p. 339)

The message is first and foremost a declaration. It is good news about God. It is the story of what God has done in and through His Son Jesus Christ, our Lord and Saviour. He has established His Kingdom. True, the full manifestation of the Kingdom is yet to come. We await the final consummation. But the Kingdom of God has been inaugurated. The time has been fulfilled. (Stott, 1964, p. 176)

In briefest outline, this message contained: (1) A historical proclamation of the death, resurrection, and exaltation of Jesus set forth as the fulfilment of prophecy and involving man's responsibility; (2) A theological evaluation of the person of Jesus as both Lord and Christ; (3) A summons to repent and receive the forgiveness of sins. (Mounce, 1960, p. 257)

In Paul *euangelion* has become a central concept of his theology. It means the familiar good news: that God has acted for the salvation of the world in the incarnation, death, and resurrection of Jesus. In so far as this event is already promised in the Old Testament, the Old Testament belongs to the gospel. (Becker, 1976, p. 111)

The gospel is to be found in the Bible. In fact, there is a sense in which the whole Bible is gospel, from Genesis to Revelation. For its overriding purpose throughout is to bear witness to Christ, to proclaim the good news that he is lifegiver and Lord, and to persuade people to trust in him. . . .

The Bible proclaims the gospel story in many forms. The gospel is like a multi-faceted diamond, with different aspects that appeal to different people in different cultures. It has depths we have not fathomed. It defies every attempt to reduce it to a neat formulation. . . .

Nevertheless, it is important to identify what is at the heart of the gospel. We recognize as central the themes of God as Creator, the universality of sin, Jesus Christ as Son of God, Lord of All, and Saviour through his atoning death and risen life, the necessity of conversion, the coming of the Holy Spirit and his transforming power, the fellowship and mission of the Christian church, and the hope of Christ's return. (Lausanne Committee, 1978b, pp. 12–13)

The crux of the Good News is that God has acted decisively in Jesus of Nazareth to inaugurate an age of salvation in which all who call upon him in faith and confess him as Lord will be made right. God offers reconciliation with himself and with an alienated world through his Son. We who were far away from God are now able to come close because of the incarnation, death, and resurrection of Jesus Christ. We who were enslaved by a variety of "powers" are now able to be set free. A vast array of metaphors and expressions are caught up in the reality of this message and made vitally alive for all who hear and believe. The irreducible minimum of the Gospel is the person of Jesus Christ, the living Word of God, who must be encountered and submitted to for one to enter the Kingdom of God. It is Jesus Christ who gives evangelism its dynamic and who is its basis, form, and content. Because the gospel is more than a formula to believe (though it is a pattern of sound words), because it is not simply a fixed kerygma which must be slavishly mimicked, because it is a living Word, it cannot be fully or finally expressed in a single statement or creed. It can only be approximated by statements that will vary according to the audience being addressed, the cultural and historical context, and the theological tradition from which a person speaks. This does not mean that there is no identifiable core to the gospel, but rather that it is a unity that exists in diversity, a single message that has many valid and important expressions.

Above all else, the authentic witness to and proclamation of Jesus Christ serves as the center of the gospel. It is he who must be proclaimed in evangelization if it is to have or find any authenticity. In the proclamation of Jesus other basic themes of the Bible will find their subsidiary and supporting places. So also the ramifications and demands of the gospel in a given context will have their powerful effect when they grow out of the witness to the living Christ.

It is important to acknowledge that the Good News must be lived as well as verbalized. Those who follow the One who submitted to the cruel death of the cross cannot expect a life free from suffering and sacrifice as they seek to evangelize the world. The evangel is not simply the message Jesus proclaimed. It is also the reality that Jesus lived, the Kingdom which he brought. The evangelist must live the evangel if it is to have any credibility or authenticity.

DEFINING EVANGELISM

In the light of the brief New Testament description of evangelism, we want to define evangelism in a way that will be useful when planning strategies. Numerous definitions have been suggested. The Evanston Assembly of 1954 described evangelism as "the bringing of persons to Christ as Saviour and Lord that they may share in his eternal life" (Stott, 1975, p. 39). Michael Green in his magnificent book, *Evangelism in the Early Church,* speaks of evangelism as "proclaiming the good news of salvation to men and women with a view to their conversion to Christ and incorporation into his Church" (1970, p. 7). The Anglican Archbishops' "Committee of Enquiry into the Evangelistic Work of the Church" of 1919 in England declared that evangelism is "to so present Christ Jesus in the power of the Holy Spirit that men shall come to put their trust in God through Him, to accept Him as their Saviour, and serve Him as their King in the Fellowship of His Church."

The Lausanne Congress on World Evangelism (1974) gave a more detailed definition:

> To evangelize is to spread the good news that Jesus Christ died for our sins and was raised from the dead according to the Scriptures, and that as the reigning Lord he now offers the forgiveness of

sins and the liberating gift of the Spirit to all who repent and believe. Our Christian presence in the world is indispensable to evangelism and so is that kind of dialogue whose purpose is to listen sensitively in order to understand. But evangelism itself is the proclamation of the historical, biblical Christ as Savior and Lord, with a view to persuading people to come to him personally and so be reconciled to God. In issuing the Gospel invitation we have no liberty to conceal the cost of Discipleship. Jesus still calls all who would follow him to deny themselves, take up their cross, and identify themselves with his new community. The results of evangelism include obedience to Christ, incorporation into his church, and responsible service to the world. (Douglas, 1975, p. 4)

All of these definitions express various aspects of evangelism. They are all responding to the Bible and its various statements and portraits of evangelization seen in the early Church. Our problem is to be *biblically responsible* and yet at the same time find a definition of evangelism that can be used *within a strategy perspective.* There probably is no single definition of evangelism that could be universally accepted, but the basic intent of the word can be expressed simply:

> *To evangelize is to communicate the gospel in such a way that men and women have a valid opportunity to accept Jesus Christ as Lord and Savior and become responsible members of his Church.*

Several facets of this definition need to be spelled out. First, everyone comes to each new experience with his own knowledge, attitudes, behavior, and relationships, which are modified by that experience. Evangelization can be described as offering knowledge ("to communicate the gospel") which will change attitudes and lead to new behavior ("accept Jesus Christ as Lord and Savior"), and which will establish new relationships both between the individual and the Creator and between individuals ("and become responsible members of His Church").

Second, this definition is intentionally silent on the specific phrasing or expression of the gospel other than to indicate that it leads a person to embrace Jesus Christ as Lord and Savior. We believe there is a heart to the gospel and have attempted to point to that heart through the statements of a number of writers. The Willowbank Report gives a good statement of the broader range of matters that are drawn into that center. But it is impossible to specify a single expression as universal since the gospel can be communicated in a variety of ways. Which elements of the basic message should be presented in what time sequence, and which points of contact and needs must be addressed, will all vary from place to place and people to people. The important thing is that all of the claims of the gospel are communicated to those whom we hope will respond to Christ's gracious offer of forgiveness.

Third, there has been some debate as to whether the definition of evangelism should include the winning of disciples. Both John Stott and J. I. Packer criticize the Archbishops' definition for including a desired end ("that men *shall* come to put their trust in God . . . ") in the definition (Stott, 1975, pp. 39–40). In this way it appears that evangelism takes place only when people actually commit themselves to Christ. For them evangelism is to "announce the good news, irrespective of the results" (Stott, 1975b, p. 69). We have included commitment to Christ as part of our definition because it serves an extremely useful focus in planning strategy.

Let us assume for the moment that "the *purpose* of evangelism is to give men and women a valid opportunity to accept Jesus Christ as Lord and Savior." Let us also agree that this is a good definition for the purposes of discussion. Now the difficulty with such a definition is not that it is wrong, but that when the time comes to put it into practice, we need some way of *measuring* its accomplishment. We need to know whether we have actually practiced evangelism. The only way we can know this in any comprehendible way is if we define what the *results* of evangelism should or might be.

According to our definition there are a number of possible results: (1) A person can accept Jesus Christ and become a part of a worshipping fellowship of Christians. (2) A person can accept Jesus Christ, make a decision to follow Christ, but not join any local expression of the Church. (3) A person may understand the claims of the gospel, have a grasp of the fundamentals of the Good News, and yet not be ready to make a commitment. Such a person is evangelized in one sense, having been given a valid opportunity, but remaining indecisive. (4) A person can make a conscious, informed decision to reject the offer of salvation and remain outside the body of Christ. Such a person also can be viewed as evangelized if the communication was valid within the cultural context.

The first response is measurable and observable. We can see that a person has joined a fellowship of believers and is living a life which to the best of our knowledge shows the marks of Christian growth and maturity. It is much more difficult to measure the other three responses, especially for results, since there is the possibility for a change of mind at some future date.

Therefore, while the *purpose* of evangelism may be to give people a valid opportunity to accept Jesus Christ, the simplest (measurable and accomplishable) *goal* of evangelism must be to bring people into the fellowship of a local body of believers. Certainly this is what Jesus meant when he said, "Go and make disciples. . . . " When this is compared with the response to Peter's preaching on the day of Pentecost, during which three thousand people became disciples, we can come to no other conclusion. That we have no assurance that all of the men and women who join a local fellowship are necessarily Christians should not keep us from operating on the assumption that the probability that they are Christians is much higher than the probability that they are not.

Thus we can distinguish several aspects of our definition:

The *nature* of evangelism is the communication of the Good News.

The *purpose* of evangelism is to give individuals and groups a valid opportunity to accept Jesus Christ.

The *goal* of evangelism is to persuade men and women to become disciples of Jesus Christ and to serve him in the fellowship of his Church.

Fourth, we need to define what we mean by "a valid opportunity," for it is a vague and undefined phrase. It is true that it is difficult to measure when or whether a person or group has had a valid opportunity to accept Jesus Christ. Studies in communication as well as our own personal experience show that mere exposure to the proclamation of the gospel or some other message is not necessarily sufficient to provide the understanding and motivation to make a decision about it. Sometimes the message is phrased in words we really do not understand. Or it may be presented by someone who is part of a group we dislike. Or perhaps we were simply not paying much attention when the message was being declared. There are a thousand reasons why exposure is not the same as successful communication. To be sure, there must be exposure, but it must also be understood and retained long enough for a person to act on it.

We see a number of ways to assess whether or not a person or group has been given a valid opportunity to respond to Jesus Christ.

1. The gospel, and not some substitute, must be communicated.

2. The messengers who proclaimed the gospel must be authentic disciples of Jesus Christ. They must be people who themselves have submitted to the demands of the gospel.

3. The message must be phrased in the language and idioms, the thought forms and world view of the listeners who are being asked to make a decision. For example, if the listeners are illiterate, the message must reach them in an oral form.

4. The means of communication must be suited to the social structure and communication patterns common to the people. If an important message from God is normally shared by older men at a special feast, the gospel ought itself to be communicated in a similar fashion.

5. The witness to Jesus Christ must be sustained long enough to be comprehensible to the average person of the group being evangelized. We cannot conclude that a village has been evangelized simply because we have preached there one time.

6. Ultimately, a valid opportunity implies the work and presence of the Holy Spirit. Paul's preaching was not in words of wisdom, but in demonstration of power. It is the Holy Spirit who must intervene in the mixture of personalities, culture, message presentation, and methods to open the hearts of the hearers and give them a faith response to Jesus Christ. The Holy Spirit is indispensable for whatever is necessary in miracles of love and healing.

A valid opportunity is thus not a simple matter of throwing the words of the gospel out into the air, hoping that they might find a responsive hearing. It may take weeks of careful and sustained proclamation and explanation. A person may have to hear the message a hundred times before he or she comprehends this strange, new doctrine. Even Paul, speaking in one of his native languages, was misunderstood when he preached in the market at Athens (Acts 17:18). Some thought he was preaching about "foreign gods"—one named "Jesus" and the other "Resurrection" (in the Greek the feminine noun "resurrection" could be understood as the name of a goddess). How much exposure, what use of the traditional channels of communication, what rephrasing of the authentic gospel message will be necessary will vary and is definable only in terms of the particular qualities and background of the evangelizing agent and those being evangelized.

EVANGELIZATION AS A PROCESS

There are some helpful distinctions which will guide how we use several terms. *Evangelization* is the total process of announcing the Good News and bringing people into discipleship with Christ in his community. Evangelization should be seen as a process to be enhanced, rather than a goal to be achieved. The Bible gives us no numerical definition as to when the goal of world evangelization will be reached, only the situation that will surround it (Mt. 24:14).

In contrast, *evangelism* generally means the specific acts or methods associated with the process of evangelization. When we speak of the evangelization of a people, we refer to the total context of circumstances, evangelism events and approaches, personal contacts, and media programs that move individuals and groups through a decision-making process that confronts them with Jesus Christ. Most of our goals deal with the specific events of evangelism rather than the overall evangelization process. Goals are needed for measuring progress and for effective communication with other Christians and organizations. But it is one thing to measure the decisions and new church members that are the by-products of a crusade, and quite another to enhance the process of evangelization by producing communities of Christians who have a desire to bring others to Christ.

We must recognize that while the task of a given act of evangelism might be completed and put behind us, the process of evangelization continues unabated until Christ himself returns: "And this Good News about the Kingdom will be preached through all the world for a witness to all mankind; and then the end will come" (Mt. 24:14). On one hand, this Kingdom has arrived. It has been announced in the person of God's Son, Jesus Christ. To accept citizenship in the Kingdom is to first see oneself as standing outside the Kingdom, alienated and separated from God, and then to accept the gracious gift of salvation offered through trust and saving faith in Jesus as the Son of God.

On the other hand, the Kingdom has not arrived. It is yet to come in its fulness. We who now partake of the Kingdom have been given only a foretaste of the full power and peace of that coming Kingdom. We exist in the tension between a Kingdom come and coming. Biblical eschatology does not give a specific time for the coming of the Kingdom. There is a tension between sayings that stress the imminence of the Day of the Lord and those that indicate an indefinite delay. As George Ladd indicates about the synoptic Gospels:

> They leave the reader in a situation where he cannot date the time of the end; he cannot say that it will surely come tomorrow, or next week, or next year; neither can he say that it will not come for a long time. The keynote is: "Watch therefore, for you know neither the day nor the hour." (1974, p. 210)

Evangelization must continue. We must be preoccupied with the spreading of the Kingdom of God even as we watch for the coming of the Kingdom. In acts of evangelism and social action, in special programs of compassion and nurture, we must prepare ourselves and help others to prepare themselves for the King's coming.

CHAPTER 8

Defining Your Mission

We have looked closely at the meaning and dimensions of mission. We have tried to clarify what evangelization involves. Now we face the question of mission definition: How do we decide *who* to evangelize? None of us can take responsibility for the evangelization of the whole world. We have to discover that part of the total process for which God wants us or our church to accept responsibility. Paul was an apostle to the Gentiles. His own sense of calling and identity with the task of evangelization of the first-century Roman world focused on only a part of that world. He did not try to go east into the Parthian Empire and beyond to India. Nor did he consider it his job to stay in Palestine and continue evangelizing the Jews of that region. Paul attempted to evangelize only one part of the world—the gentiles of the Roman empire. We too need to define what part of the world we are to evangelize.

ASSUMPTIONS FOR MISSION DEFINITION

In order to determine where we might do the greatest good for the Kingdom of God, we will follow a number of basic assumptions (these are justified and developed in other parts of the book):

1. People can be most meaningfully viewed when compartmentalized or segmented into sub-cultural social groupings of various types.

2. The communication of any message or the expression of compassion will be most effective and meaningful when it acknowledges and makes use of the characteristics of these sub-cultural groups (Engel, 1979, p. 32).

3. The definition of mission, including evangelization, begins with the selection of a specific sub-cultural group (and within that group, some smaller unit such as a particular community or a special segment such as youth).

Such assumptions go counter to the traditional focus of many missions and much popular thought that centers on a *country*. In the past many missions came into existence to evangelize a given *geographical* area, for example, the West Indies Mission, China Inland Mission, Red Sea Mission, and Afghan Border Mission.

To some extent these assumptions also go counter to the basis on which a significant amount of methodology is presently based: the hope that the majority of a geographical region can be reached effectively through a widespread trade language, or lingua franca. Trade language evangelism and church planting have been adopted for a number of reasons. Practically speaking, many cross-cultural evangelists have paled at the thought of learning two or even three languages in order to function effectively within a country and with a specific people. A missionary from Germany going to Kenya would have to have some command of English and Swahili in order to deal with many governmental and trading situations. If he or she also went to the Turkana, an additional language would have to be learned. Many Turkana know neither English nor Swahili. Also, the issue of Christian leadership training (based on the Western college or seminary model) in a former colonial situation where there are dozens, if not hundreds, of language groups has made it appear best to adopt a single, trade-language approach. As a result of these practical considerations, workers in evangelism and education have often ignored sub-cultural differences.

This has fundamental implications for Bible translation as well. We do not want to make pronouncements here about the difficult problem of vernacular vs. popular language usage. However, we do want to point out that the decision to function in a trade language rather than a vernacular language is a decision to define one's mission. Assuming that an audience can be reached by a trade language can narrow the effective contact which we have in a given geographical area without our realizing it (Wonderly, 1968, chapters 1–5).

Using a trade language has not always been bad. But it has meant that:

1. Many Christians have been selected from among a people on the basis of their command or use of the trade language. This choice has discriminated against the women of a society who often do not use the trade language.

2. Many trade language situations select the modern sectors of a people, those who are assimilating to a dominant surrounding culture (e.g., Spanish or Ladino culture in Central America). The church thus becomes identified with rejecting traditional life and language. For example, in Central America among the Mam Indians, the Christians show relatively little interest in the vernacular translation. Their church services are conducted in the trade language and they only participate in the larger church hierarchy which uses the trade language. Consequently, the church has little to offer the traditional mono-lingual Mam.

3. The educated leaders of the church are trained in terminology and perspectives that are foreign to their primary cultural identity. When asked to utilize some of the concepts of the New Testament in order to interpret God's action in Christ, they find themselves at a loss in the vernacular. They do not know a good word or phrase to translate what they have learned in the trade language where they never had to face many of the practical issues which face them in the traditional culture. Furthermore, they are taught "standard solution" methodologies for handling various evangelistic and pastoral problems, methodologies which may not touch the traditional culture at its key pressure points. As a result, there is a shallow, often misguided encounter between the Christian faith and the life of a people.

4. Because of the dependence on the trade language, mono-lingual individuals who exhibit gifts of natural leadership are passed over in the church for younger persons who have lower potential for leadership in the traditional culture. Community leadership patterns tend to be bypassed in favor of those that can be enhanced only by the trade language in formal educational experiences modeled after the West.

5. The cross-cultural evangelist remains on the outside of a social system which, by the nature of the language choice, is never really understood. Language is a key component of the meaning system of a people (see chapter 11) and cannot be bypassed in attempting a trans-culturation of the meanings of the gospel for a specific people.

In short, our assumptions reject the notion that mission definition can stop with the selection of a country or a major trade language. Rather mission must focus on a specific sub-cultural grouping of people. Selecting a given people group within their language and political context is crucial for mission definition.

THE NEED FOR MISSION DEFINITION

Many missionaries and mission agencies are frustrated when faced with the complexities of the modern world. We know that there are over five thousand distinct language groups and over two hundred nation-states. Hundreds of thousands of villages currently have no indigenous witness to Jesus Christ. How do we go about deciding what to do, where to place personnel, which people to evangelize and which not to evangelize? These are serious and difficult questions which can occupy a great deal of time and effort as we try to discover our part in evangelization in this generation.

We need to define mission because of at least two basic realities: First, we know that communication is effective only when it is aimed at specific, limited audiences. This is what we see happening in the New Testament. There is no "shotgun" approach, sending the same message in the same form to all audiences with the vague hope that somebody somewhere might be struck by the truth. The early Church carefully adjusted the form of the message so that it would be understandable and persuasive to different audiences. When Paul preached in the Jewish synagogue, he recognized both Jewish members and Gentile God-fearers who followed the Old Testament law and prophets. His message was tailored to be understandable and appealing to them (Acts 17:22–34). In Athens, when addressing Greeks who had little or no contact with Jewish traditions, he changed his approach. He knew they were saturated in current Epicurean and Stoic philosophy. His message was filled with allusions to and statements about those philosophies (Acts 17:22–34). Although in both cases the evangelistic intent shines through his words, it is apparent that Paul knew the specific characteristics of the audience he addressed, and that this made a great difference in how he expressed the gospel. (In our section on "Describing a People" we will develop this theme in greater detail.)

Second, our current approaches have been less than satisfactory. Of course this varies from mission to mission. A quick survey of Protestant agencies with a combined staff of over four thousand missionaries indicated that none was satisfied with his field selection process. Most had no criteria by which to select a new field. For those churches and groups where the individual missionary has a great deal of latitude in field selection, the frustration was even greater. Daniel C. Hardin of the Churches of Christ writes:

> The fact is that many missionaries use little objective judgment in selecting their fields. When this writer is asked what influenced him to go to Korea, he usually replies that it was God's guidance. That answer seems necessary because the only other alternative is to call it a matter of pure chance. He did not search for the best place, ask the advice of responsible elders, study the literature, or use any of the tools and resources available but merely accepted an invitation to go to Korea and trusted that it was God's will. He is not ashamed of that decision to go to Korea because it was honest and based upon all that he knew back in 1957. Today, however, he feels that it would be extremely rash to ignore the many avenues of help that are open and blunder into a field without any preparation or selective planning. (1978, p. 22)

One can say without too much contradiction that the field selection process has not been well studied and that generally it turns out to be a difficult, arbitrary process. Colonialism in the past and the problems of gaining residence visas in the present have had more to do with the selection criteria than any other factors.

In what follows we will examine mission definition in teams of criteria for field selection, mission definition, theology of field selection, the impact of church tradition, specialization, personal needs, geopolitics, and apparent needs.

FIELD SELECTION CRITERIA

Field selection can be done from two different perspectives: the perspective of the individual missionary and the perspective of field executives. The organization will be necessarily concerned with a wider range of questions in field selection than the individual, though there is a great deal of overlap in a number of the factors that influence such a decision. The individual normally does not have the same range of contacts and resources for either searching for options in evangelism or for researching the possible areas into which new evangelism teams might go. Yet the actual operation of many missions is such that the initiative and concern of individuals moves the organization to consider a new area for evangelism. If specific volunteers or veteran evangelists sense a calling or a burden for a particular area or people and continue to bring it up to the organizational executives, such a concern will be examined and a new area will or will not be opened.

Field selection involves a number of criteria and factors that vary in importance from organization to organization. We will summarize the ones that were stressed in an informal survey of Protestant mission agencies before treating several factors in greater detail.

1. We must have a *mandate*, a mission which we believe God has commissioned us to pursue. From that mandate we are able to state the basic objectives or purposes which govern our existence as a mission agency and as evangelists of the gospel.

2. We must have *knowledge* about peoples who can be selected for evangelization. Not only can a people not hear unless a messenger is sent to them, but that messenger will never be sent if a people is unknown.

3. We must see a *need* for our entry. If the people is already being well evangelized by other Christian groups, we may not need to add another voice to the crowd of present evangelists.

4. We must have *personnel and resources* available to commit to the outreach. We cannot talk about field selection if our people and resources are already committed and cannot be shifted to a new area.

5. We must be *able to enter* the field. We can feel a great burden for peoples who are shut behind high political walls, but it does little good to select them for evangelism if we are unable to enter their country. It may be that other Christians from other ethnic and political citizenries can enter and we can enter and we can help them to do so.

6. Evangelization must be done *in the context of a particular culture.* If the people we wish to evangelize are in a state of warfare or under such strict laws dealing with proselytism that we cannot evangelize, we either have to change our people or change our mission. We have to go beyond need as such to the opportunity to meet the need. Can the Church be planted among this people? If not, perhaps we need to look elsewhere.

7. We must sense God's *call* to this people at this time. It may not be as dramatic or as clear as Paul's vision of the man from Macedonia, but we need a deep inner conviction borne out of prayer that God wants us to go and do the work of evangelism.

It is simple and easy to list these criteria on paper. Putting them together within an organization and community is neither simple nor easy. It takes a great deal of faith, cooperation, and hard work. We cannot underestimate the impact of the leadership of individuals who sense God's leading and push in the direction of evangelizing a new people. This is important in all deliberations about field selection. Once there is knowledge of a people with need, the process of checking it against the objectives of the mission, agency, or community, and of confirming the need and opportunity begins. Questions of personnel, resources, and call enter as it appears more and more likely that this is a context where a group might enter and evangelize. Different philosophies of ministry and organization will influence how each specific opportunity is evaluated. In fact, there are a number of important factors that influence the use of these criteria in selecting a people for evangelization.

THEOLOGY AND FIELD SELECTION

The specific understanding of the world and the mission of the Church in that world can have a profound effect on the selection of a field for evangelism. Missiological theologies give different weight to various ideas about what ought to be used to identify a people as especially deserving of the Church's attention. One of the contemporary theologies of mission insists that we ought to give priority to peoples who are currently responsive to the gospel. For example, Peter Wagner writes:

> Not all fields ripen at once. Good farm management, as well as good missionary strategy, will place the bulk of the workers in the ripest field but not abandon the others, since someone should be on hand to do the work when the harvest is ripe there, too. The most common missionary error is to deploy an excessive number of workers in fields where the harvest is not yet ripe; while at the same time in the ripened harvest fields, fruit is being lost because of lack of workers. Jesus' prayer request for laborers in the *whitened* harvest fields is the law of the harvest. (Wagner, 1971)

Under this missiological understanding, priority in field selection would be given to peoples who demonstrate openness to the gospel. While it does not advocate the abandonment of so-called "resistant" peoples, it would give them a much lower priority and a much smaller part of the personnel available to do evangelism. Such a theological understanding would give attention to developing tools for measuring or estimating receptivity and using them as important criteria for mission definition.

Another missiology might give prominence to Paul's ambition: "It has always been my ambition to preach the gospel where Christ was not known, so that I would not be building on someone else's foundation" (Rom. 15:20). Out of such a principle would come an agency or organization seeking "new tribes" or frontier peoples who have not previously had the opportunity to hear the first time about Jesus Christ. Such a mission definition would give attention to discovering where the gospel is already available and where there are peoples who for one reason or another have not had the opportunity to be evangelized, regardless of whether they might turn out to be resistant or receptive.

A missiology that stresses economic and social liberation might zero in on political and social conditions of a people. Those whose "oppression index" was high would be given special attention. The missiology of the traditional agencies which stresses the evangelization of the Jews appeals to the example of Paul and his words about offering salvation "first" to the Jews (Rom. 1:16; Acts *passim*).

Despite their differences, most theological principles are not found in isolation. One may be convinced that the theology of the New Testament advocates a principle that we give special attention to the poor and oppressed, and at the same time hold a secondary principle that advocates that among the oppressed we give first priority to those who are also responsive to the gospel. These are not exclusive missiological patterns of understanding, and they can be combined in a variety of ways. What we are pointing out is that one's theology has definite implications for the selection of people for evangelization.

CHURCH TRADITION AND FIELD SELECTION

Church traditions are quite varied and relevant at a number of levels to the process of defining mission. They affect how one becomes committed to a specific people. For some, an inner calling and even revelation from the Lord is the only way to define mission. Appealing to Acts 13 and the somewhat mystical experience of the church hearing the Holy Spirit's voice to set apart Paul and Barnabas, some churches have insisted on a similar form or experience before moving ahead with the logistics of sending evangelists and arranging for the resources to carry out specific programs.

Other traditions, while recognizing the importance of an inner confidence that God is calling an evangelist, advocate that orderliness and stewardship ought to be given more prominence in the process. Research on fields and careful surveys are carried out. Detailed reports are submitted and argued over until objective, demonstrable needs are established, and people are recruited to meet these needs. A rationally established need and the match between the capabilities of people to meet the need are given more prominence in mission definition than a mystical or semi-mystical calling. In some traditions the call is inherent in the psychological/educational performance levels of the evangelists and the job description which has been established out of careful research on a possible field for ministry.

Ecclesiastical tradition also affects the role of the individual in the process of mission definition. In centralized churches and agencies, the individual may have little say in the selection of people. For example, the Church Missionary Society has a ministry in fifty countries. When a candidate comes forward and is trained for the missionary vocation, the selection of field of ministry is set by past involvements of the Anglican Church, by the perceived needs at the moment, and how well the candidate can fulfill those needs. The church hierarchy and the previously established fields mostly define the mission. Among churches with congregational principles, such as the Churches of Christ, the individual and local church have tremendous leverage in deciding where to attempt evangelism.

It is also a demonstrable fact (though not much strategic attention has been paid to it) that in evangelization different ecclesiastical traditions have widely variant successes and failures. The Presbyterians have been extremely successful in Korea, Pakistan, and Taiwan. Fiji is dominated by the Methodists. The Pentecostal denominations have been enormously successful in Latin America, the Baptists in Burma and Nagaland (northeast India), and the Anglicans and Roman Catholics in Uganda. In each of these cases, there was significant growth in particular tribes or parts of the population, but it is clear that the ethos and evangelization approaches of some churches "fit" given peoples more than others. It is at least an important question to ask whether a given church, with its theology, missiology, distinctives, worship style, and philosophy of ministry, is likely to be evangelistically successful, given what is known about a certain people and its context.

ORGANIZATIONAL SPECIALIZATION
AND MISSION DEFINITION

Organizations, by their nature, narrow down the range of field selection. If one joins Wycliffe Bible Translators, over 96 percent of the world's population is automatically ruled out of mission definition because Wycliffe attempts to reach only minority peoples who have no Bible translation. The North Africa Mission is concerned with evangelizing only Muslims from North African countries. Organizations, like churches, bring their own traditions and specific goals into any consideration of what people to select for evangelization.

It is also true that organizations, like individuals, have particular gifts and competencies. Certain organizations, given their present personnel and history of strengths, can never reach some people groups and should not consider doing so. Specializing in certain types of ministries means specializing out of many others. An organization such as the Wycliffe Bible Translators has many skills dealing with frontier peoples and non-literate groups. Yet they do not have strength to deal with evangelization in large cities. The infrastructure of support services and personnel enable some organizations to respond to certain situations much more rapidly and effectively than others. When the Vietnamese refugees resettled in the United States after the fall of South Vietnam, it was natural that the Christian and Missionary Alliance did most of the ministering because it had a significant number of personnel who had worked previously with the Vietnamese, and who knew the language as well as some of the refugees.

PERSONAL CONSIDERATIONS

The individual or couple who is seeking where to serve needs to assess a variety of things—a sense of mission, knowledge of peoples needing evangelization, organizational connections, and church affiliation. All of these will help to clarify God's call. Gifts of ministry, educational skills, faith and vision, experience and resources, linguistic and management ability, and self-motivation are other factors that lead to a mission decision. Some even assert that a spiritual gift is essential to cross-cultural ministry (Wagner, 1971, chapter 4).

There is no doubt that motivated individuals who sense a calling toward specific peoples can have a major impact on their organization's decision to evangelize a new people. Because personnel are a *sine qua non* for evangelization, their presence or absence can spell the difference between pushing forward or simply maintaining the historic involvements.

GEOPOLITICS AND ENTRY

One of the dominant facts of current missions is the limited number of countries open to Western missionaries. While the recent opening of China portends some new challenges for the Church in the years ahead, the door is hardly open. At present there are no Western missionaries present, and none has been invited into mainland China. Evangelization by radio and by Chinese of the diaspora is taking place on a very limited scale. The number of Muslim countries which have restricted evangelization by Westerners has increased in recent years. It is still very difficult to get visas for Westerners for evangelization ministries among the Hindu castes of India.

Third World missions is still in its infancy, and the majority are still engaged in diaspora evangelization of their own peoples (Wong et al., 1973). This is, of course, a very essential part of evangelization. The overseas Chinese need to be evangelized, as do the Koreans of Los Angeles, the Vietnamese in France, and the Gujarati in London. But it does mean, if one is interested in the evangelization of China or Muslims, that new relationships and support structures will have to be developed.

We simply cannot ignore that what country a Christian is from plays an important role in the potential for gaining a hearing for the gospel. While Christians from the United States might not be welcomed or listened to, Christians from Sweden might be seen as friendly, and consequently allowed to share the gospel. Pakistani Muslims would hardly take time to listen to a Muslim convert from Indonesia (they are not viewed as Muslim in the true sense), while Christians from Syria or Jordan would be listened to respectfully since they live near Mecca. We need to assess the realistic potential for a hearing (from a human point of view) in field selection.

THE APPARENT NEEDS

Selection of a people to evangelize is also related to actual evangelization need. While it is true that all humans need Christ, not all live in contexts where they have an equal opportunity to hear about him and discover who he is. To some extent, one's theology and ecclesiastical tradition will have a strong effect on assessing the degree to which a people is already evangelized, or being evangelized, and the degree to which it is unreached. So, too, will one's view of what priority ought to be given to the potential for meeting the needs that apparently exist. If we take two peoples who appear to have similar levels of need for evangelization (both being only minimally evangelized by some criteria, such as the percentage professing and practicing Christian faith and the penetration of the population at large by Christian presence and proclamation), one of whom is responsive and would give many of its daughters and sons to faith with increased opportunity, should we consider the responsive people to have greater need for evangelization than the less responsive?

UNREACHED PEOPLE DEFINED

The Strategy Working Group of the Lausanne Committee for World Evangelization has suggested one approach to defining need for evangelization among various peoples. They define "unreached peoples" as any people group with less than 20 percent practicing Christians. Within that definition they have defined various levels of need (see Figure 8-1, p. 98 below):

1. "Hidden peoples" are those with no or virtually no practicing Christians. If evangelization is to be done, it will have to be done by cross-cultural evangelists (E-2/E-3 evangelism). These are peoples who by any definition ought to receive careful attention of the Church worldwide. Opportunity to be introduced to Christ is lowest among these peoples. How will they hear if no one is sent?

2. "Initially reached peoples" are those who have been evangelized, and up to 1 percent have become practicing Christians. Many of these will have been won by cross-cultural evangelism. A vast amount of evangelism still remains to be done.

3. "Minimally reached peoples" are those who have between 1 and 10 percent practicing Christians. By this time a great deal of near-neighbor or intra-cultural evangelism is taking place. Most who are being won to Christ are being won by people of the same people. Cross-cultural aid and nurture is probably still needed.

Unreached Peoples:

Hidden People:	No known Christians within the group.
Initially Reached:	Less than one percent, but some Christians.
Minimally Reached:	1 to 10 percent Christian.
Possibly Reached:	10 to 20 percent Christian.
Reached:	20 percent or more practicing Christians.

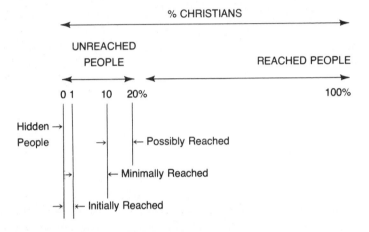

Figure 8-1   Definition of Unreached People

4. "Possibly reached peoples" are those who have between 10 and 20 percent of their population practicing Christianity. If the growth rate of the church is healthy, the cross-cultural ministry may be terminated because the church probably has the potential to evangelize the people.

The exact percentages listed are not always important in assessing need. The most important criteria is not the outsider's evaluation of evangelization need, but the insider's impression. If the insiders think that their people is "reached" when only 6 percent or 12 percent are practicing Christians, their judgment needs to be seriously considered and respected. In selecting a people to evangelize, we need to take into account the actual status of evangelism and the growth of the church. If the church is growing and has reached the status of "possibly reached" we need to look elsewhere for those we can evangelize.

It is estimated that there are three billion people in the world who do not claim Jesus as Lord. Over two billion of these live in people groups within which there are no Christians (the "hidden peoples"). They will be reached for the Kingdom across the barrier of cross-cultural communication. One rough estimate is that there are approximately fifteen thousand such people groups within the 220 countries of the world. These should be given top priority for future evangelization.

If these two billion are in fifteen thousand people groups, this means an average of 135,000 people within each group. If a maximum of 20 percent of the people of each group have to be reached by cross-cultural evangelism, then the task before the church is not to reach two billion "hidden peoples" but to reach 405 million people, or, to put it another way, an average of twenty-seven thousand people in each group. Looked at this way, world evangelization is not such an overwhelming task. We can narrow it down to a specific target within the limits of missions.

RESOURCES FOR PEOPLE SELECTION

Once we have a set of criteria which will guide us in the definition of our mission, we also need information which can serve as a basis for orienting our search for a people in need. There are a number of resources needed—some are gradually being developed, others are only in the dream stage.

Anthropologists, historians, political scientists, and others have done a tremendous amount of work in attempting to locate and understand the peoples and countries that inhabit this planet. The Church needs to exploit this large reservoir of information in order to discover critical areas of evangelization need. Every mission agency and Church ought to have a professionally trained staff that can make this information useful to the Church in a variety of ways, especially in communicating the gospel. There are already a number of specific resources:

1. *The World Christian Encyclopedia,* ed. Dr. David Barrett (1980), is a very useful beginning point for understanding the broad outlines of Christianity around the world, country by country. Because it also includes ethno-linguistic information, it can serve as a beginning perspective on the degree to which Christian faith has penetrated the various peoples of the world. It is, of course, *only* a beginning point and has to be interpreted and utilized with other sources of information.

2. The Unreached Peoples program of the Missions Advanced Research and Communication Center of World Vision in conjunction with

the Lausanne Committee for World Evangelization is developing resources, both computer and printed, for isolating and dramatizing the needs of unreached peoples in all parts of the world. The publications of the *Unreached People '79* and *'80* (Wagner and Dayton, 1979, 1980) provide examples of this kind of available information.

3. In-country surveys by joint committees are crucial for the advance of the gospel in the next few decades. Gerald Swank's *Frontier Peoples of Central Nigeria and a Strategy for Outreach* (1977) needs to be duplicated in a hundred countries. When people who have lived in a context for years can come together around a carefully done survey of church growth and evangelization needs, whether in a congress or in a more limited research team, the churches and agencies will begin to gain an accurate portrait of the needs that face us in the next generation. The *World Christianity* (published by MARC) series of studies on the status of Christianity in specific areas of the world is useful as well.

4. After an initial decision indicating the potential "match" between a mission, agency, Church, or other body, it is often extremely important to do an on-site survey. To talk with people who are more knowledgeable, to discuss the ins and outs of a situation with people who are already in the situation, is a major step in field selection. Church growth books, handbooks, and computer files can do no more than give a few clues that something is worth closer examination. A more detailed, careful check helps to clarify and refocus initial impressions.

5. Other mission agencies and churches can be approached. They will often share the work they are doing on trying to clarify future field selection. Christians are not alone in the area of trying to understand the world's evangelistic needs, and we need to make use of what others are doing. One thinks of the research unit of the Worldwide Evangelization Crusade, headed by Patrick Johnstone. This organization is developing an enormous amount of information about the peoples of the world.

PERSPECTIVE

In all of this we need to remind ourselves that God is with us. He will guide us as we attempt to meet the continuing needs of hundreds of peoples for evangelization. We are part of a large body which is enormously vital and active in our world. While we cannot take the whole burden on our small shoulders, we can make a difference for some of the peoples of our generation. As we listen to the voice of the Spirit, as we learn about the nations and peoples of the earth, as we try to discover where we will have opportunity to utilize the gifts and resources of which we are stewards, God will direct us to fruitful avenues of ministry.

We need to have a long-range vision. We are part of the growth of the Kingdom of God. While evil becomes stronger and more diverse, we need to see that the leaven of the gospel is also spreading and that the Kingdom of God is invading more and more realms of this world. While we may not see the evangelization of some of the peoples of the earth in our generation, we can help build organizations and set in motion the processes which will make possible their evangelization in the generations ahead. We need to be building bridges to the future.

This is of course a process, not a single event which we can point to in the past and say that at a given point we fully understood God's mission for us or the specific people he wanted us to evangelize. It is something that happens in the flux of our changing world. We change, others change. Our organizations and churches change. The situations in which we must evangelize change. One way of understanding this is to see the ten steps of our process as iterative. It is impossible to think about our mission without considering the methods, the people, the strategy, and God's plans. One makes an initial selection of a people, and 2) learns what he or she can about them. 3) One then considers the force for evangelism. Next, one looks at 4) means and methods. If these look practical, an initial approach is devised and 5) outcomes are predicted. 6) The question is asked, where do we fit? 7) After this is determined, we 8) make plans. If all still looks positive, we 9) act. Note that anywhere in the cycle we can abandon our initial assumption. (Best to fail on paper!)

In faith we ought to think as far as we can into the future that God has for us and then move out to act and repeat the process again.

POSTSCRIPT

Following are two recent mission agency attempts at listing criteria and questions that need to be answered in the process of field selection. Both are written from the viewpoint of the organization, but many of the questions can be adapted for an individual to use when attempting to define whom to evangelize.

A. *Development of a new ministry:*

The proposal for a new ministry should include a detailed description of the project and a satisfactory response to the following questions. Similarly, periodic review of ministries already commenced should result in satisfactory response to the same questions:

   a. Does it contribute to the main objective—development of a mature church? And to what extent?
   b. Is there mutual agreement that God is leading thus?
   c. What would be its effect on other priorities: in personnel, finance, time, energy? This should be considered at all appropriate levels, from local to international.
   d. What is the urgency of the need?
   e. Are resources available to initiate the program, and is it reasonable to expect continued resources? Are we willing to commit resources?
   f. Is it feasible geographically, culturally, politically?
   g. Is there a viable, effective church which, instead of the mission, could accomplish the project?
   h. Is any other agency able to meet the need?
   i. Is the project controllable?
   j. Is this the most effective way—are there alternatives?
   k. What are the negative and positive by-products?
   l. Is it consistent with the character and mandate of the mission?

B. *Policy for entering a new field:*

   a. Is there evident need which we can meet?
   b. Does the task to be performed come under the mandate of the mission? Is it within the stated purposes and goals of the mission?
   c. Is there a consensus of agreement by the board that it is God's will to open the area as a field of the mission?
   d. Are experienced personnel available to open the field? More than two with complementary gifts so that we can enter on a team basis?
   e. Is the area to be evangelized so widely separated geographically from where the mission is already operating that management of the new area is impossible?
   f. Will the area under consideration allow for the development of a full field? If not, is the consideration for ministry one of

placing or loaning personnel to do some limited time service assignment?

g. Is there an invitation from groups currently working in the general area, or at least an agreement from them for us to enter?

h. Do we have individuals who have a strong desire and real potential for serving in the new area? Are any of them gifted in "pioneer" or new field ministries?

QUESTIONS

Mission and the Church

1. What is the mission of God on planet earth? What is his plan for the universe?

2. What is the mission of the Church?

3. How do the various components of what the Church is to be and do fit together? Is there something which can serve to unify these various elements or identify the chief mission of the Church?

4. Are humanization and the traditional notion of evangelization mutually exclusive images of the mission of the Church? How does the alleviation of suffering and injustice relate to the priorities of the Kingdom of God? How does evangelization in the sense of gospel proclamation relate to the priorities of the Kingdom?

5. In what ways can a theology of the Kingdom of God overcome some of the contemporary polarizations in the debate about the proper mission of the Church?

Evangelization

6. What is evangelism? How does the Bible define evangelism?

7. How do you define evangelism? Are you happy with modern attempts to define evangelism?

8. What is the essential content of the gospel?

9. What types of diversity in expression are permissible in the presentation

of the Good News? How can various presentations of the gospel be evaluated in order to guarantee the authenticity and faithfulness of a new expression? 10. Should the definition of evangelism include its results? Has a person who has said no to Jesus Christ been "evangelized?" When can we legitimately conclude that a person or people have been evangelized and our task is done? 11. What does a person need to believe and be in order to be saved? 12. What relationship exists between the evangelical message, the evangelist, and the demands of the evangel on everyday life? 13. Is evangelism a goal to be achieved or a process to be enhanced?

Defining Your Mission

14. What criteria should we use to select a people for evangelization? 15. How do we define evangelistic need? Which groups of people do we consider "unevangelized" or "unreached?" What criteria do we use to determine evangelization? When does a group no longer need evangelization from groups outside its own group? 16. Where can we find information to help us discover peoples who could most benefit from our evangelism?

STEP 2

THE PEOPLE
TO BE REACHED

Considerations

A People-Centered Approach

Defining and Describing a People

Understanding the Meaning System
of a People

Understanding the Needs of a People

Understanding the Behavior of a People

The Larger Context

Questions

CONSIDERATIONS

1. The single most important element in planning strategies for evangelism is an understanding of the people to be evangelized.

2. Standard solutions to evangelize unstandard peoples not only violate the humanity of those being evangelized, but make an offensive confusion of the Kingdom of God.

3. The unity of the Church is a unity of the Spirit, not one of cultural or linguistic uniformity.

4. Evangelism that attempts, for whatever high theological reasons, to ignore cultural and social differences that exist in human society quickly turns into mis-evangelism that unnecessarily drives people away from Christ.

5. A people is definable by those common attributes that make them either reachable by a given means or difficult to reach by any known means.

6. The crucial matter in considering any group a distinct people, worthy of a special strategy and their own indigenous church institutions, is the subjective sense of group identity, not the objectively provable fact of homogeneity on a given set of characteristics.

7. The willingness to know and experience a people is always the first act of authentic biblical evangelism. Ultimately only those who not only understand a culture but enjoy participating in it are able to authenticate their witness at the deepest levels.

8. The Kingdom of God must be understandable within a people's meaning system, relevant to felt needs, and viable within their institutions if it is to encounter the inner soul of a people.

9. People do not live in the same world and simply use different labels for understanding that world. The real choice that faces us in evangelization is contextualization or confusion. The only way we can protect the purity of the message of the gospel is to embody it in the indigenous terms that are available in the culture of a people.

10. People go through a process which includes several changes of knowledge and attitudes before they are ready to acknowledge Christ as Lord and Savior. Evangelization must be intimately related to that process.

11. Evangelism begins with need as a people defines it.

12. The felt needs of a people are not irrelevant or unrelated to the fundamental spiritual dimensions of the Kingdom of God. The hunger of the body is as important as the hunger of the soul.

13. Change is possible only where there is discontent with the way things are.

14. The good news of forgiveness must be directed to the preexisting sense of wrongdoing that may be found among a people. The gospel must "scratch" where it "itches."

15. To understand the culture of a people is to understand both the glory of how the gospel can find new expression and the agony of a new confrontation with unique forms of human evil. Because culture is a mixture of good and evil, there is always an ambivalent, ambiguous relationship between it and Christianity.

16. Receptivity to the gospel is a function of the "fit" that exists between the gospel and the culture as well as the satisfaction people presently feel with the current fate in life that culture provides for them.

17. Research is the name we give for the activities that supply missing experience.

18. In attempting to evangelize across cultural boundaries, most of us do not need more education. We need complete reeducation.

19. Few if any people groups exist unto themselves. Every group in some way is related to a larger context. To greater and lesser degrees this larger context helps to define the people.

20. "The larger context" is not limited to the individual political, economic, and social systems within a country. Often these systems reach through entire continents.

21. The degree to which the larger context within which a people lives helps to define the situation and values of a people must be understood in order to understand the people themselves.

22. The political, social, and economic context sometimes can be so overbearing that they become the primary definers of the life of a people.

CHAPTER 9

A People-Centered Approach

INTRODUCTION

*T*he people who are to be evangelized are like the soil into which the farmer of Jesus' parable (Mt. 13:1–23) sows the precious seed. Not all soils or peoples are alike. Each kind will bear a different harvest, and some will yield no harvest at all. Intelligent sowing of the seed which is the Word of God is crucial to its eventual fruit. If they want a good harvest, the farmer and evangelist must do more than simply sow the seed; they must also understand the condition of the soil.

We have already determined that doing "evangelism in general" is as meaningless as trying to "farm in general." A farmer has to know what crop to grow and where to grow it. Just as the farmer must understand the nature of the seed which is to be sown to produce the crop, so we must understand the message of the Kingdom of God which we share in evangelism. We need to know the potential beauty and abundance which lies in every seed we sow. But once we are convinced of the potency of the seed to be planted, we must then carefully analyze the soil.

Different fields have different soils. Pedologists (scientists who study soil) have classified a vast array of soils, which, when combined with climatic conditions, have an enormous range of plant and animal life. Each soil type has developed under different conditions and parent material, each has distinctive chemicals and nutrients which can facilitate the growth of certain plants and retard the growth of others. The pedologist, in cooperation with the farmer, tests the various soils of fields to determine the proper measures for fertilizing, soil conservation, weed and pest control, crop rotation, and so forth.

Similarly, we need to understand the people to whom God has called us. They have developed under different conditions and parent materials. Each people has its own particular language, world view, social structure, economic and technological base, and religious sensibilities. Some "fields" are full of rocks that need to be cleared away. These may be the rocks of misunderstanding about Christianity or the rocks of deeply rooted cultural practices. Other fields will be overgrown through disuse. Prior "crops" have an important effect in depleting soils of certain nutrients. If the Muslim religion, or Hinduism has permeated the field, the soil will be different than if animism has permeated the field.

Thus, the farmer thoroughly understands what a particular seed needs to germinate and to grow in order to produce the best harvest. Even the most hardy seed will lie dormant unless soil conditions are right. As the farmer accepts the needs and conditions of the soil as a given which must be worked with, so the Christian accepts the needs and situations of the particular people to be reached. The evangelist approaches evangelization with God's love, a love that accepts people where they are and reaches out to them in their need.

In this section we will deal with a number of questions about the people we intend to evangelize. There has been a great deal of discussion about the legitimacy and value of respecting the social and cultural boundaries of a certain people.

In this chapter we will discuss the validity of *"A People-Centered Approach."* Are there biblical and theological grounds for adapting the evangelistic message and methods to the distinctive social and cultural groups we are called to evangelize? We will then deal with the question of *"Defining and Describing a People."* This will lead us to three additional chapters: *"Understanding the Meaning System of a People," "Understanding the Needs of a People,"* and *"Understanding the Behavior of a People."* Finally, in order to put this second step of describing a people in a proper setting, we will review the *"Larger Context"* within which mission always takes place.

People are found in an enormous variety of social and cultural groupings. Each grouping has its own beauty and strengths that offer a satisfying identity to its members. No one knows how many distinctive people groups exist in the world, but it is in the tens of thousands: Gypsies of Spain, Mennonite Germans of Russia, Yanamamo Indians of the Orinoco, Boston "Brahmins" of Nob Hill, Cantonese restaurant workers of Vienna, Arabs of Saudi Arabia, and Dinka cattle herders of the southern Sudan. The list is almost endless.

People do not exist as isolated individuals. As much as we might like at times to remove ourselves from the groups that surround us, we are all interconnected members of some society or subcultural group. These societies are as different as a large technological nation such as Japan or Korea and a small, face-to-face hunting and gathering society such as the Kung Bushmen of the Kalahari Desert in Namibia.

Understanding this diversity is the single most important element in planning strategies for evangelism, given an agreed upon theology of mission. All the steps of evangelization depend upon and grow out of our understanding of a people's characteristic socio-cultural qualities.

It is no accident that Step 2 focuses on the people who are being evangelized. While one might rearrange or redefine many of the other steps in the process we are describing, to either eliminate or reorder the task of understanding a people would be to alter radically the perspective of this book.

In the pages that follow we will try to make a case for a people-centered approach to evangelization. An understanding of the "soil" into which the seed of the gospel is to be sown is by far the most important component for evaluating alternative methods, roles, potential evangelists, and approaches, or for determining reasons for success or lack of success in evangelism.

THE IMPORTANCE OF A PEOPLE-CENTERED APPROACH

Alwyne Wheeler's *Fishes of the World: An Illustrated Dictionary* (1975) lists thousands of fish: fresh water and salt, denizens of the deeps and occupants of the top inches of the seas, whales and dolphins, trout and tuna, extravagantly colored tropical fish for the household aquarium and mammoth monsters like the *carcharodon carcharias,* the great white shark. In all, modern science has classified some twenty-two thousand different species of fish. Each has its distinctive size and shape, its own peculiar location and way of living that enables it to survive in the wild.

Fishing is one of the oldest and most important activities of humanity. A 4,000-year-old tomb picture in Egypt depicts fishermen pulling at their nets from reed boats. Today more than five million people make their living harvesting the bounty of the global waters. Sophisticated equipment, large-scale research institutes, and advanced graduate programs enhance a harvest of 145 billion pounds a year. Whether taken by huge nets (such as the purse seine), gill nets, spears, traps, long lines with dozens of hooks, fly reels, dredging, or trawling—each type of water life has to be carefully understood and the appropriate methods employed if it is to be used in the gourmet restaurants and kitchens of the world.

Seven of Jesus' twelve apostles were fishermen by profession. It is no wonder that he used fishing as a metaphor for their evangelistic mission: "Don't be afraid; from now on you will be catching people" (Lk. 5:10). One of his parables of the Kingdom was about the large dragnet or seine which catches all kinds of fish, both the edible tilapia and sardines of Lake Galilee and the catfish which the Jews considered unclean: "The Kingdom of heaven is like this. Some fishermen throw their net out in the lake and catch all kinds of fish. . . " (Mt. 13:47–50; McCullough, 1962; Cansdale, 1970, chapter 17). Then the fish are sorted. The unclean are thrown back into the lake just as the angels will sort the good from the bad at the end of time.

There were probably a number of things Jesus had in mind when he compared evangelism to "catching people." It is clear he was not simply talking about "going evangelizing" the way many of us "go fishing" today—as a pleasant vacation. Jesus was talking about persuading individuals, families, and groups to become his disciples.

In addition the parable suggests that just as there are different types of fish, there are different types of people. Some would have to be caught by the "cast nets" of evangelism, designed to take those living in shallow waters closer to the shore. Some would be caught only by the great dragnets hundreds of feet long, designed to catch those who inhabit the depths far from shore. Still others would be caught only by a patient night fisherman, one fish at a time.

Like fish, humans are found in many different communities and cultures, each with their own special location and habits for surviving in a world with increasingly fewer resources. Each distinctive group of people is like a species of fish. We must carefully understand each group if we are to be effective in our mission of "catching people." The methods we use, the timing and location we choose, the people who engage in the mission are *all dependent upon the distinct characteristics of those we are trying to "catch."* To try to catch tuna using a fly fisher's rod and reel is as absurd as trying to harvest trout from a shallow, icy mountain stream with a great seine net 200 feet in length! Yet we often try to evangelize peoples who have vastly different languages, cultures, histories, and social structures using a single method that was developed for evangelizing the cities of the West. Each group of people must be understood in terms of its distinctive customs and thought patterns, and must be approached with the skill and care of the fishing boat as it attempts to catch a distinctive type of fish.

It is for that reason that we begin the process of building a strategy to evangelize with the people to be evangelized.

A STANDARD APPROACH TO UNSTANDARD PEOPLES

This people-approach to strategy cannot simply be taken for granted. In fact, it is often overshadowed by another basic approach to strategy called the "standard solution." The standard solution is based upon the observation that all people share a common humanity. Beyond the peripheral differences of language, customs, and clothing, which make other people seem exotic, there is a deeper commonness. Pride, loneliness, needs for security and happiness, and the struggle for survival are part of the life of all cultures. Theft, adultery, and violence exist everywhere. Religious customs attest to the universal desire for knowledge of the unknown and a desire to control life's mysteries.

Because of this, the standard solution approach assumes that the differences between various cultural groups are insignificant. So long as one can use the language of the group, a standard methodology will work in virtually all cultures. It is assumed that a method that stimulates significant church growth in one culture will probably be useful in many other cultures.

It would be foolish to deny that standard solutions often experience partial success, and sometimes even dramatic success, when they move from one culture to another. An example of this is the saturation evangelism methodology known as "Here's Life." Campus Crusade for Christ originated this strategy in its attempts to reach cities in the United States. In places like Hong Kong this same basic strategy has had positive response and has fulfilled many of its stated goals (i.e., many people have prayed to receive Christ as Lord). In other places, however, the strategy has seen only marginal results; for example, in Kenya. Here a more rural and tribal context creates significant problems for a strategy based on media events and a common language. Even more trouble was experienced by "Here's Life Kenya" when a Western illusionist held a mass meeting event based on a "magic" show. Since most Kenyans do not understand various types of illusions and tricks, many wondered if Christianity were simply a more powerful version of the witchcraft they practiced in their traditional culture.

Several common problems afflict the standard solution approach. Often it creates tremendous difficulties for further evangelism because of the way it confuses or offends when it is not adequately adjusted to cultural differences. Frank S. Khair-Ullah tells the effect of such a standard solution approach in Pakistan:

> A 'scripture distribution' program was launched from Wheaton, Illinois. Every name listed in the telephone directory of some city or cities in Pakistan was sent a copy of the New Testament in Urdu by mail. Some addresses were changed by the time the packets arrived, some people refused to accept these unsolicited packets of the Christian Scriptures. Tons of these got accumulated in the post office, which had to be disposed of by auction as 'waste paper.' Some of us discovered this when some small merchandise was purveyed to people in envelopes made out of the pages of the Bible. Anyone who is familiar with our culture would have been horrified, for the greatest respect is accorded to all scriptures in the East whether it be the Quran or the Bible. You can imagine the chagrin of our Muslim friends who could not understand why such mass desecration of our Holy Book was carried out by the American Christians.
>
> Pakistan Bible Society, I am told, did make a protest. But they were told that some letters of appreciation did arrive at their office appreciating the distribution. How many? That we were not told. (1979, p. 570)

It is our conviction that *both* the differences and the commonness of humans must be respected in any successful approach to strategy. The people who need to be reached by the gospel are found in groups that are significantly different in terms of language, cultural traits, felt needs, life-style, modal personality, and responsiveness. In seeking an effective and meaningful hearing for the gospel, the evangelist must tailor a strategy for reaching the unreached on the basis of the particular attributes of the specific group which needs the gospel. What role the evangelist will play, what gifts and special methods need to be employed, how many Christian workers and what resources will be required all depend upon the nature of the particular group. We are convinced from careful study of approaches that have been tried by the Church, that we best respect the common nature of humanity when our strategies conform to the differences in world view and life-style among the social communities and subcultures of our world.

So important is this in our thinking that we could call this approach a people-centered strategy. While we believe there is a role and a place for standard solutions (they work well in cultures that share certain similar traits and where social change is slow), they have a very limited role and place in our day and age. We are convinced that there is no single, universal strategy that can be applied to all the unreached peoples of our world, or even a majority of them. Most of the standard solutions have been repeatedly applied in dozens of countries and hundreds of cities around the world. The net result demonstrates that they are signally unable to make any appreciable difference in reaching the nearly 2.4 billion who live beyond the current cultural boundaries of already established churches and mission efforts. Furthermore, the majority of such efforts have had only marginal effect in changing the growth rates of the churches in the societies and peoples which they were supposedly helping to evangelize.

Consequently, we reject standard solutions for unstandard peoples. They do not work, and worse, they often do more harm than good (in spite of all the organizational propaganda that trumpets "results" back to donors in Western countries).

But we are convinced that *there is a standard approach which can be used to devise strategies which will be effective for each remaining unreached group.* It is the approach that is based upon serious consideration of the cultural and contextual differences that make each people unique, and upon a problem-solving method that provides a way of understanding how that uniqueness can become part of an evangelistic strategy. In short, it is based on the conviction that God has a unique strategy for each unique people. To discover that strategy we need to respect the particularity of a people and to utilize a series of basic questions which provide the information necessary for us to make decisions about the strategy that might best communicate the gospel.

Beyond this, we are also convinced that such an approach is biblical. There are good theological foundations for insisting that the unchanging message of the gospel be incarnated in different ways for different peoples. There is clear evidence that the Bible itself sees culture and the grouping of humans into people groups as so crucial that the methods used by New Testament evangelists differed according to the audience being evangelized.

BIBLICAL TERMINOLOGY FOR
VARIOUS PEOPLE GROUPS

Beginning with the Old Testament, it is obvious that the Bible is aware of peoples—various human groupings based on one or several principles that affect the way their members live and think (Bietenhard, 1976). Of course the most outstanding division is that drawn between the "holy people" of God (*'am*) and the "gentiles" (*goy*) (Schmidt, 1964, p. 6). The main emphasis in the Old Testament falls on God's activity in creating "a people" for himself, calling out Abraham and working with his descendents to form the nation of Israel. In the process God gives them a common legal-cultural framework at Sinai, a geographical homeland in Palestine, and a centralized political structure under David and Solomon. Israel is a holy people, separated from other peoples such as the Canaanites. There is a keen awareness of these alien peoples as well as the necessity that Israel maintain its distinctiveness as a people committed to Yahweh.

Three Hebrew terms indicate a categorization of peoples. The first does so in terms of geography (*'eretz*). This term, which labels peoples as "lands" or "countries," recognizes that customs, languages, social structures come to be shared among social groups that exist within a given geographic area. Groups are also labeled as "languages" or "tongues" (*lashon*), stressing the importance of shared communication in creating a distinct people group (Behm, 1964). It is this aspect of people formation that most strategies are willing to admit as a demarcating line between distinctive groups which require separate evangelistic effort and separate church structures. The term for "tribe" or "clan" (*mishpachah*) highlights the binding quality of kinship and marriage in creating a people group. Over a long period of time, family traditions and loyalty form the foundation for subcultures as well as the distinctive customs that distinguish one group from another (Maurer, 1974).

New Testament terms are more comprehensive and set within a different phase of God's redemptive action. Whereas the Old Testament accent is on achieving a cultural uniformity in a single, holy people set apart to serve Yahweh, the stress in the New Testament is upon a unity that incorporates great cultural diversity. Pentecost is a signal that the new people of God will incorporate the vast array of tribes, clans, castes, languages, and subcultures. The miracle of tongues signals that each language group is to hear the mighty acts of God in its own tongue. The Church does not reduce the people of God to one culture or to one people in the same sense that Israel was a single people sharing a single culture. Rather, the people of God is a community sharing a common loyalty to the same Lord, confessing the same faith, and yet retaining distinctive ethnic and cultural ways of life. *The unity of the Church is a unity of the Spirit, not of cultural or linguistic uniformity.*

A number of verses in Revelation (5:9, 7:9, 10:11, 11:9, 13:7, 14:6, 17:15) envision the end of time as encompassing rather than erasing the differences that characterize people groups. *Ethnos,* translated "nation," "gentile," or "people," refers to groups of people bound together by the same manners, customs, and other distinctive features (Schmidt, 1964b). This Greek word comes closest to modern anthropological terms for labeling people groups. Of course it is true that about 40 percent of the time it is used in the sense of "gentiles" or "nations" as opposed to the Jews or the Christians. But it is clear in such passages as Matthew 28:19 and Luke 24:47 where the Church is commissioned to evangelize all the *ethnē* that it refers to Israel as well as all the gentiles. It is probably preferable to render Matthew 28:19 as "Go, then, to all *peoples* everywhere and make them my disciples . . . ," as does the *Good News Bible,* rather than "all *nations,*" as rendered by other Bible translations. The latter term indicates the notion of a political unit such as a state which may in fact have numerous "peoples" as component parts of the nation. This is true in the United States, which includes Puerto Ricans, southern Blacks, Cantonese-speaking Chinese, Navajo Indians, New England Catholics, Vietnamese refugees, midwestern farmers, and so forth.

There are those who choose to argue as does Johannes Verkuyl (1978, p. 107) that *ethnos* does not refer to "ethnic units," but rather to the whole humanity from which God is gathering his people. Though it is clear that this word can be used this way, there is still the question of the nature of those "*ethnē.*" As Schmidt notes: "In most cases, ἔθνος is used of men in the sense of a 'people,'. . . [It] is the most general and therefore the weakest [term for people], having simply an ethnographical sense and denoting the natural cohesion of a people in general" (1964b, p. 369). The commission to make disciples of all peoples does not refer simply to constituting fellowships of disciples in all the political units which are today recognized as nations. Rather it is aimed at all peoples who exist in states of natural cohesion because of shared language and life. Each unit, whatever it may be called, is to be discipled, baptized, and taught all the things Jesus commanded his apostles. In some cases these will be ethnic units. In other cases, they may be subcultural groupings or social caste units within a single ethnic unit.

A second term in Revelation stresses the broader notion of a national or political unity—*phulē,* a term which is often translated "tribe" (Maurer, 1974). It refers to a society of people who are bound together by common descent, leadership, and law. As such it covers different types of peoples, from a clan group to a large chieftainship or tribal unit with centralized political authority.

Glōssa, usually translated as "language" or "tongue," refers to a people as a group bound together by virtue of speaking and understanding the same language or dialect (Behm, 1964). Wycliffe Bible Translators as well as modern linguistics has made us keenly aware of the "babel" of over five thousand languages (Grimes, 1978). Each language has its distinctive way of labeling and categorizing the world and its experience as a people. By its distinctive use of words and concepts as well as grammar, it creates its own world of meaning that includes those who understand the language and excludes those who do not. It is a powerful and important factor in creating a distinct people group, as proven by the language riots in such polyglot nations as India and Iran. And yet a single language may encompass such a large population and be found in so many separated localities that it may itself break down into dozens or hundreds of smaller people groups.

Laos is often translated "nation," "race," or "people." It views groups or populations as bound together as a political unity, gathered under a common history and constitution, such as the citizens of the same city (Strathmann, 1967). A variety of other terms are also to be found in the New Testament: *Dēmos* is used to refer to people as residents of a single city or community (Grundmann, 1964). *Diaspora* describes the situation of an exiled or dispersed people, living in many places among other peoples (Schmidt, 1964a). Because of their common history and identity (such as the Jews in the Roman world), they retain a sense of unity and pride that keeps them distinctive in their way of life. *Patria* views people as a group who see themselves as one because of common descent from a single father (Schrenk, 1967). They might be a single nuclear family, a lineage or kindred, an extended family with servants in a household, or a caste or tribe. *Ochlos* normally designates a people who have grouped together because of some common situation or need, and not any permanent principle (Meyer, 1967). A crowd at a football game is one example of this. A mass of people temporarily unified because of some natural disaster such as an earthquake is another example.

Thus, it is apparent that there is an awareness of people groups in the Bible, an awareness that sees a variety of principles upon which groups find unity and cohesion. Various degrees and types of solidarity exist in society, and people develop their own communication patterns and cultures as a result of living together. Whether it be geography, language, political commonality, or family connections, there is a recognition that the world of humanity out of which God is creating his own people is highly diverse. There is also the assumption that whatever the process of evangelization or eschatology may mean, it does not lead to the imposition of a cultural and linguistic uniformity upon that diversity. Rather, each people is seen as becoming a "disciple" of Jesus Christ, learning to follow him in the context of its own life-style and language.

EVANGELISM AND PEOPLES OF THE NEW TESTAMENT

Evangelism in the early Church took place in the context of a variety of social and cultural groupings. Much of Acts deals with the way in which various peoples were brought into the Church by the guidance of the Spirit and the changes and controversies that surrounded this expanding circle of peoples. The clearest distinction is that between Jew and gentile. Much of Paul's correspondence deals directly or indirectly with the relationships between those Christians from Jewish and non-Jewish backgrounds. But virtually all New Testament scholars recognize more distinctions than these. There are a number of socio-cultural backgrounds that were taken into account in the communication of the gospel and later in the theological expressions and life-style adjustments that were made in various churches. The clearest of these are those parts of the Christian movement known as Palestinian Jewish Christianity (Aramaic-speaking, insistent upon rigorous observance of Mosaic law, centered in Jerusalem), hellenistic Jewish Christianity (Greek-speaking, less rigorous in observance of the law, symbolized by Stephen), and hellenistic gentile Christianity (made up of former gentile God-fearers and converts from backgrounds with little or no contact with the hellenistic Jewish synagogue). Within the gentile Christian movement one can discern differences of outlook and expression (as can be read in Colossians, Corinthians, or Romans).

The early chapters of Acts tell the story of how the gospel, though only initially received by Aramaic and Greek-speaking Jews, was gradually taken to gentile groups. In measured steps we see the Spirit moving out beyond the Jews first to the half-Jews, or the Samaritans. One of the Greek-speaking hellenistic Jewish Christians felt impelled to proclaim Jesus in Samaria (Acts 8). This is then followed by the account of the first gentile, the God-fearer Cornelius, being brought into the Church through the unusual miracles surrounding Peter's reluctant preaching at Caesarea (Acts 10–11). His household and some of his clients followed him in the baptism of faith. Finally, we have the story of the beginning of the first Church with many members from backgrounds that had no affiliation with Jewish synagogues (Acts 11). In it all there is a recognition that something new is taking place: God is changing the way in which his people would exist from a relatively mono-cultural, ethnically-based people to a multi-cultural, multi-ethnic, universal people without a center in a geographically-limited nation state.

The diversity faced by the apostolic Church was as complicated as the diversity of many modern pluralistic societies. Among the Jews there were significant differences between the various religious schools—the Pharisees, the Sadducees, the Zealots, and the Essenes. The peasants and poorer sectors of Palestine were known as the 'Am ha-aretz, the people of the land. They were despised by the Pharisees because they did not or could not keep every detail of the law. The various regions of the country of Palestine also created diversity. Galilean Jews spoke with an accent and were looked down on by the Judeans. Those who were either religiously or racially distinct (such as the Samaritans and Idumeans) were also excluded from the social gatherings of many of the more religiously strict Jews (Jeremias, 1969; Safrai and Stern, 1974, 1976; Schurer, 1973; Hengel, 1974a).

In the Roman world the diversity was even more apparent (Rostovtzeff, 1957; M. Grant, 1960; Judge, 1960; Benko, 1971). Social classes existed, with the elite senatorial and equestrian families at the top of the social pyramid. Municipal bureaucrats and veterans of the armies were also privileged citizens with special rights. Freeborn citizens (plebeians), freed slaves, "peregrini" (working class and peasantry who were not citizens of Rome), and slaves made up the lower classes that did most of the work that made the Roman world prosperous. Beyond these classes one can point to the list of conquered peoples and barbarians found within and on the borders of Rome: Lasitanians, Celtiberians, Lystrans, Ethiopians, Egyptians, Aedui, Suebi, Turdetani, and so on. Occupational groups and guilds were also specialized groupings of people who lived and worked together.

Such was the diversity that confronted the early Church. The New Testament does not mention all of the lines and divisions in the Jewish or gentile worlds because the Christian movement gained its major number of converts from only a few of these groups. Although the gospel was potentially universal, it spread only among a limited number of social groups in the first fifty years of its history. Early Christianity was congregational religion carried on by enthusiastic members who were charismatic, and who came largely from among the anonymous, petty bourgeois. These were the artisans or small business people of the towns and cities. (From its inception, Christianity was marked by artisan leaders: Jesus was a carpenter; Peter, James, and John were fishermen who owned their own ship; Matthew was a minor tax farmer; Paul was a tent-maker; Lydia a seller of dyed cloth, and so on.) The slaves who were from city households whose master had become Christian thus were probably artisans, domestics, and educated persons, and not the uneducated, unskilled slaves of the great slave farms.[1]

1. The sociology of early Christianity upon which much of this analysis is based is only minimally developed (Judge, 1960; Theissen, 1977; Gager, 1975; Malherbe, 1977; Hengel 1974a, 1974b; Nock, 1964; Sherwin-White, 1963; R. Grant, 1977; Benko, 1971). So far as we can tell, Christianity in apostolic years did not grow well among the rural peasantry (who were more attuned to magic), members of the upper levels of the military (who had a tendency to be negative toward salvation religions), the civic bureaucrats (who used religion for civic control but tended to be skeptical of its truth claims), the commercial patriciate (who were strongly this-worldly), or the economically dispossessed (including the lower levels of slavery whose lives were too disorganized and marginal to permit much preoccupation with anything but survival) (cf. Max Weber, 1968, pp. 468–517). It did not reach out to touch most of the ethnic tribal groups but rather grew largely in the same regions and among the same peoples which had been affected by hellenistic Judaism. Consequently, it was concentrated at the end of the first century in cities in the hellenized parts of the eastern and central provinces of the Roman empire. A literary analysis of the letter of Paul indicates that those he addressed had a rather remarkable degree of intellectual ability (even more so if we make the error of supposing his words in I Cor. 1:26–28 are meant to brand Christians as deriving from the illiterate dregs of the social order rather than simply the nobodies of the petty bourgeois). It is a form of petty bourgeois intellectuality which would hardly be understood by the peasant and which would seem "unphilosophical" and irrational to the aristocratic elite (as in Acts 17:32 or 26:24). The inherent bias against the rich set early Christianity against the direct interests of the growing mercantile class, though some apparently were still won to faith and house churches were established in their households. On a positive level, there seems to be a direct correlation between the life situation of this class and the formulation and adaptation given the gospel by evangelists drawn from the same class. A great deal of work still needs to be done in this area. We can only outline our conclusions and suggest some of the analyses that can be found in the New Testament on this issue.

Within the ranks of Palestinian Judaism we find the 'Am ha-aretz most responsive to Jesus and the proclamation of the gospel, though Pharisees and priests also became Christians. We have no way of knowing what percentages came from each group. Acts 11, 15, and 21 indicate that the strict pharisaic Jewish Christian was influential within the Jerusalem church. In spite of their inability to triumph over the broader Jewish Christian point of view, they sent Judaizers all over the Roman world to plague Paul and were later represented by ideological descendents in the Ebionite movement from the second to the seventh centuries. It seems judicious to assume from the victory of the broader party at Jerusalem along with the treatment of the hellenistic Jewish Christians (Acts 7, 15) that the 'Am ha-aretz (from which the twelve apostles came) and the hellenists were dominant as a numeric group.

Outside Palestine, Christianity appears to have grown around the nuclei of converted hellenistic Jews and gentile God-fearers. The God-fearers who had not become full proselytes were attracted to the form of Judaism preached by Paul. It allowed them equal status before God without circumcision and denied the religious value of the food and social scruples of strict Judaism. When we imagine the fabric of client relations as well as the ties of *collegia* (associations of guilds, corporations, clubs) and *familia* that existed among the petty bourgeoisie, we can see that a specific set of peoples comprised the large number of converts of the early Church.

In sum, the early Church grew as a congregational religion and was located in cities where Judaism was strong, primarily in the hellenized and romanized sectors of the eastern and central provinces of the Roman world. Socially, it was comprised of the petty bourgeoisie and included their domestic and artisan slaves. As it grew, it experienced a number of crises over how Christians from the various backgrounds and convictions were to relate to one another, especially Jews and gentiles, though other issues such as slave and free, male and female were also addressed. Frontier and peripheral provinces were not evangelized so that only those who spoke Greek or Aramaic came to be the dominant groups in the churches recorded in the New Testament. Whether this limitation of the social character of early Christianity was intentional is not a question that we can answer at this distance from the actors in that history. The New Testament records the various ways in which the gospel was contextualized to deal with the particular constellation of needs and ideas of those who became Christian, both Jew and gentile.

PAUL'S PHILOSOPHY OF MINISTRY

Paul declares a people-centered distinction when he acknowledges himself to be an apostle to the gentiles, just as Peter was an apostle to the Jewish peoples (Gal. 2:7-9). He never called himself an apostle of a city or a province. While he obviously had a strategy that encompassed provinces and cities as key points for evangelization, he chose them in terms of his overall consciousness of being called to evangelize a particular kind of people in his world (contra Liefield, 1978, pp. 179-180; Verkuyl, 1978, p. 51).

What is implicit in this distinction is made explicit in I Corinthians 9:1-23, especially verse 22b: "I have become all things to all men, that I might by all means save some." Paul mentions four groups to whom he deliberately adjusted his life-style and message presentation in order to gain their allegiance: Jews, those under the law, those outside the law, and the "weak." Paul's evangelism was centered on Jesus Christ, whom he proclaimed unashamedly. But when he was evangelizing the gentiles to whom he was an apostle, he sought to make the message intelligible and meaningful to them.

To those "without the law" he became as one without the law, though he lived consistently within his commitment to Christ. Paul used all his energy and ingenuity to phrase the gospel and model the Christ-centered life in a way that would be understood by a gentile. Jewish cultural scruples were set aside. The gentile was not asked to change his life by adopting circumcision or various customary food habits of the Jewish community. Instead, he or she was directly confronted with Jesus, the Lord of all and final Judge of the living and the dead, and asked to make a commitment to him within his or her own cultural context. Paul's point was that winning "the more" (v. 19) involves discovering and eliminating whatever offends or confuses (life-style, message presentation, methodology) the people to whom one is sent, as well as enhancing that which will maximize the number of those who will be obedient to the gospel.

Such a procedure as modeled and advocated by Paul necessarily involves beginning with the people to be evangelized. There must be an adequate knowledge of the group to whom the evangelist is called. What are their scruples, mores, and procedures for making decisions? To become a Jew, one must understand Jewish peoples. What adjustments must be made in methods, media, and roles if there is to be a culturally-authentic opportunity to respond to the gospel? Paul's example is a challenging one. After his conversion, Paul spent many years living in Tarsus, a gentile city. He thoroughly understood its inhabitants, knew their language as a native, and could quote from their poets and writings. He knew how to enter into their thought patterns and life-style so as to make the message and life of the Kingdom of God as clear and as compelling as possible (Acts 14:15–17; 17:22–31). His knowledge of the Jewish groups was just as deep because of his education and life at Jerusalem (Acts 22:3–5; Phil. 3:4–6). His strategy of working first with the Jews in a city and then turning to the gentiles was solidly founded on his bi-culturalism that allowed him to authentically enter both the Jewish and gentile worlds and present a contextualized expression of the meaning of the Kingdom of God.

If we did no more than to imitate Paul at this point, in spite of the continuing debates of missiology and evangelistic strategy, we would create a titanic revolution in cross-cultural evangelism.

SALVATION THROUGH HEARING THE WORD

Underlying this philosophy that the message of the gospel and the life-style of the evangelist need to be incarnated in a variety of ways for different groups of people, is Paul's conviction that salvation comes by hearing. Paul was convinced that people must *truly hear* the Lord's voice in their own context if they are to be able to call upon the Lord for salvation. Paul's words in Romans 10:10–17 remind us of this:

> For it is by our faith that we are put right with God; it is by our confession that we are saved. . . . As the scripture says, "Everyone who calls out to the Lord for help will be saved."
> But how can they call to him for help if they have not believed? And how can they believe if they have not heard the message? And how can they hear if the message is not proclaimed? And how can the message be proclaimed if the messengers are not sent out? . . . So then, faith comes from hearing the message, and the message comes through preaching Christ.

This passage includes a number of important aspects about a people-centered approach:

1. People cannot obtain salvation through their own efforts or religious activities. There is a connection between the knowledge of the message of the gospel and the faith that puts people right with God.

Salvation is something which is made available through the preaching of Christ.

2. Whether or not people are able to respond to God's love in Christ depends upon the messengers sent out to them. Whether it be a tribal, religious, occupational, or social class people, if no one is sent to preach specifically to them, then there is no opportunity to hear the message and to enter into faith. How many messengers need to be sent? As many as are necessary to proclaim Christ to all the distinct groups that inhabit the earth. Each group that is different enough in culture and self-identity to need a specifically tailored act of preaching will need a conscious strategy and a specifically sent messenger.

3. "Hearing" is used in Romans 10:14,17 in such a way that it includes the idea of *understanding* the message. The mere recitation of the message, the giving of a tract or a printed New Testament cannot be considered "hearing" unless the recipient *understands* the message. The question for Paul was not simply whether the gospel was preached but whether it was *heard*. Communication of a message is much more than simply beaming radio waves into the target audience. The audience must be listening, and the message must be such that it catches their attention and is comprehendible within their own framework of thinking. Because of the differences between groups, the message will have to be presented in different ways, using different languages, illustrations, media, and spokespersons.

4. Hearing and understanding the gospel is no guarantee that it will be accepted. Preaching Christ is not an act of propaganda or coercion. Even in this passage Paul sadly indicates that "not all have accepted the Good News" (v. 16). The goal of evangelism is to persuade men and women to put their trust in Christ as Lord and become faithful members of his Church by providing a culturally-authentic opportunity to hear and respond to the message of salvation. Yet the response may be willful rejection of God's gracious offer. Nonetheless, it is our conviction that we can only be sure that Christ is being rejected when the message proclaimed has been adequately tailored to the distinctive qualities and customs of the people being evangelized. *Too often what is rejected is a confusing and offensive mixture of the Good News and the foreign cultural trappings of the messenger.* An adequate and careful understanding of the people to be evangelized is basic to the whole process of planning strategies for evangelism.

We realize that the foregoing treatment of the Scriptures is brief and only suggestive of the material that bears on the question of the importance of beginning with the people to be evangelized. God has graciously chosen to place great importance on each one of us. He gave his Son that none of us might perish but have everlasting life. The incarnation of Jesus Christ as a Jewish boy at a particular time in history in a very parochial cultural location is perhaps the most striking parable of evangelism in the Bible. For nearly thirty years Jesus was one of the people of Palestine. He spoke their language, ate their food, and learned their customs. He watched people live and die, and heard about their struggles and questions. Only after learning about the inner soul of the Jewish people of Palestine did he begin proclaiming the Good News of the Kingdom in the power of the Spirit. He was God's apostle to the people of God, and he brought them a revolutionary message and way of living that changed the history of the entire human race.

Having accomplished his task, he then turned to those he had chosen and sent them forth: "Peace be with you. As the Father sent me, so I send you" (Jn. 20:21). They now became his apostles, sent to declare the same good news, to love various people groups, and to understand their inner thoughts so well that their message would transform life and society wherever it was heard and received in faith.

We who are sent to continue this mission today cannot act as though we are greater than our Lord. We too must incarnate a strong and patient love that communicates the Good News in a clear and compelling way. This message will vary with each messenger and with each distinctive people group. But we can have the assurance that it is Christ who sends us. He gives us his Spirit to be our strength, peace, and counselor in the midst of the ambiguities and difficulties of ministry.

CHAPTER 10

Defining and Describing a People

*I*f we are agreed in principle that evangelization as a process is best thought of as taking place within the boundaries of peoples, then we need to know what a people group is. How do we decide that a collection of individuals and families are sufficiently similar to one another to be considered a distinctive people group? How do we put boundaries around a specific population and say they are a people who merit a distinctive strategy, a distinctive sending of evangelists so they might truly "hear" the Good News? How dissimilar do two peoples have to be before they need their own specially tailored contextualization of the gospel, their own separate indigenous church institutions?

THE DEBATE ABOUT MONO-ETHNIC CHURCHES

These are not easy questions. Almost everyone recognizes the legitimacy of separate strategies and even institutions for peoples who speak separate languages. We see no reason for forcing Kikuyu to learn Luo or to participate in worship and Bible study in a language that is not native to them. But it becomes much more controversial when we deal with differences between peoples of the same language, differences rooted in social class, caste, race, or education.

There is a significant debate about the mono-ethnic (or mono-class, mono-language) churches resulting from people-oriented evangelization. The problem centers on the question of the legitimacy of indigeneity versus the imperative of the unity of the Church (Lausanne Committee, 1978a; Wagner, 1978; McGavran, 1979; Shenk, 1973; Conn, 1976; Dubose, 1978). We are not going to try to resolve the problem. There is need for a more highly developed theology of culture and social structure before many of the issues can be settled.

Furthermore, there is a often a very real dilemma between the imperative for demonstrable unity based on reconciliation between separate peoples and the imperative to respect the distinctive indigeneity of each unique people. The rich variety of culture should be preserved by the gospel, not destroyed. Yet the very preservation of it often gives continuing support to attitudes of superiority and exclusiveness that are incompatible with a discipleship that demands love and justice. The attempt to transcend cultural differences often leads to a non-indigenous, artificial church that loses its potency to evangelize the group from which it was derived. Each church, if it is to be truly indigenous, must be rooted in the soil of the local culture of its people.

The answer to this dilemma has yet to be produced. The Church Growth movement has stressed the demonstrable historical and contemporary fact that mono-ethnic churches tend to grow more rapidly than those that attempt to be multi-ethnic. David Barrett's survey of churches world-wide indicates "that people join mono-ethnic churches everywhere; and only join [multi-ethnic] conglomerates where there is no mono-ethnic alternative" (1979, p. 276). The pragmatics of evangelism, communication, and social relationships which produce leadership are deeply rooted in sociological and anthropological facts that cannot be banished or ignored by the wave of a magical theological wand. Evangelism that attempts for whatever high theological reasons to ignore cultural and social differences that exist in human society quickly turns into mis-evangelism that unnecessarily drives people away from Christ. Yet we must observe that the Church Growth advocates need to do a better job at relating the "homogeneous unit principle" (that people like to become Christians without crossing racial, linguistic, or class barriers) to a more serious and profound theology of the Church and its unity than they have produced thus far.

The critics of the Church Growth movement at this point have offered a number of commendable theologies of the Church and its unity. In attempting to approach the question of church growth, they have forced us to take a more serious look at those convictions about Christian oneness and fellowship that produced a costly and transforming discipleship in the apostolic Church. Church growth that does not go on beyond numbers counted on membership lists is defective. The quality of discipleship produced is crucial and cannot be ignored in evaluating the desirability of certain types of growth. But these critics have produced very little in the way of significant contemporary or historical scholarship to show that their theological formulations have resulted in either more rapid evangelization of peoples or higher levels of mature discipleship.

We cannot wait until this issue is settled to engage in evangelism nor wait to develop more potent tools for devising evangelistic strategies. There are thousands of peoples who need to have indigenous churches in their midst if they are to be confronted with the power of the Kingdom that Jesus proclaimed. We can only hope that both sides of this argument will continue to dialogue in a spirit of Christian openness and love, and will demonstrate their true commitment to evangelization by planting many of those churches.

MEMBERSHIP IN GROUPS

Throughout our lifetime we spend much of our time in groups with other people. We are born into a family. As we grow older, we become part of play groups and school classes. Later we are members of clubs and associations, we form cliques or crowds of friends, and we work in organizations that require us to be part of various types of working groups. Out of these group experiences we learn the vast majority of the things we know. We are shaped and molded to understand and conform to a variety of customs and ideas. Our personality is formed from the way people have related to us, especially in families and friendships.

Groups are crucial to the way we become humans, to the way in which even God's people live and minister. The whole concept of *koinonia* is based upon the notion of a group of people who are unified by the Spirit, who express and experience love and commonness as they live in relationship to one another. Paul's image of the body of Christ is an attempt to capture the web of interdependence and care which is to be part of the new people God is forming from those who have been called into his Kingdom.

Social scientists have coined an enormous variety of terms to classify the fantastic range of human groups. Some of these are nuclear family, extended family, moiety, deme, sib, clan, kindred, and lineage. Others are social class, caste, status groups, voluntary associations, formal organizations, primary groups, secondary groups, and reference groups. Residential groups are classified as villages, hamlets, towns, cities, and suburbs. Still other terms describe whole societies: band, tribe, chieftainship, and nation. This list, of course, could easily be multiplied.

We have come this far without being very precise about what we mean by a "people." How can a "people" be defined?

WHAT IS A PEOPLE?

We may say that a "people" is a collection of humans who see themselves (or are seen by others) as culturally distinct from other groups. They share certain cultural traits such as language, religion, values, and often a common history. Usually there is a degree of pride associated with the life-style of the group. Members feel that their way of life is right for them and is better than the customs and ideas held by other groups. Usually they wish to cultivate the cultural elements which they see as important and to pass them on to the next generation. Normally they marry others of the same group (outside those kinspersons with whom marriage would be considered incest).

Such groups as the Chinese, the Japanese, the Germans, the English, the Egyptian Arabs, the cattle-herding Maasai, the Sikhs of India, and the rural Javanese farmers are all examples of a people. They participate in a common culture and speak a common language. But for evangelistic purposes we must be more accurate and precise. A people in our sense is a smaller and more culturally uniform group than these examples.

The Chinese are an ethnic group made up of hundreds of peoples with dozens of spoken dialects: Mandarin, Cantonese, Teo-Chiu, Wu, Hakka, Amoy, and so on. Many of these spoken dialects are as different from one another as English is from German. But there are also Chinese who no longer live on the mainland: 3.6 million live in Indonesia and no longer speak any Chinese dialect, and an equally large group in Thailand have intermarried and have taken on Thai names, nationality, and language. The world's one billion Chinese peoples are found in nearly ninety-six nations in addition to their large concentration in the homeland. They are divided into a large number of distinctive communities and social groups that have strikingly different social customs and attitudes. They would have as much difficulty being socially intimate with one another as an American and a German, or an Oxford-educated industrialist with a semi-literate dockworker.

What we are interested in is a group of people who, because of their similarities, tend to think in broadly common ways and therefore will react in generally the same way to a given evangelistic strategy. *A people is definable by those common attributes that make them either reachable by a given means or make them difficult to reach by any known means.* At this point we must turn to sociology and anthropology to help us in clarifying the different types of human groups and what it is that defines some of them as "peoples."

DEFINITIONS OF SOCIAL GROUPS

The most basic postulate of social science is that human attitudes and behavior are largely derived from membership in groups. We humans think the thoughts we think, have the knowledge we have, pursue certain goals instead of others largely because of what we have learned, consciously and unconsciously, from the groups to which we give our loyalty. We are all shaped and molded by the groups of which we were and are or even hope to be a part.

Scientists have yet to achieve a satisfactory classification of social groups. The same group can be classified in a variety of ways: by size, openness, organization, relationship to the larger societal groups, membership procedures, value homogeneity, permanence, focus of interest or function of group, and so forth. All of these characteristics can be important for understanding a given social group, but they are not all equally important for a definition of a people.

Broadly we may distinguish four distinctive categories of groups (utilizing the schema of Robert Bierstedt, 1970, pp. 272–301):

1. Statistical groups

These are groups created by the imagination of the scientist. The scientist places people into groups on the basis of a chosen trait; for example, the number of red-headed or left-handed people in the population. Most frequently these are demographic groups, statistical classifications that do not take into account whether people so classified see themselves as a group or whether they ever interact with one another.

This is not to say that statistical groups are unimportant. It may be very important for a person in the car business to know how many families bought new cars last year, or the number and location of Mercedes-Benz owners, even though those groups never see themselves as a group (until there is a recall of their car because of an unsafe feature). It is important for a radio broadcaster to know how many people listen to the radio and what their age profile is. Statistical groups can be important for certain types of activities, especially in mass media and marketing. But this is not the kind of group we are referring to when we speak of a people group. People groups may form from what were at one time statistical aggregates, but our interest is in groups that already have a group identity.

2. Societal groups

These are groups which have similar identities and common traits such as age, sex, skin color, style of clothing, language, accent, residence, common interest, health problems, and so forth. Shared interests (and differences) lead to the formation of social groups in specific localities that serve to utilize those shared interests for accomplishing common goals. Whether or not more specific groups form, there is an awareness of "we-ness," of being a distinct group in contrast to other people in the society. Examples might be the aged, teenagers, blacks, Southerners, the blind, Bostonians, occupational groups, hippies, and so on. What distinguishes these groups from the statistical aggregate is that they have a subjective awareness of the trait by which a statistician might classify them as a group.

The importance of this inner sentiment of similarity cannot be overestimated. It serves as the basis for the formation of the types of groups which we term "peoples." Only on the basis of this sentiment can a group identity be formed and the other two types of groups arise.

3. Social groups

These are groups in which people actually associate with one another. These include friendships, families, congregations, neighborhoods, clans, and classrooms. These are groups that have a degree of self-identity as well as a degree of allegiance and loyalty, and oftentimes a feeling that the people and ways of the group are better than those of similar groups. What distinguishes the social group from the societal group is that in addition to an awareness of similarity in some given set of traits, there is a network of interaction. People actually associate with each other. They spend time with one another, and make friends (and enemies) from this group. They discover a broader set of values. They help one another during a crisis, take trips together, and gossip to one another. Outsiders also see the group as distinct and treat its members accordingly.

This group is most important in the formation of personality and culture and its passing on from one generation to another. This is where people learn to conform to a relatively uniform set of customs and values. This is the group that people consult when they are in the process of making a decision. This is where people learn what it means to be a teenager, or a female, or member of the Dayton family. It is this type of group we normally think of when someone talks about social groups.

4. Associations

This is a group which is formally organized around the pursuit of a common interest or goal. Such groups have become enormously important in modern societies; for example, the Grey Panthers for the aged, IBM for making computers, the National Organization of Women for furthering the interests of females, the First Presbyterian Church of Old Hollow, and the cub scout pack of Burbank School. All of these groups are formally organized with constitutions or rules for procedure and qualifications for membership. In most cases, people become part of the organization on a voluntary basis.

The importance of this type of group in the modern world hardly needs comment. Formally organized business organizations increasingly dominate all economic processes in the industrialized and industrializing countries. Multi-national corporations are in some cases more powerful than the nation states they span. Much of the overseas and cross-cultural ministry of the Church is carried out in associations such as the Protestant mission agencies or the Catholic mission orders. Many associations are very influential in shaping a person's identity.

OUR DEFINITION OF A PEOPLE GROUP

A people group is more specific than most societal groups but usually more general and less well defined than an associational group. We define a people as:[1]

> A *significantly large sociological grouping of individuals who perceive themselves to have a common affinity for one another.*

1. This definition follows that of the Strategy Working Group of the Lausanne Committee for World Evangelization (see Dayton, 1979).

Essential to the definition is the notion that a people "perceive themselves to have a common affinity for one another." They subjectively consider all the people in a given grouping to have similar characteristics and see these similarities as a sufficient basis for acting together as a distinctive group.

To some extent, this emphasis on the subjective feelings of people as a basis for defining them as a "people" differs from the classic definition of a homogeneous unit found in Church Growth literature. There, as McGavran defines it, a homogeneous unit is "a section of society in which all members have some characteristic in common" (1970, p. 85; see also Lausanne Committee, 1978a). The stress in that definition is upon some *characteristic* or trait that is shared in common. Our definition stresses the resulting *subjective sense of peoplehood* or identity which is derived from shared characteristics. We all share a large number of things with many people. What is crucial for the formation of a people is the way in which those characteristics are subjectively given meaning and used to define what it means to be a part of this group instead of another. We also chose *not* to use the rather distinctive term "homogeneous unit" for the following reasons:

1. The term "homogeneous unit" is misleading in that it implies a homogeneity in the members of a social group that may or may not exist. What is essential is a sense of group identity, not an objectively provable fact of homogeneity based on a given set of qualities or characteristics. A people may be highly homogeneous and yet not sense that they are a social group. Or the characteristics of a people may be highly diverse, and yet they may share several traits that lead to a strong sense of affinity, to the formation of social groups and intimate interaction. It is the *awareness* of shared characteristics that is crucial, not the fact of similarity.

2. "Homogeneous unit" has been misused as a scientific concept. It is such a broad and elastic term that there is virtually no group to which it cannot be applied (James Smith, 1976, draws a different conclusion from this fact). Consequently it does not really distinguish between the different types of social groups we discussed above. It can apply equally well to a statistical group as to an associational group.

3. The term is often applied after the fact. Only after rapid church growth is observed does one search for some similarities in a group that might explain why they shared the need to be jointly responsive to the gospel. It thus becomes a circular observation. If there is rapid growth, it *must* be due in part to growth in a homogeneous unit.

The term is particularly difficult in urban settings where people belong to a variety of overlapping social and societal groups. The term is not problematic in tribal, ethnic, or caste settings where there are strong divisions between peoples. But it is problematic in cities. It is true that many cities maintain wards where highly-bounded groups live and work, separated from other groups (this is especially true in the late developing countries). In these cases, people are like "urban villagers" (to use Herbert Gans' term) and can be dealt with as "homogeneous units" (as is the case in Bombay, India, or the tribal settlements in Kinshasa, Zaire). But this is distinctly not the case for Tokyo and the non-ethnic parts of New York City, Boston, London, Paris, Rio, and hundreds of other cities.

Our definition stresses the fact that the things which people share in common—be it language, religion, ethnicity, residence, occupation, health, class or status, caste, legal situation, or some combination of these—bind people together in subjectively defined social groups. They come to see themselves as a people and others begin to treat them as distinctive; for example, the Urdu-speaking Muslim farmers of the Punjab (who share language, religion, occupation, location), the Welsh working-class miners (ethnicity, occupation, class), or the white, swinging singles in North American apartments (race, marital status, lifestyle, and residence). Each of these groups has several characteristics that differentiate them from other groups and types of people in the nations in which they live.

"Affinity" means that individuals are primarily attracted to those with whom they have something in common. This does not mean that there must be actual interaction for individuals to be considered part of the group; rather, there must be the *potential* for interaction.

"A significantly large" sociological grouping indicates that the group must be large enough for people to find their *primary* group identity in it. Individuals have varying ties to different social, societal, and associational groups. In one sense, a single nuclear family can be considered a people. It meets all the criteria of the definition, and certainly for children it is often the most significant social group with which they identify and make their decisions. At the other end of the scale, a social class may be considered a people to the extent that it has a sense of affinity and group identity. Often a social class is more like a statistical category. Technically speaking, social classes are horizontal divisions of the total society whose members differ in prestige due to differential access to valued resources and positions of power. Even though members of the same class may share certain traits, they may seldom act together.

But where they do, they may be considered a people. So even a rather large group can be considered a people provided it has a clear sense of affinity.

In the end the criterion of significance for size *must be derived from evangelistic goals.* The group must be large enough to warrant the special effort and caring that is part of a distinctive strategy for reaching a people group. The group should not be so large and diverse that it cannot be adequately and effectively reached by a single strategy. In too large a group, there is the possibility that some people will be offended or confused by approaches that do not relate to their needs. The opposite is also true. In too small a group (unless one is dealing with the whole of a tiny ethno-linguistic group, such as the forty Tasaday of the Philippines) there is the possibility that certain families and communities, who really are similar enough in life-style and who see themselves as similar to the communities on which the strategy is focused, will be excluded and overlooked.

The important thing is that people have a sense of belonging to a group. When we discover the pride that a Yir Yorunt, or a Kafir, or a Boston Brahmin, has in his or her customs and symbols, then we can begin to incarnate adequately the message of the gospel in a way that will make the best sense and give them a valid opportunity to accept Christ.

RESOURCES FOR DESCRIBING A PEOPLE GROUP

There are many avenues by which a person can come to identify and describe a people group. It is a problem and adventure which has preoccupied missionaries, government administrators, and anthropologists for many years. Sociologists have devised many tools for describing the groups that are found in cities and industrial societies, just as anthropologists have developed techniques for dealing with smaller communities, especially in cross-cultural settings. Missionaries likewise have made a significant contribution through their experiences of living in cross-cultural contexts and through their own surveys and studies.

A number of resources are now available to the person who is interested in understanding a specific group of people. We will touch on only a few, but we are confident that they will be sufficient to *begin* the process.

1. Unreached Peoples Questionnaire

This questionnaire[2] is an attempt to secure the *minimum* amount of information an outsider might need to describe a people group. It is explicitly oriented to the issues of evangelization and therefore contains questions dealing with the status of church growth and evangelization efforts among a people group. It asks questions about the following:

— The identity of the people. Who are they? Where are they located? How many are in this group?

— The elements that distinguish and unify the group. These include things like language, ethnicity, kinship, shared occupation or residential area, common religious customs, and so forth.

— The languages used by the group; not only those languages which are spoken or read but also those which are used for education, trade, and religious and evangelization purposes.

— The religious commitments of the people. How many are Christians? How many practice their faith? What about non-Christian religious or secularized commitments?

— What type of Christian witness does this people have? How open are the people to religious change or Christian commitment?

— What are the crucial needs of a people? How do they see their own spiritual and physical needs?

This questionnaire is only a simple expression of *what* needs to be known, not *how* one comes to know it. For that reason it needs to be supplemented with the information sources and techniques that are found in the following resources.

2. Manuals and handbooks

There are many manuals and handbooks that provide essential information for describing a people. It is not possible or even necessary to list them all. We will suggest only a few, most of which have more extensive bibliographies for the person who desires further information.

A number of books deal with the question of *what* one might want to know about a group, and thus provide categories and terms for labeling various kinds of observed customs and social groupings. *Notes and Queries* (Royal Anthropological Institute, 1951) has been a standard

2. This is the 1979 version of the questionnaire that has undergone considerable testing since first developed in 1974. A copy of this questionnaire may be found on pp. 491–495 below.

handbook for social anthropologists. It is especially useful in understanding peoples who are non-Western and live in small communities. George Peter Murdock, et al., *Outline of Cultural Materials* (Human Relations Area Files, 1971) is more of a catalogue of categories for classifying descriptive material from all types of societies. Thomas and Betty Brewster's *Language Acquisition Made Practical (LAMP)* (Lingua, 1976) is another guide which suggests not only what but how to go about acquiring information about a group while in the process of learning their language.

Many other books deal more with *how* to gather information through research rather than giving detailed statements of what ought to be looked for. One of the best is *Doing Fieldwork: Warnings and Advice* (Wax, 1971). A briefer treatment of the same issue is found in *Field Methods in the Study of Culture* (Williams, 1967).[3] Sociologists have also tried to provide guides and training materials for researching social groups. *Fieldwork* (Junker, 1970) has been a standard work for many years. It should be supplemented with other standard texts. *The Research Craft* (Williamson, et al., 1977) and *The Practice of Social Research* (Babbie, 1975) are two among many. *How Can I Get Them to Listen: A Handbook on Communication Strategy and Research* (Engel, 1977) is an excellent, non-technical introduction to survey research for Christians seeking to design and evaluate communication strategies for evangelism.

3. Scientific surveys of peoples

One of the best resources available is the vast array of books and articles produced by professional anthropologists, sociologists, political scientists, and research institutes. There are literally thousands of studies of peoples from virtually every country in the world, most of which have been published in European languages. Their quality varies

3. There are a large number of similar studies. Many are enjoyable and provide significant insight into the problems of studying peoples in a wide range of differing settings. Elenore Smith Bowen's *Return to Laughter* (1954, 1964) is a semi-classic fictionalization of the fieldwork experiences of Laura Bohannan. Hortense Powdermaker's *Strangers and Friends* (1966) is interesting reading about a woman's research in four different groups. Other studies and essays may be found in: George Spindler, ed., *Being an Anthropologist: Field Work in Eleven Cultures* (1970), Morris Freilich, ed., *Marginal Natives: Anthropologists at Work* (1970); David Maybury-Lewis, *The Savage and the Innocent* (1965), and Paul Rabinow, *Reflections on Fieldwork in Morocco* (1977). Holt, Rinehart, and Winston is publishing a whole series of paperbacks edited by the Spindlers: "Case Studies in Methods of Anthropology."

greatly, of course. Some are based on only a few months to a single year of research. Others are the result of multiple approaches and many years of careful study by several scientists. Used in conjunction with personal experience and checked against further research, such studies can be invaluable in describing the customs and life patterns of a people.

The easiest way to discover what is available is to gain access to the anthropology library at a nearby university or college. The best and most complete collections are to be found at major graduate centers which have a doctoral program in anthropology. The Peabody Museum library at Harvard University is an outstanding collection with a superb catalogue for anyone researching a people that has been studied by anthropologists. Other such universities are the University of Chicago, University of California (Berkeley), Yale, Cornell, U.C.L.A., University of Washington, Stanford University, University of Michigan, and Washington University. In Europe, significant collections can be found in London, Paris, and Berlin.

There are collections of surveys of peoples that can give a person quick access to further studies; for example, Frank LeBar, et al. have edited standard works on Southeast Asia: *Ethnic Groups of Insular S.E. Asia* (Human Relations Area File, 1972), Volumes 1 and 2; and *Ethnic Groups of Mainland S.E. Asia* (HRAF, 1964). The University of Texas publishes the standard encyclopedia on Central American Indians. Edited by Wauchope and Vogt, volumes seven and eight of the *Handbook of Middle American Indians: Ethnology* (1969) give a detailed survey of what is known about a large number of such groups. *Muslim Peoples* (Weekes, 1978) lists three hundred groups and provides descriptive articles for the ninety-six Muslim groups each numbering over one hundred thousand. Evans-Pritchard, the British anthropologist, has edited a popular twenty-volume series on *Peoples of the Earth* (1973) that might be found in a public library. Though quite dated, George Murdock's survey, *Africa* (1959) is still useful for an overview of the hundreds of African tribes. *The Peoples of South Asia* (Maloney, 1974) is a brief overview of the Indian sub-continent and can be supplemented with *The People of Asia* (Bowles, 1978) and *Atlas on India* (Schwartzberg, 1977).

4. Missiological studies

More case studies of church growth and evangelization are becoming available. The William Carey Library (1705 Sierra Bonita Ave., Pasadena, California 91104) has published a large number of research projects dealing with specific countries, peoples, and churches. Many of them contain brief summaries of the groups' cultures.

Some, such as *The Gospel and Frontier Peoples* (Beaver, 1973), are of special interest because they display estimates of the evangelization of various peoples in addition to giving cultural information.

Unreached Peoples '79 and *Unreached Peoples '80* (Wagner and Dayton, 1978, 1979) are part of an ongoing series of research annuals which describe unreached peoples and list large numbers of other peoples for whom some descriptive information is stored in the computer facilities at the Missions Advanced Research and Communication Center (MARC) of World Vision International.

The World Christian Encyclopedia, edited by David B. Barrett (1980), gives evangelization information on some twelve hundred major ethnic groupings in some 220 countries of the world. Patrick Johnstone at the Worldwide Evangelization Crusade headquarters in England also heads a program to detail the evangelization needs of various major ethnic groups around the world. When combined with the more detailed information gathered by the Unreached Peoples Program at MARC, the information in the *World Christian Encyclopedia* and other anthropological information are very useful in describing peoples.

5. Secondary literature

Encyclopedias (such as the *Britannica*) will often have brief descriptions of peoples. One of the most useful series for further bibliography as well as overviews of most large ethnic groups in a country is the *Area Handbooks* published by the United States Government, and researched and written by the Foreign Area Studies of the American University. More than seventy of these handbooks are currently available. Almost all devote one or two chapters to detailing the names and interrelationships of major ethnic and social class groups in a country.

6. Personal observation and skills

The best source of information for describing and understanding a people group is personal, sympathetic contact over a long period of time. One cannot simply read about a particular people. A people must be *experienced*. Only as we become identified with the people to whom God calls us, only as we enter into their life-style can we begin to understand their sense of pride, their joy at meeting another of "their own kind." Only then can we understand and appreciate the beauty of their way of life and how God wants to enhance it with the leaven of the gospel.

It is not easy to enter into the life of another people. There is a sense in which we all remain outsiders to people who are not part of our personal roots. Yet some people achieve remarkable degrees of intimacy. There are skills that can be learned and utilized in developing the ability to become a part of another people. If we say that God has called us to evangelize a particular people, one way we *show* our love is through the care we take in understanding what makes them distinctive and in understanding how the gospel speaks uniquely to them as a people. As we will discuss later, this willingness to know and experience a people is always the first overt act of biblical evangelism. It may well be that only those who can come to enjoy the way of life of the people they are evangelizing will ultimately be able to authenticate their witness within a people.

THE ADVANTAGES OF A PEOPLE-CENTERED APPROACH

It is useful at this point in our discussion to enumerate some of the advantages of shifting the emphasis of missions from political boundaries to people groups. In some ways these advantages might be stated as follows:

It attempts to see the world as God sees it. The Lord of the universe is not only concerned with the political boundaries formed by humans, but is also concerned with relationships to one another.

It mobilizes the Church world-wide. By removing the emphasis on missions as being a ministry which crosses political boundaries, it makes the church in every country responsible not only for the other countries of the world but for the people groups within that country.

It is a response to the Great Commission. The Lord tells us to go to all peoples.

It makes the task understandable. It is very difficult to comprehend the task of mission within a country of any size. It is not difficult to understand the task when a people is well defined.

It defines a realizable goal. The discouragement of missions is the seeming impossibility of bringing an entire country to Christ. When a people is defined numerically, and when the task of mission is seen as nurturing these people until 20 percent are active in Christ's Church, then the goal becomes realizable.

It sharpens the sense of God's call.

It defines the preparation needed. Too often in the past missionary preparation has been defined by a particular "field" (usually meaning a country). Often this type of preparation is not adequate to get on with specific tasks.

It helps communicate the task of mission. Mission agencies and churches are prone to think of *countries* as places where they have a ministry. When the people group is used to define the work being done, then the fuzziness of trying to think about the whole country disappears.

It changes the emphasis from sending to reaching. The Church is not in the business of sending missionaries. It is in the business of reaching peoples and making disciples.

It helps recruiting. When a task is well defined and understandable, it is much more likely to attract those whom God has prepared for that specific task.

It discourages the erection of artificial national boundaries. One of the major dilemmas faced by missions today is the institution of the "national" church. When a mission agency from Denomination X plants a church within a country and says "This is the X Church in this country," it is in effect setting itself up for defeat. As this church identifies its sense of being with its nationality, it quickly assumes jurisdiction over the entire national boundary. There might be hundreds of unreached peoples still within the country which the newly planted church has no current capability to reach. And yet because it is the *national* church, it feels that it must discourage expatriate missionaries from its own denomination from entering its borders.

It models cross-cultural mission for the younger church. Most world evangelism is going to be carried out by some local churches. The difficulty is that too many younger (and older) churches think that this is the only way of moving forward in evangelization. When the mission agency seeks to plant a church among a *people*, it demonstrates to this church that it has a responsibility to plant a church among another people.

It assists coordination between mission agencies and churches. It does this by being specific about a people that we are attempting to reach and inviting others to participate with us.

It makes strategy specific. When strategies cover a large number of peoples, they are seldom effective for any one. As a consequence many strategies are seen as ineffective, when really they might be very effective if applied to just one people.

It defines the total cross-cultural mission task. The task of mission is not to reach three billion people. The task of mission is to plant a viable church within every people group in the world.

Finally, its strength is prayer support. Prayer aimed specifically at pleading with God to shower his mercy on a particular people is intelligent, consecrated prayer.

CHAPTER 11

Understanding the Meaning System of a People

*T*o describe a people is one thing; to understand them is another. Understanding is the chief currency of successful evangelism. It enables us to touch the inner springs of life and dramatize how Christ cares about the hurts and aspirations of every person in every cultural group. It enables us to say the right word at the right time because it opens channels of communication. It enables us to learn as much from those we share Christ with as they learn from us. But it is not a currency that is easily earned.

When we think of the greatest parable of the New Testament, the living incarnation of God in Christ, we are overwhelmed by the manner in which God demonstrated his caring and understanding. He became one of us, lived under the law, humbled himself even to the point of assuming the place of a convicted criminal. He lived in Palestine for thirty years, listening, asking questions, studying, observing, and absorbing the life of those about him, before he began to proclaim the Kingdom of God. Jesus understood the Jewish people so well that everyone who heard him marveled—"No one teaches like him," they said. Jesus Christ thoroughly understood the people to whom he communicated the message of God. We who claim to be his disciples can do no better than to follow his example.

THREE DIMENSIONS FOR UNDERSTANDING A PEOPLE

Understanding a people is at the heart of planning strategies for evangelism. It serves as the basis for all the steps that must later be considered and planned. An awareness of the various facets of a people enables us to see how best to communicate the gospel. Charles Taber has written:

> The evangelist, before planning his approach, must discover what assumptions the hearer holds about reality, truth, and value; and more important, must be keenly aware of what problems deeply trouble the hearer, so that he can maximize the fit of the Gospel presentation to the hearer's needs. This is what Jacob A. Loewen has called "scratching where it itches." Such an adaptation presupposes on the part of the evangelist more or less extended, more or less intimate contact with the hearer in a variety of social situations, and a keen sensitivity and awareness of what social scientists call the paramessage of the situation. True evangelism rarely flourishes in isolation from the whole of life, it rarely succeeds in reaching and transforming a man by operating in vacuum or at a distance. (1973, pp. 121–122)

The next three chapters will deal with the major elements which we feel are important in understanding a people group. Insight into the nature and characteristics of a people is a basis for selecting from a variety of possible strategies, approaches, methods, and roles. Perfect understanding is not possible or even necessary. But there are some things which are essential to a self-conscious, intelligent strategy for evangelism.

To probe deeply into the heart of a people is to go much deeper than the objective descriptions in the Unreached Peoples Questionnaire (see pp. 491ff), or emphasized in the books listed in "Resources for Describing a People Group" (see pp. 140–142). It is to consider the motivating forces that move a people to act the way they act. It is to see the world the way they see it. Understanding a people means discovering their general answer to the question: What is life all about?

While there is no simple scheme that will pull back the veil and disclose the answer to the outsider, there are a number of areas which are crucial to the understanding of a people. We find it helpful to stress three dimensions of a people's life: meanings, needs, and behaviors (including institutions and relationships). As evangelists, we are looking for several types of "bridges" over which the gospel can be conveyed

(McGavran, 1955). There are "bridging concepts and symbols" within the language and lore of a people which can serve as conduits for Christianity (Richardson, 1974). There are "bridging needs" which are close to the inner psycho-social-emotional concerns of a people and to which the gospel and Christians can minister and speak. There are "bridging customs, behaviors, and relationships" which can be tapped to embody and support the Christian faith in a culturally authentic way as it is born in a new people group.

Each of these three dimensions is crucial because of its significance to the success of evangelism. The first dimension deals with what people think and how they think—their perceptions and perspectives as they attempt to construct meaning from their world. Only bridging concepts can make the Christian faith understandable to a people. If the gospel does not make sense to them, they will reject it. The second dimension stresses relevance. The gospel must meet the deepest aspirations, needs, and motives of a people or it will be rejected because it is peripheral to life. The third dimension is concerned with the roles, social structures, institutions, and relationship networks which structure a people's way of life. Behavior patterns and relationships are important to the cultural viability of Christian faith and the actual manner in which evangelism can be carried out. Christianity has to be incarnated through certain external action patterns which must find authenticity not only as a response to the gospel but also as a response from within the cultural patterns of a specific people. *If Christianity is not culturally authentic, it can never gain the vitality it needs to transform a culture from within.*

We will examine each of these three areas in the next three chapters.

THE MEANING SYSTEM OF A PEOPLE

People continually attempt to make sense of their world. They cannot live comfortably when everyday human living makes no sense to them. Consequently, they develop a system of meaning that gives order to the world and their experiences. It tells them what the universe is like, why they exist, what they can expect from life, how to understand death, and how to communicate with others about common experiences and ventures.

The meaning system of a people is comprised of symbolic or cognitive maps which provide labels, perspective, interpretation, explanation, and coherence to life. Once a person has learned the meaning system of a people (all children are consciously and unconsciously trained into their parents' meaning system), he or she then tends to perceive and understand the world in terms of that system. It is as though we are all born extremely nearsighted, unable to make much sense of the impressions received by our brains until we put on the glasses provided by our parents.

There are a number of components that together make up the meaning system in which we all participate (Hesselgrave deals with these in detail, 1978c, pp. 121–271). The most significant are:

1. Language

Each language is a symbolic system of codes which labels the world and thus assigns meaning to it. Through these verbal symbols people can communicate with one another. But each language labels the world differently. People do not live in the same world with different labels; rather, because their labels are different, they live in different worlds. Language is fundamental to every people's identity and ability to survive as a relatively unified group that cooperates in joint ventures. So much has been written on the importance of language to the communication of the gospel. Some excellent examples are works by Brewster (1977), Larson and Smalley (1972), and Eugene Nida (1957, 1964, 1974). Apart from a grasp and understanding of the actual verbal communication patterns of a people, it is doubtful that an evangelist can enter into the mind of a people and adequately communicate the gospel.[1]

1. It is late in the day to produce another sermon on the importance of language learning and the use of the vernacular. Apparently there is still a serious question in many mission circles as to the fundamental importance of language in evangelization. At the 1979 meeting of the American Society for Missiology, Dr. Nida summed up more than thirty years' experience and acquaintance with more than 3,000 missionaries: "Despite the valiant efforts of numerous missionaries to master strange unwritten languages and the considerable success which a few persons have had in doing so, verbal communication for the most part has been poor and often seriously misleading. Almost all early Bible translations in so-called 'new languages' have been found to be seriously deficient. Many of them are so literal that people have found them difficult to understand. In Africa, for example, many persons have had to read the Scriptures in English, French, or Portuguese first in order to know what they meant in their own native languages. . . .

"In comparison with the level of linguistic adequacy in the Scriptures, the level of missionaries' proficiency in oral use of Third World languages has been even worse. Despite the fact that most of the languages in Africa south of the Sahara have tonal distinctions which are extremely important, not only in dis-

2. Hermeneutics

Languages have codes which can be used to label experience and identify its components. The hermeneutics of a people refers to its system for interpreting and understanding the significance of that labeled experience. It has to do with how people think, the processes by which they interpret, explain, and understand the basic information received through the language and sensory experience coded by that language. How do they formulate conclusions? What role does intuition play as opposed to the linear, syllogistic reasoning so popular in the West? What counts as evidence? What is considered an adequate explanation for a "reasonable" person? How do they go about the process of persuading people of a new idea or practice? To what do they appeal in order to get the potential convert to see the wisdom of changing his or her mind? Hermeneutics deals with how the language is *used* in order to reach the conclusions which guide actions and provide certainties. It has to do with the principles that govern the thinking process of a people faced with explaining a myth, a gospel story, or an everyday event.

3. World view

When we consider a people's *total response* to their universe, we consider their basic assumptions about experience (Hiebert, 1976, p. 356). A world view is "the central governing set of concepts and presuppositions that [a] society lives by" (M. Kraft, 1978, p. 4). It is a framework into which all other thoughts and concepts are placed; it is a set of themes that pattern the perceptions of what is real and unreal, what is possible and impossible (C. Kraft, 1979, p. 53). It acts as a gestalt within which all other understanding of the world takes place. Normally the hermeneutical and language systems of a people reflect, give expression to, and reinforce the world view, and thus provide a self-sustaining, mutually reinforcing meaning to all of life. The different world views held by different peoples lead to radically different conclusions about life's mysteries. When Paul was bitten by a poisonous snake

---

tinguishing words but in marking grammatical relationships, very few missionaries have ever learned to use the tones correctly. . . .

"Though for the most part missionaries were often conscious of their linguistic handicaps and desired more time and help in learning local languages, the mission boards which sent them to the field were usually far less sensitive to the problems of verbal communication . . . On numerous occasions I have pled with missionary leaders to take more seriously the problems of verbal communication, but only rarely have I experienced a positive response" (1979a, pp. 2-3).

(Acts 28:1–6), the people of Melita concluded that he was a god because he did not die. Had a modern Western scientist been there, he or she probably would have come to a different conclusion because of his or her radically different world view. Differences in assumptions about the reality of the spirit world, the appearance of gods in human form, or the existence of microscopic things called toxins—all produce very different and, at times, incompatible perceptions and explanations of events or texts.

These three components must be understood in terms of their religious system if we are to understand how a people gives a distinctive meaning to its existence and experiences. Every people has its own distinctive philosophy and religious commitment that give specific content to its world view. These are found in myths, stories, folk tales, or scriptures that explain who God is, what the spiritual realm is like, and how these relate to human life and activity. Even the various rituals and attempts to relate to the unseen world contain implicit if not explicit assumptions about what God or the goddesses, gods, and spirits will do for humans and what humans must do to avert evil and guarantee the good. Religion as a system of meaning is one of the central expressions of how language, hermeneutics, and world view aid people in their quest for significance.

BEGINNING WITH A PEOPLE'S UNDERSTANDING

The meaning system of a people is important because it serves as the context by which people come to listen to the gospel. We all learn by moving from the known to the unknown. However confused, wrong, or inadequate a people's ideas might be when measured against the revelation of God through Christ, they nonetheless serve as the starting point, the known from which a people ventures into the unknown of Christian faith.

People come to the gospel with prior notions of justice, mercy, love, law, and evil. They already can explain why people get sick and how the supernatural is involved in getting well, the meanings of various types of dreams, the nature of time and space, and the reality and activity of a spirit world. They have definite ideas about how God speaks to humans and what he can be expected to say. All of these ideas affect the way in which they will hear and interpret the gospel. Evangelization must come to terms with the meanings it encounters in cultures. If it does not begin with the language, the ways of interpreting messages, and the world view of a people, evangelization will not make sense to a people.

We normally think of the importance of the meaning system in connection with Bible translation (Nida, 1964, 1974; Wonderly, 1968; Kasdorf, 1978). The problem is patent: How can this meaning, this phrase, this concept be adequately expressed in this particular language, for a people who have this particular type of world view? How can the meaning and impact of what Jesus said be conveyed so that people will understand what the Kingdom of God is about?

The problems found in Bible translation are symptomatic of the larger problem of the transculturation of the gospel into foreign social institutions and structures. The gospel must be translated not only in word but also in deed. We do not know exactly what Jesus would have said in a different social structure. We have to discover for ourselves what he would have said to a particular people. Jesus commanded that we make known "all things whatsoever." This is a large task in our own meaning system, much less in a foreign one, but that is part of the challenge and demand of evangelism.

> God Himself took the risk of translation when He became incarnate, when He translated the Word into our stumbling language—and misunderstanding is inevitable. The offer of salvation becomes a stumbling-block. His translation—His offer of self-giving and self-effacing love—led directly to a cross. But the cross of risk and suffering is inscribed anew upon every translation as soon as an attempt is made to express the message in new terms. (Sundkler, 1963, p. 57)

It is not possible to outline briefly the variety of techniques and approaches that have been developed to uncover and utilize the meanings and symbols already present in a given culture. That this question is a major concern and bone of contention for missionaries and missiologists is evident from the large number of articles and books dealing with the issue (to cite a few: Kair-Ullah, 1976; Accad, 1976; Loewen, 1976; C. Kraft, 1977; Ahrens, 1977; Hwang, 1977; Taber, 1978; Corwin, 1978; Kelley, 1978). The journal, *Gospel in Context* (1564 Edge Hill Rd., Abington, Pa. 19001), also has numerous articles dealing with the question.

INDIGENEITY OR CHRISTO-PAGANISM?

The concern with how the essential meaning of Christian faith is expressed in a human culture is a natural one (C. Kraft, 1979a). The validity or non-validity of communication and incarnation of the Kingdom is at stake. There are tensions and difficulties. From the very start, ambiguous choices have to be made by people who are not well informed as to the consequences of those choices for the ultimate evangelization of a people. What one Christian group may consider a compromise and confusion of the message, another group may view as a creative breakthrough in linking Christian meanings with traditional symbols and meanings in a given people (Yamamori and Taber, 1975). What is one's indigeneity is another's Christo-paganism.

Yet the risk is unavoidable. Without the attempt at indigenization the result inevitably will be confusion, offense, and often a worse form of syncretism. Without indigenization there is no meaningful confrontation of religious systems and no intelligent opportunity to say yes to Christ (Nida, 1960, pp. 184–188). How one draws the line between an indigenization of Christian action and meanings and a syncretism that adulterates and nullifies the power of the gospel is not a problem peculiar to the newer places where the gospel is spreading. Penetrating questions have been raised about the "purity" of the Western forms of Christianity. Many argue that American evangelicalism is itself a syncretistic version of "Christo-Paganism" ("Christo-Americanism") with a heavy overlay of consumerism, the "American Way of Life," individualistic self-fulfillment, narcissism (Lasch, 1979), and other elements which nullify some of the key components of true discipleship (Herberg, 1960; Berger, 1961; Sider, 1977; Quebedeaux, 1978).

We can say (with hindsight in many situations) that God is able to lead us as we attempt to interrelate and correlate the truth and life of the gospel with the life patterns of a people. It is not a simple or direct process, as any study of the New Testament background will reveal. Words and symbols (such as resurrection, agape, logos) were appropriated by the early Church as it attempted to be both faithful to the revelation of God and meaningful within the culture and language of the Roman world. Certain terminologies and approaches were rejected as incompatible (Bruce, 1977). In very brief and schematic fashion, Jacques Ellul captures this process in a model and suggests that it happens in all the contexts into which the word of God comes:

> If in contrast we study the relation between the culture of the time and the expression of revelation, we find a complex interplay of adoption and adaption. In a given cultural and historical setting, the intervention of revelation takes the following course. First, we have appropriation; the message of God uses the cultural modes of

a specific time and place and enters into them. Then there is contradiction; the difference between the content of revelation and
that of the particular culture becomes apparent, perfect adaptation
is seen to be impossible, and the greater the appropriation, the
more glaring is the contradiction. Then there is expropriation; the
cultural schema or concept is absorbed by the content of revelation
and the cultural sense is expropriated in favor of the revealed sense,
as, e.g., in such words as resurrection or even God. (1976, p. 164)

This is a process that is being explored in depth today by modern
biblical scholars. Even a work such as the *Theological Dictionary of the
New Testament* (Kittel and Friedrich, eds., 1964–1974) demonstrates
repeatedly how the Greek and Hebrew contexts of biblical revelation
did not fully convey the gospel. But their use by the Church over a
period of time transformed their meanings so that they increasingly
came to communicate the essential gospel message. It also demonstrates
how the early Church did not resort to "borrowed" words, transliter-
ated from another language and culture context in order to preserve the
holy meaning of a concept thought impossible to convey through their
own native tongue. They entered into the world they were evangelizing,
understood its meaning systems as best they could, and boldly gave
witness to Jesus Christ as the Lord and Redeemer of all people.
Several parts of the "Willowbank Report" on gospel and culture
address this same issue:

God's personal self-disclosure in the Bible was given in terms of
the hearers' own culture. So we have asked ourselves what light it
throws on our task of cross-cultural communication today.
The biblical writers made critical use of whatever cultural material was available to them for the expression of their message. For
example, the Old Testament refers several times to the Babylonian
sea monster named "Leviathan," while the form of God's "cove-
nant" with his people resembles the ancient Hittite Suzerain's
"treaty" with his vassals. The writers also made incidental use of
the conceptual imagery of the "three-tiered" universe, though they
did not thereby affirm a pre-Copernican cosmology. We do something similar when we talk about the sun "rising" and "setting."
Similarly, New Testament language and thought-forms are
steeped in both Jewish and Hellenistic cultures, and Paul seems to
have drawn from the vocabulary of Greek philosophy. But the
process by which the biblical authors borrowed words and images
from their cultural milieu, and used them creatively, was controlled
by the Holy Spirit so that they purged them of false or evil implica-

tions and thus transformed them into vehicles of truth and goodness.

Sensitive cross-cultural witnesses will not arrive at their sphere of service with a pre-packaged gospel. They must have a clear grasp of the "given" truth of the gospel. But they will fail to communicate successfully if they try to impose this on people without reference to their own cultural situation and that of the people to whom they go. It is only by active, loving engagement with the local people, thinking in their thought patterns, understanding their world-view, listening to their questions, and feeling their burdens, that the whole believing community (of which the missionary is a part) will be able to respond to their need. By common prayer, thought and heart-searching, in dependence on the Holy Spirit, expatriate and local believers may learn together how to present Christ and contextualize the gospel with an equal degree of faithfulness and relevance. (Lausanne Committee, 1978b, pp. 7–8, 14)

The particular formulation of the faith of a given time or people never exhausts the total meaning of the gospel (Webber, 1978). But the necessity for formulation in terms of the meaning system of a given people is indisputable. Unless the authentic gospel is given in the language and thought forms of the people being evangelized, true evangelization cannot take place.

WHAT A PEOPLE KNOWS ABOUT THE GOSPEL

Unless we are dealing with a completely unreached people ("a hidden people"), we begin with a situation where people already have some knowledge of Christianity. Even among the "hidden people," there are some who have knowledge or a great deal of understanding about Christianity. This diversity of experience and understanding must also be taken into account when devising strategy.

We know people go through several changes of knowledge and attitude before they are ready to acknowledge Christ as Lord and Savior. The process of internalizing and evaluating the meanings of Christian faith continues even after such an acknowledgment is made. This is not a radically new idea. Sociologists have recognized for many years that individuals and groups move through a process in coming to a decision. Studies on the diffusion of innovation (e.g., new health care ideas, agricultural techniques, or species of plants) also conclude this (Rogers and Shoemaker, 1971; Engel et al., 1973; Janis and Mann, 1977; Toch, 1965).

A number of attempts have been made to develop some kind of coherent model or scale of the way in which people go through the process that leads to a commitment to Christ (Tippett, 1977; Lofland, 1977; C. Kraft, 1979, pp. 328–344). Building on the work of Viggo Søgaard, James Engel, director of the Graduate Program in Communications at Wheaton College Graduate School, has suggested one model which stresses particularly the dimension of information gathering and evaluation (Engel and Norton, 1975; Engel, 1977, 1979; Søgaard, 1975). People come to know only gradually that there is something about which they can make a decision. They then go through a process by which their understanding of that alternative is raised. Eventually they come to a point where they have enough information to decide whether or not they will act on it and make a decision.

We have taken the basic framework of the "Engel Scale" and have modified it to produce our own version of the spiritual decision scale. We have also combined our modified version with Søgaard's idea that at each point of increasing understanding of faith, a people can feel positively or negatively about what they have learned. The resulting scale (Figure 11-1) becomes a powerful way of viewing the process that is happening among a people. In an extensive discussion on the application of this scale, Engel (1979) has focused primarily on the *individual*. We have modified the scale in terms of *groups,* and this is why we have made the final steps, +2 and +3, behaviors of a *community.*

What this scale suggests is the importance of understanding where a people or an individual is located in terms of understanding the Christian faith. Evangelistic activities must be planned in harmony with a people's understanding of the gospel. At one extreme (−7) are those who have no direct knowledge of the gospel. This would include those who are too young to have a cognitive awareness of God's love in Christ. But it would also include those adults who know only what they have discovered through nature, conscience, and the truths in their traditional culture.

Others have a greater awareness of the Christian faith. Some (−6) only have an awareness that there was a person called Christ or that there are people who call themselves Christians. Others have more information: they know some things about Christ and his plan of salvation (−5). But these do not yet comprehend the basic ideas and message of the gospel. It may be obscured by lack of contextualization or identification with foreign elements, or it may be mixed up with incorrect ideas (as is true of Muslim ideas about Christian notions of Christ and

THE PEOPLE PROFILE

DECISION POINT		% 25 50 75	ATTITUDE + 0 −	RATE OF CHANGE
NO AWARENESS	−7			
AWARENESS	−6			
SOME KNOWLEDGE	−5			
KNOWLEDGE	−4			
IMPLICATIONS SEEN	−3			
PERSONAL NEED	−2			
CONFRONTATION	−1			
CONVERSION				
RE-EVALUATION	+1			
INCORPORATION	+2			
PROPAGATION	+3			

Figure 11-1   The People Profile

God). Then there are those (−4) who can state in at least simple terms what the Good News is about.

Up to this point the scale suggests points of understanding that, though not easily measured, can be objectively distinguished. The points that follow are more subjective and also more difficult to measure. Those at −3 have come to understand that the facts of the gospel apply to them, and that if these facts are true, they demand commitment and faith. At −2 the person senses that the gospel is something which he or she needs. There is an awareness that commitment to Christ will bring about a change in a person's life. Such a person or group, having arrived at this point in the process, and provided the basic attitude is positive, is ready to be challenged to become a disciple of Jesus Christ (−1).

At each of these points the basic attitude of the people is crucial. It may be that as a people comes to learn more of the meaning of Christian faith, it will become more negative. Not all who learn what the Kingdom of God is about will welcome its demand for repentance and change. One of the authors was told by a number of missionaries that the Baliem Dani in 1978 were as a whole quite knowledgeable about the gospel and for that very reason rejected it. These powerful leaders said that they knew Jesus was powerful and wonderful, but that they had too much to lose in the old religious-political system which they controlled if they agreed to allow their people to follow Christ. They knew that they would have to give up their involvement with the spirits. They sensed that they would no longer be able to control the people and gain the upper hand politically and economically. Of course, the opposite is equally true. Negative attitudes may be dispelled as people truly come to understand the great gain that is offered in God's gracious gift of life through his Son. Evangelism sometimes entails working on an attitude change rather than introducing new information. The goal is both an understanding of the true meaning of the gospel and a positive response to it.

A positive response to the challenge brings about what the Bible calls conversion or the new birth. The Holy Spirit regenerates those who turn in repentance and faith to embrace Christ as their Lord and Savior. Those who reject this step retain only a "head" knowledge of the gospel. They can recite the fundamentals of what it means to become a Christian, but they do not truly know God.

Following such a decision is the critical period of time when the commitment is reevaluated (+1). There is an inner conversation as well as the outer one when others find out that a person or family has become Christian. Was this a good step? Are we going to continue to affirm faith in Christ and follow him even when it is inconvenient? During this time, one's decision for Christ is either confirmed and strengthened or denied and weakened. Incorporation into a fellowship (+2) refers either to the formal joining of a local congregation or the informal associating with a group of fellow believers. In either case it marks the point at which new Christians are interacting with others who have also decided to become disciples of Christ. Some (+3) have reached the point where they are already engaging in the propagation of the gospel by which they were saved.

ASSUMPTIONS AND ANALYSIS OF THE PEOPLE PROFILE

Having sketched the meaning of the various points along this continuum of relationship to Christ, we will now spell out some of the assumptions which underlie this scale:

1. While the scale gives the impression of being rather monolithic, implying that everyone goes through the same set of steps, this is not a necessarily so. This is a *model*, developed to highlight certain *common* patterns of movement toward decision. It might take one person only twenty minutes to traverse from −6 to +1 while another might take twenty years. People might also skip one of the steps, or some positive attitudes toward Christ might coexist with very little understanding of the fundamentals of the gospel.

2. Although the scale is a linear one, the *process* of a group or person coming to Christ may not be linear at all. It is, however, very difficult to portray a non-linear decision process. This model is thus a compromise. But it suggests at least some of the questions we need to ask about a people and the gospel. How much do they understand the gospel and how do they feel about it? What more do they need to know and experience before they will be ready to be challenged to receive Christ in an intelligent and valid way? We are forced to begin with an understanding of where a people is before we begin dumping our pre-digested theology. We can "fine tune" our presentations of Christ so that a people is given information that harmonizes with what it already knows and needs to know in order to make a decision. In other words, it is a tool of selection, rather than a strict sociological description.

3. The scale suggests that the goal of communicating the gospel is to move people in their decision process toward Christ. In recent history there have been only two "acceptable" ways to measure success in evangelism: (1) the number of "decisions for Christ" (−1 to +1) and (2) the number of church members (+2). But there are two additional ways to view the evangelistic task.

First, the ultimate goal of this scale is to form a group of people who will *propagate* the gospel. The history of missions is filled with examples of efforts to plant a church without considering how that church could become a missionary church. We cannot be content simply with "decisions" which we then cavalierly "turn over to God." Nor can we be content with simple incorporation into a fellowship. We are interested in the *process* of evangelization, not in simply recording decisions for Christ.

Second, we need to give more importance to the so-called "pre-evangelism" events and steps. So much value is placed on decisions and church members that evangelists often neglect other parts of the evangelization process that may be essential in challenging large numbers of people to receive Christ. It also enables us not to have false expectations about methods that do not and really cannot function to produce decisions, even though they help to move people from ignorance to an awareness of the fundamentals of the gospel.

4. While the scale centers on the question of what a people knows and comprehends about the gospel, Engel and others also insist that there are more dimensions which must be understood in order to perceive a group's movement toward Christ (Engel, 1977, p. 31; Fraser, 1979). One must understand how a group *feels* about the subjects that are part of the gospel, what important life-style motivations and needs will affect the way a people hear the gospel, and the style by which the group contemplates and registers decisions regarding a change in religious allegiance. So the scale does not stand alone in charting the spiritual decisions process. It is one tool among several.

When we attempt to apply this scale to ministry contexts, we begin to discover, as has been said, "The cleanness of theory is no match for the mess of reality." It looks more "scientific" than it can ever be. It is very difficult to measure many of the steps, especially −2 and −3. But this should not hide the fact that there are at least five steps that are easily measured (though nothing is measured *easily* in social science!): The two end points (−7, no awareness of Christ, and +3, active propagators) are easy to determine, and also those points in which people say they have made a decision to follow Christ or are participating in a fellowship of Christians. The fifth point that can be reasonably established is whether a person is aware of the Christian faith, even though the degree of awareness may be difficult to decide (whether −6 or −5 or −4).

We can establish at least the broad positions of people within a group. Trying to nail down the specifics may be too much to hope for or even try. The simplest way to apply the scale is to make statements about where people within the group are *generally* located at a given point in time and where they ought to be *generally* located at the end of a given set of evangelism events. We also want to know the rates of change from one point to another. Such information helps us to measure progress, to tailor our communication efforts to the actual understanding level of a people, and to communicate to fellow Christians the reasons behind the particular strategies we have chosen.

Despite all of this, there are some counter-balancing qualifications and questions. First, conversion is in fact a multi-dimensional reality. Many times people come to Christ, not because of what they have come to know and understand about him, but because of a crisis experience. One of the findings of the study of Dr. J. W. Pickett's *Christian Mass Movements in India* (1933) is that the motive for entering Christian faith had nothing to do with the subsequent quality of Christian life. What was crucial was the quality of the teaching and shepherding that took place shortly *after* people made the decision to become Christians. What that study indicates, as well as other studies, is that it is possible for people to *know* or *understand* (in a cognitive sense) very little about the fundamentals of the gospel or about who Jesus is other than that following him is a positive thing. Only *after* becoming a Christian in these cases does one understand the fundamentals of the gospel and its personal implications. Those who entered the Church for mundane reasons or little understanding became strong Christians only if they were well discipled after commitment. An unpublished study of conversion and spiritual growth in Brazil conducted by MARC in 1970 also stresses the importance of discipleship *after* the decision (+1).

In many contexts, for example in areas where there is an animistically-based Islam, people come to Christ out of a crisis experience during which they have discovered the power of Christ. The "knowledge" they have is experience-based and oriented to the solution of rather self-interested, mundane problems. The entry point which brings them to faith is an experience of divine healing or something that is viewed as a miracle: the casting out of a demon, an unusual answer to prayer, and so forth. In Egypt for a period of time, the combined divine healing and vivid preaching ministry of a Coptic priest was bringing many Muslims to faith. The same may be said of many converts of the Pentecostal movement in Latin America. It is the *demonstration* of power in the name of Christ that impresses people in need, not just a statement about Christ's power by an evangelist.

If in fact we discover that people are going through a different process than that modeled by this scale, *we need to change our scale and develop one that will help us conceptualize the actual process.* Only as our evangelism is in harmony with the way God is at work moving people toward Christ, can we give it its most effective shape. The scale which we have used is *Western* in its origin. But even in the West we can discover significant groups of people who come into faith through a more experience-centered process than is portrayed by the scale. As stated before, this is only a model and a tool. It must be modified and reformulated to fit the people we are trying to understand. They will go through a process as they come to faith, and our understanding of that process will contribute substantially to our ability to design approaches to foster evangelization. We are dealing with people who have an inherent drive for meaning, an inner urging that finds expression in language, hermeneutics, and world view. As we attempt to project the message of the Good News into their context, we need to be sure that we take into account what they already know and what they need to know to understand the Kingdom of God.

This scale will be used in a number of places throughout the balance of this book. It will be used to help us understand the selection of people and means and methods. Most importantly it will be seen as an effective planning tool in designing strategies for reaching an unreached people.

CHAPTER 12

Understanding the Needs of a People

E vangelization always takes place in the context of need. When we study the ministry of Christ, we are impressed at the way in which he always responded to the needs of people: he healed the blind, the lame, and the lepers, blessed the children, fed the hungry, instructed those who sought truth, forgave the guilty, accepted the outcasts, and reassured the fearful. He was sensitive to the deep needs of people and broke the social taboos and conventions of his day if they prevented him from helping those in need.

The words that Christ shared about the Kingdom of God were not only masterful expressions within the meaning system of the Jewish world of his day but they also addressed the needs of people. He did not give the same message to everyone who sought him out. He spoke of living water to the Samaritan woman at the well, he told Nicodemus that he must be born again, he urged the rich young man to sell all he had and give it to the poor. To each he particularized the meaning of the Kingdom according to his or her needs.

NEEDS ARE DEFINED BY A PEOPLE

Needs are never encountered in an abstract or disembodied fashion. Needs are defined in particular ways by the meaning system and culture of a people. What the affluent American sees as an absolute necessity for daily living is an unimaginable luxury for the poor in other countries. Need is thus relative to the people, their definitions of the world, their expectations, and their past experiences. The meaning system of a people thus not only shapes the way they perceive (and do not perceive) the world but also shapes their needs.

Just as the gospel needs to be contexualized within the meaning system of a people, so *it also needs to be contextualized within the needs of a people as they define them.* It is the height of foolishness to try to get a people to change their language so we can tell them the Good News in our own language. It is equally wrong to force them to redefine their needs so we can use our own experience of the way the gospel has met our needs to show how it can meet theirs. We need to accept a people's language as a given. We need to learn its vocabulary, grammar, meanings, and styles in order to translate and inculturate the message of the gospel in the most adequate way. We need to "particularize" the Good News in the meaning system of a people (Hesselgrave, 1978c, pp. 135–141). We must labor to learn the aspirations, needs, drives, motivations, and fears of a people in order to translate the meanings of the Kingdom so they address the needs of a people.

We heartily affirm the spirit of the following statement from the Willowbank Report:

> There is the humility to begin our communication where people actually are and not where we would like them to be. This is what we see Jesus doing, and we desire to follow his example. Too often we have ignored people's fears and frustrations, their pains and preoccupations, and their hunger, poverty, deprivation or oppression, in fact their 'felt needs,' and have been too slow to rejoice or to weep with them. We acknowledge that these 'felt needs' may sometimes be symptoms of deeper needs which are not immediately felt or recognized by the people. A doctor does not necessarily accept a patient's self-diagnosis. Nevertheless, we see the need to begin where people are, but not to stop there. We accept our responsibility gently and patiently to lead them on to see themselves, as we see ourselves, as rebels to whom the gospel directly speaks with a message of pardon and hope. To begin where people are not is to share an irrelevant message; to stay where people are and never lead them on to the fulness of God's good news, is to share a truncated gospel. The humble sensitivity of love will avoid both errors. (Lausanne Committee, 1978b, p. 16)

The felt needs of a people are not irrelevant or unrelated to the fundamental spiritual dimensions of the Kingdom of God. We believe that Jesus Christ is Lord of all. This means his activity encompasses all that is human. The hunger of the body as well as the hunger of the soul is deeply impressed upon the love of God. Clothing, housing, and health are all part of the concern of the Church—"What God the Father considers to be pure and genuine religion is this: to take care of orphans and widows in their suffering and to keep oneself from being corrupted by the world" (Jas. 1:27). Jesus began his ministry in Galilee by characterizing his ministry with the words of Isaiah: ". . . to bring good news to the poor . . . to proclaim liberty to the captives and recovery of sight to the blind, to set free the oppressed and announce that the time has come when the Lord will save his people" (Lk. 4:18, 19). Jesus touched all of these needs as he went about Palestine proclaiming the Kingdom of God.

Jesus did not deal only with subjectively felt needs. His own commitment to the Kingdom of God made him constantly aware of the objective discrepancy between what the world is and what his Father's Kingdom is. Until Christ reigns in every heart, and the peace and love of his Kingdom rules all human existence, there will be a need to proclaim and live out the Good News of his Kingdom. Jesus always began with felt need and used it to demonstrate the power and relevance of the Kingdom.

NEEDS ARE SHAPED BY CULTURE

Anthropologists look upon culture in part as an adaptive mechanism. Culture provides a people with the ideas and tools they need to meet their physical, psychological, social, and spiritual needs. But no culture is completely successful in meeting all the needs of its people. One of the results of sin is that culture has demonic as well as admirable qualities. Every society has unresolved tensions which are frustrated by other aspects of the world and culture. There is also what Kant called the "social unsociability" of people. People are drawn together in friendship and cooperation by irresistible needs and culture patterns. Yet at the same time they find this intimacy to be the occasion for conflict and tension. Humans are sociable and antagonistic at the same time.

Communal life is also to some extent a competitive struggle in which some people are more disadvantaged than others in their people group. The various valued aspects of personality, physique, intelligence, wealth, and so forth, are unevenly distributed, and people have different levels of satisfaction about their lot in life. Resentments, tensions, anxiety, fears, and drives are some of the subjective needs of a people group. These needs, which motivate life and give it its emotional texture, are the "daily bread," the everyday humdrum existence of a people group.

Knowledge of these needs is crucial to evangelism for several reasons. Studies of religious groups and other societies indicate that people are reluctant to make new religious commitments. For the most part they prefer to keep the traditions (with small modifications) which they inherited from their parents. They are wary of religious claims that come from groups outside their own tradition. Oftentimes this is coupled with a tendency to punish or reject those who embrace a new religious faith. Unless there are strong feelings of dissatisfaction with the current tradition, people are very unlikely to give attention or serious consideration to Christian faith as an alternative to what they already experience.

For conversions to take place on a significant scale, there normally have to be certain tensions and problems that push people and groups out of their normal equilibrium. These might be such adverse physical conditions as famine or poverty, disease, natural disaster, or war. Or they might be less objective disturbances such as racism, oppression, migration, social discrimination, and ridicule (such as the ridicule experienced by the lower castes in India who now make up 95 percent of the Church in South India). In the midst of these tensions, people often become more open to new ways. *Change is only possible where there is discontent with the way things are.*

People must feel that these situations are disruptive before they can be open to the gospel. Often this is described as "responsiveness." This means that there are people groups and individuals (such as Cornelius, Acts 10–11) who already consider the Christian faith to be an answer. After a suitable evangelistic appeal, they are ready to believe. It is no accident that large movements into the Church have occurred under situations of significant socio-cultural change and largely from among parts of the population who have felt disadvantaged.

Sometimes needs are not very conscious. In fact, there is often an interactive effect between the agent who brings a new way of life and the needs to which the agent appeals. The individual or group may be only dimly aware of how strong it feels about some situation or need until it is focused and brought to its awareness. Normally, appeals do not create the need into which the offered solution fits, but rather bring the need into sharper focus. Because of this, it is at times difficult to label a people as "responsive" or "resistant" to the gospel. It may be that they are resistant to the evangelizing efforts of one agency because of the way it phrases the gospel or applies it to the needs of the people. The agents themselves may not be attractive to the people. Another agency with a different approach that is tied into the deeply felt needs of the people may initiate a movement toward Christ. Were the people resistant or responsive?

DISCOVERING FELT NEEDS

How can we uncover the needs of a people? It may seem simple-minded, but often the best way is to ask them! But one must be sure to ask many people, not just two or three. One can ask later respondents to react to what earlier respondents said. Part of the sensitivity of being God's servant is demonstrated in truly listening to people's needs. There is no substitute for a fundamental empathy and rapport that opens life to life and reveals basic human issues in a social grouping.

Of course there is also no substitute for other kinds of objective data which help us to discover felt needs:

1. Rituals and/or magic often indicate heavy emotional involvement on the part of the actors. Anthropologists tell us that one of the major functions of religion is to relieve anxiety (Malinowski, 1954; Howells, 1948). Religious and magical rituals serve to still a person's anxieties and fears, to maximize a person's confidence that the unseen world is working in his or her favor, and to provide the guarantee of success that technology and current knowledge cannot. Ritual indicates that the culture's technology and means cannot secure an important end for the individuals.

When one thus observes a great deal of ritual in healing, one can conclude that there is an important felt need for good health in the face of a number of illnesses. The network of "superstitions" is a cultural map to additional felt needs. The use of astrological charts, charms, or divination are all indications of some felt need that cannot currently be met by the culture. This is true primarily of ritual that is not part of a calendrical cycle, such as Christmas or Easter (which often tend to be routinized and related not to some anxiety but to basic cultural ideals).

2. A second place to look for indications of need are in the ideals of a culture. Every people has some ideas about what an ideal adult is like, both in the personality or characteristics of the individual and in his or her career goals. One can ask people about these ideals and can also observe the characteristics of the people who have attained the highest respect within the society. Being aware of the things that hinder a

person from attaining the ideal provides clues again to the felt needs of a people. What things in the environment, in the competition with other peoples in the region, or in the social customs hinder a person from becoming all he or she would like to be? How can that discontent be connected with Christ's power to set free and fulfill?

3. Another indication of felt needs in a culture is legal disputes. Conflicts, disputes, and disagreements arise in every human society. What are they about? How frequent are they? How many people get involved in them? How difficult are they to settle? Answering these questions will inevitably lead to a description of some of the areas of need which are causing people to clash as they try to meet their needs.

4. Another approach to felt needs is to observe the behavior and attitudes of Christians in the local church. What are the common "temptations" of the young Christian? Of the older Christian? Where the body of Christ is adequately meeting the needs of a people, temptation will diminish significantly. Where there are unmet needs, or a form of Christian faith that is not dynamically incarnated into a people's way of life, the people will find alternative solutions to their problems. An example of this might be the widespread use of healers and diviners, even by Christians, in Bantu Africa. The Western Church has brought physical healing which relates very well to the material and physical causes of illness, yet the Church has not answered the question as to why one person is sick and not another, or why one experiences misfortune and another good luck. The witchcraft in Africa has helped to explain this natural evil, but the Church has done little to provide a substitute to replace this witchcraft. The underlying need that leads to the temptation to resort to witchcraft thus remains unmet and many Africans continue to meet the need in a traditional manner.

The sum of all these approaches is to describe the context of a people's subjective need. A Christianity that does not have direct relevance to the life struggles and anxieties of a people is seen as alien, foreign, and odd (Loewen, 1975, pp. 3–26).

GUILT AND THE GOSPEL

Every society has some standards of right and wrong. They are found in the ideals as well as the behavior of a people. They are often very similar to the moral law of God (Lewis, 1947). Their application or importance, however, may be radically different from our own ethical ideals.

The guilt people feel will most frequently be related to their ideals and standards for right and wrong. The gospel must be directed to pre-existing guilt. T. Wayne Dye has given a detailed example of how this worked among a people of New Guinea:

> Back before [the Bahinemo] had had Christian teaching, I tried to translate Jesus' list of sins in Mark 7. As each sin was described, they gave me the local term for it. They named other sins in their culture.
>
> "What did your ancestors tell you about these things?" I asked them.
>
> "Oh, they told us we shouldn't do any of those things."
>
> "Do you think these were good standards that your ancestors gave you?" They agreed unanimously that they were.
>
> "Well, do you keep all these rules?"
>
> "No," they responded sheepishly.
>
> One leader said, "Definitely not. Who could ever keep them all? We're people of the ground."
>
> I took this opportunity to explain that God expected them to keep their own standards for what is right, that He was angry because they hadn't. Then I pointed out that it was because they fell short of their own standards that God sent His Son to bear their punishment so they could be reunited with Him.
>
> This was a crucial step toward their conversion. For the first time the Scriptures were linked to what God was telling them through their consciences. Within a year most of the people in that village had committed themselves to Christ.
>
> Since that day in 1967, they have never lost the awareness that in the Bible God is concerned about their daily behavior and not just talking about strange taboos. Since then, they have changed their source of authority from inherited tradition to the Scriptures, and they have been learning how Christ through His Spirit can come inside them and give them power to attain the standards they could not keep before. (1976, pp. 39–40)

The need for forgiveness is an objective one. We all stand before a holy God as guilty rebels who have sinned against his glory. No one is righteous in the presence of God. How God reveals our separation from him varies greatly. It is at the point of felt guilt that the gospel must offer repentance and comforting words of forgiveness.

People who are without Christ are lost. They have wandered away from God and are separated from him. Like the lost sheep, the lost coin, and the lost son of Luke 15, they need to be found. As ambassadors of Christ and heralds of the King, it is our task to share the Good News and give people the opportunity to respond and be found. It was this that motivated Jesus to spend time with the despised sinners of his day—he was finding those who were lost and reuniting them to their Creator and Redeemer.

But lostness is expressed in a variety of ways. Just as there are skid row bums and poverty crime, so there are country club bums and white collar crime. Alcoholics, workaholics, respectable lawyers, and tyrants are all lost and need to be found. They experience their alienation from God, other people, and themselves in a variety of ways. One person may be carrying a burden of guilt because of something in the past. Another may have only a general sense of malaise and boredom with life. Whatever the reason for alienation, they all need the same Savior. They all need to become part of the same Kingdom. They all need the same Spirit alive in their hearts. But the drug addict will need an awareness of God's power for his or her own particular lostness just as the successful, ulcer-afflicted, top executive will need to see God's love and forgiveness in quite a different way. Again, the gospel must "scratch" where it "itches."

Another example of this can be seen among the BaHima of Uganda:

> It is a truism of the revival movement that the material of confession varies according to the social milieu. Those of the pagan BaHima pastoralists are mainly to do with infringements of tribal prohibitions—drunkenness leading to wife-beating; various dietary infringements; quarrelling at watering places; desertion of one's family; adultery as tribally defined—but also with breaking the Protectorate or codified Native Law—perjury in court, visiting diviners, hut-burning, and the like. (Stenning, 1964, pp. 271–272)

Such examples could be multiplied (Hile, 1977; C. Kraft, 1976; Loewen, 1976). If we consider our own pilgrimage with the Lord, we see that he is always meeting us as and where we are. It is wrong to assume that God will encounter a people with different experiences and culture in the same way he has encountered us or even the peoples of the New Testament.

CHAPTER 13

Understanding the Behavior of a People

*W*hen we evangelize other people who are part of our own society, we often do not think deeply about how they think, or what they need, or the way in which they live. We know intuitively what they are like because we are one of them. We feel that there is little need for serious training in how to relate to world views that differ radically from our own traditional Western philosophical and scientific world view within which most of Christian theology has been expressed.

However, when we have to deal with peoples whose experience, socialization, and language are dramatically different from our own, we begin to realize how much we take for granted in evangelism. We realize that we need to learn a great deal before we can begin to transculturate the meanings of the Kingdom. We discover that we do not simply need more education, but a complete reeducation (Hesselgrave, 1978c, p. 71). We must learn about a new meaning system, a new way of looking at need, and a new way of acting and interacting. We need to see the gospel in a new light, to discover what it means apart from our own culture.

CULTURE AND CHRISTIANITY

The meaning system and needs of a people are two central aspects of the culture of a people. We must understand them if we are to com-

171

municate and relate the gospel in a meaningful way. But there are other facets of culture which have a particularly important bearing on the communication of the gospel and the establishment of an indigenous fellowship of Christians. This chapter deals with behavior patterns. *Behavior patterns are the organized modes by which a people goes about meeting its needs in institutions, roles, social structures, and customs.* Various customs and ways of organizing people can act as either bridges into the Kingdom or walls that keep people out of the Kingdom. Once a church is established, it has to discover many of its patterns for everyday living, worship, and service in the common patterns already available in the cultural heritage of its people.

Culture is a mixture of both good and bad elements. From a theological viewpoint, we have to affirm the dignity and value of culture (Lausanne Committee, 1978b, p. 6; C. Kraft, 1979). Humanity is a creation of God. The commands given to our ancestors included the cultural activities of controlling nature, existing in families, and reproducing. Even in a fallen world, much of culture functions to hinder the self-centeredness of humans, and to bring people together in small groups where love can grow and life can find meaning. Culture provides the means for achieving the good ends decreed by the Creator for his creation. Art, social organization, technology, agriculture, and science are all reflections of the Creator.

But culture can also be evil. Selfishness exists in many social structures and customs. Warfare, pride, disputes, oppression of the weak and defenseless are all found in cultures and social structures. No culture is perfect.

Even the truth of God is exchanged for a lie in various religious systems. Humans have repeatedly chosen to find their own righteousness instead of that offered by God. Because culture is a part of the fallenness of humanity, it will change significantly as it is impregnated with the gospel. Just as the inner person is changed by the Spirit of God at conversion, so the culture is affected by Christians as they live out the new dynamic of their life in Christ. As the whole lump of dough is gradually leavened, so the Kingdom of God, which is present in the church, will gradually affect every part of a culture (without creating a new so-called "Christian culture").

The gospel not only utilizes culture in communicating the meanings of the Kingdom, but also stands in judgment over human cultural adaptations. It thus exists in dialectical tension with culture, incarnate in it yet continually breaking out of it to find new wineskins for its fresh, new dynamic. Consequently, there is always an ambivalent, ambiguous relationship between Christianity and every human culture. It has the potential for great good, or for a confusion that unnecessarily undermines the achievement of evangelistic goals.

Sometimes people resist the gospel not because they think it false but because they perceive it as a threat to their culture, especially the fabric of their society, and their national or tribal solidarity. To some extent this cannot be avoided. Jesus Christ is a disturber as well as a peacemaker. He is Lord, and demands our total allegiance. Thus, some first-century Jews saw the gospel as undermining Judaism and accused Paul of "teaching men everywhere against the people, the law, and this place," i.e. the temple (Acts 21:28). Similarly, some first-century Romans feared for the stability of the state, since in their view the Christian missionaries, by saying that "there is another King, Jesus," were being disloyal to Caesar and advocating customs which it was not lawful for Romans to practise (Acts 16:21; 17:7). Still today Jesus challenges many of the cherished beliefs and customs of every culture and society.

At the same time, there are features of every culture which are not incompatible with the lordship of Christ, and which therefore need not be threatened or discarded, but rather preserved and transformed. Messengers of the gospel need to develop a deep understanding of the local culture, and a genuine appreciation of it. Only then will they be able to perceive whether the resistance is to some unavoidable challenge of Jesus Christ or to some threat to the culture, which whether imaginary or real, is not necessary. (Lausanne Committee, 1978b, p. 13)

THE "FIT" BETWEEN THE GOSPEL AND CULTURE

We assume that the gospel is a message for all peoples, that the Lordship of Christ can become a dynamic reality within every culture on earth. Conflict between the gospel and culture cannot always be predicted once we have divorced culture from the particular expression it might have in the culture of the evangelist. We view the practices of infanticide, suttee, foot-binding, human sacrifice, slavery, and head-hunting with a bit of historical distance. We view the issues of polygamy, caste, international economic systems, and totalitarianism in politics with a bit more interest since they are matters being debated and struggled with at the present time. We can see the depth of the issues and do not yet see the outcome.

Every culture has institutions and social structures which appear on the surface to be incompatible with the gospel. The Church eventually will have to address these matters, but at the starting point it is usually futile to get a people to express repentance for matters about which God is not yet speaking to them. Yet eventually they will have to consider the validity of key elements of their behavior and cultural patterns in the light of God's revelation. When should these issues be raised and how should they be addressed? What behaviors and institutions must be challenged from the very beginning as part of the call to repentance and the Kingdom of God?

On the one hand, there must be the realization that a change of allegiance to Jesus Christ is a radical and deeply significant event. Jesus is a challenge to the very center of a people's world view and religion. As Lord, he allows no rival. There is thus a necessary confrontation at the point of conversion. Yet there is another side. Conversion should not "de-culturize" a person, removing him or her from tribe and family, and forcing the adoption of the evangelist's culture as a part of the process of conversion. While every aspect of the cultural past comes under the scrutiny of Christ's Lordship, this does not necessarily mean that the past will be rejected.

We must always remember dialectical relationships when we assess the potential "fit" between the gospel and culture. We always live in tension: We are a part of the world, yet we are not partakers of its spirit or ruling powers (Jn. 17:14, 15). We must ask two questions: First, what social structures should we utilize to proclaim the love of God? How do we incarnate the acts of service and love within a culture's behavioral patterns? In what ways is the culture of the people closer to the biblical norms of love and caring than our native culture? We must face the very real and significant fact that the gospel will be incarnated in the cultural patterns of this people and some of those patterns will be more suited to such an expression than our "Christian" cultural patterns.

The second question is a difficult one: Are there some common cultural practices that are clearly prohibited *by the Scriptures* (not simply our Westernized interpretation of them)? What are they? How important are those practices in the life-style of the people? How deeply rooted are those customs in the needs and meaning system of the people? How difficult will it be to change those practices? Are these matters that ought to be raised during an initial encounter with the gospel or are they matters that ought to be left to the gradual process of evangelization?

Neither question is easy to answer. As stated previously, customs are ambiguous mixtures of good and evil. Customs are also dynamically interrelated with many other customs and institutions so that the effect on the others of changing one cannot be predicted. Often it takes years to sort out the ambiguous elements of culture. One needs only to be reminded of the new attitude toward polygamy, which was once, for the most part, a universally proscribed behavior (Hillman, 1975). Once the Church believes that a certain custom is wrong, or that Christians ought not to participate in a certain institution (such as the early Church's ban on the gladiatorial games, reluctance to participate in the trade guilds where sacrifices were made to patron goddesses and gods, and stand against Christians acting as soldiers in the army), there will be opposition from within the people group. Those whose interests are threatened (as was the case with the silversmiths, led by Demetrius of Ephesus, whose trade in images of Diana was threatened by so many becoming Christian) will rise up to oppose and subvert the gospel. But the gospel must and will take a stand on many issues around the world. What effect that stand will have upon the progress of the gospel in a people needs to be assessed if we are to have adequate plans for the mission of evangelization.

MANY FORMS OF CHRISTIANITY

As each new culture comes to know Christ, it learns to express the gospel in its own unique way. This diversity of Christian expression among communities can be used as a tool for evangelization: one community might be loud and emotional, another quiet and contemplative; one liturgical, another unornate; one emphasizing the gifts of the Spirit, another cultivating the inner fruits of the Spirit. In assessing the "fit" between gospel and culture, one must take into account particular biases and traditions of a particular people. Perhaps a people would relate best to a charismatic, teetotaling, anti-polygamist, separatistic form of Christian faith. Or perhaps a liturgical, drinking, polygamy-tolerating, ecumenical, non-charismatic Christian faith would do much better.

What we are saying is that there is a legitimate diversity of commitment and life-style within true Christian groups. Pentecostals, Presbyterians, Lutherans, Baptists, and Episcopalians are all part of the Church universal. The potential fit between a culture and these various traditions is not the same. We ought to look for a maximal fit—that point at which the message of the gospel is the clearest, and unclouded by the unnecessary cultural baggage of the evangelist or his or her agency. The diversity of experience and conviction within the universal Church ought to used when seeking to evangelize the enormous diversity of unreached peoples.

UNDERSTANDING THREE FACETS OF BEHAVIOR

Since a great deal has been written on understanding the social structures, institutions, and roles of other cultures, we will mention only three areas which need emphasis.

1. "The silent language"

A basic part of human behavior is "nonverbal" communication.[1] This kind of communication includes the physical characteristics of people, body language (messages sent by gestures and motions of the body), spatial relationships, temporal relationships (such as punctuality, length of various events, seasons), paralanguage, body contact, and aesthetics (Hesselgrave, 1978c, chapter 31 explores these areas in detail). The potential for miscommunication between people who have learned different systems of nonverbal communication is too well known to those who have crossed cultural boundaries. Apart from the reinforcement of the verbal message by the nonverbal, one is quickly (and justifiably) seen and understood as hypocritical, cold, uncaring, and strange. It is in this area that much of the reeducation needed for the cross-cultural worker must take place (Nida, 1979b).

2. Social structure

The Church Growth movement has repeatedly called attention to this aspect of human behavior. People are ordered into various groups: kinship, tribal, communal, and organizational. There is a vast mosaic of social classes, castes, ethnic units, occupational groups—all with various degrees of status and respect, privilege and prejudice, life-style and opportunity. People relate to one another on the basis of their position in the social structure and both admit or deny various degrees of intimacy because of who they are.

1. Edward T. Hall's books have been particularly influential in this area.

The church almost invariably grows in relationship to the known characteristics of the social structure of the people being evangelized. An understanding of the structure not only suggests reasons why some people seem responsive and others resistant to the gospel, but also suggests some of the key people to approach if the gospel is to be given a respectful hearing by the people. Leaders who sponsor the preaching of the gospel can greatly facilitate the *hearing* of the gospel. Yet they can also effectively squelch the hearing of the gospel, for if they turn away from the gospel, a large part of their followers will also turn away.

The social structure is also important for understanding what kind of role the outsider is to play (see chapter 29). How the missionary fits into the culture and what he or she can do, has a great deal to do with the social structure and the position which the people have assigned to the missionary (Loewen, 1975; Cohen, 1963).

Many of the debates about ethics and questions of mission strategy focus on the nature of social structures such as family (polygamy vs. monogamy, male dominant vs. egalitarian, nuclear vs. extended), caste (should we allow single caste or multi-caste churches?), class (all the institutions from educational to occupational that classify people), political organization (multi-partied democracy vs. single party totalitarian states), economic organization (capitalist vs. socialist), and so on. Because social structures influence human behavior, they must be considered when deciding what implications the gospel will have in a particular social context. Christians have very strong feelings about social structures, and so do the people who are being offered the gospel. If we do not understand the how and why of a people's social structure, we could very easily mix up our own evaluations with the message of the gospel and inadvertently restructure the society.

For further reading, we suggest books by Donald McGavran (1979), William Smalley (1979), Al Krass (1974), Eugene Nida (1960, chapter 5), David Hesselgrave (1978c, Part VII), Marvin Mayers (1974, pp. 81–191), Paul Hiebert (1976, chapters 7–17), and Alan Tippett (1971).

3. Institutions

Every society organizes in order to solve its common problems. Over time it develops formal and standarized patterns for handling various affairs of life. An institution is an organized way of doing something that is customary among a people. Institutions include such things as marriages, funerals, festivals, laws, worship, and so on. Institutions provide the pattern for much of public behavior. The individual does not have to dream up a pattern for each occasion but must rather learn the one that is available and act it out in the appropriate setting.

A major part of understanding a people involves understanding its institutions. Knowing the expectations that go with being a host or a guest, a patron or a friend, a stranger or a mediator can open or close the relationship which one might wish to form with others in the culture. The books which we referred to under social structure also contain many examples of the importance of this aspect of human behavior, and we refer our readers to this literature for more detailed treatment.

If we want to incarnate Christianity within a people, we must understand their meaning system (language, hermeneutics, world view), their needs and aspirations, their social structure and institutions, and their "silent language." Together these form a whole which gives a people a distinctive group identity. Through their culture and practices, we will have to transculturate the meanings of the Kingdom of God. There is little that is more challenging or rewarding than to plant the seed that gradually grows into the body of Christ. The Holy Spirit in conjunction with Christian leaders who rise up in response to the gospel will carry each church through the process of growing in grace and truth as it faces the variety of decisions of how to show the love of God in this particular, unique situation.

RECEPTIVITY AND RESISTANCE

As evangelists, we all wish we knew the degree to which a people will be responsive to the gospel message. If we could predict the behavior of acceptance of a particular people, it would be much easier to engage in the sometimes arduous and lengthy task of learning another culture.

Figure 13-1 is a scale to help our understanding where a people is in their readiness to respond to the gospel:

This tool, of course, asks only for an overall estimate, an average for

What is your estimation of their attitude toward the gospel?

−5 −4	−3 −2	−1 0 +1	+2 +3	+4 +5
Strongly Opposed	Somewhat Opposed	Indifferent	Somewhat Favorable	Strongly Favorable

Figure 13-1   The Resistance/Receptivity Scale

a particular people group. There may be individuals or sub-groups within the people who differ substantially from the mean of the group. This is characteristic of any group—there are often some individuals who know a tremendous amount about Christian faith living among people who on the average only have a dim awareness of Christianity. But it is still helpful to try to characterize the group as a whole. We need to be both careful and realistic in making such an estimate. This is demonstrated by studies that show the self-fulfilling nature of labeling a people's potential attitude toward the gospel as resistant (David Liao, 1972, offers a case in point). Some have even argued that we discard the category of "resistant" since every people will resist evangelization if it is culturally insensitive.

The receptivity or resistance to Christian faith in any given instance is due to a number of variables:

1. *The degree to which a people is satisfied with its present fate in life.* If their own religion and magic give satisfactory answers to their questions, they will not give much hearing or consideration to any alternative religion.

2. *The degree to which the rest of their life is changing.* New immigrants or people who have recently moved from their traditional habitation are more open to new ways and ideas. So are minorities who are away from their normal communities and are no longer surrounded by friends who support their old religious identity.

3. *The cultural sensitivity of the gospel presentation.* A great deal of the resistance among many peoples around the world is due to the cultural insensitivity of evangelists. Many times, people are asked to give up parts of their identity in order to become Christians; for example, many traditional Western Christians are opposed to polygamy, and insist that the practice be discontinued (even though David was a polygamist *and* a friend of God, as well as numerous other Old Testament figures).

4. *The agent of the Good News.* Because of their ethnic and political origins, some people will be given a more respectful hearing than other agents of evangelization. The young, Western-educated person is not always the best evangelist!

5. *The relative fit between the gospel and the cultural patterns that are presently dominant in a social group.* There are some customs which the gospel does not condone. The Thessalonians had to turn away from idols to serve the true God. A deeply rooted religious system that stands

in opposition to Christ will resist the gospel. This is also true of a people that profits greatly from crime. This is not to say that drug traffickers, prostitutes, thugs cannot be won to the gospel. It is only to recognize that the very system of which they are a part stands against the demands of discipleship, and this creates a natural resistance to the gospel.

Assessing receptivity or resistance to the gospel is basic within a strategy for evangelization. If a people is extremely receptive—like Cornelius, they are ready to believe and only await the words of life— then almost any method or strategy will reap a great harvest. Mistakes will be easily rectified and forgotten. If, on the other hand, a people is strongly resistant to Christian commitment (even assuming a culturally sensitive approach in evangelism), then, in most cases, even the best of strategies will fail.

It is in the middle range that strategy differences can make substantial differences in the results. With good strategy, a large hearing for the gospel is possible whereas a poor or weak strategy simply will not break through the indifference or neutrality to stir up the desire for a better way of life. A difference in approach, or in the agent who attempts evangelization, or in the tradition of Christian piety, can produce either a large, virile Church or a small, struggling body.

THE ROLE OF RESEARCH

The evangelist must know not only the gospel but also the people to whom he or she is communicating. This is not easy. It takes careful and serious work in libraries, in the field talking with anthropologists and missionaries, and preeminently in personal contact with the people themselves. Unlike the farmer who can "scientifically" and objectively examine soil conditions and qualities without influencing the results, we are not able to stand outside the system we are attempting to understand. The very process of trying to discover various facets about the culture, attitudes, understandings, and needs of a people change us as well as the people we are trying to understand. Furthermore we understand the people from a particular vantage-point. We come with our own cultural background, meaning system, and needs. All three of these influence the questions we ask and the answers we perceive. We need to understand our own culture as a basis for understanding another (Stewart, 1971).

We often do not do serious research on our own type of people when we plan evangelism for them because we are one of them. We have experienced the needs, attitudes, customs, and meaning systems which are part and parcel of our way of life. But we need to do a great deal of careful and sensitive research in order to understand a group about which we know nothing. Of course there are limits. We cannot forget our ultimate goal, which is to evangelize a particular people to the glory of God. We can spend a lifetime doing research and never get around to doing the thing that originally motivated the research. It is research for evangelism, not for its own sake. On the whole, however, there is far too little understanding of a people before evangelism is attempted, and research should continue even during the process of evangelization.

What we have suggested in this section is only a beginning.[2] There are many other important things that need to be known and appreciated about a people.

2. Research in missions is not a recent invention as indicated by the extensive studies conducted between 1900 and 1925.

CHAPTER 14

The Larger Context

INTRODUCTION

*P*revious chapters in this section have focused on the particular people we are attempting to reach. By definition our people group is almost always smaller than the national boundaries which encompass it. (We realize, of course, that at times the people group will reach across the national boundary.) How ideal it would be if every people existed on an island! But people almost always exist within a larger context, and we have to understand this larger context if we are to understand the people. Just as we have to understand the individual within the context of his or her family, and the family within the context of the clan, and the clan (or its equivalent) in the context of the larger group, so we must understand a people in the context of the peoples that surround them.

The areas in this chapter could easily encompass a book. But since it is not our intent to deal extensively with an entire country, but only to sensitize the cross-cultural missionary to the need for understanding, we will limit ourselves to a brief sketch. We will deal with the political, economic, social, religious, and the Christian church aspects of the larger context to see how they might combine to permeate the very essence of a people. Finally, we will consider a larger spiritual context which we will call "the powers of the air."

THE POLITICAL CONTEXT

Since every people exists within a national boundary, the immediate question for any cross-cultural missionary attempting to reach a people from the outside is the question of freedom to enter the country and the freedom to proclaim the gospel. There are obviously many countries that do not permit the entry of foreigners, let alone the entry of foreigners for the purpose of proclaiming another religion. In other countries, the political system is closely related to the religious system. This is particularly true of Islamic states. These governments also prohibit the entry of foreigners who wish to proclaim another religion.

The next question would be the degree of religious freedom allowed in the country. In some countries, it is a civil offense to change one's religion without a great deal of legal process. Other countries greatly restrict the growth of some religions by forbidding large meetings or the building of meeting places. We need to ask about the freedom to move about within a country. Some governments also greatly restrict the internal movement of their citizens.

Popular terminology divides the world into the First World, the Second World, and the Third World. The First World is the world of the West, the Second World is the world of Communist/Marxist domination, and the Third World is the so-called "developing" countries. Such terminology self-righteously assumes that the First and Second Worlds are already "developed." (We find this categorization distasteful, both to ourselves and to those who live within the so-called Third World.) Over half of the world's population and a majority of unreached peoples live within these developing countries. What do we mean by developing or development? In a larger sense, the term refers to the attempt to provide the Third World with the same type of technological amenities that are available in the Western world. There is a tacit assumption that life is better in the "developed" world and that their forms of society are to be emulated. Many governments are seeking to carry out development or modernization within a political system modeled after the First or Second World. This kind of modernization will have tremendous impact upon all of the peoples of the country. In some countries the government, in what it believes to be the best interest of the total nation, is carrying on a program that totally neglects the peoples who may be geographically or socially isolated from the mainstream of the population. In the rush toward modernization in other countries, roads and new industries are shattering traditional cultural ties. We need to familiarize ourselves with the impact of modernization on a people. What has been the experience of other people groups within the country? Will ethnic or tribal groups be allowed to maintain their ethnicity and their tribal ties? What are the government's future plans for urban groups, for example, those living in high-rise dwellings? What are the government's plans for transportation systems, especially roads? The construction of a new road that will connect a previously inaccessible group with a center of modernization will have great social impact.

One of the most difficult problems for the cross-cultural missionary is his or her view of the political system within a foreign country. We live in a day in which the West has made a great deal of "human rights." Since most Western missionaries come from countries that have some form of democratic process in which the people have a choice in deciding upon their leadership, it is very difficult for them to recognize the appropriateness of a one-party system of government. A totalitarian government is even more difficult to recognize. Are you and/or your agency ready to operate within the political environment? Will you be able to limit yourself to announcing the coming of the King and his Kingdom, or will the demands of that Kingdom force you to take some form of action that will antagonize the foreign government?

In addition, most Westerners live in countries in which there is little overt "bribery." (We put the word "bribery" in quotes because there is often a very fine line between a "tip" and a "bribe." For example, if you fail to give a tip to the usher in a Paris theater, chances are not only you will hear about it, but so will all the people seated around you.) Many countries have cultural traditions of personal payment for services to those in government. In the view of the people there "It has always been like this. This is the way things are." Regardless of how you decide to operate within such a context, you first need to understand it from the viewpoint of the people there and the potential impact it might have on your ministry. (Often we are surprised to discover that Christians within a particular country find this situation quite normal.)

What is the spirit of nationalism within this country? Many countries work hard at building national unity. They view this as the only way to break down the natural barriers between the various cultural groups within their borders. The government works energetically to hold up the "nation," no matter how new, as the ideal for all people. Often this results in the government viewing some particular group as unpatriotic or even revolutionary. It is interesting to note that the northern tier tribes of India, Burma and Thailand, which are predominantly Christian, are all viewed by their governments as having tendencies towards revolution. These governments are very sensitive to outside contacts with these people. One needs to consider this particular group's view of its government, and how that view might be modified by the introduction of Christianity. Will this present a problem, or will it be helpful?

Many governments have very strict rules on record, particularly about religious activity, but they seldom enforce these rules because they believe that the resources brought into the country by outside missionaries are useful to the country. What is the situation in this country?

What are the work rules within this country? There was a time when the cost of carrying out missions through national workers was only a very small percentage of the cost of supporting an expatriate. In many countries this is no longer true. In the same way that the Western countries have adapted social security systems and minimum wage laws, so many developing countries have established work laws which dictate one's ability to hire and discharge a person, the amount he or she must be paid, and even the number of people that can be hired. These and other work laws can have a decided impact on one's ministry.

THE ECONOMIC CONTEXT

Modernization brings economic instability. Countries with large national resources often have built up their dependency upon the export income generated by these resources to a degree that their entire economy is tied to fluctuations in the price of raw materials.

What is the history of this particular country's economic stability? What is the rate of inflation? What is it predicted to be? Is the country moving into an era of greater or lesser economic stability? When was the currency last devalued? Does the government have a policy which pegs its currency to the currency of another country? What will be the inpact of this upon you and your agency?

Are there import restrictions? Are needed materials already available within the country or will they have to be imported? How is the wealth distributed? Is it in the hands of a few powerful families or groups or is there a growing middle class?

What is the impact of all of this on the group that you are attempting to reach? Are they economically exploited or oppressed? Can they become economically self-supporting?

THE SOCIAL CONTEXT

Most societies have a distinct system of class or caste. Often the boundaries of these are blurred to an outsider, but almost always they are well understood by the person within the system. The caste system in particular has had a marked impact upon the growth of Christianity through the years. A well-defined caste naturally tends to ignore what happens in another caste. Thus, if one caste becomes Christian, it may become an obstacle to Christianity within another caste. We need to know how our particular group is viewed within the country, particularly if it is one caste among many.

The class system in general is less rigid than the caste system. The typical developing country has a small upper (wealthy) class, a somewhat larger middle class, and a very large lower class. We need to know where our particular group fits within or across these class boundaries and what the impact of Christianity will be upon their position in the class. For example, in Brazil the rapid growth of Christianity has impressed a Protestant work ethic on many of the lower class settlement areas which has resulted in a considerable increase in material wealth.

This raises the natural question as to the possibilities of migration across class lines. Has it happened in the past? Will it be possible in the future? If it is possible, how will the higher class view those who are moving into it?

Different countries have different educational systems. Many countries have an educational system which is designed to select only the most capable and move them on to a higher education. The majority of their citizens receive only a very minimum education. Other countries provide an educational system only for those who are willing to enter into it. This usually excludes those in geographically isolated places or nomadic groups. The impact of the educational system on society may be negligible or very extensive. Some countries have made higher education such an important goal that the number of university graduates far exceeds the number of positions for such graduates. This produces unrest. At the other extreme, there are those countries which need to import university graduates in order to maintain the political and economic system of the government. Christian missions have traditionally been concerned with education. How much education will be needed within the group that we will be attempting to reach? How much of what is needed can be provided by the government?

This opens up the whole question of government social services. In addition to education, this includes health services, welfare and agricultural assistance, and family planning. These services may be either a help or a hindrance to the gospel. The government's interest in the people and our concern can either enhance or impede our ability to meet the felt need of the people.

A subset of social services and the educational system is the question of literacy. Literacy is not a *necessary* prerequisite to Christianity. Many people have heard the gospel message, and have memorized and incorporated it into their belief system without being able to read. Although the world illiteracy rate appears to be decreasing, there is a common belief that *functional* illiteracy is increasing. It is one thing to *teach* someone to read. It is quite another to actually motivate them to read. If the social and economic life of a people does not require them to read in order to function, there is little likelihood that they will read at all. We need to know the statistical literacy and the functional literacy of a people we are attempting to reach. We need to know whether outside forces are working toward making this people more literate or less literate.

THE RELIGIOUS CONTEXT

We have already touched on the problem of the dominance by another religion within a country. Often a religion, particularly Islam, will be closely aligned with the government. Followers of the dominant religion may act to prevent our people group from allying itself with another religion, even though followers of the dominant religion may have no interest in another religion.

Our definition of religion also includes secular forms of belief such as Marxism, which rejects the need for a higher power outside mankind. A strong resistance to any form of traditional religion exists in many Marxist countries.

Hinduism, while not as militant as Islam, also seeks converts. Hinduism has a surprising ability to absorb Christianity into its system, and to accept Jesus as a Son of God without giving allegiance solely to him. If we are attempting to reach a group that follows Hinduism, we need to consider how the surrounding Hindu population will react as we seek to win them to Christ.

THE CHRISTIAN CONTEXT

Although the number of Christians may be small, and there may be no Christian church among the people we are attempting to reach, there may be other major groups of Christians within the national boundaries. The leadership of these Christian churches, particularly of those churches that consider themselves national denominations, may think that anything that goes on within their national boundary should be done under their aegis. This is particularly true for those of the same denomination. For example, if a Christian group has a strong Reformed tradition, they will likely see other Reformed Christians as natural parts of their church. Their spoken or unspoken response to outsiders is, "This is our country. We will carry out the evangelization of our own country." Some churches hold this view even though they may have little interest in the other non-Christian groups within the country. This is not a simple problem. Much of this exclusiveness is reinforced by a spirit of nationalism within the country. This exclusiveness is a natural response to years of colonial rule, a rule in which the churches of the West often participated. Christian love demands that we attempt to relate to our brothers and sisters wherever they are found. The possibility of disagreement always exists. The time may come when, like Barnabas and Paul, we have to go our separate ways. But we must first understand and appreciate the Christians who are already there.

It is helpful to analyze the extensiveness of the work of each significant church within the country. Often they are unaware of the fact that they are not cross-culturally sensitive and that many groups find it quite difficult to enter into their fellowship.

This leads to the question of cultural differences within the different churches. In the providence of God, people-group movements have often resulted in a church which is ethnically or culturally based. This kind of church often appears foreign or alien to other people within the country, in the same way that another tribe or caste may feel foreign or alien. The very fact, as we discussed above, that this particular group has accepted Christ may deter others from considering Christ. Sometimes the church may be made up of converts from a religion of which our group disapproves. For example, if the church is predominantly Hindu, and the people we are trying to reach are Muslim, it is not likely that Muslim converts will feel comfortable among Hindu converts.

In some countries the church has been nationalized. The government has forced all of the Christians into one national church, as in Japan at the outset of World War II. We need to consider whether or not the people in our group would have to become part of a national church if they became Christians.

Often we are surprised by the political views of Christians in another country. We are startled to discover that they approve of a government that we feel is oppressive. We are surprised to find that there are Christians who also consider themselves Marxists. We have a responsibility to first ascertain whether these people are Christians.[1] If they are not, but later become Christians, how will they align their political views to Christianity?

IMPACT OF THE LARGER CONTEXT

We have dealt with the various contexts above as though they operated independently. Obviously, this is not true. There are interactive systems at work, systems which are intimately connected and interdependent. To attempt to deal with one without considering the other is an exercise in futility.

Very seldom will it be possible neatly to define a people without considering the larger context. O that the world were made up of the traditional anthropologists' islands! Here and there around the world we will still find tribal groups which are isolated sufficiently from other people groups that their most significant context is the geographical one. At the other end of the scale would be a people group within a vast urban setting. Here we are faced with the problem of defining a group, many of whose members participate in other groups. It takes a great deal of thinking and some prayerful guessing to decide what would be the best way to define them. The affinity of any group in an urban setting is continually threatened by the political, economic, and social structures within which it exists. A great deal of study needs to be done in this entire area.

It is important for us as North Americans to realize that Christians in other continents believe our questions are upside down. For them the "larger context" is the *primary* question. Foremost among those who feel this way would be Christians in Latin America who see themselves in the midst of a vast power struggle. They see fellow human beings pushed and stressed by economic forces that are out of their control. A handful of landowners may control their entire country. Struggles for power between industrialists and landowners may be continually changing in the context within which people live. Dictatorships limit their freedom. The life of their country is controlled by the multinational corporations of the North. Social structures oppress them. Many Christians in Latin America therefore see the need for a "liberation" theology which will speak to the needs of these oppressed peoples.

1. We must begin our approach with Christology. If the people have a high view of Jesus as Lord and Savior of mankind, we have a firm base upon which to build.

We cannot ignore this last view. The forces of society do shape and mold any group of people, and one can easily argue that before isolating any "people group," one must first examine larger forces within which they exist. The fact that in the approach we are describing in this book we have not asked these "higher level" questions does not mean that we do not understand the need to ask them. Rather, for this study we have restricted ourselves to the more limited context. However, we do appreciate this larger context, and have attempted to reflect this when we ask, "What is the perceived need of this people?" and "What do we believe is their basic need?" The questions of the larger context discussed in this chapter all bear upon the definition of need.

THE POWERS OF THE AIR

We would be remiss if we did not conclude this section with the recognition that the context within which we work includes spiritual dimensions that are far beyond our understanding and control. Paul has said, "For we are not contending against flesh and blood, but against the principalities, against the powers, against the world rulers of this present darkness, against the spiritual hosts of wickedness in the heavenly places" (Eph. 6:12). This immediately draws us out of the secular world of the social sciences and into the larger dimension of the world in which we live. Anthropology can help us to understand man's origins and capabilities. Psychology can give us insight into the inner workings of a person's mind. Sociology can give us clues about the societies within which individuals operate. But the mystery of evangelism remains. With all of our knowledge, with all of our study, with all of our preparation, we are still only channels of God's power. Before further analysis of what is needed to reach an unreached people, we need to examine the rest of Paul's words:

Take the whole armor of God. We need to stand ready for the onslaught of evil around us.

Gird your loins with truth. We are not manipulators using half-truths. We are people who claim to have the Truth.

Put on the breastplate of righteousness. The demands of the gospel are the demands of righteousness.

Shod your feet with the equipment of the gospel of peace. The gospel brings both inward and outward peace. Those who share the gospel need to be at peace with themselves and their tasks.

Protect yourself by taking the shield of faith. The world is immense, and its problems are vast and complex. We are but a small band of men and women with an unbelievable task. We need to set our goals and our statements of faith before us.

And with this all we take the helmet of salvation and the sword of the Spirit which is the word of God. This is our basic equipment. Our warfare is carried on not by us but by the power of the Spirit, the word of God hidden in our hearts.

Pray at all times in the Spirit, with all prayer and supplication. To that end, keep alert with all perseverance, making supplication for all the saints (Eph. 6:13–18).

WE DO NOT HAVE VERY MUCH CONTROL

All of the above and the preceding chapters might leave one with the impression that if we do our homework well enough, and if we lay our plans well enough, things will turn out the way we have planned. But this is not always the case. We will have very little control over our immediate situation, let alone the larger context we have discussed here. But it is through attempting to understand by the hard hours of sometimes discouraging research that we often find the information that will make us effective. Attempting great things for God sometimes means attempting to get a great understanding!

HOW MUCH DO WE NEED TO KNOW?

Because of all this studying, one might easily wonder whether we will ever get around to *doing* anything. How much do we really need to know? Where do we begin?

One way of answering this question is to think of the context within which we work as a series of concentric circles. At the very center would be people that we are trying to reach. Encompassing that would be the political context of the country. Between these two circles would be other circles of the social system, the economic system, and the religious system. How much we need to know will depend upon how close these circles are to our particular people. For example, if we are dealing with a group that is quite isolated from any religion or direct government contact, we may need to know more about the major religion of the country or the mechanics of the government beyond that which we need to know in order to gain entry into the country. If our group is surrounded on all sides by another religion, obviously what that other religion is attempting to do with our group is extremely important.

The question of a larger context, like all questions, is one that we can seldom answer in detail. Again the importance lies in asking the questions, not in finding all of the answers.

QUESTIONS

A People-Centered Approach

1. How is a "people-centered" approach different from traditional methods of doing evangelism?
2. Is there biblical precedence for seriously considering the cultural differences that exist between peoples? Should the church maintain or preserve those cultural differences?
3. Did New Testament evangelists engage in strategies that were conditioned by the cultures of the people they were attempting to evangelize?
4. Is the Christian evangelist to consider herself or himself as sent to a geographic area (a country or land) or to a people? How did Paul or even Jesus view his calling as an evangelist?
5. When can we say that a people has "heard" the gospel? How many distinct or unique sendings of evangelists are necessary if the Great Commission is to be fulfilled?
6. Should our primary orientation be toward ensuring the purity of the message or toward ensuring an understanding of the message? Is this a false dilemma?

Defining and Describing a People

1. What is a "people"?
2. What are the various kinds of human groups? Which ones are suitable for specially tailored strategies of gospel communication?

3. How do we decide if two groups are sufficiently different from one another to require separate strategies for evangelism and indigenous church institutions? Does this question have to be answered differently in urban populations where people have multiple group memberships than in rural or tribal/ethnic/caste settings where people belong only to one group?

4. What do we need to know about a group in order to describe it in a preliminary fashion? (The Unreached Peoples Questionnaire is relevant here; see the Appendix).

5. Where can we best research that information about a people in order to answer those questions? What resources are available for research?

Understanding the Meaning System of a People

1. Beyond the information we gather to *describe* a people, what do we need to know in order to *understand* them?

2. How do we go about "translating" the meanings of the Kingdom of God so that they make sense in a new cultural context? Do we have to be concerned with the language we are using?

3. How do we draw the line between what is genuinely indigenous and yet an authentic expression of the gospel and that which is also genuinely indigenous but an inauthentic expression of the gospel (what we usually call "syncretistic" or "Christo-pagan")?

4. What kind of process do people go through in coming to faith in Jesus Christ?

5. Can those who have an adequate and accurate grasp on the implications and personal relevance of the gospel still say no to Jesus Christ? (In a way this question is asking whether we believe the major problem facing evangelism is one of communication—"if only they *knew*"—or whether there are other factors that are important so that even those who *know* at times say no to Christ.)

6. What is the ultimate goal of evangelism? Bringing people to an awareness of the meaning of the gospel? Persuading people to become committed to Christ? Increasing the number of faithful members of the church? Increasing the number of active propagators of the gospel? All of these?

Understanding the Needs of a People

1. How did Jesus deal with human need in his ministry? What was the relationship between his helping people in need and his proclamation of the Kingdom?

2. Why is it important that evangelism deal with the felt needs of a people as it defines them rather than as we might think it ought to define them?

3. How do we discover people's felt needs? How do we avoid simply reading our own understandings of needs into the life and situation of peoples in cultures different from ours?

4. How do we preach repentance? To what types of things are we to connect the call for repentance? What if a people does not feel guilty for some of the things which we know to be sinful from our understanding of the Bible?

The Larger Context

1. To what extent does the political context within which a people lives help to define the mission?

2. How can the social and economic contexts work to redefine the basic values of the people?

3. Are there times when the first thrust of evangelism must be to correct the social, political, and/or economic system in order to address the true needs of the people?

STEP 3

THE FORCE
FOR EVANGELIZATION

Considerations

Qualifications

The People Available

The Organizations Available

Recruiting and Training

Questions

CONSIDERATIONS

1. The work of Christ flows out of a commitment to the body of Christ. Too often Western individualism has bypassed this biblical principle.

2. The entire Church is potentially available for the evangelization of any people.

3. There is a close relationship between people to be reached and the people that God has set aside to reach them.

4. Missionaries should be viewed by themselves and by the people they are attempting to reach as a mission community, rather than a group of individuals.

5. The "para-church" agency or community is the basic vehicle through which the Church communicates Christ to the world.

6. The structure of the mission agency should be designed to fit the task at hand and the people to be reached. The structure is needed but should be an outcome rather than a requirement.

7. Presently there are not enough cross-cultural missionaries to reach the unreached peoples of the world.

8. The day of the Western missionary is far from over; indeed, it has just begun.

9. The missionaries who are available are mainly working in the wrong areas.

10. Some mission agencies should withdraw from the areas in which they are working.

11. God is just as interested in reaching people as sending missionaries.

12. There are thousands of young people willing to be trained, but existing North American missionaries are not equipped to receive and train them.

13. There is no vocation into which it is more difficult to be accepted than the missionary vocation.

14. The training of a cross-cultural missionary is equivalent to the training of a medical doctor and should be viewed as such.

15. The average layperson's view of missions is inadequate and must be changed.

16. Change must begin with the local church.

CHAPTER 15

Qualifications

O nce we have gained an initial understanding of a people with whom we wish to share the gospel, the next logical consideration is whom to send to reach them. From the thousands of men and women serving in Christ's Church who is to make up the specific force for evangelism? As we will see, this second step is closely related to the question of means and methods. Although we see Christ's work as the work of the church, and not just the individual, it will be useful to consider what qualifications an individual needs to become a missionary. We will then move on to consider both the individuals and organizations available (chapters 16 and 17). We also have some strong convictions about the way men, women, and organizations ought to be recruited and trained for the missionary task. Chapter 18 will attempt to suggest a new model for missionary training.

ADEQUATE FAITH AND VISION

During the last decade there has been a new interest in spiritual gifts, and many books have been written on this topic.[1] Some see spiritual

1. For a good overview and an excellent bibliography, see C. Peter Wagner, *Your Spiritual Gifts Can Help Your Church Grow* (1979).

gifts as well defined and limited. Some go further and say that many gifts were given only to the apostles. Others have an open-ended view of gifts. They view the *charismata* in the Bible as suggesting only that everyone is gifted in such a way as to fit into the body of Christ.

Whatever one's view of gifts, it seems evident to us that faith is, in many dimensions, a gift which is given to some Christians in greater measure than others. There is, of course, a basic faith necessary for salvation (Rom. 5:1ff and Rom. 10:17ff). In a very real sense all of the Christian life is a life that is lived in faith. Paul tells us in II Corinthians 5:7 that we walk through this life by a faith which lives in hope. Paul described himself in Galatians 2:20 as living by the faith of the Son of God. Christians are known as those of the same "faith" (Gal. 3:7). It is the shield of faith that protects us against the fiery darts of the evil one (Eph. 6:16). When Paul is concerned about a people, he inquires about their faith (I Thess. 3:5ff).

But there is another dimension to faith, one which evidently varies between individuals. In his exhortation about the spiritual gifts of the church at Corinth, Paul speaks of faith as a gift of the Spirit (I Cor. 12:9). Later on (13:2) he implies that there is a quality of faith that can make things happen—"so as to remove mountains." This sort of faith is closely related to the idea of vision. Those who have this sort of faith have an ability to envision the world in a different way because they are confident that it is God's intention that the world be different from the way it is now. Their vision focuses on a particular situation or a group of people, and gives them the ability to set goals and to make statements of faith for the future. Without this vision, without this "ability to cast a net into the future," the Church cannot move forward. We would see this qualification as working itself out in the life of an individual and an organization. Within an organization, there may be only a few who have this gift, but without it the mission is greatly jeopardized.

A DEMONSTRABLE LIFE

This book is written primarily for those in Western Christianized societies. It is often very difficult to distinguish between Christians and non-Christians in such a society.[2] But in spite of the difficulty of noting

2. C. S. Lewis once responded to those who wondered why some non-Christians appeared to act so much better than Christians that one first had to know where Christians had begun in order to see what a difference had been made!

outward appearances, the Bible assumes that there is a fundamental difference in the way a Christian lives out his or her life. Often Christians have difficulty describing what this difference is, whereas non-Christians may be able to identify easily that something is different. We are reminded of a secular management trainer who spent time consulting for a Christian organization. His view was that the primary forces in an organization were position and power. But he sensed a "third force" within this Christian organization which he could not define, but which he had to acknowledge. Somehow he found that the people within this organization dealt with one another from a different viewpoint.

People will work out their Christianity in different ways. We are all affected by our genetic and social heritage, the situation in which we exist, and the things to which we are committed. The Christian life is a life lived in tension. Nevertheless, a necessary prerequisite for demonstrating a Christian life in another culture is an ability to demonstrate a Christian life within one's own culture.

PRIORITIES

Individualism is almost synonymous with the West, particularly with America. Horatio Alger stories may have taken on new forms, but most Westerners are still entranced with the idea of the individual making it against overwhelming odds. The cult of the individual has almost reached the point of alienating us from one another.[3] This individualism is not biblically based. Striving to outperform others is a worldly concept which needs to be constantly reexamined.

It is to counter this that we would like to suggest three levels of Christian priorities within which we can set qualifications for a cross-cultural missionary. We feel that these priority levels, these levels of commitment, are universal and not just for the missionary and missionary organization. In another culture they might be stated in another way. We have stated them this way in response to our own Western culture.[4]

3. For a good overview, see Christopher Lasch, *The Culture of Narcissism* (1979). For an interesting introduction to American culture see James Stewart's *American Cultural Patterns: A Cross-cultural Perspective* (1971).
4. For further discussion on this subject see Edward R. Dayton and Ted W. Engstrom, *Strategy For Living* (1976) and *Strategy For Leadership* (1979). For an application of these principles to the local church, see Raymond C. Ortlund, *Lord, Make My Life a Miracle* (1974).

Our three levels of commitment are:

1. Commitment to God and Christ.
2. Commitment to the body of Christ, his Church.
3. Commitment to the work of Christ.

The order of these levels of commitment is tremendously important. No one will argue with the first priority, commitment to God and Christ. As Christians, we see our allegiance to the Trinity as given through the salvific work of Christ. Our allegiance is based upon what he has done for us, and this makes us distinctively Christian. Unfortunately, too many Western Christians move directly from their commitment to Christ to attempting to serve him directly. They fail to see that when they became Christians they were automatically incorporated into a new relationship, a relationship so unique that Paul can only compare it to the human body (Rom. 12 and I Cor. 12). The work of Christ is carried out by his body, the Church. Individual Christians are gifted to fit into this body (Eph. 4:4–13). This body finds its ability to work through the power of Christ: "from him the whole body joined and held together by every supporting ligament, grows and builds itself up in love, as each part does its work" (Eph. 4:16). "To each man the manifestation of the Spirit is given for the common good" (I Cor. 12:7).

> The body is a unit, though it is made up of many parts; and though all its parts are many, they form one body.... The body is not made up of one part but of many.... As it is, there are many parts, but one body. The eye cannot say to the hand, "I don't need you!" And the head cannot say to the feet, "I don't need you!"... But God has combined the members of the body and has given greater honor to the part that lacked it, so that there should be no division of the body, but that its parts should have equal concern for each other. If one part suffers, every part suffers with it; if one part is honored every part rejoices with it. (I Cor. 12:12–26)

The work of the *individual* is to become a working part of the body. The work of the body, the Church, is to carry out the work of Christ (Trueblood, 1961).

When one examines the biblical data on goals that we should set for ourselves as the body of Christ, there is little doubt that the major emphasis is one of *relationships*. Only three times in the New Testament is the word evangelist used. The New Testament writers talk very little about a strategy for evangelism. Almost universally, their assumption is that people will be changed by the witness of the lives of those who have been transformed by the power of Jesus Christ.

In recent years there has been an increasing recognition that discipleship is based upon relationship, and that evangelism is a natural result of the people of God who are in right relationship with each other. Jesus not only said, "By this all men will know that you are my disciples, if you love one another" (Jn. 13:35), but he also prayed that the disciples "may all be one; even as Thou, Father, art in me and I in Thee, they also may be in us, *so the world may believe that Thou hast sent me*" (Jn. 17:21).

As Christians we are charged with the task of taking the gospel to all people. But in the face of a world that is desperately seeking to find examples of Christ-like lives, we are often surprised at how the missionary community has placed the priority of the task before the priority of caring for one another. In one early survey conducted by MARC of the missionary population of Brazil, the question was asked, "To whom are you responsible?" Almost 50 percent of the respondees answered, "To the Lord Jesus Christ alone!" Many missionaries questioned the right of the surveyors to even ask the question.

It is not difficult to surmise why missionaries (of all people) might have problems with authority, and at the same time may not sense the need to be committed to one another. One of the gifts sensed by a missionary is an ability to go it alone, to be dependent upon God and oneself when face-to-face with discouraging odds. The "faith mission" system, in particular, tends to select this type of person. From the very beginning of the missionary experience, the candidate is asked to raise his or her own support and to set up lines of communication with those in the home country who can offer additional prayer or financial support. The candidate is usually asked about his or her call to a country, rather than to an organization. And in many missionary field organizations, the candidate is not only permitted to make his or her own decisions about where to work, but may be expected to do so.

The result of this kind of experience is that missionaries too often continue to live as individuals. Even though they may be living next to each other, they demonstrate little of the "body life" for which the world yearns. Often they attend missionary prayer meetings where the work is prayed over at great length, but the gut-level needs of the individual are seldom mentioned. Failure is often viewed as individual failure, rather than group failure. Prayer letters back home seldom mention that another mission group may be at work a mile away.

We recognize that this emphasis on these three levels of priorities may force us to reexamine the concept of "missionary call." But is not God's call first to *be*, then to *do*? And would this not say that more emphasis should be placed on commitment to the group, to the Church that was called to reach people for Christ rather than to the task?

There are many who will immediately reply, "Missionaries are sent to other countries to proclaim the gospel, not to start their own little church for missionaries!" There is no doubt in our mind that proclamation must include a verbal announcement that people are separated from God and the only way open to them for a new life of reconciliation is through the saving grace of Jesus Christ. But if gospel *does* change lives, then a major portion of the "proclamation" is going to be the changed life of the missionary.

All of this discussion naturally leads to the question of personal gifts, the question of being properly fitted into the body.

INDIVIDUAL GIFTS

As we have discussed above, the Bible indicates that God has fitted each Christian with particular qualities or attributes which we have come to call gifts.

To ask whether the Christian has spiritual or natural gifts is a moot question. The Christian is a whole person. He or she is indwelt by the Holy Spirit and empowered by that same Spirit. All that he or she has is given from God to be used for God. But there is a need for sober evaluation. Paul admonishes us, "For by the grace given to me, I say to every one of you: Do not think of yourself more highly than you ought, but rather think of yourself with sober judgment, in accordance with the measure of faith God has given to you" (Rom. 12:3). This appears just before Paul's statement about how we are all members of one body, and how we are gifted to fit into that body. There are many ways that one can go about discovering one's gifts. There are well-developed, secular testing systems that will highlight an individual's strengths and weaknesses. If we are a part of the Church, we should expect members of the body to affirm the gifts that we have.[5]

5. For a good example of how this has been carried out in one local church, see Elizabeth O'Connor, *Journey Inward, Journey Outward* (1968).

PROPERLY FITTED INTO THE BODY

If the individual has not demonstrated an ability to fit into a local body with his or her own culture, he or she will certainly have difficulty in acting out Christianity in another culture and helping those within that culture to understand the body of the Church. The local church has a great responsibility to struggle against the natural push of the Western culture towards individualism. The Western culture of the 1970s has been moving more and more toward letting the individual "do his own thing." The culture always naturally influences the Church to follow along.[6]

This understanding of one's gift, this fitting into the body of Christ, assumes a self-understanding on the part of the individual. This self-understanding is very important to those who would be part of that force for evangelism that crosses cultural boundaries.

CROSS-CULTURAL SENSITIVITY

Much of Western society, particularly the United States, has very little appreciation for cultural differences. The average middle-class American has very little understanding of the extreme difference in value systems between the middle and the lower end of the lower class within the United States. The experience of most Americans in their local church settings is mono-cultural. The mono-culturalism of the average American church is the natural result of people with common interests and a common affinity for one another. Whether this is natural for Christ's Church has been and will be hotly debated, but the fact remains that most Westerners do not know how to relate to people of another culture. Nor do they understand their own cultural eccen-

6. For those who would wonder whether the Church actually does this, we would point to an example from the United States. In 1950 the norm in most churches in the United States was that women should wear a hat to church or, at the very least, have their heads covered. In 1975 the norm in most churches in the United States was that women were not required to and indeed few wore hats within the church. In 1950 women wore hats because of the biblical injunction that women's heads should be covered in the house of worship (I Cor. 11:10). Few sermons have been preached, and no articles have been written, that we know of, speaking out against this change. And yet twenty-five years later the biblical admonition has somehow been reinterpreted (see also Webber, 1978).

tricities (Stewart, 1971). They, like the people of most cultures, passively believe that the way they do things is the right way. Without knowing that they are doing it, they interpret each other's body language, manners, and mannerisms as normative. When they think about "planting a church," they normally think about starting another church similar to theirs.[7]

How then does one discover whether one has cross-cultural sensitivity? In the next section we will discuss the need for adequate preparation. Part of this is obviously both an intellectual and an experiential understanding of the differences between cultures and an exploration of one's ability to work within those differences. One of the indications would certainly be an ability to accept and love people from one's own culture. A good foundation for cross-cultural sensitivity is an ability to see people as people and to love them as they are, even as one disagrees with their values.[8]

ADEQUATE PREPARATION

We will have more to say about training in chapter 18. In that chapter we will propose that medical training is a model for the kind of training required by the cross-cultural missionary. Again, we need to emphasize that we are speaking primarily to the Western missionary and Western organization, although much of this will fit those who are seeking to carry out cross-cultural ministry within a similar format.

If one examined the educational qualifications of those working in the first century of the modern missionary era, one would discover that missionary candidates were well educated for their day. There was a growing emphasis on the need for theological preparation and research. Few people realize today the extent of the research that was done in cross-cultural missions in the latter part of the nineteenth century and the beginning years of the twentieth century. The amount of information and research compiled for the historic Edinburgh missions conference in

7. See Ron Fisher in "Why Don't We Have More Church Planting Missionaries?" *Evangelical Mission Quarterly,* October, 1978.
8. One of the tensions faced by mission organizations is that individuals who are self-determined and single-minded often tend to be rigid in their acceptance of others whose views are different from their own. This is all the more reason to have people fitted into a body (see also Mellis, 1976).

1910 was so vast that to this day much of it lies uncollated in the Library Tower of the Union Theological Seminary in New York. Most missionary libraries have copies of the extensive mission atlases that were produced during the first quarter of the twentieth century. But by 1960 both the need for research and the emphasis on the formal educational preparation of the missionary reached its ebb. Why did this happen? Why was the great emphasis on education and research into the missionary task left in such disarray?

One can speculate that there is a strong correlation between the decline in the mission agencies associated with the mainline denominations in the United States, those associated with the present Division of Overseas Ministry of the National Council of Churches of Christ of America, and the numerical growth of the "faith missions." The *Occasional Bulletin* of the Missionary Research Library[9] pointed out in early 1960 that the numerical size of the missionary force associated with the DOM and that associated with the Evangelical Foreign Mission Association (EFMA) and the Interdenominational Foreign Mission Association (IFMA) was, for the first time, equal. Indeed, the EFMA/IFMA group was obviously growing at a much greater rate. Inherent in the founding of many of the faith missions was the idea that formal qualifications were not as important as a willing and ready heart. J. Hudson Taylor, founder of the China Inland Mission (now the Overseas Missionary Fellowship), was an advocate of such a system, which had great initial success in China.[10]

One can also speculate that the correlation between the anti-intellectualism of the early Pentecostal movement and the anti-intellectualism within mainline conservative Protestantism within the United States was a reaction to the liberalizing tendencies in the early twentieth century. Science and the scientific method became highly suspect. Conservative Christians between the 1920s and 1950s had great difficulty with the idea of applying the scientific method to the task of evangelism.

A return to the earlier view of the value of formal education and study and the usefulness of appropriately applied social science can be seen in the founding of the Institute of Church Growth at Northwest Christian College and the subsequent moving of that Institute to the

9. Price and Orr, 1960.
10. It is interesting to note that at the end of his missionary career, Taylor himself questioned the wisdom of allowing all who were willing and able to come into the missionary enterprise.

School of World Mission of Fuller Theological Seminary by Dr. Donald McGavran. The founding of the Missions Advanced Research and Communication Center (MARC) in 1967, and the subsequent founding of graduate schools of mission study pushed the movement along. There is a growing recognition that the complexity of the world is such that effective cross-cultural evangelism can be enhanced only by a more methodical study of social sciences and the newly defined discipline of missiology.

A DEFINITE CALL

Western Christians have defined their sense of place, their sense of God's leading, and their sense of vocation by expressing it as "God's call." As we will discuss in chapter 28, this expression is only loosely defined, and mostly refers to some form of mystical communication between the individual and God. We think that in this sense one needs to experience, on both an intellectual and emotional level, a definiteness about what one is to do and where one is to fit into the body of Christ. As we have previously mentioned, although we see that such a "call" is given to the individual, the Bible asks us first to be called into the body, and then to see ourselves as part of a body that has a definite task. The difference between the local church and the mission agency is primarily one of goals. The local church is called upon to carry out two contradictory tasks. On the one hand, the local church is called to help the poor, the needy, the lame, and the blind. It accepts into its membership anyone who affirms Jesus as Lord and looks to him for salvation. At the same time, the church is called to "go forth" on a mission with which it has been entrusted. Lame and blind members are also to go forth. The "para-church" agency is a natural response to this dilemma. "Healthy" Christians have been temporarily moved out of this setting and set aside for a particular task. This means that, for the moment, they are relieved of the wider task of the church and fitted for a special vocation.

Each Christian who undertakes the task of cross-cultural missions, the task of leaving one's local church and setting forth to establish a new one, needs to have a real understanding of how they individually fit, first into the local body of which they are a part, and second, into this special group (para-church). We see no set pattern for how this is to be accomplished. Prayer, meditation, biblical study, and circumstances will all obviously help. Perhaps as important of any of these is the affirmation by other members of the local body that they, as the body of

Christ, sense that this individual has those attributes needed to accomplish the particular task.[11]

11. The practice of some Latin American churches of first identifying leadership gifts within an individual before training them for leadership seems much more appropriate than the Western system of allowing people to choose the ministerial vocation and then to train for it often quite independently of affirmation by a local body.

CHAPTER 16

The People Available

*I*n Step 2 we looked at the people that God wanted to reach with his living word. Often we quickly move on to "how?" without first recognizing the more important question of "who?" People and methods are intimately entwined. We cannot apply a method unless there are people equipped to carry it out. There is little use in calling people who do not know how God wants them to go about their task.

We have designated the people God will use to reach another people as the *force for evangelism*.[1] "Force" is a very appropriate term. God intends to use his people to reach those whom he calls to be his people. Every Christian in the world is potentially a member of this force, and in one sense every Christian is always a part of the task of world evangelism. We go forth into all the world not only with our persons, but also with our prayers and resources. Outwardly, Christ's church is divided into hundreds of different denominations, but the Bible assures us that mysteriously we are all part of one body. We are all a total force. One could also picture it as a large sun. At the core is the body of Christ, fired and empowered by the Holy Spirit. Radiating out from this sun are particular beams of energy, special task forces from this body, which

---

1. This apt phrase was first suggested by Frank Ineson. See Ineson, Frank, and Read, William, *Brazil 1980* (1973), Monrovia, MARC.

have been designated to reach a particular people. The source of their power rests with the total body. Their direction is determined by a particular need. Not every Christian is called or capable of reaching every believer. Only a few are especially equipped and chosen.

It is important to realize that God is more interested in *reaching people* than *sending missionaries.* Romans 10 tells us that all who call upon the Lord will be saved. God will use those who are sent to bring a people to a saving knowledge of himself. The people to be sent need to be fitted to the people to be reached. What is the need and the context in which God wants to meet the need? Whom has God called and equipped to meet that need? Attempting to answer the second question will often force us to further define the first one. Attempting to answer the means and methods question will drive us back to reconsider what we have said about the force for evangelism.

Ultimately, the makeup of the force for evangelism will be determined only after we have completed our entire strategy. It is not enough to decide who will go. There is usually a large support force of those who will stand with the missionary in providing resources, training, communication, and prayer. But in this chapter we will be primarily concerned with selecting those who are to go.

Go where? What barriers will have to be crossed? There are many questions to be asked in discovering whom God has chosen for a particular task. Remember Gideon's experience? God gave Gideon a series of tests to trim down his force to those few who were particularly equipped. If there are no Christians among the group we want to reach, then cultural barriers will have to be crossed. This means that from the thousands of Christians who may have a desire to reach this people, we will have to find those who are able to bridge the cultural barriers. There will be other tests to consider: Who will be acceptable to those we want to reach? Who is available? Who is called? Who is qualified? Who is able?

The purpose of our evangelism is to establish a community of people in relationship to one another and in relationship to God. We are calling people from one kingdom into another. God has commissioned the people of his Kingdom, and has designated them as his Church and his body. God's people are to be the agents of evangelism. They are to go forth in the strength of their community. Some will have to be separated from the local body as a special agency. But their effectiveness in calling people to a new community will be directly related to how effective they were in their own community.

People in a community sometimes find it necessary to create a structure or a formal way of relating to one another. It is helpful in thinking about the force for evangelism to consider how such structures operate and what kind are needed.

This chapter then will focus on how, from all the Christians potentially available as evangelists, we discover those whom God has set apart to reach a particular unreached people.

In most of what follows we will assume that the individuals needed are already within existing mission organizations or that the mission organizations have within themselves the ability to find and attract these people. We will leave it to others to discuss the structure and formation of mission organizations.

WHAT IS THIS PEOPLE LIKE?

At Step 1 we described a people. This was an important first step. Now we must consider who is the most likely person(s) to communicate the gospel to a particular people.

The Engel/Søgaard Scale, with an accompanying rate of change scale, gives us a compact overview of a people. In the balance of this chapter we will discuss cultural distance, who is available, who is acceptable to the people, who has experience, who believes he or she has been called, and what are the qualifications needed. All of these questions can only be answered in light of the context, in light of the people we are trying to reach. The Engel/Søgaard Scale helps us see a people at a glance. In Figure 16-1, we have shown profiles of three people groups: A, B, and C. Before proceeding further, consider what force for evangelism will be most effective in these three different cases.

Half of the people in group A are unaware of Christianity. Their number is decreasing by 5 percent each year. Another 40 percent have some awareness, but their attitude about what they do know is very negative. This group (-6) is increasing each year by the same amount that those at -7 are decreasing. There are a small number who have some knowledge of the gospel (-5), but their attitude is also negative and their number is constant. There are no people beyond this. There is no church. What does this tell you about the qualifications for those who are to reach them?

The people in group B are all aware of Christianity. There is no one at -7. About 25 percent are at -6, 50 percent at -5, and 10 percent at -4. Notice that all of these are very positive about what they do know. There is a small church—2 percent at $+2$. The church has a positive

Figure 16-1   Three People Profiles Compared

THE PEOPLE PROFILE	PEOPLE A			PEOPLE B			PEOPLE C		
DECISION POINT	% AT THIS POINT 25 50 75	ATTITUDE + 0 −	RATE OF CHANGE	% AT THIS POINT 25 50 75	ATTITUDE + 0 −	RATE OF CHANGE	% AT THIS POINT 25 50 75	ATTITUDE + 0 −	RATE OF CHANGE
NO AWARENESS −7	▇		−5% year						
AWARENESS −6	▇	X	+5% year	▇	X	15% year	?	X	−5% year
SOME KNOWLEDGE −5	▪	X		▇	X	20% year	?	X	+5% year
KNOWLEDGE −4				▪	X	20% year	?	X	+5% year
IMPLICATIONS SEEN −3									
PERSONAL NEED −2									
CONFRONTA-TION −1									
CONVERSION									
RE-EVALUATION +1				.5%	X	20% year			
INCORPORA-TION +2				2%	X	20% year	?	X	−2% year
PROPAGATION +3				1%	X	20% year			

215

attitude and is changing (growing at a rate of 20 percent per year). What does this tell you about the qualifications for the force for evangelism?

The people in group C have a very different profile. Those who are not Christians have a neutral to negative attitude about Christianity. Those who are Christians are declining slightly each year and feel only neutral about their religion. None of them is a propagator. What does this profile tell you?

WHAT IS THE CULTURAL DISTANCE?

The peoples of the world are separated by a number of barriers. The most obvious of these are geography and language. But they are also separated by cultural barriers, which are much more subtle blocks to communication. We have already discussed the need to understand the culture of the people we are trying to reach and have given a number of references for further study. As we think about the force for evangelism, we need first to identify the relationship of the culture of the people to be reached to the various cultures in which Christ's Church finds its expression. Just as we can think about the geographical distance, so we can think about cultural distance. Will it require an E-0, E-1, E-2, or E-3 evangelist? (See pp. 5–6.)

WHO IS AVAILABLE?

Having said this, we can begin to examine what kind of Christians might be available.

First, are there any Christians among this particular people? We can get a quick answer by looking at the +2 on the Engel Scale which describes the people. The fact that there are church members does not, of course, mean that they will automatically begin to witness in their community. There are stagnant churches all over the world which have no real desire to trouble their waters by bringing in outsiders. So we must also consider their attitude toward local evangelism, as well as the ability of others to motivate them to become effective evangelists, if indeed they are lethargic. In some cases there is little probability, from the human viewpoint, that they will reach out to their own people group. In other words, although there is a church already there, it appears as though some form of outside intervention is needed.

This discussion naturally leads to another question: Are local Christians still culturally acceptable? Evangelistic methods of the past often produced a local church which extracted people from the culture in such a way as to set the local church over and against the culture. Instead of the local church becoming the sweet perfume of Christ to its own group, it became an offense to them. For example, when a religious minority, such as Hindus in a predominantly Islamic culture, comes to Christ, their former cultural patterns and the very fact that they are viewed by others as a mixture of two religions may make them unacceptable to those around them, even though they speak the same language and live in the same geographical area. The situation is not peculiar to any particular area. It is found within Western as well as non-Western countries.

If there are no local acceptable Christians, what local Christian body is culturally akin to this group? The answer to this question is not always obvious. Many times there are Christians who are very similar to another group, but who are geographically separated from this group. During the mid-1970s, missionary Peter McNee, a member of the New Zealand Baptist Mission, did a survey of Bangladesh (McNee, 1976). He discovered that there was a pocket of Garu people in northern Bangladesh who were geographically separated from the main Garu body further west. When he pointed out to the strong church among the latter group that there were other Garus who were not Christians, they were quick to evangelize this newly discovered group. So it does not follow that those who are physically closest to a group will indeed be most useful in evangelization. They may not be. However, it is very useful to consider that all Christians of the world are potentially able to reach this particular group and attempt to bridge their cultural distance. Another example would be converts from Islam in an entirely different country. These converts might have a much better understanding of how to communicate to the Islamic mind and could be much more acceptable to them.

WHO WILL BE ACCEPTABLE TO THE PEOPLE?

Who will a people perceive as able to meet their needs? The primary entry point to a people is through their perceived needs. Are there

Christians who will be viewed as able to meet these needs? For example, if the people perceive their need as one of economic assistance in the form of community development, are there Christian agencies available to carry this out? If this people has a perceived need to be freed from the tremendous spiritual forces surrounding them, are there Christians available who understand such demonic forces and the need for an encounter with them? For example, the people of the Seychelles Islands are predominantly Roman Catholic and Anglican. However, their Christianity is actually Christo-pagan, and a majority of them also practice voodoo (similar to the voodoo of Haiti). It has been suggested that the Pentecostals in Brazil are best qualified to reach these people because they understand the need for an encounter with demonic forces.

What are this people's cultural biases? We might believe that a neighboring tribe can best reach this people. After all, they live in the same geographical context and come from a similar religious background. However, the barriers of tribalism may limit their effectiveness. The church in Pakistan in the 1970s was predominantly Hindu and had great difficulty in finding acceptance among the predominantly Muslim community.

What is the political orientation of this people? First, there may be national boundaries which certain members of the church will be unable to cross. The national differences between the two countries legally exclude them from entry. Even if they are not legally excluded, there may be strong political ideologies which will separate them. The gospel has marvelous ability to adapt to and transform those of many different ideologies, but we should be blind to such differences when we are attempting to reach out to those who do not know Christ as Savior.

Who will be acceptable theologically? There is a wide diversity of theological *emphasis* within the Church. Some will place strong emphasis on the power of the Holy Spirit to overcome spiritual powers. Others will emphasize the form of order and church worship, and they will feel strongly that these should not be modified by culture. The New Testament has several examples of such diversity. Early in the book of Acts (chapter 7), Christians are grouped together in different language and cultural settings. In Acts 15, the Jerusalem Council asks the new church in Antioch not to "eat any food that is unclean because it is offered to idols" (Acts 15:20). On the other hand, Paul, in writing to the Corinthians (chapter 8), evidently felt no burden to place such a rule upon that church. If you believe it is unbiblical to allow for such differences and that all churches should be alike, then this will not be a useful distinction for you. However, if you believe that the Bible permits a wide diversity of emphases, then this becomes an important question. In chapter 22 we will discuss the kind of church that could come from this group. The theological emphasis speaks directly to this consideration.

What churches exist in this country? Unfortunately, local churches are not immune to nationalism. The Presbyterian Church in a particular country may have strong feelings about other Presbyterians doing evangelism in their country (see pp. 187f.). Local churches in the area may have already formed their own opinions as to what is needed to reach this people, even though they are not reaching them. Some outsiders may be acceptable, others may not be. Then, too, the local church may not *need* any help. A missionary executive once offered to send more missionaries from his agency to Chile. The response was, "The Holy Spirit is doing a great work among us, and we are very busy. When He is finished with us, we will try to help you. Meanwhile, please don't send us any more missionaries!" Also, during the early 1970s, the Presbyterian Church in Mexico requested the three North American Presbyterian denominations to temporarily withdraw from Mexico in order to permit the Church to gain its own sense of self-identity.

Who will be acceptable to the local church already among this group? One might immediately conclude that any individual or agency who is effective in reaching a particular people should be acceptable to an established local church. The difficulty is that some members of the church may be concerned about an individual's different doctrinal views. The biblical injunction to think about each other's needs demands that we take into account, to the extent it is possible, the viewpoint of many different Christians.

What other groups are working with this people or in this area? This would have to include not only those who were living in the area, but those who are attempting to minister to the area through radio, correspondence courses, and other evangelistic methods. Can we relate to these groups? What will be the obstacles or advantages to our cooperating? As we will see in the chapters on means and methods, one method, or a group emphasizing one method, will not be the only thing needed. Again, let us remember the idea of the total *force* for evangelism. We recognize that doctrinal distinctives and views of Christian life can separate various mission agencies. However, many Christian agencies use secular tools and work alongside secular agencies, even while they reject cooperation with other *Christian* groups.

WHO HAS HAD EXPERIENCE?

Some may have had experiences with particular people. Others may have had experiences with a similar people. Still others may have had experiences that will be needed after we have selected the appropriate means and methods. The head of a good-sized denominational mission recently sought counsel from us about how his mission should select an unreached people. There are so many unreached people groups that members of the mission were wondering where they could begin. We asked him, "What groups are you reaching now?" We then asked him the next logical question, "Are there other groups similar to the ones that you're now reaching?" As it turned out, there were, indeed, other groups within the same country.

Is there a church or a mission working with this people now? If so, what has been their experience? Have they seen significant church growth? Do you have any idea why they have been effective or ineffective? For example, are there some individuals who have been particularly instrumental in reaching these people? What have they learned from their experience? What are their plans for the future? All of these questions will help us in understanding where others fit and where we fit. It is helpful to remember that these questions will always be asked with a bias, our own personal bias. This cannot be helped. If we are acting as a researcher, wondering how to reach a particular people, we will have one bias. If we are acting as a consultant to another group or agency, our bias will be different again. Finally, if we are wondering whether we should be personally involved in reaching this people (see Step 7, "Your Role"), then we will have another bias. These questions are designed to provoke understanding, not necessarily to provide specific answers.

Who has had experience with a similar people? Where there has been positive experience, why did things turn out the way they did? How can we learn more about what others have done? Are these churches or agencies candidates to be the ones to reach this particular people? Often mission agencies, in their desire to reach out to the entire world, forget to capitalize on their capabilities. As we illustrated above, instead of searching for an unreached people similar to ones they have already reached, mission agencies tend to think in geographical terms and, in one sense, have to begin all over again.

Who has had experience in this country? There are many cross-cultural barriers within a national boundary, and many times it is more difficult for those within a country to cross than those from outside a country. However, common sense speaks to the need to assess what God has been doing through his church within this national boundary, particularly among and through the citizens of this particular nation.

WHO BELIEVES HE OR SHE HAS BEEN CALLED?

God moves in mysterious ways. His Spirit touches the minds and hearts of individuals and organizations, and moves them in ways which they often do not understand themselves. As Christians we need to be sensitive to the Spirit's leading. God leads in many ways, but eventually his leading is expressed by members of his body with such simple statements as, "I believe this is what God is calling me (us) to do." If God is leading you to reach this people, one way of making certain that you are part of his total force for evangelism is to discover others who are also being led. Who has been gathering information about this people? What research agencies can tell you more about this people? Who has had a prayer burden for this particular people through the years?

THE GOING COMMUNITY

In chapter 15 we expressed the view that biblical priorities demand, first, commitment to Christ; second, a commitment to one another as members of his body; and third, a commitment to the work of Christ. Work is built upon the foundation of the first two commitments. We must change the idea of sending an individual missionary to that of a going church.

By this we mean a *community* of missionaries who have established themselves as a community *before* they move into a new culture to proclaim Christ. This, of course, is not a new idea. William Carey and his two partners considered themselves a church from the beginning of their mission and constituted themselves as one as soon as they landed. The history of missions is replete with stories of bands of men and women who knit their hearts together during the long sea voyages that carried them to the people of their calling. But in a day of jet travel and individualized, Westernized Christianity, perhaps we need to reexamine the idea that although the individual missionary may at times be an expediency, the missionary band, the *going* church is much more biblical and profitable.

We begin with the concept of gifts. *There needs to be a gifted com-*

munity. In Ephesians 4 Paul writes that gifts are given to different members of Christ's body for both the work of the ministry and the building up of the body. It is through the body that the ministry is to be carried out. Seldom, if ever, is one individual gifted for the entire missionary vocation. When moving into a new culture the missionary is faced with the diversified tasks of learning the language, building bridges into the community, maintaining facilities, understanding the culture, translating the Scriptures into the thought forms of the people, and teaching those who respond to Christ's gracious invitation. Not only are few gifted to this extent, but few are capable of understanding their own cultural presuppositions and personal biases. They need the continual corrective of those who understand both them and their culture.

This brings us to the second point. *There needs to be a self-understanding community.* Most of us are aware of the need for self-understanding and acceptance of ourselves as persons. But every person in every culture has great difficulty understanding his or her own cultural biases. These go so much deeper than simple things like table manners and forms of greeting. Different cultures *think* in different ways. To the Westerner who has been brought up on the whole concept of linear and logical thinking and who sees time as a string of events moving toward an ultimate culmination, it is incomprehensible that someone in another culture would think about time in any other way (Stewart, 1971). We need help from each other. Most of us are much more perceptive about how other people communicate and listen than we are about how we communicate and listen.

The Lausanne-sponsored discussion on Gospel and Culture[2] (LCWE, 1978) highlighted the additional *need for a hermeneutical community.* If the gospel is to be translated into a culture that is different from the culture of the missionary, the missionary must attempt to understand what the Scripture is saying to this other culture. This is no simple task. The only human control we have on how we handle the Scriptures is the continual cross-checking of what we think the Spirit is saying with what others believe is the most accurate and appropriate translation. Eventually this hermeneutical community *must* be joined by those from the culture into which the gospel is being communicated, for no matter how strongly we divest ourselves of our own cultural biases, in the end they will (and perhaps should) remain. The missionary is only the bridge between two cultures.

2. See the Willowbank Report on *Gospel and Culture* (LCWE, 1978).

The going church must be a caring community. Depending upon the circumstances of the situation, there will need to be a division of labor based upon necessity for the situation and for the gifts that they have been given. There have been too many missionary situations for which the major task of the missionary was to stay alive in a hostile environment because there was no one else there to establish a support base. Even more important is the need for a fellowship. The missionary community cares not only by giving physical assistance but by giving spiritual comfort and admonition.

There needs to be a witnessing community, for witness is carried out not just by what we say, but in how we live. We witness to the power of Christ in our own lives by how we care for one another. The people in the culture to which we are called may have great difficulty understanding our thought forms and even our expression of the gospel. But they cannot help but see the love that we have for one another. Time and again we have heard missionaries testify about how differently they were viewed when they had children or when their parents visited them. They were seen as people in community, and the community that they were attempting to reach saw for the first time that they too were people in relationship.

Finally there is a need for *a researching and understanding community*—a community which is listening to what this new culture is saying and discussing the implications of the gospel for this new situation.

All of these characteristics can be learned in a missionary situation, though the obstacles are very great. Is it not a much more biblical and effective way to establish these relationships *before* starting a new work? Once such a community is established in a field situation, it in turn can accept new individual members because it will have already established itself as a caring community.

It is encouraging to discover a number of mission agencies who have successfully adopted this approach. The Agape Program of Campus Crusade for Christ is training people as teams. Overseas Crusades is establishing a team as they move into new areas. The key is to become committed as a team *before* leaving for the field rather than making a commitment after being in the field.

Different peoples require different forms of communication to understand the gospel. The missionary of the 1800s usually came from a large, extended family and an environment where community life was part of living. All over the United States and Canada today we read about new efforts to establish Christian communities. Evidently we have lost something which we desire to find again. Rather than export our own sense of loneliness and alienation, would we not do well to use the occasion of our going to reestablish a community for ourselves and for the people to whom we go?

HOW TO BEGIN

Having said all of this, where do we begin? There are so many variables, so much to consider. Some will be approaching the problem from the viewpoint of their individual calling. Others will be approaching the question of selection as members of an agency. What do we do?

The answer is found in what we have called "planning strategies for evangelism, the ten-step process on which this book is based." (Let us again remind you that these ten steps are meant to demonstrate the planning process, not necessarily the evangelistic endeavor itself.)

Actually this entire process can be used at each step as illustrated in Figure 16-2.

Here we have tried to show the cycles within the cycle. It is an iterative process. We begin by defining what we think our mission should be in the same way one proposes a thesis. Let us suppose that

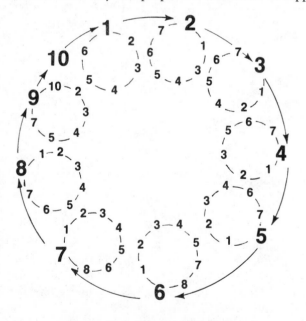

Figure 16-2   The Iterative Cycle

you tentatively decide to *define the mission* as reaching the Javanese on the island of Java in Indonesia. With this tentative thesis you move on to the next step.

You *describe the people* as best you can. You discover that there are approximately seventy million Javanese, about sixty million of whom live in a rural setting. They have a religious mixture of Islam and traditional religions. You conduct research from secular and religious sources about the country of Indonesia where the Javanese are found. You learn that Indonesia is a country of thousands of islands spread over almost three thousand miles with many different cultures and a central government operating out of Djakarta. You gather further information about the country through secular and religious sources.

With this brief survey you move on to look at the *force for evangelism*. Using the *World Christian Encyclopedia* you find that there is a large church which succeeded the early Dutch Reformed Church. You also find a sprinkling of smaller churches and a number of mission agencies involved on Java. From the *World Christian Encyclopedia* you also get some indication as to the degree of growth among this particular people.

Probing further for *means and methods* you read some of the literature about cross-cultural attempts to evangelize the Javanese, as well as attempts by local churches. You learn that radio broadcasts using the traditional Javanese music were first introduced in the 1970s. You discover that some of the local churches have been effective in reaching rural Javanese in non-Muslim villages, but that there has been little impact on villages which have a strong influence of Islam.

Putting all this together you *define your approach*. You decide to concentrate in East Java in the area of Malang where there has been some responsiveness and a Bible school.

With this general approach in mind you *anticipate outcomes*. You decide that a church could possibly be planted and established by your mission in three years, and that you might be able to expect three additional local churches in five years.

Now comes the question of *your role*. Remember, planning strategies is not primarily about what others should do. We are attempting to find *our* role in God's economy. You ask questions about your agency or group. How will they be received by the people? How will they be received by the Christians who are already there? Do you have the ability to carry out this approach? The necessary resources?

Let us interject here that in any of the previous steps you might have decided that this was not the place for you to work. For example, as you looked at the force for evangelism, you might have decided that there are others who could do a much better job than you. As you looked at necessary means and methods, you might have concluded that the ones that were needed were not the kind that you were prepared to carry out. When you analyzed anticipated outcomes, you might have concluded that you really could not see any possible outcomes. Or, when the time came for you to examine your own role, you might have decided that you were not the one or the agency to reach this particular people. In other words, at any one of these steps you may have narrowed the definition of your mission by *eliminating* the Javanese.

Assuming that in your preliminary thinking you still felt good about reaching the rural Javanese of Eastern Java, briefly sketch out how you would go about it. *Make plans.* See what these tell you, what further insights they give you.

Since this is a plan for planning, you have already carried out the next step—*act.*

The final step is *evaluate.* What do you think about your plan? Are you the one to do this? Look at the mission again. What do you see now? Perhaps it looks good. Notice that the circle has closed and you are back to defining the mission. "But," you might respond, "I've already done that." Here again we need to see the repetitiveness of the cycle. You obviously do not have enough information to evangelize the rural Javanese in the area of Malang. All you have really done is to make a decision to keep probing and learning. Depending on who you are and how much you already know about Indonesia, you might decide to invest a considerable amount of time in further research. You might decide that it would be worthwhile to send a survey team to Indonesia. Again you would go through the same cycle that we have described above, only in this next step you would have learned a great deal more. In fact, one could imagine that you or your agency could send four people to Malang only to discover two years later that you had chosen the wrong people to reach. "What a waste of time!" someone might exclaim. No, we are always learning. As we have pointed out earlier, no one can predict the future. We can at best only approximate our understanding of God's will and attempt faithfully to carry it out on the basis of our understanding. It is far better to have gotten to the point of knowing that you were the wrong agency to reach a particular group of people and to withdraw than to press on regardless of what you now understand. We know that this is foreign to much thinking and practice, but we maintain that in God's business there are no successes or failures. There is only obedience.

CHAPTER 17

The Organizations Available

WHY PARA-CHURCH ORGANIZATIONS ARE NEEDED

*T*he phrase "para-church" has come to mean an organization made up of Christians which is doing work for the Lord outside the direct control of the local church or denomination. There has been, and probably will continue to be, considerable debate as to whether this is an appropriate term. There are those who would believe that there should be no distinction between the local expression of Christ's body and those who have been set aside for a specific task. In the previous chapter we recommended the idea of the going community. At the same time we recognize that this community, especially if it is to attempt a cross-cultural mission, must be made up of a special group of Christians. We cannot randomly choose people from a fellowship in a local church and say that they are the ones for the task. There is the "set apartness" of Acts 13:2 which is an important part of the total work of the Church.

The para-church differs basically from the local church in its goals. The local church has two conflicting goals: the goal of building up the body of Christ and nurturing one another, and the goal of sending forth those into the work of the Church. This nurturing includes the care of the "walking wounded." These conflicting goals can never be reconciled within the local church.[1]

However, any other Christian organization is formed for a specific purpose, and by definition must select Christians from local fellowships who are specifically gifted for the task. Regardless of what one may call such an organization, there is a difference between it and the local church. A mission agency cannot take its walking wounded with it. Certainly the mission will have to care for those who are wounded in the midst of the task. But ultimately, if they do not recover, they will have to be returned to the nurturing environment of the local fellowship.

ORGANIZATIONAL STRUCTURES

If the force for evangelism is to be a going church, a group of Christians in relationship to one another, committed to a common task, then the members of this church will need to find some formal way in which to relate to one another. If their ability to express the love of Christ as a community is important to the evangelistic task, then we need to understand how such a relationship can be formed. There are a variety of relationships in any organization, and there are a number of theoretical models which describe these relationships which are, in many respects, like an organization. Christian executives spend a great deal of time considering the type of organization that would best suit the task to which they are committed. One gets the feeling that if we could find just the *right* organizations, we would have an answer to all of our difficulties. We need some way of thinking about an organization, some way of picturing these relationships.

One model that is helpful in understanding the force for evangelism is based upon the purpose and goals of an organization. This model is particularly useful for thinking about reaching another people with the gospel, because it focuses on why an organization exists (Dayton and Engstrom, 1979).

The *boundaries* of this model (Figure 17-1) are established by an organization's purposes and goals. As we will see later, purposes are why we attempt to do something. Goals are the specific measurable

1. In *Strategy For Leadership* (1979) Ed Dayton and Ted Engstrom point out that this is the reason why all the leadership and management of the local church is so extremely difficult. Because of this conflict of goals, the local church is the most complex of all organizations.

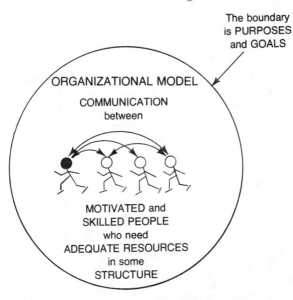

Figure 17-1   An Organizational Model

events we hope will come about. This model focuses not on what the organization is going to do, but on what it wants to accomplish.

Motivated and skilled people who have *adequate resources,* a good *communication network,* and an *appropriate structure* are needed within this boundary of purposes and goals.

Boundaries

Once we have clearly stated our purpose, we have taken the first major step. It is to this purpose that we call others who have the same sense of God's calling them to accomplish something for him. In our particular case we are talking about a mission, the purpose of which is to proclaim salvation in Jesus Christ and to call people into fellowship with him. However, purposes need to be further defined so others know specifically what we intend to do. We mentioned earlier the mission executive who stated that the goal of his mission was "To lay Japan at the feet of Christ." This is a high and noble ideal, but it is expressed in such broad terms that it is meaningless. We will cover this in detail in Step 6—"Anticipated Outcomes." Suffice it to say here that the clearer we can be in stating our goals and purposes, the more likely we are to attract motivated and skilled people.

Skilled and motivated people

As others have pointed out, it is much easier to attract people who are already motivated than to motivate people to a new undertaking.[2] We attract motivated people by clearly stating our purposes and goals. In this case our purpose is to reach a particular unreached people with the gospel of Christ by clearly defining that these are the people that we intend to reach and these are the ways we intend to reach them. We will attract those who want to reach them through these methods and, conversely, not attract those who are not interested. An organization that views itself as primarily involved in carrying out a function, such as a Christian radio broadcast, will attract the right people by being very clear about its purposes and goals. A good example of how clear goals and purposes attract and motivate people is the experience of Wycliffe Bible Translators. Wycliffe's general purpose is to make the Scriptures available to all peoples. But they reduce this to the language of a particular people. The goal then becomes very clear: "To reduce the language of the _____ people into writing and to translate the New Testament into this language by _____." The fact that Wycliffe, as of 1979, had more members in its organization than any other cross-cultural mission is the natural result of clearly stated purposes and goals.

But people must not only be motivated, they must also be gifted and skilled.[3] This means that they must have the adequate training and experience. It does little good to have people with willing hearts if they are unable to carry out what they would like to do. A great desire to drive an automobile does not insure that an inexperienced driver will be able to start the car and keep it on the road.

Adequate resources

Motivated and gifted people will not be able to reach their goals unless they have adequate resources. These resources include finances, materials, prayer support, and a variety of physical needs.

Communication

Communication between human beings is much more difficult than most of us recognize. There are a variety of ways to communicate:

2. See Maslow (1972).
3. We are purposely not distinguishing between gifts and skills here. "Natural" abilities, learned skills, and spiritual gifts are all equally important.

speech, writing, body language, symbols, appearance, actions, and so forth. These appear in different ways in different people. People have different needs for different types of communication. Devising a way of keeping people informed of their progress against their goals and their relationships to others is a key ingredient. If there is a group of motivated, gifted people who have adequate resources to carry out the task, a good communication system between them, and a common purpose and specifically identified goals, then there is a high probability that they will reach their goals.

Organizational structure

An effective organization must have good communication, and this means that some form of structure or organization will be needed.

There are a wide variety of organizational models.[4] In some cultures decisions are reached by group consensus. Such a structure will be different from one in which decisions are made unilaterally by recognized leaders. Some of the attributes of an effective structure include: a clear picture of the lines of authority, responsibility, and communication, a way of defining the different tasks of the individuals in relationship to the group's goals, a system of evaluating and reporting progress against goals, and a way of handling problems within the group.

In selecting the force for evangelism, we need to go further than individual gifts and roles. We need to describe some form of structure. The model that we have described is a useful tool in formulating such a structure. Do not forget to test any proposed structure against the culture in which it is operating. A major problem in establishing Christ's Church within different cultures has been the missionaries' insistence that their cultural norms are and should be normative for the culture in which they seek to communicate Christ's love. There is a high likelihood that the resulting church will tend to model itself after the community from which they heard the Good News. There are too many cases where when the mission withdrew, or turned the structure over to the church, the church members felt it necessary to fill all of the roles in the structure that was brought to them with their own members. The weight of carrying such a structure is often deadly to the life of a newly formed church. The *ideal* structure would be a structure that was very similar to organizational structures already within the society. Often this will mean that the structural form of an organization within a country will be quite different from the structural form of the country of the cross-cultural missionary.

4. See E. Dale (1967).

PRIORITIES FOR THE CHRISTIAN ORGANIZATION

Earlier in this chapter and in chapter 15 we laid out the three levels of Christian priority. It follows that these three levels of priority—commitment to God and Christ, comitment to the body of Christ, and commitment to the work of Christ—should be part of an organization. Christian organizations are unique. The forces working within an organization normally come from the force of one's position or the force of power belonging to each individual. But there is a "third force" operative in Christian organizations (p. 28). It is the power of the Holy Spirit. In a way unlike that in any other each individual within a Christian organization is guided by this common Third Force.

There is a common allegiance to something higher than the organization itself. Secular organizations may have an allegiance to the profession which transcends or modifies the allegiance to the organization, but Christians have an ultimate allegiance. This ultimate allegiance can be used positively or negatively. Too often Christian organizations use this allegiance in a manipulative way. They place demands upon their members which put them in a position of being tools rather than people. Christians have a biblical model for what an organization should be like: "Those parts of the body that seem to be weaker are indispensable, the parts that we think are less honorable we treat with special honor" (I Cor. 12:23). There is no room here for an organizational structure which assumes that leaders give directions and followers carry out the tasks without regard to their relationships to each other.[5]

THE EXISTING ORGANIZATION

Up until now we have been discussing the force for evangelism as though it were a wide open and unsettled question. We have discussed organizations as though they had not yet been brought into existence. Often, however, those conducting the strategy to reach a particular

5. In recent years, modern secular management theory has been discovering what Christians should have known all along. Harry Levinson and other management theorists who emphasize a behavioral view of management have pointed out the effectiveness of people in their work is tremendously dependent upon how they feel about one another. Organizations are more and more being viewed as organisms. The machine-like model of the Industrial Revolution is being rapidly discarded. For a good discussion on the behavioral approach to leadership and management, see Levinson (1968) and Herzberg (1966).

people are already in an organization. We will discuss the role of the individual and the organization in the total strategy in chapter 29. However, there are some things about organizations which can be noted here in the context of identifying the force for evangelism.

Any organization which is seeking to determine if it should reach a particular unreached people or how it can go about reaching an unreached people needs to ask all of the questions asked above. It is just as important to decide that this organization is *not* God's chosen instrument to reach a particular people as it is to decide that it is God's chosen instrument.

If after all of this research an organization decides that it is not the one that God is calling to a particular people, then it needs to pass on the thinking and research it has done to others who may be more qualified. This is a key idea. If we think of ourselves as being part of a total body, then we need to believe that our research can be used by others.

AN ORGANIZATIONAL CHECKLIST

There are a number of questions that an organization can ask about itself in seeking to decide whether it is the organization qualified to go to a particular people.

1. Do we have enough information about this people? Do we really understand them?

2. Have we adequate information at hand? Have we done adequate research?

3. Are we already working in this country?

4. If we are not working in this country, do we understand the complexities of working within this particular national boundary?

5. Have we ever worked with a similar people, a similar culture? What have we learned from this? Were we effective? If we were not effective, why do we think we will be effective now?

6. Do we have people available, or will we have to train them?

7. Do we have adequate mature leadership to move into the field?

8. What would be the size of the group that we think will be needed to reach this particular people?

9. How long do we think it will take before a church is planted?

10. How long do we think it will take before that church has the ability to evangelize (E-1) the people within its own group?

11. Are we able to expand the present organization to carry this additional responsibility? Should we move from the place where we are now working? Is this an opportunity for withdrawal?

12. Can we expect a wide base of support from those who give us financial support?

13. Will we be able to communicate what we are doing in such a way as to build the necessary prayer support?

14. Will our present structure fit this new need or will we have to change our structure?

15. Will any organizational changes meet a great deal of resistance, or will they be welcomed? Are we able to change?

16. Will we be able to work with others who are working in the country or amongst this people? Will we be welcomed by the local church that may be there or others working among this people?

17. Is there another organization that can do just as good a job as we could? Why are we the ones? Have we really sought the mind of the Spirit? Is there a general consensus among our group based upon prayer and meditation?

A THIRD WORLD AGENCY

We are attempting to see the world through Western eyes, to understand what we, as part of Christ's Church, are called upon to do. This naturally raises the question as to whether there is a group or organization from the Third World who could be used. There is a great deal of interest among local churches in supporting Third World missionaries.[6]

We in the West naturally tend to look for cross-cultural mission agencies that are similar to ours. It is too early to tell whether this Western view of how missions should be supported and organized is appropriate in other non-Western countries. Some agencies indicate that we should not be concerned with Western structural concepts. As an example, the Missionary Prayer Band in India originally was

6. The existence of a growing number of Third World mission agencies was first pointed out by Wong, Larson and Pentecost in *Missions from the Third World* (1973). For further reading in the status of Third World missionaries see Nelson (1976) and Clark (1971).

founded to pray for non-Christians. This prayer naturally led to people being sent forth from the group as itinerant evangelists. There was little formal structure. To put it another way, if one finds within a particular country, such as India, a wide diversity of cultures which can be physically reached by available transportation systems among which one can live in a manner very similar to the culture from which one has come, then the type of organizational structure required will be quite different from that of the overseas mission.

At the end of 1970, the vast majority of Third World missions were diaspora missions, Japanese going to Japanese-speaking people, Koreans going to Korean people, Hindi-speaking Indians going to Hindi-speaking Indians. A Western agency needs to give careful consideration as to whether the mission team will be able to come into a particular country without going to the major expense of transporting Westerners to a culture and a life-style that may be considerably more foreign to them than for someone from within the same country (Wong, et al., 1973).

MISSIONS IN PARTNERSHIP

One way forward is through a concept of partnership in missions, to *assume* from the very beginning that our agency cannot go it alone and that one of the tasks of the mission is to enable the force for evangelism which already exists within a country to be brought together. This is a difficult role to play. It is hard to take leadership and still assume the kind of servant role that is required if natural suspicions about an outsider are to be allayed.

SUPPOSE THERE IS NO MISSION AGENCY

As we begin the decade of the 1980s, there is a growing dissatisfaction among many young people with existing mission organizations. As we discuss in the next chapter, becoming a missionary is a difficult undertaking. The policies and procedures that govern so many existing agencies, their concern about their ability to raise the necessary support, and the complexities and tasks that they are already undertaking make it difficult for them to easily venture out into new fields.

The task of beginning a new mission agency is not insurmountable. The experience of the Churches of Christ who send missionaries directly from their church is a good beginning point (Elkins, 1974). There are great weaknesses and great strengths, too, of this particular system. Probably the greatest strength is the warm and supportive home base provided by a local church which is also operating as a mission board. The major weakness of the Churches of Christ approach, and the problem that faces every new agency, is the lack of knowledge and experience. Too often a fervent heart replaces a fertile mind. The task of cross-cultural missions *is* a difficult one. The major difficulty with forming a new organization is the absence of people who have experience in forming and leading organizations. How often we reinvent the wheel! The way to begin is to consult with those who have been there and then to describe an ideal organization five to ten years in the future. The ideal will seldom stay constant but it helps to think about the future (organization).

Our counsel for those seeking to start a new mission agency is not easy to accept. It involves a great deal of homework, and learning what others have learned. We would suggest that going through the planning process described by the ten steps in this book is an excellent way to begin. We put the problem in its correct perspective by focusing in on a particular people and then attempting to see what would be necessary in order to reach that people. But before launching out with a new organization, we strongly recommend reading a survey of what others are already doing. Fortunately, for the potential missionary from North America, the *Mission Handbook: North American Protestant Ministries Overseas* (Dayton, 1976 and Wilson, 1980) is a valuable resource. Many new and successful agencies have begun in the past ten years. Far more have failed before they got off the ground.

It has also been our experience that established mission agencies are very open to well-organized programs proposed by those outside the agency. Often these agencies have incorporated such programs into their overall structure.

WHERE DO WE GO FOR MORE INFORMATION?

Where do we go for more information about what others are doing? How do we discover all we need to know? Before asking this question, we need to ask: "How much information do we need?" The answer may seem rather trite: "Just enough"—just enough information to help us to move ahead in our planning and in our actions. Planning strategies for evangelism is a *process*. No one can accurately predict the future.

Any goals that we set to reach a particular people are, at best, statements of faith. Our information will always be imperfect. Plans cannot be made just once. They need to be continually remade as God shows us new light and as we gain new knowledge.

CHAPTER 18

Recruiting and Training

THERE ARE NOT ENOUGH MISSIONARIES

*T*he population of the world in 1980 is 4 billion 200 million and growing at the rate of 1.8 percent per year. At that rate, there will be 6 billion 214 million persons in the world by the year 2000.

The number of people who claim to be Christians in the world is somewhere between 1 billion and 1.2 billion. As best we can tell, Christians also multiply at the rate of 1.8 percent per year. Thus by the year 2000 there will be 4 billion 666 million people in the world who do not acknowledge Jesus Christ as Lord and Savior. There are fifty to fifty-five thousand Protestant missionaries, and approximately forty-five thousand missionaries from the Roman Catholic Church. The growth rate of both Protestant and Roman Catholic missionaries lags behind both the growth of the Christian population and the growth of the total world population.

Over 2 billion non-Christians in the world are separated from any Christian witness by cultural barriers. In other words, there are no Christians who live in their midst who are potentially able to communicate the Good News.

THE DAY OF THE WESTERN MISSIONARY IS NOT OVER

There are still thousands of people groups that are only going to be reached by those with material resources such as are found among the Christians of Western nations. The demand to make disciples of all nations has not been withdrawn from this group. Often the national boundaries which are closed to citizens of one Western country are not closed to citizens of another Western country. In addition there is a need to be faithful, waiting in anticipation for the days when new opportunities arise. As these pages were being written, vast changes in China, after thirty years of hostility to the West, were going on. This is a good example of our need to be prepared.

Even if mission agencies from the West focused only on countries open to them, the number of unreached peoples within *these* countries far exceeds these agencies' present potential to reach them. It is estimated that 200,000 missionaries from the United States and Canada could effectively be put to work by the year 2000.

What would it take to have 200,000 effective Protestant cross-cultural missionaries by the year 2000? Really not very much. There were, in 1976, about two thousand new missionaries entering the total North American force each year. That number would have to be increased to ten thousand a year. The amount given to North American Protestant missionaries in 1975 was $656,000,000. By the year 2000 that amount would have to increase at an average rate of 7.5 percent per year to $3,452,000,000 in order to support the missionary force.

The number of mission agencies would not have to grow at all. Of the 620 agencies that were listed in the eleventh edition of the *Mission Handbook* (Dayton, 1976), there were only thirteen agencies with more than 500 North American personnel overseas. That number would have to increase to about 175 agencies. At the InterVarsity triennial missions conference at Urbana, Illinois, in December, 1976, over nine thousand young people indicated a willingness to serve overseas. Three years before, five thousand expressed a desire to serve.

Some mission agencies are already growing at the necessary rate. The Southern Baptist Foreign Board and Wycliffe Bible Translators increased from 4,707 in 1972 to 5,360 in 1975, or a 13.9 percent increase per year. At this growth rate these two agencies alone will have 122,000 staff in the year 2000.

From 2.9 million members, the Mormons fielded twenty thousand missionaries in 1975. At their present growth rate they will easily have one hundred thousand by A.D. 2000. The Mormons *expect* every Mormon young man to serve a two-year mission assignment, supported by himself and/or his family, *before* he begins a vocation. If there are 10 million mission-minded Christian families in the United States alone, and each one has a son under twenty-one years of age, 10 percent or one million would be short-term missionaries today. Include a daughter, and you have two million.

CURRENT MISSIONARIES ARE NOT FOCUSING ON THE TASK

In 1975 only 25 percent of the North American mission force was attempting to plant churches (Dayton, 1976). Dr. Ralph Winter has estimated that only about 5 percent of those missionaries were doing pioneer work—work among people where there was no existing church. In other words, 95 percent of the North American missionaries were working among the one billion people who were in groups that already have a church, while only 5 percent were attempting to reach the two billion "hidden people" (Winter, 1978; Douglas, 1975).

SOME MISSION AGENCIES SHOULD WITHDRAW

If a mission agency in a particular country is primarily involved in the support of a national church rather than church planting or evangelism, then one must conclude that either the agency has turned from church planting to church support or else it somehow believes that if the agency makes the church strong enough, the church will be able to do the job of evangelism within the country. In the early 1970s, few evangelical or faith missions advocated this latter view. However, more and more mission magazines and pamphlets are attempting to educate their constituencies that this is the best way forward. This is a disturbing trend. In some ways it is very natural, for if the mission has been effective in establishing a church, that church ought to be able to do the task. But why is it necessary for *a foreign mission* to carry out that task? Why are not more agencies withdrawing from a particular field? (As used here, "field" means a particular people group.)

The answer can perhaps be found in the difficulty that an established mission agency has in renewing itself on a particular field. All organizations tend to organize themselves in a way which will create stability. This is basically built into the human system. Each of us would prefer the "ideal organizational structure" which would permit us to get on with the job. A concrete structure is preferred over a constantly changing structure. As we seek organizational stability, it is very easy to make "comity arrangements" between individuals and sub-groups that will effectively build walls around the things that we are doing. Evaluation of original goals is discouraged. Work becomes more important than the purpose for which it was originally instituted. Newcomers into the organization soon learn that in order to move ahead they had best defer to the wisdom and age of older members.

The most stabilizing influence, the group most resistant to change, is the *field* force of any agency. These are people who have learned to cope with situations the hard way. After learning a language, learning a culture, learning to survive in a hostile environment (climatic and social), it is not easy to adapt to change on a *continuous* basis. The model of those who have gone before is easily accepted as the best way of doing things. It is difficult enough to work in a strange environment without introducing the idea of continuously adapting to a new environment. Thus, *very few mission agencies plan for success.* Very few count on the fact that their efforts are going to result in a growing dynamic church which can take over the work. They seem to assume that they will *not* be successful. Their churches will *not* become self-supporting, self-propagating, or self-governing. The idea that the missionary is there to "work himself out of a job" is beautiful in theory, but often excruciatingly difficult in practice.

Here then is the challenge to ourselves and to others who plan to be in the business of evangelizing some part of the world:

1. Is the agency increasing or decreasing the amount of outreach to unreached peoples?

2. If it is decreasing, should it change its program?

3. If it sees itself with a strategy of evangelism that in practice boils down to developing a local church, is it scripturally valid and politically sound?

4. If such an analysis shows that this agency is not doing evangelism with the unreached, who should?

5. Should the agency withdraw to regroup and replan?

GOD IS AS INTERESTED IN REACHING PEOPLE AS IN SENDING MISSIONARIES

A major dilemma to the mission enterprise today is that we in the West have become educated to support missionaries rather than missions. The majority of the forty thousand North American missionaries are supported as individuals or couples. In most cases the agency involved has worked out the formula for the amount of funds missionaries will need in the country in which they serve. Local churches and individuals have been invited to participate in supplying funds for this "support." Part of this encouragement has been through the medium of the person of the missionary himself or herself. The pros and cons of "deputation work" have been widely discussed elsewhere, and it is not our purpose here to evaluate the historical effectiveness of this means of finding an answer to the mission task. But it is an historical fact that there are thousands of missionaries who have adequate support to get them to the field and maintain them while they are there, *but do not have enough funds to carry out the task for which they have been sent.*[1]

This equating of mission with the missionary conveys a subtle message: God is more interested in missionaries than he is in missions. It is our contention that God is just as interested in reaching people as he is in sending missionaries.

There is a real need for mission agencies (and missionaries) not only to count the total cost of their strategies but to present this total cost to those from whom they are expecting financial and prayer support. The type of planning that has been advocated in the ten steps outlined in this book should result in a very comprehensive picture of what is being attempted. This picture needs to be shared with boldness.

Some mission executives have argued that the local churches are already having difficulty in supporting the individual missionary. They wonder how any church can possibly increase its support to cover project funds. However, the experience of the second half of the 1970s indicated that there was no shortage of funds if the need was adequately presented. World Vision International, a Christian service agency, raised more funds for overseas work through existing local churches by presenting needs and projects than any other agency did in presenting the needs of people (missionaries).

---

1. Another interesting by-product of this approach is the difficulty of the agency to find funds for the overall management of the task. Field missionaries become jealous of giving "our money" to headquarters!

In the same way that clear purposes and sharply focused goals motivate people to take part in the mission task, so these definitive purposes and goals will attract the needed financial and prayer support.

THOUSANDS OF YOUNG PEOPLE
ARE WILLING TO BE TRAINED

Thousands of young people are willing to be trained, but the mission agencies are not equipped to train them. We mentioned above that at the Urbana 1976 collegiate mission conference, nine thousand young people indicated a willingness to serve overseas, and yet previous history shows that only a small percentage of that nine thousand will ever attempt to become involved in overseas service. Why is this so? The calling of "missionary" is not at present accompanied by a well-defined career path. This lack of a clear career path is the result of many things. There are some Christians who do not believe that much more than a "definite call" is required. But the major obstacle appears to be a lack of commitment by those involved in the missionary vocation to prepare well-equipped men and women. A major difficulty is the failure of more mission agencies to set aside personnel who are called and qualified to train others.

Few agencies have training programs that meet their own needs. An exception, and a worthwhile model, is Wycliffe Bible Translators, which not only trains people in language acquisition, but puts them through an environmental stress situation which attempts to foresee the real experience. (It should be noted that Wycliffe has the advantage of not having to train their staff to work in a particular language.)

There are evidently few nearby cross-cultural experiences available in English. Training in the United States or Canada does not give the same result because the candidate can easily step back into his or her own culture. At the same time, there is no apparent problem with asking young people to meet high requirements. For example, the Christian and Missionary Alliance requires that a missionary spend two years in a pastorate. From another view, in 1977 thirty-seven thousand individuals in the United States received a Ph.D. Most of these did this on their own, working in the formal educational system. Evidently, there was adequate motivation to keep working years past the B.A. The problem seems to be that churches, agencies, and schools are not agreed on the need and method of certification. (It is worth noting that most of those Ph.D.s had to learn, at least to read, *two* languages.)

One mission professor stated:

> There's still a prevailing notion that one can major in any subject in college or seminary and be a good missionary. No special courses are necessary! Most leading missions have a minimum requirement—one year of Bible—nothing is said of missions! I think this is a great mistake. To go overseas without missionary anthropology, cross-cultural communication, area studies, missionary life at work—to say nothing of the history of missions and non-Christian religions, is an act of consummate folly![2]

THERE IS NO JOB MORE DIFFICULT TO GET THAN THAT OF A MISSIONARY

This is the natural result of what we have discussed above. Most people assume that anyone who wants to become a missionary can easily do so. To show the real difficulty, let us imagine that becoming an engineer was analogous to becoming a missionary. A young person decides that he or she would like to become an engineer. He or she wisely starts asking different companies who utilize engineers about what he or she should do in order to be an engineer. One company tells him or her that all he or she needs is a one-year history course. Another company tells him or her, "No, what you really need is seven years of training in the engineering sciences." The third organization responds that all that is needed is a strong desire to be an engineer.

Our prospective engineer gives up on the organizations and decides to ask some of the universities. He or she finds that there are about two hundred and fifty graduate and undergraduate schools that offer engineering somewhere in their curriculum, but he or she can find only one school in the whole United States and Canada that teaches nothing but engineering at a graduate level and only twenty-three that teach nothing but engineering at the undergraduate level. Comparing their courses, he or she discovers there is a great deal of discrepancy as to what engineering is all about.

Further discouraged, our engineering candidate turns to friends and members of the local church. "What is engineering all about?" the candidate asks. Some say that engineering is a very exotic profession with lots of excitement. Others say that engineering is hard work. Still others reply that as far as they can see, being an engineer means giving up a lot.

2. J. Herbert Kane in a letter to Edward R. Dayton dated April 4, 1979.

This is almost a direct analogy to becoming a missionary. There are literally thousands of young people who have written letters seeking to find out how to become cross-cultural missionaries. Something is wrong.[3]

MISSIONARY TRAINING IS EQUIVALENT TO MEDICAL TRAINING

Acquiring the job of a missionary is extremely difficult. There is probably no profession which requires a higher level of commitment, education, and spiritual insight. Yet, there is probably no profession that has paid less attention to its potential members. The difficulty is not that there are no graduates who desire an overseas Christian career, nor graduate schools interested in training missionaries. The difficulty is that the profession is not geared for on-the-job training. The result is too many poorly trained missionaries, too many talented men and women who are challenged to go but never make it overseas, too many complaints from national churches that missions and missionaries are insensitive to their situations. How could this be rectified? What would be a good model?

As a point of departure, let us examine the training required to become a medical doctor. After completing undergraduate work in "premed" the student enters a three-year medical school associated with a teaching hospital. Here there is a daily mixture of classroom, laboratory experience, and direct experience with patients. As the student advances in training, he or she is given more and more opportunity to work with patients on a one-to-one basis. At the end of this time the person graduates and is certified as an M.D. However, the education is far from over. The next step is an internship, actually working as a doctor in the hospital under the supervision of other doctors. This normally takes from one to two years. But still the education is not completed. Before the doctor can move out to practice in society, he or she spends another one to two years as a resident in a hospital. Here he or she supervises the work of interns and gains further insight into the medical profession. It is our contention that the "doctor of souls" requires just as much preparation as the one who cares for the body.

3. A number of people are struggling to overcome this situation. Intercristo, an agency involved in attempting to match up individuals with mission opportunities, now publishes a semi-annual *Directory of Christian Work Opportunities*. Many undergraduate schools are beginning to offer mission courses that include a cross-cultural experience.

When one draws analogies for the mission profession from the medical profession, one equates the hospital with the field or the cross-cultural environment. Herein lies our first major obstacle. There is a tremendous need for the equivalent of teaching hospitals within missions. Mission agencies need to accept as part of their God-given task the on-the-field training of younger missionary candidates. The sad fact is that although many mission agencies have excellent opportunities to do this as a result of the growing number of short-term missionaries, most mission agencies, and particularly the missionary staff on the field, view these short-termers as an annoyance.

But there is still another difficulty, and this is one of perception. In our discussion above we have used a number of terms to designate where someone is in his or her medical experience—premed, medical student, intern, resident, practicing doctor. These terms are all understood by those in the West. We do not expect medical students to perform major operations.

Our familiarity with the word "missionary" has hindered its accurate definition. Since the word is derived from the word "mission," the meaning we assign to it will directly reflect our concept of what is involved in the mission of the Church. If one believes that all activity carried out in the name of Christ is the mission of the Church, then it follows that anyone so involved is a missionary. However, if one believes that the primary mission of the Church is the propagation of the faith, then the only missionary is the one so involved. But in none of this is there any indication of level or degree of experience and/or responsibility of the missionary. Most students of missiology would be quick to say that becoming an effective cross-cultural communicator of the gospel requires skill, training, and experience. And yet we have no way of describing and naming such levels of experience beyond indicating how many "terms of service" the individual may have served overseas. The adoption of a more descriptive system is long overdue, in terms of the individual in the missionary force, the constituency supporting that force, and the management of the force. The adoption of adjectives such as the student, candidate, apprentice, assistant, associate, and senior, would give us at least six levels of training and experience. These terms would introduce the idea that there is an *entry point* into this honorable profession, and that there are higher levels toward which to move and toward which to work. Such an understanding would have an immediate impact on the missionary candidate, the missionary, and those who support him or her. If it were well understood that one does not expect an assistant missionary to produce results, but rather to be in the position of a learner or an apprentice, then the drive to prove to oneself and others that one is really filling a God-given call would not produce the load of guilt that is found in so many young missionaries. The more experienced missionaries, in turn, would be able to see themselves as trainers. Too often, senior missionaries seem to deal with newcomers as though the only way they will ever learn is through the "school of hard knocks." One of the tasks of the senior missionary would be to train assistant and associate missionaries.

Second, viewing the missionaries in this way would also indicate the need for continuing education. There is much to be learned from the world of books, the world of discussion, the world of reading what other people have done before; in other words, the academic world of the graduate school. If it were recognized that every assistant or associate missionary should be spending part of his or her furlough time in such ongoing education, then the younger missionary would not feel guilty about having to justify the cost or the time involved in such education.

Third, the adoption of such distinctions would encourage the mission agency to think of field assignments in terms of teams, rather than just individuals. It would be logical that if a new field was going to be opened, one would send a senior missionary who in turn would be supported by a given number of missionaries, associate missionaries, and perhaps assistant missionaries. This would also help the field missionaries, who have a tendency to be self-sufficient, to see the need to relate to each other. It would be an unheard of thing for an assistant or associate missionary to be sent to open up a new work by himself or herself. Either their qualifications would be such that they would be promoted to a higher level at a very young age, or the work would not be started until a sufficiently qualified person could be found. This again would relieve a great deal of guilt that comes from failure of young men and women to carry out the task that might seem very simple to others who have done it before, but which is very difficult if there is no one there to coach.

This approach to the missionary task opens up an entirely new world for recruiting and missionary education and training. By recognizing that it is impossible to make the leap from layperson to professional missionary in the brief span of a year, missions would give their potential candidates a career path to follow. Local churches too would have a better understanding and would be able to support their own people.

What follows is an example of how this might work:

Let us begin by accepting missionaries not as candidates (who may or may not make it) but as accepted apprentices. They could enter the program at any time during or after their junior year in college. They would be taken under care by a mission agency in the same way that some churches take candidates for the ministry under care. At the same time they could be taken under the care of their local church. The agency would agree to give them spiritual, financial, and educational guidance, and the apprentice would agree to abide by the regulations of the agency. Next, the agency would design a program which assumes that it will take at least eight years before the candidate moves through apprenticeship and internship to full missionary status. During this time the intern would receive additional education, on-the-job training, and exposure to a wide variety of cross-cultural experiences.

On the basis of having accepted him or her into the program, the agency then encourages individuals and churches to support this person in the same way they would support a person overseas. The agency would educate donors to understand that part of their support is to put missionary apprentices through an intensive training program.

Assume that one year of the intern's first term "on the field" would include a year of training in cross-cultural communication, probably at a graduate-school level within the culture—what might happen to a typical college junior under such a program? In April the college junior would be accepted into the program. During that summer he or she would have a short-term experience overseas under the guidance of field staff. At the end of the summer there would be a two-to-three week briefing/learning time in which the apprentice would be asked to view the summer's experience in light of his or her previous expectations and to lay plans for the following year. During the senior year and beyond there would be monthly apprentice/intern news bulletins about what others were doing and about what was going on within the agency. Arrangements would be made with the college or university for a two-to-four-week between-semester intensive course somewhat like that given by the Summer Institute of International Studies.[4]

If the apprentice had no Bible school or seminary training, plans would be made for two or three years of additional theological work combined with on-the-job training. Status would be changed from ap-

4. In the late 1970s there were a good number of undergraduate schools who had such programs available. Specialized programs such as those available at the William Carey Library in Pasadena, California and the cross-cultural study program of the Fuller School of World Mission are a tremendous step forward.

prentice to intern. It would be assumed that the intern is going to work a twelve-month year with two weeks of vacation.[5]

At the end of this formal education, the intern would go overseas for his or her "first term." (In a secular medical program this would be called a residency.) During the language-learning phase, there would be intensive courses in cross-cultural sensitivity with an emphasis on the candidate understanding the culture from which he or she comes as well as the one within which he or she is hoping to work. At the end of the first term would be a nine-months study course, hopefully at a seminary or training school in another country, which would include not only studies in the social sciences, but an emphasis on theology in a different culture.

At the end of this time the intern would receive his or her first regular "furlough," during which a decision would be made as to whether the intern would return to the same field on which he or she had been studying and whether the intern would continue his or her career with this particular agency. (The option would be open to join another agency.)

At first glance this proposal may seem almost impossible, particularly financially. However, the amount of funding required for each candidate is clearly spelled out and if a portion of this funding, say 10 percent, was put into a church's general fund to carry out such training, there is no reason why it cannot be managed. There *is* an obvious minimum size to such a program—at least ten apprentices would be required to make it viable.

The program has the advantage of presenting to potential candidates an immediate road which they can travel, a road which is open-ended to the future. It would be a major step in reeducating some of the constituencies of the various agencies about the need for this type of education and the need for flexibility in approach. It would demonstrate to churches (in which many of these missionaries would work in the future) that North America intends to send men and women who are prepared not only spiritually, but intellectually and emotionally.

Figure 18-1 (see p. 250 below) illustrates this proposal. Such a proposal is not for every mission agency. However, when one considers that eighteen agencies in North America comprise half of the total missions force, other agencies should be challenged to join together on some major rethinking of present candidate and educational programs.

5. In our Western society, which views anyone who is still in school or who has not yet taken a full-time job as a "pre-adult," this might go a long way to having them viewed as adults!

Figure 18-1 A Model for Missionary Training

TRAINING AND EXPERIENCE LEVELS	TYPE OF PREPARATION		EXPERIENCE
	CLASSROOM	FIELD TRAINING	
LEVEL I – Pre-Mission: Four to five years of undergraduate work.	College Undergraduate: Bible, sociology, anthropology & theory of language, French or Spanish.	One year formal education in another culture and language.	Four summers or interterms with two different agencies and fields.
LEVEL II – Mission Training: Three to four years of graduate work.	University graduate study: theology, biblical studies, Greek, missionary anthropology and sociology, communication theory and practice.	One to two years of field work in area near expected service.	Field work done in cooperation with and under supervision of selected mission agency.
LEVEL III – Intern: Two years of language acquisition and people study.	None	Coaching by senior missionary and former professors via correspondence. Language study.	Assignment to specific people group. Language study among group.
LEVEL IV – Associate Missionary: Two to six years of work on field.	Nine months of field work at School of World Mission at end of field work. Review, evaluate.	Supervision by senior missionary.	Work with mission team attempting to evangelize assigned group.
LEVEL V – Missionary: Two to six years of work on field.	None	Supervision of associate missionaries.	Decision on assignment to new field or continuance in present field.
LEVEL VI – Senior Missionary: Four to eight years of field work and teaching.	Two years of graduate study leading to PhD or equivalent.	Teaching of trainees and interns. Field evaluation assignments.	Decision to return to a people or to a field teaching situation.

THE CHALLENGE OF TRAINING

There is a growing recognition within the missions community that cross-cultural training in communicating the gospel is imperative. The founding of the School of World Mission at Fuller Theological Seminary in 1965 was shortly followed by schools of world mission in other seminaries.[6] American Christian and Bible colleges, which produced the major portion of missionaries for the faith missions in the decades following World War II, have also greatly expanded their curricula and are now offering graduate courses. Fuller has now expanded its program to include a cross-cultural studies program for college graduates with no previous cross-cultural experience. Many other programs either provide or encourage students to participate in cross-cultural experiences.

But the need still remains for training centers *within* other cultures. Some beginnings have been made. Daystar Communications' intensive six-to-eight-week training courses in Nairobi attract students from all over the world. But what is needed is a school that has direct access to and oversight of existing attempts at cross-cultural ministry. The task of training missionaries on the field must be viewed as the *highest* missionary calling, not a necessary interruption of the real task. A large agency or a consortium of smaller ones needs to inaugurate such a training center. The Wycliffe Bible Translators have given us the model. Others need to follow.

THE AVERAGE LAYPERSON'S VIEW
OF MISSIONS IS INADEQUATE

Many mission executives and a number of thinking missionaries know there is a need for some radical changes in both our philosophy of mission and the means by which it is carried out. But most of them are convinced that "You can't beat the system." They are convinced that their supporters support only a certain philosophy of mission. We believe that they are fooling themselves.

What is the average layperson's view of missions?

6. The School of World Mission at Fuller was designed to retrain existing missionaries and national evangelists. Admission to the program was dependent upon previous cross-cultural experience.

— Mission is carried out by individual missionaries—men and women of exceptional faith and dedication, and it is carried out through individual programs.

— Mission is carried out on a shoestring budget. One of the major indications of the dedication and spirituality of the missionary is his or her willingness to "make do" on an impossibly small income.

— Most missionaries work in areas where there are few, if any, other mission agencies.

— The basic qualification for a missionary is spiritual dedication, rather than training and education. The latter may be necessary for "specialized" ministries, but for the evangelist a knowledge of Scripture and some knowledge of the language are the basic requirements.

— The churches begun by the missionaries are, of course, very grateful to them and need the missionary's presence to help them mature spiritually.

— Peoples of other lands, particularly non-Western peoples, are like children who need the guidance of more sophisticated Westerners. They cannot be trusted to adapt the gospel to their own culture.

— The younger, and usually poorer, churches are not to be trusted with large no-strings-attached funds.

— The number of missionaries supported by a church or recruited by a mission is a direct indication of the success or effectiveness of the church or mission.

This admitted caricature is the result of a self-reinforcing system of recruiting and fund raising. Young people who feel called of God to serve in a foreign land must believe some, if not all, of these things. In order to present themselves and their work as worthy of financial and prayer support by their lay constituency, they must usually espouse these views.

THE LOCAL CHURCH CAN CHANGE THE WORLD

Some years ago we were involved in designing a training seminar for local churches. We entitled it "The Local Church Can Change the World." It is from the local church that "healthy" members are sent forth and undergirded with wisdom, prayers, and resources. One of the positive signs of the times is the growth of the Association of Church Missions Committees which, under the banner of "Churches Helping

Churches In Missions," is attempting to act as a bridge between mission agencies and local churches. The genius of the ACMC is that it is completely ecumenical or transdenominational. It accepts membership from any local church. It desires to push no particular doctrinal emphasis other than that of a firm biblical faith. Hundreds of local churches are finding not only new financial resources that they can make available to the missionary task, but a new interest in the world that lies outside their own country. The impact and influence of one local church can be seen in the experience of the United Presbyterian Church. At one time over half of the overseas missionaries serving under the United Presbyterians came from only *six* Presbyterian churches throughout the United States.

Concerned and effective Christians are always found in the context of the local church. Relationships within the body are what inspire new passion and vigor. Ultimately, the local church will change the world.[6]

7. For more information about the Association of Church Missions Committees, write to ACMC, 1021 E. Walnut Street, Suite 202, Pasadena, CA 91106.

QUESTIONS

Qualifications

1. How would you describe the faith and vision necessary for a missionary?
2. In what sense should the missionary have demonstrated the Christian life before being qualified for the missionary task?
3. How does Western individualism fit into the whole concept of mission?
4. What do you believe are the basic priorities of Christian life?
5. How do individual gifts fit into the missionary task?
6. How can one demonstrate cross-cultural sensitivity?
7. What is the role of the "call" in deciding on the force for evangelization?

The People Available

1. What is the cultural distance of the people that you are attempting to reach? On the basis of this, who has appropriate experience?
2. If there are Christians in this group, are they culturally acceptable to the rest of the group?
3. If there are no acceptable local Christians, what local Christian body is culturally closest to this group?
4. Who will this people see as able to meet their perceived need?
5. What cultural biases do these people have that would preclude a certain group or individual from reaching them?
6. What is the political orientation of this people?
7. Who will be acceptable to this group theologically and ecclesiastically?

8. Are there local churches already in this country? If so, what are their attitudes about this people?

9. Who will be acceptable to the local church that may already be among this group?

10. What other groups are working with this people or in this area?

11. Who has had experience with reaching a similar group?

12. If there are already people working there, would our agency be acceptable to them? Would they welcome us or resent us?

13. If there is a group already working, are they experiencing success in reaching these people?

14. Who believes that he or she has been called to reach this people?

15. What kind of experience should a missionary team have? What gifts will be needed? What training will be needed? What resources will the force for evangelism have to bring with it?

16. What steps will have to be taken to insure that missionaries go as part of a missionary *community*?

17. What do means, methods, and goals tell us about the qualifications of the force for evangelism?

The Organizations Available

See the organizational checklist on pp. 233-234.

Recruiting and Training

1. Why do you think there are not enough missionaries?

2. Why do you think it is true, if it is, that the current missionary force is not focusing on the unreached people of the world?

3. Why is it so difficult to become a missionary?

4. What do you believe are the steps needed to prepare adequately a cross-cultural missionary attempting to reach a specific people group?

5. How can we help the average layperson to see the mission task as it really is?

6. Why is it important that the local church see that it needs to be involved in mission?

STEP 4

MEANS
AND METHODS

CONSIDERATIONS

1. The right use of the right means is not the key to success in evangelism. Nor is leaving the results in God's hands alone.

2. Many of our arguments about methodology are futile because we have not distinguished method as performance from method as principle and method as philosophy. We simply are not arguing about the same thing.

3. More and more we are inserting technology between us and those we seek to evangelize. Our contacts are increasingly more impersonal and fleeting. Yet all our studies indicate that the nature and length of contact is the single most important element in evangelism.

4. The multiplicity of peoples we face requires a multiplicity of methods. Every method excludes some types of people from authentic witness and must be complemented by other methods that include them.

5. We cannot protect the vital role of the Holy Spirit in evangelism by denying the means of the Holy Spirit. Methods play a causal role in producing the effects we seek.

6. Differences in methods produce very real differences in the size of churches, the quality of discipleship, the spiritual formation of Christian community, and the emergence of indigenous leadership.

7. Methodology that is ill conceived and applied without regard for the culture and context of a people leaves us with no humanly justifiable reason for believing that anything is happening that will further the evangelization of a people.

8. We do not have as much control over the effects we produce as we would like or even think.

9. We must be continually modifying a method as we evaluate its results.

10. Wherever we look to discover models of ministry, we ultimately will have to incarnate them in terms that make sense for the particular people we are evangelizing.

11. The very people we seek to evangelize may themselves be able to teach us the best methods by which they can most effectively be evangelized.

12. There is something contradictory about trying to create an indigenous church by using Western methods.

CHAPTER 19

Defining Means and Methods

INTRODUCTION

A nyone who has farmed knows that using up-to-date equipment that is in perfect working order is no guarantee that there will be a bumper crop. Much more is involved than simply tools or techniques. Climate, plant diseases, bad soil, faulty fences that do not keep animals out, and a variety of other things have a bearing on the ultimate size and quality of the harvest.

Although we cannot simply assume that applying the right methods inevitably leads to the large harvest, we can guarantee that using the wrong methods in farming is the quickest way to failure. When the seed is misplanted, when a dry land crop is irrigated, or an apple orchard harvested with a tomato picker, the results are disastrous.

Means and methods in farming and in evangelism are continually changing. Some are very simple, for example, the digging stick or hoe which is used in a large part of the world. Others are more complex, such as the wooden plow pulled by a draft animal. And some are extremely complex and powerful, such as the modern diesel tractors that pull large plows and cultivate enormous fields. Through experience people discover new uses, and they modify old tools to suit new soil conditions or new plant species. Evangelism likewise has a wide range

261

of means and methods that are in the process of change. Whether we talk about becoming a Christian through a friend, or use a printed tract, or engage in a country-wide saturation evangelism campaign, we are aware of a great variety of means and methods for carrying out evangelism.

This section of the book deals with how means and methods fit into an overall strategy for evangelism, how we go about selecting the appropriate tools and techniques, and where and how we go about developing models for evangelism techniques. There is nothing mysterious or magical about tools or techniques. Tools are simply the instruments we use to achieve our goals. A technique is a way in which tools, labor, and skill are put together so that we achieve our goals effectively and efficiently. We cannot engage in evangelism without utilizing some means and methods. To change our world we have to *do* and *be* some things. Much of our doing will be mediated by the tools we use and the techniques or procedures within which they are used.

We should also point out that our analogy breaks down at this point. Unlike farming, the actual tools or methods are so completely tied up with the people doing the evangelism that their effects cannot be separated from the people who use the tools. Farming is much more mechanical than evangelism. Several farm laborers (assuming a minimal level of skill and understanding of the crop and tools) can be sent into the same field with fairly similar results. But many of the methods and means of evangelism are such an extension of the people using them that very different results can be produced from the same method or tool among the same people.

Unlike farming, evangelism does not permit standardized techniques and tools. If one could imagine a world where apples were different shapes and sizes, growing on different plant structures depending on the country, or a world where rice in one country grew underground like peanuts and in another grew underwater like kelp in the sea, one might have a more accurate picture of the difference culture makes in our attempt to develop standardized means and methods for evangelizing the world. We can take a tractor or plow or pesticide to another country and it will work in basically the same way (given the proper soil and climatic conditions) in the production of the same crop. But we cannot expect an evangelism method or means which has been effective in communicating the gospel in Atlanta, Georgia to have the same kind of effectiveness in Nairobi, Kenya or Madras, India.

Unlike farming, it is more difficult to determine the effects of evangelism methods. Evangelists can continue for years and never know whether they are using the best methods, whether they are turning as many away from Christ as they are attracting, whether their results can be attributed to a particular method or to something else. This is partly the result of the slipshod attitude that God alone is responsible for the results. It is partly due to our unwillingness to have light cast upon the results of our sacrificial labor (sometimes we fear *knowing* we have failed more than failure). It is partly because we have had the wrong criteria for evaluating what we have done. We have counted our working hours, the people working and attending meetings, and the tracts we have handed out. We have counted everything except the resulting harvest. We simply do not know very much about the methods and effects of evangelism.

This section has three chapters. We will first define means and methods. Next we will present a theory of selection. Finally, we will present some resources that will aid in finding means and methods.

DEFINITION

We probably all have an immediate understanding of what a "method" is. We call our method of discovering and validating knowledge the "scientific method." Or we talk about various training methods: the oral-aural method of language learning is very popular. The Suzuki method is an approach to teaching children how to play musical instruments at a very early age. We speak of the method an artist uses in producing a work of art. There are sales methods, steel production methods, methods to treat illness, and methods to prevent pregnancy.

In general terms, a means or method is a regular or orderly way of doing something. It is a standardized procedure for accomplishing a definite result which is based upon past experience and/or research. It is a prescription for action which tells us how to go about doing something once we have decided what we want to accomplish. It normally assumes that a given set of tools or technology is available and orders them into a scheme so individuals do not have to reinvent a process for achieving a given goal. A method disciplines our action and thought by providing guidance to what we do and how we approach a given task. As such, a method aims at a given degree of efficiency and effectiveness. It attempts to answer the question "how" as systematically as possible.

METHODS AND CUSTOMS

By their very nature means and methods are very close to culture. A culture is made up of thousands of methods for accomplishing the various activities that make up the sum and substance of human life. Many of these methods are called "customs" because they are cultural practices that are based upon long-standing traditions and practiced by a large majority of the people who share a given culture. For example, Americans eat breakfast by using silverware. Their food is put on plates which are set on tables which we normally sit next to in chairs. The food itself is only a narrow range of the foods we eat, and it is prepared according to customary methods. Our "custom" of breakfast is a method by which we nourish our bodies and begin a new day.

Yet it sounds odd to call such a thing a method. Normally we use the word to refer to some procedure or mode of action that is more self-conscious. Methods refer to uniformities in social action that are adapted to goal-oriented interests of people and are not the result primarily of custom. As such they are usually more open to change and to an establishment of procedure based on a rational approach of testing the results in order to discover the most efficient means to a given end. This is, of course, only a very relative distinction since a method can become customary or become associated with the sanctions of some norms which make any rational examination of it taboo or any attempt to change it heretical. In these cases the method becomes an end in itself.

METHOD MANIA

The Western culture is a method-oriented culture. Jacques Ellul has probably done the most acute analysis of this fact (1964, 1965, 1967, 1976). In every area of life the "technical phenomenon is the main preoccupation . . . ; in every field men seek to find the most efficient method" (Ellul, 1964, p. 21). Education, politics, personal adjustment, oil exploration, athletics, organizational administration, and transportation are all swept up into a frenetic drive for technical progress. Sometimes means and methods become so important that we lose a sense of the ends for which the means were employed.

Countless numbers of books have been published because of our never-resting desire to know "How to. . . . " Even the Christian life is not immune to method mania. Dozens of books have been published on how to discover an abundant and fulfilling life. The answer is often a mixture of a positive outlook on life, faith in God, and the right use of some given means or methods to bolster the former attitudes. Louis Schneider and Sanford Dornbusch's *Popular Religion: Inspirational Books in America* (1958) documents this in detail. Faith itself has been instrumentalized so that we are offered a "spiritual technology" which will deliver the Holy Spirit, healing, wholeness, and prosperity if we follow a set of prescribed disciplines.

Christians have not always felt comfortable with this orientation or the way it has infiltrated current evangelization perspectives. If anything there is a history of debate and acrimony about almost every basic innovation in evangelistic methodology from the time of Charles Finney (1792–1875) to the present. While Finney argued that a "revival" (what we would call a successful evangelistic crusade) "is a purely philosophical result of the right use of the constitutional means," many of his contemporaries were troubled by the reduction of the role of the Holy Spirit implied in such a view (McLoughlin, 1959, p. 84). Finney meant "inevitable" success by his use of the word "philosophical":

> The connection between the right use of means for a revival and a revival is as philosophically sure as between the right use of means to raise grain and a crop of wheat. I believe, in fact, it is more certain and that there are fewer instances of failure. (McLoughlin, 1959, p. 85)

Many of the current contemporaneous methodologies that are touted as a heaven-sent answer to the challenge of evangelization for today are equally suffused by Finney's perspective!

In the history of debates about methods one thing is certain: those who innovate a new and successful methodology invariably carry the day and the next generation of evangelists. It is difficult, in a pragmatic world, to argue against results, especially when one cannot show equal or better results from alternative methods. Logically, it is also difficult to try to argue that there is little or no connection between means and ends, even if they are evangelistic means and ends. We may not know a great deal about how methods are causally connected to the conversion of unbelievers and the growth rates of churches, but we cannot conclude that methods are irrelevant to the communication of Christ or the conversion of the lost. We reap what we sow here as in the other departments of human endeavor. We *know* methods are relevant because of the experience and study of the Church world-wide.

Yet we cannot be so naive or messianic about our methods as Finney and some of his descendents appear to be. There is far more to evangelization than simply the right use of the right means. We are not dealing with the operation of physical and organic laws, but with people who are far less uniform and predictable than plants. We have already alluded to the fact that human factors are involved (personality, competencies, gifts, rapport, etc.) in evangelism in a way that can have major impact on the effectiveness of a given methodology. However we approach the question of methods, we must be humbly aware that they are only *one* of the components of a strategy. True, they are an important and critical part, but they are not sufficient in themselves to guarantee effectiveness or success. The right methods do not insure a large response to the gospel. Again we deal with human factors that transcend considerations of the efficiency of a given means to achieve an end. Pope Paul VI has well said:

> The first means of evangelization is the witness of an authentically Christian life, given over to God in a communion that nothing should destroy and at the same time given to one's neighbor with limitless zeal. . . . St. Peter expressed this well when he held up the example of a reverent and chaste life that wins over even without a word those who refuse to obey the word. It is therefore primarily by her conduct and by her life that the Church will evangelize the world, in other words, by her living witness of fidelity to the Lord Jesus—the witness of poverty and detachment, of freedom in the face of the powers of this world, in short, the witness of sanctity. (1976, p. 28)

A DEFINITION OF MEANS OR METHODS

We define *means* or *methods* as humanly devised tools and procedures with an associated pattern of action and organization aimed at achieving some result or change in the world.

1. Methods are human creations designed to serve the interests of human groups. Even if they are derived or based on what is perceived to be a biblical pattern (as Roland Allen or Ian R. Hay may claim for the methods they advocate), they are based on a human's understanding of that biblical pattern. Most frequently, what is heralded as a biblical method is in fact a historically-limited statement of philosophy or one

set of disputed methods as opposed to another. A brief survey of such biblically-based methodologies will show the many different understandings of what the Bible says. Furthermore, because they are human creations, methods are relative, limited, subject to time, improvement, and change. Their legitimacy comes from the degree to which they serve the will of God in mission at a given point in time among a specific people.

2. Methods are a grouping of tools and procedures. Every method assumes the availability of certain tools which are then ordered into a definite relationship and utilized to produce results. A visitation-evangelism method, for example, might include the use of letters, printed literature, the phone, certain transportation facilities, and a training program to equip staff for the actual evangelistic encounter. This procedure takes a variety of other available "means and methods" and organizes them into a new entity for effecting change.

3. A method also implies some type of standardized or regularized behavior on the part of people. It specifies how the tools and procedures are to be used, in what sequence, and by whom. It attempts to coordinate activity and relationships between people in order to maximize effectiveness. A saturation evangelism program such as "New Life for All" in Africa produces a set of coordinated activities which church people are trained to engage in. The use of the "Four Spiritual Laws" booklet as an evangelistic method is an example of an attempt to standardize a verbal presentation of Christ.

4. Methods are oriented toward ends or goals. The question of method is, technically speaking, a question of the best *means* to an end. For example, we can do many things with a screwdriver: tighten or loosen screws, pierce a hole in a piece of paper, pry open a tight window, or even stab a person in the back. None of the ends is inherent in the nature of the screwdriver even though it can do some of those tasks more efficiently than others. But it is also true that there are some things that a screwdriver cannot do: it cannot turn a rusted bolt or cut a piece of glass. Methods are intended to achieve certain results, to do some tasks and not others. Each has a limited scope of ability to achieve change in our world. They can be legitimately evaluated only against their ability to reach certain goals. But unless they are evaluated in terms of their performance against aims, they cease to be "methods" and increasingly become ends in themselves.

METHODS AS PRINCIPLES AND AS PERFORMANCE

We need to make other crucial distinctions that will help us gain a broader perspective on the importance and limitation of methods in strategy. We are aware of the difference between the requirements of a position or role and the actual performance of a person who holds that position or plays that role. Two women might both be presidents of companies, but the way they fill the role of "president" may be quite different. We would have little difficulty in describing what a father or a mother is expected to be and do in our culture. Or we could observe what a particular father or mother actually does and on that basis describe what a father or mother is. In one case we have described what they *ought* to do, in the other, what they do.

The same distinction can be made about language. Grammar describes the rules and principles of the language, what is considered good form and how words are to be used. In one sense such a set of rules describes the language. But the performance, the actual speaking of the language, is another thing. Often the spoken language is different from the description of the rules and principles that are supposed to govern its use.

Methods can be approached on both levels. From one point of view we speak of a *method as the set of principles,* the prescriptions that have been formulated for guiding behavior in order to produce effects. We can pick up a manual that describes how In-Depth Evangelism works, or a manual that is used to train people in undertaking friendship evangelism such as *Evangelism Explosion* (Kennedy, 1973). These describe a method from the point of view of grammar, the way it is supposed to work, the plan for action. From another point of view we speak of *methods as actual performance,* a method that unfolds itself in an actual evangelism event. In-Depth Evangelism as it is carried out in Guatemala or Evangelism Explosion, or as it is put into action in the First Trappisterian Church will differ in significant ways from the principles found in manuals describing the method. The method as a pattern and the method as practice are two related yet separate matters.

This distinction is important when we discuss or evaluate the usefulness of methods in different contexts. Take a list of commonly characterized methods such as:

Ashrams or retreat centers	Film strips
Tracts	Gospel records
Cassettes	Mass Crusade

Door-to-door visitation
Mail campaigns
Television programs
Drama presentations
Newspaper advertising
Medical evangelism
Industrial evangelism
Open Air preaching
Camping programs
Christian schools
Athletic contests
Correspondence courses
Recreation centers
Music concerts
Bible translation
Home Bible studies
Christian magazine

Personal witnessing
Bus ministry
Crisis centers
Literacy classes
Healing services
Counseling
Evangelism survey
Movies
Billboards
Revival meetings
Social service
Prayer breakfast
Telephone evangelism
Christian books
Dialogues
Church services

These examples are actually *classes* of similar methods, of similar "grammars" for achieving goals in specific contexts. One can abstract common traits in the list, because each example has similarities which are variations on a theme. All camps and camping programs have some common elements—they are away from cities and home, they are normally in session during the summer, they stress activity and involvement in the out-of-doors, and so forth. They all operate from a similar orientation of principles. But each program has its own particular scheduling, organization, age and class group. One camp might stress baseball, archery, and basketball, and another might focus on water sports and horseback riding. Some are explicitly aimed at evangelism; others are aimed at enhancing the quality of understanding and leadership in Christians.

The same thing can be said of methods which aim at communicating the gospel door-to-door. Some door-to-door visitation is done unannounced while other versions call only on "contacts," such as visitors who have attended some service at the church. Literature may or may not be given out. The principal purpose of the time may be seen as getting to know the family with the aim of later revisiting those who seem interested, or it may be to press for an immediate decision for Christ. For some groups, visitation is a way of "putting in time" for a church requirement (such as the Jehovah's Witnesses). Each program of door-to-door visitation has a different training program and utilizes a different "pitch" or approach. The "housing" areas visited differ and present various problems in visitation (from manyatta complexes made of dhom palm in Northern Kenya and high-rise apartments in Singapore to the suburban single family dwellings of Los Angeles or the squatters' huts on a hillside in Brazil). In each case the pattern or basic concept is applied, modified, and practiced somewhat differently.

METHOD AS PHILOSOPHY

Finally, we may speak of *method as philosophy*. Many of the more comprehensive methodologies have explicit assumptions and abstract principles that serve to legitimate and explain the rationale for a certain structure of activities and organization, that is, they present themselves as philosophies of ministry. This component is clearly seen in Evangelism in Depth. Orlando Costas has written:

> The generic term *In-Depth Evangelism* stands for a worldwide evangelistic movement which had its *formal* inception in an experiment carried out in the Republic of Nicaragua in 1960. It can be succinctly described as an effort to *mobilize the church of Jesus Christ with all of her resources for a comprehensive witness in the world*. It represents, at once, a dynamic evangelistic concept, a comprehensive strategic methodology and a coordinated, functional program. (Costas, 1975, p. 675)

Costas then develops each of these latter three elements. As a "concept" (what we are calling method as philosophy) In-Depth Evangelism has a comprehensive view of the world, the Church, and the message of the gospel. It is this view that gives theological rationale and depth to the methodology. As a "comprehensive strategic methodology," In-Depth Evangelism aims at the mobilization of all Christians in their local context for the continuous witness to Jesus Christ. It is based on Ken Strachan's thesis that "the successful expansion of any movement is in direct proportion to its success in mobilizing and occupying its total membership in constant propagation of its beliefs" (Roberts, 1971, p. 86; see also Roberts, 1967; Peters, 1970).

The method as a pattern aims at mobilizing Christians in a region through consciousness raising about Christian responsibility for witnessing, analysis of needs and resources, planning for action (both local visitation efforts and special campaigns on a regional or national level), coordination of the effort of many churches and Christians, and evaluation. The most common elements at this level are the formation of prayer cells, the training of laypeople, the visitation program for reaching every home, and special campaigns.

Seen as practice, the method "can take many different programmatic forms" (Costas, 1975, p. 687). Costas then briefly describes how the basic concept and strategic methodology was applied in a nation-wide effort in Cameroun, a denominational effort in South Vietnam, a program strategy for a local congregation in North America, and a city-wide interdenominational effort in Santiago, Chile. In each case there was significant modification of the pattern as it was adapted to different contexts, cultures, and scopes. Costas argues that ". . . In-Depth evangelistic programs are relative to the needs, cultural characteristics, historical circumstances, and resources of the church everywhere. *There are no fixed program patterns*" (Costas, 1975, p. 693).

It is helpful to keep these three levels distinct (even though practitioners of many methods do not). It enables us to separate the propaganda and ideology that often becomes part of a method from the actual results of the method. At times the philosophy of the method is so dominant that it hides the fact that the method as practice is not achieving its goals. It also keeps us from arguing at different levels. When we criticize a method, we may be speaking of it as practice, while its defenders or practitioners may be hearing us criticize not only the actual implementation and results but the biblical philosophy that has been so carefully worked out to justify and strengthen the method's adoption. It also helps us be more sensitive to the cultural dimension in methods. We may continue to believe in a given philosophy of ministry or methodology while radically changing the pattern and practice of a method in response to changing social and cultural contexts. Much of the problem of Western methodology in cross-cultural evangelism is a confusion of the three levels, so that the "Four Spiritual Laws" or "Sermons from Science" movies or some other method is exported at not only the philosophy level but also at the pattern and practice level.

In sum, we define means or methods as humanly devised tools and procedures with an associated pattern of action and organization aimed at achieving some result or change in the world. In addition, we distinguish three levels of methods: philosophy of ministry, an ideal pattern or plan for action, and an actual practiced set of behaviors and relationships which have measurable results in the real world.

CLASSIFYING METHODS

No clear way of classifying methods for evangelism has been developed. Part of the problem is that so many things are called methods that it is very difficult to know what to do with all of them. Also, as we have noted, methods exist at several levels, from philosophies of ministry to specific, implemented programs. There are a number of ways to distinguish, or at least call attention to, some of the qualities and dimensions of methods that need to be considered in a strategy. Some might be:

— the degree to which a method is biblically grounded or justified
— technological sophistication required by the method
— involvement of the laity vs. implementation by experts
— length of time for the method to complete one cycle of its plan
— relative financial cost
— relationship of the method to local congregational life ("church" vs. "para-church" methods)
— relevance of the method to a given goal of evangelism

Each one of these is an important dimension. We will look at four areas which have particular relevance and importance in classifying methods.

1. *Contact between the evangelist and the lost*

Many studies indicate that the most significant element in church growth and conversion is the personal relationship network that is formed by the evangelism encounter. John Nevius writes that this is what produced the greatest number of conversions in China nearly one hundred years ago: ". . . by far the greater proportion is to be referred to private social intercourse" (1958, p. 84). Marion Cowan describes a Christian movement among the Huixtan Tzotzil of Mexico which grew largely because of the influence of family. Half of the eighty cases studied had been brought to Christ through the influence of "blood" relatives (consanguineal), and the other half through relatives by marriage (affinal). Only three were non-kinsmen (1962). Studies of church growth in Japan have revealed the importance of this factor as well. The early missionaries began schools for training college-level students in Western sciences as well as the faith of Christ. Those who entered the schools were the opposition samurai who had been overthrown by the

Meiji restoration and felt that their only future was in acquiring Western skills and knowledge to utilize in a new Japan. Consequently, the Church began very strongly among educated, urban individuals (a social distinction it has kept to the present day) (Yamamori, 1974; K.J. Dale, 1975; Thomas, 1959). The method that was chosen created relationships of such depth that the ex-samurai became Christians in large numbers.

By contrast, the schools which developed in Africa did not start within an educated, literate population. Mission schools had to begin at elementary levels, and consequently the Church became identified with education and children. The older men of tribes did not convert or attend the Church which was so strongly tied to literacy and children (Shewmaker, 1970). The method created a Church identified with Western people, education, and those seeking jobs in the developing economy in the cities. It alienated the older generation and those who chose to remain rural or traditional in their life-style.

Thus one way of classifying methods is by the type and nature of relationship they form or utilize between Christian evangelists and those being evangelized. There are long-term and short-term methods. Evangelism through schools would be an example of a long-term method. Handing out tracts to strangers on a street corner would be a short-term method. Of course methods can be varied so that the relative contact is extended. A tract can be utilized in an evangelism effort that turns into a long-term friendship. So-called itinerant evangelism need not be a one-time preaching method, but can be extended into a longer-term program. Al Krass writes about how a village would be visited once a week for a full year if the people there showed definite interest after the initial itinerant presentation. The gospel was preached and explained each week at an agreed upon time to as many as were interested:

> The Evangelical Presbyterian Church has a rule that inquirers shall receive regular Christian teaching for a period of at least one year before baptism. Therefore, we did not have to raise the question of acceptance or rejection, or of baptism, the sign of acceptance, until at least one year had passed. (Krass, 1969, p. 245)

We can also classify methods on the basis of whether or not they are bringing people into direct contact with the evangelists. Direct methods would involve a face-to-face encounter with people. Scripture translations, radio broadcasts, advertising, and correspondence courses which stand behind and support more direct encounters and relational evangelistic methods, are examples of indirect methods. Because of technology, more and more of our methods are far more impersonal and fleeting than they were a hundred years ago.

We can further classify methods on the basis of the type of relationship they utilize or create. Visitation evangelism can utilize either completely "cold turkey" approaches where people are contacted simply because they live in a certain residential district, or it can focus (as Evangelism Explosion does) on people who have visited our church. It can also be redesigned so that only close friends or family relatives of people who already are Christians are visited.

2. Types of people reachable by the method

We already mentioned the method utilized by early missionaries in Japan: higher education. By its very nature it excluded the lower social classes of Japan who were not educated or literate. We need to realize that all methodologies exclude some people. If we do not, we will never realize the narrow range of people we can reach with a given method. How many of our methods assume that people must be able to see or hear or walk to a public setting? Do not most of our methods automatically exclude the deaf, the blind, and the handicapped (Judson, 1975)?

One can construct a large list of limiting factors. We will mention only a few examples. Printed literature assumes not only literacy, but also a certain educational and age level to understand the vocabulary and concepts. Tracts or literature exclude the illiterate or the very young. They also exclude those who do not understand the language or dialect. Radio broadcasting assumes the availability of adequate receivers and an interest in Christian programming as opposed to competitive stations. Radio excludes those without access, interest, or time to listen to the programs. Crusade evangelism requires people to come to a central location at a given time. It automatically excludes all those whose work hours are at the same time or who are sick or handicapped and cannot come to a public setting of that type. Nor does it normally reach the rural areas. When it is advertised in the normal mass media channels it excludes those whose source of information does not include the mass media. Mailing Bibles to those listed in telephone books excludes all who do not have telephones or whose address has changed since the telephone book was printed.

These are only a few very crude examples of how methods can be classified by their limiting factors. Listening to the promotion of various dynamic Western evangelism agencies we could easily believe that if we just gave enough money so that these agencies could mail Bibles to every name in all the telephone books of the world, or could export a saturation evangelism methodology like "Here's Life," we could evangelize the whole world! There is little understanding that the multiplicity of peoples require a multiplicity of methods, and that every method, by its very design, *excludes* certain peoples who will be reached only by a complementary method.

In the past, we have assumed that those who have not been reached must have *something wrong with them*. Heaven knows how hard we have tried, how much money we have spent to reach the world! There has been little awareness that many peoples have been excluded because there was *something wrong with our methods*.

One example is the nomadic peoples who inhabit semi-arid and arid regions stretching from Morocco through Africa, into the Middle East and up into Central Asia. The Church has never evangelized them and never will until and unless it finds new ways to communicate Christ in an oral and non-sedentary fashion. It is significant that in all the strategy papers developed for examining the evangelization of the peoples of the world at Lausanne (1974), not one was devoted to the nomadic peoples. No doubt such evangelization will require nomadic "pastors" whose livelihood will be herding animals, wandering from water-hole to water-hole, and following the best pasture. So long as we insist that people be sedentary (like ourselves), we will not see any modern-day Abrahams who move with their camels, asses, and sheep, and worship God on dozens of knolls and around scores of camp fires. We will have to develop "caravan churches" as the Assemblies of God have developed for the nomadic Gypsies of Europe.

The same thing is true for rural evangelism. The methods we use are for a different type of person than the one found in small farming hamlets and villages. It is estimated that of the 2.44 billion people who live in Asia, nearly 1.6 billion of them (65.5 percent) are farmers. Many of them are not included in any of the current methodologies to evangelize the lost. Consider the 1971 survey of a rural farming area (seven hundred farmhouses surveyed) which was within two hours of Tokyo:

> We were very surprised to discover that 97 percent of those farmers had never heard the Gospel. The other three percent had heard through radio or by receiving a tract when they had been in the city. The nearest church to that farming village was about a one-hour walk, and it was a weak church of about twenty members. (Cho, 1975, p. 625)

Different approaches must be taken from the standard mass techniques or urban-based methodologies if farmers are to be reached. They are excluded by 99 percent of the current evangelistic methodologies being employed in Asia today. Dr. Cho relates the extraordinary tale of a Japanese evangelist's vision for rural evangelism. His approach was to learn the technique of growing strawberries and then to settle in a very poor village.

> At first he did not say he was an evangelist or even that he was a Christian. But silently he made a new strawberry patch, and grew his berries. The farm people noticed this peculiar stranger and watched him curiously. At Christmas he harvested many fine strawberries, and made a greater profit than any of the farmers could have imagined. They gathered at his house and begged him to teach them how to grow strawberries in this way. For the first time, he told them that he was a Christian. He arranged that if they would come to his house every Sunday and hear what he had to say, he would teach them how to grow strawberries. Now that entire village is Christian, and he is not only the pastor of the church, but head of the village. Not only has evangelism had good results, but that village has become famous for strawberry production. (1975, pp. 628–629)

This is representative of the kind of thing that needs to happen all over Asia (in modified fashion). It is quite a different approach from hitting a village with "gospel bombs" (tracts wrapped in cellophane), or a preaching blitz that comes once without invitation. It also does not assume that the farmer, even if he has a radio and tunes in, can understand the rather sophisticated, urban-oriented programming Christian radio offers. Dr. Cho adds:

> I think that the ideal evangelistic worker for the farming villages should be able to increase the income of the farmers, build up their cultural life, and actually become one with them in their community life. He should plough and live and suffer and cooperate with the farmers, and love their souls and lead them to the Cross. The farm villages need workers who will touch them skin to skin and communicate to their hearts. (1975, p. 629)

3. The functional focus of the method

We can also classify methods by their results. What are the chief effects of an implemented program of evangelism? What consequences does it have for good or ill? Every method has a particular "competence," that is, it can effect some changes far better than other methods.

For example, the approach of the Summer Institute of Linguistics is one of the finest for producing a translation of the New Testament in the language of minority peoples who traditionally have not had a written orthography for their language. It also has had good success in stimulating the birth of Christian churches among those who have received these translations. But the methodology and limitations under which S.I.L. works have not been optimal for the development of a church identity. The infant churches at times grope along with little guidance in terms of what name to choose for their church, whether to build a chapel, and what relationship they ought to have with other Christians (Tuggy and Toliver, 1972, pp. 123–124).

When we think of radio as a method of evangelism, we can see how the notion of a method's "competence" can help us take a more realistic approach to its use. Research indicates that radio functions best as a means for creating awareness of Christ rather than in stimulating a specific commitment to Christ. Yet a great deal of our programming is theoretically aimed at inducing a decision. It is difficult to raise funds for a program that is aimed at moving a person or group along the spiritual decision process or at changing attitude in a more positive direction, even though this is its real forte. Radio is also very effective at the discipleship training end of the spiritual decision process. When integrated with a perspective that sees the full process of evangelism and utilizes a mix of methods to deal with the various stages or steps in that process, radio can begin to fulfill its promise for evangelism.

The same types of analysis and questions can be given for medical approaches, education as a part of evangelism, newspaper advertising, and correspondence courses. All of these are legitimate, and in some cases highly important approaches to achieving our goals. But we cannot suppose that any of them can do all the tasks that need to be done in the evangelization of a people. Just as the surgeon has many specialized tools for doing different types of surgery, the evangelist must be aware of different evangelism methods.

4. Complexity of the method

Another way to distinguish methods is to place them on a continuum of complexity. By complexity we mean the number of people involved in carrying out the method, the level of training, skill, and education necessary to perform according to minimum standards, the length of time the method will be applied, the resources required, and possibly the number of people who will be evangelized in a direct and sustained fashion. On the basis of such a continuum we might distinguish, in very broad terms, three general types of methods:

(a) Tools are the simplest element. These include such things as questionnaires, tracts, or advertising brochures. They usually have little in the way of a philosophy, or a plan or pattern of action.

(b) Further up the scale are programs. Here several tools are combined in an approach to stimulate evangelism. Programs take place over a significant period of time and involve the efforts of several people. The visitation of contacts who come to the church by the pastors and the visitation committee members might be an example of such a program. Or a church might be financing and staffing a "mission" or daughter church that will be planted in another section of the community.

(c) "Grand plans" are the most complex methods. These are often aimed at mobilizing many churches, perhaps whole denominations, in a process of evangelism that takes many months or even years. These usually come with a highly developed philosophy of ministry as well as a training program. They also may come with several models of how the basic philosophy has been implemented into a specific pattern or program and what the results and problems have been as it has been implemented in different contexts. In-Depth Evangelism, New Life for All, Here's Life, Evangelism Explosion, Crusade Evangelism (à la Billy Graham's "cooperative evangelism") are all recent examples of "grand plans" in recent decades. A methodology can also be incorporated into a very elaborate organizational structure which carries out a program of evangelism in cooperation with regular congregations and denominations. The YMCA movement in its earlier years is an example of this.

CHAPTER 20

Theory of Selection

Some years ago, the well-known mission theorist John Nevius wrote: "Let us bear in mind that the best methods cannot do away with the difficulties in our work which come from the world, the flesh, and the devil, but bad methods may multiply and intensify them" (1958, p. 10). A concern for methods, their effects, their relationship to the Holy Spirit, their justifiability, and their integrity, is not a new phenomenon in Christian thinking. Controversy over methods, over even the thought that methods have any causal role to play in the work of converting people, can be found in almost all generations where there have been active advances in evangelization.

SHOULD METHODS BE AN ISSUE?

Some of our contemporaries believe that methods are not a basic issue in evangelism, if an issue at all. For example, at a conference of mission administrators in Chicago where it was suggested that had the Emperor of Japan become a Christian the whole nation might have been won in a day, Dr. H. Kraemer replied: "I never did agree with you Americans. You seem to have the idea that by getting together and using the proper methods you can do anything. You leave out of consideration the operation of the Holy Spirit" (quoted in Douglas, 1975, p. 243). About evangelism in India, Dr. K.N. Nambudripad said:

> There seems to be no mathematical relationship between method and results, although this is only an impression. One missionary goes to a tribal area and wins thousands to Christ while others sweat and labor for decades and nothing seems to happen. In some institutions, like hospitals, no one is converted, while in others many are converted....
>
> There is no recognizable pattern between methods and magnitude of converts. (Douglas, 1975, p. 793)

The denial that methods are important in the work of God has a long and honored tradition as one of the perversions of a type of Calvinist theology that went to the extreme of trying to protect the very important action of the Holy Spirit by denying the means of the Holy Spirit.[1] One of the most famous statements of Protestant missions was one made to William Carey: "Sit down young man. When God wants to convert the heathen, he will do it without your help." In 1792 Carey responded by publishing his famous *An Enquiry into the Obligation of Christians to use Means for the Conversion of the Heathen* (1961). He even argued that the mariner's compass was a key tool for reaching the lost of the world. He then went out to Serampore and demonstrated how God could work.

While one would like to say that the remnants of this tradition are no more than clichés and shibboleths today, the fundamental attitude that rebuffed Carey continues to reappear in the most unusual and, at times, unfortunate places. In raising the issue of the selection of methods, we are agreeing with Carey: God does use means, and not all means are equally good instruments for carrying out his will. It is obscurantist to deny that methods have a causal role to play in producing the effects we seek and ultimately see in evangelism. It is a form of bad faith to act as though God does his work without the use of his people as they engage in active proclamation of the Kingdom through a variety of means. There is a very demonstrable correlation between the use of various

1. Not all Calvinism has gone to this extreme. Even the Westminster Confession of Faith recognizes "secondary" causes as part of the picture: "God from all eternity did by the most wise and holy counsel of his own will freely and unchangeably ordain whatsoever comes to pass: yet so as thereby neither is God the author of sin, nor is violence offered to the will of the creatures, nor is the liberty or contingency of second causes taken away, but rather established" (Chapter 3, "Of God's Eternal Decree").

means and their effects. Even granting that this is not a one-to-one correlation does not lessen the reality that differences in methods and approaches produce very real differences in the size of churches, in the quality of discipleship, in the ability of those churches to reproduce themselves within their context, in the rapidity with which leadership arises to meet the problems of a new Christian community, and so on.

To be concerned with the means which the Spirit uses in evangelism or in the communication of the gospel is not to diminish the Holy Spirit or to attempt a subtle repeal of faith in favor of the "arm of the flesh" (cf. Hesselgrave, 1978c). If we were Christian wheat farmers we would not foolishly pretend to be as ignorant and backward as possible so we could give the Sovereign Lord the opportunity to supply our needs and bring in the harvest. When we translate the Bible into a previously unwritten language, we do not discontinue using modern linguistic methods and simply depend on the Holy Spirit to give us the words and sentences. Means and methods are not enemies of God's divine activity in our efforts. He is pleased to work through means as we trust him to do that which we as humans can never do, even with the best of means. John R. W. Stott has some wise and applicable words:

> Some say rather piously that the Holy Spirit is himself the complete and satisfactory solution to the problem of communication, and indeed that when he is present and active, then communication ceases to be a problem. What on earth does such a statement mean? Do we now have liberty to be as obscure, confused and irrelevant as we like, and the Holy Spirit will make all things plain? To use the Holy Spirit to rationalize our laziness is nearer to blasphemy than piety. Of course *without* the Holy Spirit all our explanations [or methods] are futile. But this is not to say that *with* the Holy Spirit they are also futile. For the Holy Spirit chooses to work through them. (1975, p. 127)

WHAT DIFFERENCE DO METHODS MAKE?

Methods are not abstract entities that have no relationship to the people who carry them out or the context in which they are carried out. In the hands of a great surgeon a particular surgical technique might save the life of a person, but in the hands of another surgeon it might not be successful.

What difference does the presence or absence of love make when people are communicating the gospel with the same methodology? Or cultural sensitivity? Or the nationality or race of the communicator? Methodologies and means produce effects not simply because of a correct ordering of tools and sequence of communication, but also because of who uses them and the way in which they are used. Nor are effects a simple matter of attributing differences to the quality and depth of prayer of one church or organization versus another. We all know that prayer is a crucial reality in the life of the Church, and that it is indispensable in its abilities to activate and make fruitful God's gifts for ministry. But we can also point out two groups with virtually equal levels of "piety" or "spirituality" (so far as we can humanly tell) of which one is experiencing significant advance in evangelization and the other is facing an unresponsive situation. Why?

The means chosen to achieve goals make a significant difference in the outcomes that result as action is taken. Some methods are better means to our ends than others, given the mix of people who will be doing the evangelizing, the theological structure which we bring to bear on our understanding of the nature of the task and our goals, and the context within which we will be evangelizing. Consider the following example:

> *Case study 1:* Two gifted and dedicated lady missionairies were sent by their missionary society to Northwest China. Their mandate was to evangelize and plant congregations in a cluster of villages. They spoke fluent Chinese; they labored faithfully and fervently. After a decade, a small congregation emerged. However, most of its members were women. Their children attended the Sunday School regularly. The visitor to this small congregation would easily detect the absence of men.
>
> In their reports and newsletters, both missionaries referred to the "hardness of hearts" that was prevalent among the men. References were also made to promising teenagers who were opposed by their parents when they sought permission for baptism.
>
> *Case study 2:* In 1930 a spiritual awakening swept through the Little Flock Assembly in Shantung. Many members sold their entire possessions in order to send seventy *families* to the Northwest as "instant" congregations. Another thirty *families* migrated to the Northeast. By 1944 forty new assemblies had been established and all these were vitally involved in evangelism. (Chua, 1975, p. 968)

In both cases the goals were the same. They both set out to evangelize and establish new growing churches in the same region of China. Both were "orthodox" and dedicated. What "caused" the difference in results? The most obvious reason is the difference in the force for evangelism which led to quite a difference in approach and methodology. Chua Wee Hian analyzes the differences in this fashion:

> Consider the case of the two single lady missionaries. Day by day, the Chinese villagers saw them establishing contacts and building the bridges of friendships with the women, usually when their husbands or fathers were out working in the fields or trading in nearby towns. Their foreignness (dubbed "red hair devils") was enough to incite cultural and racial prejudices in the minds of the villagers. But their single status was something that was socially questionable. It was a well-known fact in all Chinese society that the families constitute basic social units. These units insure security. In Confucian teaching, three of the five basic relationships have to do with family ties—father and son, brother and younger brother, husband and wife. The fact that these ladies were making contacts with individual women and not having dialogues with the elders would make them appear to be foreign agents seeking to destroy the fabric of the village community. A question that would constantly crop up in the gossip and discussion of the villagers would be the fact of the missionaries' single state. Why aren't they married? Why aren't they visibly related to their parents, brothers and sisters, uncles and aunts and other relatives? So when they persuaded the women or the youth to leave the religion of their forefathers, they were regarded as "family-breakers."
>
> By contrast, the Little Flock Assembly in sending out Chinese Christian families sent out agents that were recognizable sociocultural entities. Thus the seventy families became an effective missionary task force. It is not difficult to imagine the heads of these families sharing their faith with the elders of the villagers. The grandmothers could informally transmit the joy of following Christ and of their deliverance from demonic powers to the older women in pagan villages. The housewives in the markets could invite their counterparts to attend the services that were held each Sunday by the "instant congregations." No wonder forty new assemblies were established as a result of this approach to church-planting and evangelism. (1975, pp. 968–969)

As is apparent in this example, methods made a difference, but only as part of a wider set of things: the agents of evangelism, the cultural expectations of the people being evangelized, and the focus of evangelism on a particular part of the Chinese social structure. In one case the whole family was being evangelized by whole families. In the other the women and children were being evangelized by single women who were foreigners. And the results were dramatically different. Methods are patterns of action that are utilized by people. The force for evangelism will have a major effect on the success or failure of a method to achieve goals.

The effects of methods also depend on where a people is located on the resistancy-receptivity scale. At the extremes of this continuum, methods do not seem to make much difference. Where the gospel is forbidden among a people, no amount of superior methodology from the hands of loving and skilled people will win such a people. And where a people is coming into the Church faster than it can assimilate them, almost any method will reap a large harvest; though even here a bad method can slow the harvest and even stop it in its early phases. Methods most obviously make a critical difference in the middle range of the scale. Where groups are moderately resistant or moderately responsive to the gospel, the selection of proper methodology can make enormous differences in moving a people to a more favorable attitude or in confirming them in the feeling that Christianity is foreign to their life and interests.

The actual cultural patterns, institutions, and social structure of a people will also affect the way a method functions. Major differences in the applicability of a method can be the result of slight differences in values and outlook. A careful study of methods and approaches might lead one to conclude that the best way to evangelize the Philippine barrios is to win families, to bring whole networks of relatives into the church at or about the same time. To do this one develops a strategy of building friendships and contacts with the male heads of these families, not realizing that the cultural head of the family there is the woman. A method focused on the woman rather than the man would result in different outcome. A similar example of this is given by David Hesselgrave:

> Missionaries working out of Manila have found that the house-to-house survey method of making contacts for evangelistic campaigns which has been relatively successful in Manila meets considerable resistance in outlying villages. City-dwellers are more used to doorbell-ringers and their rather prying questions. Village-dwellers are suspicious of the motives of strangers who invade their quiet communities asking personal questions and inviting them to meetings sponsored by outsiders. On the other hand, missionaries have found that the villagers are often responsive when local

friendships are established and utilized, identity and purposes are clarified, and the message is given by precept upon precept over a period of time. (1978c, p. 371)

Although methods make a real and critical difference, they are not always crucial in the outcomes of a given strategy. Where there is a well-conceived methodology, suited to a given context, applied in a skillful and sensitive fashion, and motivated by the love of Christ, people will be given a valid opportunity to discover who Jesus Christ is and decide whether or not they will trust him. But where the methodology is not well considered and is ill applied, there is no humanly justifiable reason for believing that anything is happening that will further the evangelization of the people.

We do not have as much control over the effects we seek as we would like or even as much as we might think we do. Working with and among other humans is an endlessly exciting and frustrating experience. We are continually learning and revising our ideas about how things work in a given group and social setting. What we thought would produce good turns out to effect the opposite because of our inability to control all the factors that go into changing human lives. Consequently we are continually thrust back on our trust in the Holy Spirit who alone can open our eyes to new ways of doing things, who can transform the most recalcitrant and obdurately resistant heart, and who can turn defeat into victory in ways beyond our imagination. We choose methods and revise them in the light of our experience, and then we gradually grow in our understanding of a particular people and the way God is pleased to work among them. We may not be able to control the effects we seek as completely as we would like, but we can accept responsibility to grow in our knowledge and skill in sharing Christ in a way that encounters people at the deepest levels of their existence.

Finally, there is no "one best method" for a given context. The idea of "one best method" derives from the scientific management movement that centered on Frederick W. Taylor. Applied to industrial production techniques, the notion of careful, systematic study of the work process in search for the "one best" way of organizing and implementing the task has led to most of the tremendous productivity advances of the twentieth century. But it is not entirely applicable outside of the more highly controlled and predictable environment of a factory making a product. There may be several highly effective methods for bringing a people to an understanding of Christian faith and to the point of commitment. Allen J. Swanson points out two rapidly growing Independent

Churches in Taiwan which contrast in many ways, including their methodologies:

> The point is that there is no one set pattern to church growth. One group has large, ostentatious churches, and the other does not. Church polity and organization are almost opposite one another. One pays the leaders from the national headquarters and the other is completely anonymous and by faith. One uses tongues and faith healing, the other only secondarily. One appears to have money, the other does not. One uses a seminary and the other does not. One uses Mandarin and the other Taiwanese... yet both use translators. One relies heavily upon spiritual revival meetings, the other stresses intensive lay training. One has three sacraments and a fairly worked-out theology, the other makes no reference to sacraments and minimizes theology. And yet both grow. They grow because they practice the doctrine of the priesthood of all believers. They grow because they are churches of the soil belonging to the Chinese and served entirely by the Chinese. They grow because all are vitally concerned with their walk in Christ and in sharing this life with others. They grow because the Spirit blesses their churches also. (1971, p. 218)

CONSIDERATIONS IN THE SELECTION PROCESS

In order to communicate Christ in all his fulness, there must be change at four levels: knowledge, attitude, behavior, and relationship. Any process of selection must evaluate means in terms of how they are able to stimulate or induce change at each of these levels. We tend to evaluate the people we are seeking to change in terms of our own needs, world view, and methodologies. We are generally more optimistic about the ability of our imported methods to produce the changes we seek than is borne out by the past experience of the Church in cross-cultural settings. Until we are able to see our methods and means through the eyes of those we seek to evangelize, we will be rationally unable to relate our means to our goals.

There are a number of criteria which can be applied to the selection of methods. We will sketch but a few of them under three broad categories.

1. Biblical/ethical criteria

Christians cannot always reach for a means that is justifiable solely on the basis of results. A study of the history of the Church reveals how

Christians resorted to many highly questionable means. The desire to see the Muslim yield allegiance to Jesus Christ was a commendable goal. The use of force in the Crusades can never be justified. There are ethical and moral criteria which restrain the Church from using physical force as a means of evangelization. As Augustine said, the only force to be used in convincing non-Christians to become Christians is the force of love.

We cannot use deception to further the progress of the truth. We cannot limit the freedom of people by using propaganda or psychologically conditioning regimens in order to induce "voluntary" decisions to follow Christ, such as those used by the Unification Church as documented by Christopher Edwards in *Crazy for God* (1979). Packaging the gospel in a high pressure or deceptive fashion in order to increase the number of responses for Christ is also wrong. (Studies show that most of these converts do not understand what they are doing and most of them have no intention of becoming members of some fellowship of Christians.)

We also cannot use methods that change the nature of the gospel. Some methodologies have utilized high amounts of entertainment in the process of attempting to share the Good News. When does the entertainment become the end and the religious content no more than an accoutrement? Mass advertising has to be protected from turning the gospel into a slogan or an image which is used to stimulate a certain emotive response apart from the freedom of the person. How much of the "hidden persuaders," as described by Vance Packard (1951), can be incorporated without turning proclamation into manipulation?

A truly biblical set of criteria must prove its worth as more than a mono-cultural set of biases that have been handed down by tradition. Too often the selection process is short-circuited by the consciences of culturally provincial Christians who try to legislate for other Christians. They have already "selected" the proper methods and the rest of us better fall in line. It is at this point that Romans 14 and other Pauline passages are important. There are times when it is difficult to find consensus among Christians about what is ethical or right in a given context. It is at that point that love and the freedom we allow other Christians is tested to its utmost. If we cannot let one another stand or fall in the eyes of our common Master but insist that people agree with our standards, we will continue to have an uncreative, stifling ethos that will quench the Spirit as he moves us out in new directions.

One of the more recent examples of this (now far enough behind us to be less emotional) is the introduction and use of rock music as a means for communicating with young people in the hippie generation. There was little question that the method was extremely effective in attracting large crowds of young people who were turned off to the traditional music and attitudes of the established American churches. But many in the Church raised "biblical" and "ethical" questions about the use of the "devil's" music, associated as it was with the drug culture, loose sex, and rebellion against authority.

With the spread of "contemporary" gospel music in Christian circles, rock and other forms of music are more widely accepted as means for evangelism and even worship. Many now conclude that the debate was misguided, that the questions raised were not matters of biblical standards but rather matters of taste and culture to which the Bible is largely indifferent. One can also think about some of the now almost laughable debates that went on in evangelical circles one and two generations ago about the use of movies and television for evangelism. What seemed such gallant stances for morality now appear to be misguided, ill-informed prejudices.

Applying biblical standards in method selection is difficult to do, and it cannot be done on the basis of our own experience in our native culture. The criteria we use must be carefully examined in a cross-cultural setting. They must be very clear matters of principle and ethic and must be applied within the meaning context of the people to be evangelized.

2. *Strategic criteria*

If we place the question of selection within the strategy cycle which we are using as our model, we can list the types of criteria that might be used to evaluate a particular method:

— Does the method relate to our goal of evangelization?

— Does the method fit the culture of the people who are being evangelized? Is it a method which they could themselves utilize in continuing the evangelization of their own people after we are gone? Will the method confuse or offend the people?

— Can the methods be utilized by the potential force for evangelism? What are the minimum technological and educational levels if the methodologies are to be implemented in an acceptable fashion? How will the force for evangelism feel about the methods? Are they biblically justifiable or ethically legitimate?

— What kind of role will the method create between the evangelists and the people being evangelized? Does it create the kind of direct contact which seems to be the hallmark of dynamic movements of evangelization? What role will laypeople have in the implementing of the method? What about "experts"? Will the method make the church dependent upon outsiders?

— What resources are required to initiate the method or to continue its operation? Are those resources available? Will they be available after we leave?

Each of these could be more detailed, but this suggests the kind of approach which is inherent in the cycle which we are advocating for planning strategy. By utilizing it in this fashion, we can become aware of the tools and techniques we need to use in order to do the work of God. The selection process carries us out of our lethargy and irresponsibility and forces us to give good reasons for the methods we design for evangelization.

3. Methods and the people profile

One aspect of the strategy cycle is worthy of separate treatment because of its importance. We need to place our methods against the people profile and seriously consider whether they suit the attitude and knowledge which the people currently hold toward the gospel.

In Figure 20-1 (see p. 290 below), we have added to the Engel/Søgaard Scale a place for means and methods. This decision scale essentially sub-divides a people group in a way that helps us select means and methods. If we see most of the group at −6, that has a great impact on our method selection. It also helps us decide where we will begin. For example, suppose we had a group that was uniformly spread at 30 percent at −7, 30 percent at −6, 30 percent at −5, and 20 percent at −4, with a very small church at +2. All had neutral-to-positive attitudes about what they knew. We might elect to apply a separate method to each subgroup or to concentrate first on only one subgroup. Our "method" for the other subgroups would be to do nothing.

There are several additional questions that we need to ask before we choose a method. Does the method(s) take them through a process so that they are moved closer to a decision for Christ? Does it attempt to challenge them for commitment too soon? Does it respect the common patterns by which they deliberate about major decisions that affect religious allegiance? Does it utilize their social structure in terms of the decision-making patterns that require the cooperation or consensus of certain individuals?

Figure 20-1   The People Profile and Means and Methods

DECISION POINT	THE PEOPLE PROFILE			FORCE FOR EVANGELISM			MEANS AND METHODS		
	% 25 50 75	ATTITUDE + 0 −	RATE OF CHANGE	% 25 50 75	ATTITUDE + 0 −	RATE OF CHANGE	% 25 50 75	ATTITUDE + 0 −	RATE OF CHANGE
NO AWARENESS −7									
AWARENESS −6									
SOME KNOWLEDGE −5									
KNOWLEDGE −4									
IMPLICATIONS SEEN −3									
PERSONAL NEED −2									
CONFRONTATION −1									
CONVERSION									
RE-EVALUATION +1									
INCORPORATION +2									
PROPAGATION +3									

YOUR RESPONSE

The means and methods that are suitable for one step in the process may have little or even negative value for other steps. Furthermore we must be sure that in moving part of the group along the process we do not damage the potential for moving the other parts of the group at different steps in the same direction. We must seek methods that will effect the changes that are needed in terms of the actual location of the group in its pilgrimage.

PERSPECTIVE ON THE SELECTION PROCESS

Not all the questions we have listed are of equal value. We have to keep in mind our ultimate goal: to plant and equip a church for continuing evangelization. We are moving people through the spiritual decision process so that they are eventually faced with the decision to accept Christ as Lord of their life. If a method passes most of our tests or criteria for selection, but in the end does not produce a church or harvest the fields that are ripe, then it is irrelevant. We are not evangelizing in the way we sometimes go fishing: to engage in a pleasant diversion. We are ambassadors for Christ and stewards of the gospel. We are co-laborers with God, engaged in proclaiming his Kingdom, and we cannot be indifferent to the results of what we do.

We have no calling to make a name for ourselves by discovering another key to evangelization or innovating a method that will outshine the method of a rival organization. We cannot allow our methodologies to become sacred, and we cannot lose contact with the basic questions that motivated their creation in the first place: are they effective in evangelization? Do they move people forward in the spiritual decision process? Do they create fellowships of people who are equipped and motivated to get engaged in evangelization among their own people and around the world? No method, however dramatic its success in the past, can continue to maintain its potency if it does not change with the times. It is a human product and is subject to the same limitations to which all human creations are subject.

It is like the engineer we knew who was heavily involved in newspaper evangelism, placing ads in college papers in order to spread the gospel on campuses. Unfortunately the messages tended to be abrasive and insensitive. When told how great it was that someone was trying to reach the campuses, he would praise God and redouble his effort. When told the ads were more offensive than helpful (a follow-up of the responses to his ads indicated that most who wrote in were angry and consequently not open to personal evangelism), he would not listen. He could not be told that his hundreds and thousands of dollars might be spent more effectively by utilizing a different method or means.

The selection process can never be more than a series of points in time. We never select a method forever but must be continually re-selecting it as we evaluate what actually happens as we experience its results. Any means or method has the potential to subvert the goals for which it was originally selected. We find it all too easy, having invested a great deal of time and effort, resources and emotions, in our methods, to identify with them and to see any objective examination of them as a threat to our own identity. The criteria by which we originally selected a method fade into the background and are never reapplied to see if our evaluation of a means still holds true. We find ourselves hanging onto a method that has outlived its usefulness and is now actually keeping us from innovating or selecting a more effective approach.

CHAPTER 21

Finding Means and Methods

*F*inding means and methods to carry out the mission we believe
God is calling us to do is a critical part of planning strategies for
evangelization. We have suggested in a number of places that the ultimate answer to that question is dependent on the context within which
evangelization will actually be done. There is a logic to a situation
which must be responded to if we are to meet a people at the point of
their need, in terms of their meaning system, and through their cultural
forms. Methods that are not responsive to the people who are being
evangelized are at best no more than irrelevant and at worst (too frequently the case) positively confusing and offensive. Wherever we look
for models of ministry, we will ultimately have to incarnate them into
terms that make sense for the particular, unique people with whom we
are sharing Jesus Christ.

METHODS AND THE STRATEGY CYCLE

Methods are considerations that come after several more basic decisions. Looking for methods to use in evangelism makes little sense
unless one has a fairly clear idea of (1) the task (mission definition),
(2) the context within which the mission will have to be accomplished
(an understanding of the people), and (3) who will have to woman and
man the method (the force for evangelism). Methods are *means*. Until

the *ends* are clarified, it is very difficult to look for or create a method that has any meaning. It would be like going shopping for farm equipment without knowing what crop was to be grown, how large the farm was, or what the soil and terrain was like. The best of tools do no good if we try to use them to do something they were not designed to do.

But once the parameters of ministry are established, methods can be sought and developed in a meaningful way.

Our prior decisions help us to evaluate the suitability of each possible ministry model for evangelizing a particular people. This is important because there are no universals in methodology. By working in terms of the logic of the situation as we understand it, we are forced to discover hidden resources of creativity and understanding that God will give us. Seeking unique strategies is a longer and more demanding process, less secure than simply applying "standard solutions to unstandard situations." But in the end it is far more significant and fruitful.

Our basic philosophy in this matter affects our approach to the search for means and methods. We believe there are no sinful tools, only sinful people who can misuse them. We are free in Christ by his liberating Spirit to cast our net for methods as far and as wide as possible. At the same time we must recognize that we are capable of self-deception and corruption. We must continually bring ourselves and our programs back to the biblical and strategic criteria that serve as the norms for what we are doing. We cannot take the proud attitude that our education, civilization, organization, and history hold all the answers, or even the best answers, to the future evangelization of the peoples of the world. We recognize that the very people we seek to evangelize may themselves be able to teach us the method by which they can most effectively be evangelized.

We must approach our evangelism with the realistic awareness that we know very little about how to sow the seed, or water and harvest the crop. We will have to do far more than simply sensitize ourselves to the cultural dimensions so that we can know how best to plug in our standardized solutions. Completely novel approaches which have never been taught in seminary or college and which are not written up in any missiological journal may have to be devised. We need to be ready and flexible to do just that.

NEW TESTAMENT EXAMPLES

When the Old Testament people of God wanted to gain strength and guidance to face their own situation, they often looked back and remembered what God had done in the past; how he had delivered his people and heard their prayers. We need to remember what God has done in evangelism in the past. A keen awareness of how he has worked in the past and its meaning for our contemporary evangelism situations can strengthen us and give us new creative insight about evangelism.

There are many who would loudly agree with this procedure and insist that the most important means and methods are found in the Bible. The real issue in methodology, they might say, is captured in Roland Allen's book title: *Missionary Methods: St. Paul's or Ours?* (1962). We fail in evangelism, this point of view argues, not only because we have unconfessed sin in our community (as Israel did at Ai—Joshua 7), or because of the worldliness and resistance of the people being evangelized; rather, we fail because we are trying to do *God's* work with *our* methods. If we were to rediscover the methods followed in the Bible, we would experience a new surge of success.

This view is based on the notion that the Bible not only reveals the way we can be right with God and the purposes for which we are to live, but also God's own unique evangelistic approaches and methods. To what extent is the New Testament pattern of evangelism normative for us today when we live in a different social order with different cultural patterns? Is there a pattern for evangelism which we must follow if we are to be faithful stewards of the gospel?

This is a delicate subject. We believe there is a fundamental evangelistic message which finds its normative expression in the New Testament (see pp. 75–79), but it is not equally clear that the New Testament espouses a normative methodology (Coleman, 1963; R. Allen, 1962). The life of our Lord as well as the early Church exhibits the principles of good communication, organization, and cultural sensitivity which are applicable in any situation or context. We also believe there are ethical and normative criteria in the New Testament which are important in evaluating methodologies (see pp. 286–288). All of these elements, however, bear on any type of methodology, not just the methodology of the New Testament. It is not our duty to carry out our mission in the same manner as did the apostolic Church. It responded to its context, and we must learn from the early Christians how to respond to *our* context. As Michael Harper has written:

> We need to distinguish in the Bible between what is a fixed and unalterable truth—which does not change either in the course of time or in the context of cultural variety—and where the passage is describing how the Holy Spirit inspired people in an *ad hoc* situation. In this latter instance, we are not to follow slavishly how people were led *then*, but to learn from the example of their re-

sponse to the guidance of the Spirit, and expect ourselves to be led by the same Spirit, though perhaps in a quite different manner.

In other words we have to distinguish between what is exemplary in scripture and what is mandatory. (1978, p. 24; see also Peters, 1975)

The real problem raised here is the freedom of the Church and the Christian. We have tended to make the New Testament example mandatory. We have tended to confuse forms with functions, to read history back into the book of Acts. A careful survey of the early Church yields no clear model of ministry methods in the sense of program patterns or implemented practices. The apostles were not so concerned with passing on a methodology as communicating a message, sharing a life and love that could transform human experience. Evangelistic methods and approaches have to be implemented in terms of those basic spiritual realities, but the New Testament is not a handbook of specific evangelistic methods. It does not provide a detailed blueprint for successful evangelism. Indeed it provides broad principles which can be utilized for developing philosophies of ministry in order to undergird and legitimate the wide range of differing patterns and practices which we will have to implement as we devise methods for the unique peoples of the world. Methods are effective as means to our goals only within specific contexts. We must continually change our means as the context changes in order to preserve and achieve our goals.

Michael Green, who has made the most recent, comprehensive study of evangelism in the early Church, has this to say about methodology in the New Testament:

> There does not seem to have been anything very remarkable in the strategy and tactics of the early Christian mission. Indeed, it is doubtful if they had one. I do not believe they set out with any blueprint. They had an unquenchable conviction that Jesus was the key to life and death, happiness and purpose, and they simply could not keep quiet about him. The Spirit of Jesus within them drove them into mission. . . .
>
> Their methods on the whole, while varied, were unremarkable. There is no key to instant success to be found by ransacking the methods used by the early church. . . .
>
> Perhaps [the priority of personal conversation] is the greatest lesson we can learn from the early church in the very changed situation of our own day. The most effective method of evangelism and the most widespread, in the long run, in its results, is conversation evangelism, where one who has found Jesus shares his discovery, his problems, his joys and his sorrows with one who is still

groping in the dark. There is no joy like introducing a friend to Christ in this way.... If all Christians set about doing this, they would not need much other methodology from the early church. (1975, pp. 165–166, 168, 171–172; see also Green, 1970, ch. 8)

What Green is suggesting is that it is not the specific *forms* of methodologies in the New Testament that are lasting in their example to us so much as the fact that all those forms created the kind of direct contact between vital Christians and those who needed to hear the Good News which led to conversions. In personal conversation, whether the result of open-air preaching, teaching in the synagogue, or the reading of a literary work like the Gospel of Luke, Christians were continually and avidly witnessing to the power of Jesus Christ. Personal and direct contact was crucial in the spread of the gospel then, and it is now.

There is no simple relationship between the degree of success in evangelism and the similarity of a contemporary method to forms of the methods of the New Testament. Methods, even those of the apostolic Church, are relative to the people being evangelized. Where conditions and cultures are somewhat similar to those of the first century, similar methods will be effective. But where there are large differences, changes in methodology will be necessary if we are to carry out the unchanged mandate of mission.

All the knowledge, techniques and methods which humanity has accumulated need to be put to work. God makes available to each generation those tools which are essential to carry out his task. We study the Bible because it shows us the type of dynamic and motivation that ought to lie behind our contemporary communities and evangelism. The Bible gives us a concrete perspective from which we can view our own day. We can learn from the early Church how we can respond within our new situations and creatively discover God's strategy for today. But we do not learn from the Bible that we ought to make an anachronistic attempt to force all times and situations into the *ad hoc* patterns of the New Testament models.

THE EXPERIENCES OF OTHER CHRISTIANS

A second source of methods is successful evangelism models.[1] We study what others are doing, measure them and their philosophy against

1. The literature in this area is almost inexhaustible, even though most of it is unsystematic, impressionistic, and rather "soft" from a scientific point of view. Almost all of the "Church Growth" case studies in various countries contain

our mission criteria and understanding of Scripture, and then adopt those methods which seem appropriate. This has been a strong thrust of the Church Growth movement: to discover where the Church is growing rapidly, and to focus attention on those situations so that the wider Church can learn from successful models of ministry. With its strong pragmatism, the Church Growth movement looks for what actually produces new converts (not simply growth by "proselytism" or transfer) and sees to what extent those methods and approaches can be used in a variety of other contexts. The movement wants to clear away all confusion and unsystematic thinking about methodologies and to force the Church to examine fairly and fully whether or not what it is doing actually will lead to church growth.

Interestingly enough, the current results of the movement's research seem to bear out at least a number of principles which might be simplified and schematized as follows:

(1) Evangelization occurs when the Church makes it a priority goal and concentrates resources and people on seeing new, faithful disciples added to the fellowship of the community of Christians. Evangelism does not just happen. It is the result of concern and commitment:

> Churches which are not growing are usually churches in which the responsibility for growth is all loaded onto one person, usually the minister. On the other hand, a church where everybody is working for growth, where everybody is concerned that the Gospel be known, that is a church which grows. Where everybody works at getting obstacles out of the way, where everybody learns as

---

sections relevant to the explication of methodology as it bears in various contexts on growth or non-growth of churches. Some of the more explicit, methodologically oriented studies include: Neil Braun, *Laity Mobilized: Reflections on Church Growth in Japan and Other Lands* (1971); George Peters, *Saturation Evangelism* (1970); Donald C. Palmer, *Explosion of People Evangelism* (1974); Malcolm Bradshaw, *Church Growth Through Evangelism-in-Depth* (1969); Janvier Voelkel, "The Eternal Revolutionary: Evangelical Ministry to the University Student in Latin America" (Unpublished Thesis, Fuller Seminary); Max Ward Randall, *Profile for Victory: New Proposals for Missions in Zambia* (1970); Lyle L. Vander Werff, *Christian Missions to Muslims: The Record* (1977); B. V. Subbamma, *New Patterns for Discipling Hindus* (1970); Stan Shewmaker, *Tonga Christianity* (1970). There are a great many articles in *Church Growth Bulletin* (1969–1977), edited by Donald A. McGavran, Vols. I-XI, dealing with specific methods and approaches to a wide range of peoples and circumstances. Section VI, "Evangelistic Strategy Papers and Reports," in *Let the Earth Hear His Voice* (Douglas, 1975), pp. 481–982, presents brief statements on many current evangelistic methodologies.

much as possible about the growth of the church, where the church board or session spends half its time planning for church growth, there church growth occurs. (McGavran and Arn, 1973, pp. 12–13)

(2) Large increases in the Church have occurred where the evangelizing agency has respected the socio-cultural boundaries and decision-making mechanisms present in the society. Where *peoples* have been allowed to come into the Church as *peoples,* often in movements of multi-individual, mutually interdependent decisions, the Church has incorporated large parts of society (Tippett, 1971; Cook, 1971; Read, 1965; Pickett et al., 1973; McGavran, 1955). This is a reflection of our emphases in chapters 11, 12, and 13. Where a particular sub-cultural set of needs have been met, where a people's meaning system has been utilized, where cultural forms have developed so as to conform to the life-ways of a particular people, it has been invariably easier for a people to understand that Christian faith is not a matter of abandoning family and culture, but more a matter of bringing it all under the Lordship of Christ.

It is evident that people receive the gospel most readily when it is presented to them in a manner which is appropriate—and not alien—to their culture, and when they can respond to it with and among their own people. Different societies have different procedures for making group decisions, e.g., by consensus, by the head of the family, or by a group of elders. We recognize the validity of the corporate dimension of conversion as part of the total process, as well as the necessity for each member of the group ultimately to share in it personally. (Lausanne Committee, 1978b, p. 22)

(3) There are a wide variety of methods which have been effective in creating an evangelistic situation through which the Church has been able to grow. Some of these methods and approaches today would seem rather objectionable to our current ways of thinking. Yet we can only admit that they worked in a particular context. The Icelanders became Christian when the pagan seer, Thorgeir, uttered the decree at the All-thing that from thence "all men shall be Christians and believe in one God . . . but leave all idol worship, not expose children to perish, and not eat horseflesh" (McGavran, 1970, p. 25). It took many years for that new law to work its way into the actual beliefs and practices of Icelanders, but it turned the tide. We probably would not communicate the Christian faith in a country in that way today! Witness bands, mass crusades, small house churches, a system of elementary and secondary

schools, ashrams—a wide variety of methods have been used successfully in evangelization. We agree with Melvin Hodges' conclusion: "There is no single method for raising up churches" (1973, p. 32). There are many methods, and not all of them are equally fruitful or effective. But none of them can claim to be the exclusive narrow path to significant progress in evangelization. As McGavran observes about methods among a responsive population:

> Among such populations the choice of method is a minor matter. The Nevius method, the Chandra Singh method, the tent-teams, the unpaid witness, the paid leader—all will multiply congregations. But some methods will multiply more than others and some better than others. Some will lead more rapidly to self-support and others will delay it. Some methods appear foreign, generate resistance, or create non-productive churches. Others appear indigenous, generate goodwill, and stamp in patterns possible of indefinite reproduction. (1959, p. 129)

In some ways these three principles are crucial contributions of the Church Growth movement. It has not primarily been a movement that has discovered a new methodology or clarified one method as more biblical than another. Rather the movement has heightened the importance of having evangelism as a priority in the Church. It has also insisted that the priority be understood in terms of making faithful disciples from converts, and in measuring "disciples" in terms of those who are involved in a fellowship of believers (rather than being satisfied with vague, glowing reports of decisions and attendance at meetings). As the movement has applied this philosophy within an historical and comparative research framework, it has become more apparent that church growth has occurred through "people movements" which have been generated and fostered by a number of different methodologies. When methodologies are evaluated in the crucible of church growth, different approaches appear to be effective in different contexts.

THE EXPERIENCE OF PSEUDO-CHRISTIAN AND OTHER RELIGIOUS MOVEMENTS

A third source of methods has been models developed from the study of pseudo-Christian and non-Christian religious movements (e.g., Hesselgrave, 1978a). This is an area worthy of much larger exploitation than has been the case in the past. The Christian movement is not alone in seeking to win the allegiance of the peoples of the earth. There has been a variety of Christian-derived movements. Some clearly have been within the mainstream of Christian life and faith, and others clearly have been beyond the boundaries of Christian identity. Each takes up the cause of evangelization in terms of its own distinctive message and structure.

One might point to the enormously vital and diversified African Independent Church movements, many of which are within the bounds of Christian tradition (Barrett, 1968; Turner, 1967; Daneel, 1971; Murphree, 1969; Sundkler, 1961; Loewen, 1976). The church which has grown up in the wake of Simon Kimbangu is the largest non-Catholic, non-Protestant Christian body in Zaire. These are not simply splinter groups with little to add to our current knowledge of how people are brought into a movement.

One may also point to studies of such movements as the Iglesia ni Christo (a unitarian movement with nearly one million members, concentrated in the Philippines), or the zealous lay Buddhist movements of Japan such as Sokka Gakkai and Rissho Koseikai (Tuggy, 1974; K.J. Dale, 1975; Braun, 1971; McFarland, 1967; Hesselgrave, 1978a). Or one might look at studies of Independent Christian churches in Taiwan (Swanson, 1971), or mainline and minority denominations and cults in the United States (Kelley, 1972). The list can be expanded enormously. There are many flaming causes and prophets in our generation. Many of them are able to generate the movements of the future with a message, a method, and an organization that captures the loyalty and devotion of significant numbers of people. When compared with the traditional methods of slowly growing Christian churches, dramatic contrasts appear. Those differences demonstrate how traditional methodologies are uncreative, unresponsive to the characteristics and needs of the people being evangelized, and unnecessarily Westernized in character.

Some may feel this to be a dangerous source for methods. What can the Marxists (Hyde, 1966), Mormons (O'Dea, 1957; Arrington and Bitton, 1979), the Moonies of the Unification Church (Lofland, 1977; Edwards, 1979), or the Muslim movements teach us?

The final answer to such questions depends on our understanding of what happened in the New Testament Church. To what extent did the early Church learn from other movements? To what extent did it borrow elements of methodology and church structure from environing groups? Why do we feel "borrowing" a methodology is an illegitimate or shameful affair? We learn most of what we do that way. Perhaps the most honest even if humbling response might be to say, Yes, we are bankrupt and need the stimulus of these other groups to become creative and fresh again!

A careful study of the New Testament against its background reveals that many aspects of the early Church were adopted from other groups as it "seemed good" to them and to the Holy Spirit. Their organization as community and their worship were patterned after the Jewish synagogue out of which many Christians came. They recognized that there were many things that were good and true, right and honorable (Phil. 4:8) in their society which could be baptized and used in the new Christian life-style.

Further, it must be pointed out that these pseudo-Christian or non-Christian movements are making a good and judicious use of social and cultural mechanisms. The Mormons, for example, are growing at a rate of two hundred thousand a year. How much of that growth is due to the wise use of good communication methods? If we view a movement as Satanic, does that preclude the acknowledgment that it might be doing the kinds of things the Christian Church should be doing in meeting the needs of people? Perhaps one of the implications of Jesus' words that we be as wise as serpents and as harmless as doves is that we ought to learn from the good examples of bad people without adopting their values or evil motives.

THE MEANS AND METHODS
OF THE PEOPLE BEING EVANGELIZED

Evangelization never enters a situation devoid of techniques and methods for communicating important messages similar to the message of the gospel. Every society has a communication network by which important news is conveyed throughout various levels and groups. This may be no more than the word of mouth that is carried by a traveler as he or she travels from one campsite of a nomadic people to another. Or it may be as modern and sophisticated as a satellite-borne television image of events which are occurring halfway around the world. There are traditional means for communicating information that will lead to a change in religious allegiance.

When we enter a new situation, we tend to think of it in terms of our solutions, in terms of the methods and means from our own social and cultural experiences. This is true even when we attempt to be culturally sensitive and learn the meaning systems, the language and customs of another people. Our almost innate bias is to perceive cultural information through a grid of predetermined methodologies. Such a bias blinds us to one of the most important creative sources of new methods for accomplishing the goals which we have: the people to be reached have indigenous ways of communicating to their culture. There are several examples of this.

In early Meiji Japan (1868–) Western ideas and life-style became popular. The works of a number of key Western writers such as Rousseau, Robert Louis Stevenson, and Jules Verne were translated into Japanese. Shakespeare's plays were also translated, but were not understood or appreciated. The Western dramatic mode did not fit the traditional Japanese dramatic mode. Only after Shakespeare was translated into the mode of the traditional Japanese drama (the Nō play) did he gain great popularity in Meiji Japan.

There is a traditional way for making important announcements or conveying significant news among the Baliem Dani of the highlands of central Irian Jaya (Indonesia). A powerful or influential man will send an invitation to neighboring clans and hamlets. All will assemble on a given day for a feast. The pig, the most valued and prestigious source of meat, will be butchered and cooked. Everyone will feast on the meat and the fat will be smeared on important guests. As the people finish their pig meat, the person who called the celebration will stand and make his announcement in a traditionally stylized form. Everyone knows that the message is extremely important and will give great attention and weight to what is said. For weeks the message will be discussed as people till their yams and exchange goods. If the missionary is thinking about preaching the Good News and wants it to be seriously considered, he should learn that the Baliem Dani already have a method for doing that!

Chuck Kraft attempted to devise a methodology for evangelizing villages based on this premise among the Higi of Nigeria:

> I once asked a group of Nigerian church leaders how they would present the Christian message to the village council. They replied, "We would choose the oldest, most respected man in the group and ask him a question. He would discourse at length and then become silent, whereupon we would ask another question. As he talked others would comment as well. But eventually the discussion would lessen and the leader would talk more. In this way we would develop our message so it would become the topic for discussion of the whole village." I asked them why they didn't employ this approach in church. "Why, we've been taught that monologue is the Christian way," they replied. "Can this be why no old men come to

church?" I asked. "Of course—we have alienated them by not showing them due respect in public meetings," was their reply. (1973, p. 50)

We cannot ignore the methods within social groups. Oftentimes it is *only* when we utilize their methods that we are able to stimulate a deep and powerful encounter with the gospel that will penetrate the whole population.

DEVELOPMENT AS EVANGELISM

Earlier we considered the relationship between evangelism and social action (see pp. 64–66). Here we want to examine how development can be a very powerful method for evangelism. We cannot deal with the specifics of the methodologies of development. There are other books which attempt to deal with such matters on a much broader scale (Long, 1977; Dickson, 1974; Bodley, 1975). That development is an authentic expression of Christian love that reaches out and touches people both in their proximate, immediate needs and in their ultimate need for knowing the true God and Maker of the universe, has been repeatedly demonstrated. Those who suppose it is sub-Christian, detracting from the true mission or the Church, and those who dismiss any attempt to share Christ in the midst of compassionate service as unfair, inauthentic, or coercive are in error. That it *can* detract from the mission or be used in a coercive manner is not in question. We are simply asserting that a love that responds to the real needs of people will often find itself engaged in development that has very real evangelistic impact. Those who have made evangelization an integral part of their compassionate service in hospitals, health education by extension (R. and S. Seaton, 1976), and agricultural uplift have seen people become Christians and have discovered how God cares for all of life. Those who have carried out evangelism that is motivated by love have found themselves entangled inextricably in the life concerns of the people they were evangelizing. An example of this is found in the "Faith and Farm" project in Nigeria:

It is geared primarily for the farmer and his household who make up 95 percent of the population of Nigeria. The aim of this highly successful project is to train African Christians to teach other farmers and their families to recognize that Jesus Christ is

Lord of every part of their lives. As a result, starchy, low-yielding crops have been replaced by nutritional foods with reinforced proteins. Inefficient hand-tools have been replaced by more practical instruments. Harvested crops have been properly stored and protected from the ravages of white ants and other termites. But more. Children sick and dying from disease and malnutrition have been given a new lease of life by a regular reinforced diet, and thousands of unemployed school-leavers have been given not only useful occupations but a new-found dignity and a fulfilment in a rewarding enterprise. . . .

In the northeast area of Nigeria, where the work has been extended, one incident took place which is not in isolation, and serves to illustrate the evangelistic by-product of this kind of program. One of the Faith and Farm agents saved the grain store of a Muslim and his family and protected his valuable millet and guinea corn against destruction by white ants. This was all the family had for the year. Quietly the African Christian farmer shared his skill and knowledge as he worked alongside the Muslim farmer in preserving his crops. Later the Muslim inquired, "What makes you give up your time and come to help me?" The farmer replied, "Because we want to be like our Master, Jesus Christ, who fed the people when they were hungry." And that day the Muslim farmer listened with sympathy to the Gospel message for the first time, and he began to understand it. (Hoffman, 1975, pp. 703–704)

FINAL CONSIDERATIONS

Much of what we have said both presupposes and will require a great deal of research in the future. The effectiveness of many methods is simply not very well known. There have not been many professional evaluations of the actual effects, positive and negative, of given approaches. Information has been researched because it either confirms the wisdom of an effort or gives a basis for an article that will trumpet success back to missionary supporters. Much of the information has been irrelevant to the fundamental goals which we claim to be pursuing. If we are about the business of making disciples, then it is disciples we must count! Not the number of prayer meetings we attend, or the number of handbills or tracts we hand out.

A great deal more research on the indigenous means and methods for communication, for organizing to form community, and for leadership and planning must also be done. If we desire an indigenous or "dynamically equivalent" church to grow in each people of the world, we must begin to utilize methodologies that are equally indigenous instead of imposing more Westernized technology onto situations.

Along with research we need to conduct more pilot experiments in which we deliberately try out new approaches on a small scale with careful evaluation. We can theorize, object and counter-object, plan and replan until we are tired of the whole process. But until we begin to carry out new experiments to solve old problems, until we discover more effective and efficient ways of doing old tasks, we will never find the means and methods that will carry evangelization forward in the next half-century.

QUESTIONS

Defining Means and Methods

1. What is a method or a means?
2. What role do methods play in producing the evangelistic results we seek?
3. What criteria are important for understanding the usefulness and limitations of a method?

Theory of Selection

1. What differences do means and methods make in producing the evangelistic effects we seek?
2. How do we relate the work of the Holy Spirit in evangelism to our methods?
3. By what criteria ought we to evaluate methods in order to select or create ones to evangelize a given people? (See the many questions listed on pp. 286-289.)
4. Are there biblical and ethical norms which rule out certain means for achieving our goals? What are they?
5. How do we evaluate the methods we have selected to see if they need to be changed or exchanged for better ones?

Finding Means and Methods

1. What can we learn from the New Testament that will help us to devise more effective methods?

2. What indigenous means and methods for communication and organization can be utilized for evangelism? Have we considered them *before* resorting to non-indigenous techniques?

3. Have we checked the experience of other Christian groups who have attempted to evangelize the same people or groups? What methods and approaches seem most effective? Can we use them?

4. What pseudo-Christian or non-Christian movements seem to have significant impact on the people we wish to evangelize? What can be learned from the way they communicate and organize to achieve their goals? What methods seem most responsible for their impact? Can we use them?

5. How can evangelism be an integral part of our other activities, such as development, health care, and so forth?

6. What pilot projects need to be undertaken in order to test or develop new methods for evangelization? Are we engaged in such experiments? Why not?

STEP 5

ANALYZING
THE STRATEGY

Considerations

Planning the Strategy

Assumptions

Questions

CONSIDERATIONS

1. God has a particular strategy for each people. Our task is to uncover that strategy and become a part of it.

2. Strategies are always dynamic. They are always time-bound.

3. The ultimate strategy should always involve the formation of a dynamic church.

4. Church growth is seldom linear. The diffusion of innovation is normally encyclical.

5. The major problem with many planning efforts is the failure to discuss the assumptions upon which they are based.

6. The most difficult assumptions to uncover are assumptions about ourselves.

CHAPTER 22

Planning the Strategy

W e have been following the rational process of first looking at the
people whom we believe God wants us to reach, examining the
force for evangelism to see who might be the ones most able to reach
them, and then discussing the various means and methods that might be
used to reach them.

We now come to Step 5: "Analyzing the Strategy." Although on paper
this approach looks quite linear, we have noted that it is actually an
iterative approach. It is impossible to think about the people that one
intends to reach without thinking about how to reach them. It is just as
impossible to disassociate the people who might reach them from the
means and methods that might be used. Through the process of reflection and answering a series of questions, one can accumulate enough
data to plan an initial strategy, to make a preliminary statement as to
the overall approach one would use to reach a certain people.

As we discussed in chapter 5, a strategy is both inclusive and exclusive. By defining what we *will* do, we often define what we will *not* do.
Making and refining a strategy statement is a very useful process. Initially, we have very little understanding of how to reach a particular
people. We gather information. We try to understand God's will for this
particular people. Eventually we hope to complete a plan and then to
act. We have tried to show this process in Figure 22-1. To the left is the

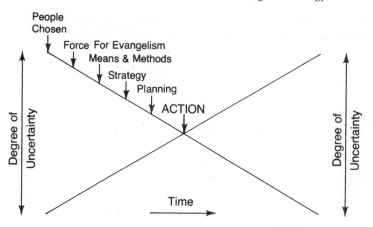

Figure 22-1   Degree of Planning Uncertainty

point in time when we start planning. Within the confines of the cone on the left, the degree of uncertainty about what to do decreases as we move toward a point of action. Somewhere along this planning stage we have to make an initial statement about our strategy. This will lead us to the completion of our planning. Note that from the point of action onward the degree of present uncertainty about the future increases. In other words, the farther away things are from the point when we decide to do something, the more uncertain we are about the future. This emphasizes that we have to continually rethink our plans and strategies.

Another way of thinking about this same diagram is to think of the cone on the left as a decreasing spiral. As we go through the planning process, asking questions about the people, the force for evangelism, and the methods to be used, we gain a better understanding as to how to evangelize a people.

LEVELS OF STRATEGY

Strategies, like plans, come in all sizes. Let us assume that the primary goal of any attempt to reach an unreached people is to see an active church that comprises at least 20 percent of the group that we are attempting to reach. For this overall endeavor we need a *grand strategy*. This strategy would be a statement about how we hope God will bring 20 percent of the people within this group to a knowledge of himself in such a manner that they will move out to evangelize the rest of their group.

An intermediate strategy might be a strategy statement as to how we expect to see a church initially planted within this group.

A *short-range strategy* might deal with our procedure for moving into the group. We will illustrate what we mean by using three levels of strategy.

PHASES OF DEVELOPMENT

It is very helpful to break down the evangelism task into various phases. The Engel Scale is very useful at this point. It can become a model or a profile of where to be. In Figure 22-2 we show four profiles on the Engel/Søgaard Scale, four different stages of evangelization. In Phase 1 we show a particular people, very few of whom have any awareness of the gospel. A smaller number have some awareness but that is as far as it has gone.

As we end Phase 1 and move into Phase 2, our strategy is to give almost everyone in this group some positive awareness of Christianity. We assume that there will be a few we will overlook, who will stay at -7 (no awareness), but the majority will become aware and a small number will have moved through the entire process and become members of Christ's Church.

In Phase 3 the *missionary* task is complete. Almost everyone in this entire group has some knowledge of the gospel, but the important thing is that 20 percent of the group is now incorporated into a fellowship and a small percentage have become active propagators of the gospel.

The new and young church has to complete Phase 4. We have assumed for diagrammatic purposes that although not all have become Christians, the church has done a good job of spreading the gospel and those who are not now members of the church at least have a knowledge of the gospel, and hopefully have understood its implications. In other words, the whole group has been evangelized.

In Figure 22-2, our *grand missionary strategy* would include Phases 1-3. An *intermediate strategy* would include Phase 1 and Phase 2, and our *short-range strategy* would include Phase 1.

THE EXAMPLE OF THE TURKANA

Two examples of grand strategies for reaching the same people will help to illustrate this procedure. The people in question are the Tur-

Figure 22-2   Four Phases of Church Growth

DECISION POINT	PHASE 1 % 25 50 75	PHASE 1 ATTITUDE + 0 –	PHASE 1 RATE OF CHANGE	PHASE 2 % 25 50 75	PHASE 2 ATTITUDE + 0 –	PHASE 2 RATE OF CHANGE	PHASE 3 % 25 50 75	PHASE 3 ATTITUDE + 0 –	PHASE 3 RATE OF CHANGE	PHASE 4 % 25 50 75	PHASE 4 ATTITUDE + 0 –	PHASE 4 RATE OF CHANGE
NO AWARENESS –7	▉		0	▉		–40% year						
AWARENESS –6	▉	X	0	▉	X	+38% year		X	–5% year			
SOME KNOWLEDGE –5				1%	X	+15% year	▉	X	+1% year			
KNOWLEDGE –4				.1%	X	+10% year	▉	X	+1% year	▉		
IMPLICATIONS SEEN –3												
PERSONAL NEED –2												
CONFRONTATION –1												
CONVERSION												
RE-EVALUATION +1				.5%	X		.5%	X	+20% year			
INCORPORATION +2					X	+10% year	20%	X	+20% year	▉		
PROPAGATION +3							1%	X	+10% year	▉		

315

kana, a people group of approximately 200,000 living in the northern desert regions of Kenya to the west of Lake Turkana (formerly known as Lake Rudolf).[1] The Turkana are a nomadic people, herders of camels and goats. They follow the herds to whatever pasture lands are currently growing in what is a very sparse, arid part of the world. They move from place to place as clans, building a new manyatta (village of thatched huts) wherever they stop. Their diet consists primarily of milk and a mixture of blood—a high protein diet which produces tall, very handsome people. They are polygamists. Their economy is built basically on the trading of animals. They have an old and well-developed culture.

In the early 1960s events conspired against the Turkana with the closing of national borders to the north and to the west. A growing population and extended drought left many of them starving. In response to this the government of Kenya opened a number of feeding camps along the shore of what was then Lake Rudolf, and subsequently allowed missionaries to move into the area. The missionaries taught the Turkana to fish. Over the years a small sedentary community of fishermen was established along the lakeshore. The Africa Inland Mission established a mission station next to a small gulf on the 150-mile-long lake. Through the preaching of the missionaries and one Turkana pastor there was a small but steadily growing church along the lakeshore. Recent surveys of the Turkana living along the lake indicate that large numbers of them move back and forth between the Turkana permanently established there and those who are still herding through the wilderness.

The grand strategy of the Africa Inland Mission is to establish a church along the lakeshore that will be strong enough to evangelize the nomadic people. Part of their underlying assumption is that modernization will continue to move very rapidly through Kenya. A hard-surfaced road is now being constructed to Lake Turkana and eventually the Turkana will have to abandon their nomadic ways. Meanwhile, a strong church can be formed.

The intermediate strategy is to establish a strong church in the lakeshore community and to train and develop Turkana evangelists.

The short-range strategy is essentially survival. This is a very harsh area of the world. Rain is scarce, and dust storms are violent. To learn

1. Initial studies on the Turkana were done by Gulliver (1951). A more recent study by Raymond H. Davis is incorporated in his master's thesis (1978). A privately funded study by World Vision International was done by Bedan Mbugua.

to survive in this environment, to learn the Turkana language, and to understand the Turkana culture has, of necessity, been the short-range strategy.

There are others who also have a grand strategy to see at least 20 percent of the Turkana become Christians, but this strategy is being worked out in a different way. The underlying assumption of this strategy is that the lakeshore people may *not* be able to evangelize those who have kept their older customs. Modernization may *not* rapidly move the nomadic Turkana into sedentary situations. The grand strategy then is to establish churches among the *nomadic* Turkana.

The intermediate strategy is to plant a culturally adaptable church within one clan, so that clan can evangelize others. The short-range strategy is to become acceptable to one clan and to lead some of the key figures in that clan to a knowledge of Christ. The Kenya researcher, in attempting to obtain a better understanding of the culture of the Turkana, sought out a significant person within one of the clans. Through a series of intermediaries he eventually made friends with a Turkana diviner. He lived with this individual for some time, observing, questioning, and learning. Utilizing his understanding of Turkana culture, he established the diviner as a friend. In the course of his friendship he was able to explain to the diviner the nature and power of the person of Jesus Christ. As a result the diviner professed allegiance to Christ and set about to teach other members of his family. As of this writing, the strategy is to set aside one thatched hut within the manyatta for worship every time the clan sets up a new dwelling place.

It should be noted that both of these strategies are complementary. Stating a strategy like this gives an overall framework within which one can begin to plan. It helps others to understand what is going on, and helps them to cooperate. It helps to direct future action. The Engel Scale is valuable because it gives us specific terms for talking about where we are in our particular strategy. When it is combined with the attitudinal scale suggested by Viggo Søgaard, it gives us a diagrammatic way of seeing how we intend to move forward. It is our contention that the ultimate goal for the cross-cultural evangelist should always be Phase 4 shown in Figure 22-2 above. But the steps in between will vary tremendously.

THE DIFFUSION OF INNOVATION

New ideas are seldom accepted at a uniform rate (Rogers, 1962). In almost all human endeavor output is seldom directly proportional to input. It almost always looks like an "S"-shaped curve. In Figure 22-3 we have shown a curve with two axes—input and output. Input might be time, energy, resources, or a combination of all three. Output could be acceptance of ideas, or church growth, or numbers of people in the church. The bottom of the curve is flat because it is very unlikely that one will be immediately accepted by a culture. It takes time to gain acceptance and to be understood. But once this acceptance takes place, once a new idea takes hold, often the growth is very rapid. Near the end of the cycle—the top of the curve—those who resist the new idea become more and more evident. Whether it is "hardening of the heart" or lack of understanding, there will always be those who find it impossible to change.

This curve is useful in understanding what happens between each step of the Engel Scale. In one sense, as we attempt to help people move from one point to another, this type of curve will repeat itself. Understanding this will help us in thinking through our strategy.

CYCLES OF CHURCH GROWTH

The input-output, "S"-shaped curve is also useful in helping us to understand how churches grow. Often advocates of church growth suggest that we set goals for how our church will grow in the coming years. Vergil Gerber's book *A Manual for Evangelism and Church Growth* (1973) offers an excellent discussion of this. Church Growth theory usually deals with growth in terms of a decade, recognizing that small spurts or declines are not necessarily important. What is impor-

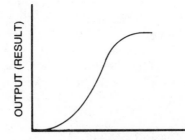

INPUT (TIME, ENERGY)

Figure 22-3   Input vs. Output

tant is the long-term growth. In our evangelistic zeal, we keep planning new strategies to win people to Christ, but we often fail to make plans to incorporate them as mature members. The East African Revival which has been under way for fifty years is a good example of this. Many church leaders in East Africa are now becoming increasingly concerned about the large number of people who become church members and profess Christ as Savior, but who do not seem to exhibit markedly changed lives. A closer examination has shown that their primary need is for teachers. A strategy which calls for church growth, but which at the same time does not call for adequate teaching, will eventually fail. As we said earlier, too often we fail to plan *for success!*

It is often better to plan for an intense evangelistic effort for a period of time, say a year, and then plan for an intense time of on-the-job training. This is working very effectively in some of the rapidly growing Pentecostal churches in Brazil. Here the new convert is immediately put to work with the church as a witness within his or her community. In his book *Dedication and Leadership* (1966), Douglas Hyde discloses how well the Communists have used this approach in their training.

If we end up with 20 percent of the members of the group at +2 (incorporation) on the Engel Scale, but with no members of the group at +3 (propagators of the gospel), then our strategy has been wrong.

DESCRIBING A PEOPLE

As we attempted to describe a people, we suggested that one can place them on a scale of movement toward Christ. By understanding that people move through a process, we can avoid the mistake of trying to move them too quickly or bypassing one of the natural steps of progression. Although our ultimate goal is always to bring people to faith and into the fellowship of Christ as active members of his body, our shorter-term strategy may be to move people only to a given step. We can see this in two dimensions. Looking back at the combination of the Engel and Søgaard scales, we may have a strategy to move people from, say, −6 to −4, or we might have a strategy to move those who are already at −4 to a favorable attitude about what they already know. On the other hand, we might have a strategy that combined both of these attempts. But by stating in our strategy what is the first goal of our evangelistic effort, we help clarify not only what we are attempting, but why we are attempting it.

THE FORCE FOR EVANGELISM

Strategy statements should include not only yourself and your agency, but also your relationship with the existing church, with other Christian agencies within the country, and with your supporting constituency. We need to encompass the total force for evangelism and to try to be as specific as possible as to who is involved.

MEANS AND METHODS

A general statement about means and methods does not have to include at this point all of the details. That will come later in our planning. For example, the means and methods that our Kenyan friend was using to reach the Turkana were to establish a relationship of trust with a significant person among the Turkana and to demonstrate by word and life that the Power of the Holy Spirit met the felt needs of the Turkana.[2]

Having said all this, we are now ready to state our strategy. Following is a sample form of such a statement:

We intend to evangelize (*name of people*) people.

We will begin with _____ group(s) on the Engel Scale.

We will do this by utilizing these methods: _____,

which will be carried out by these people _____.

It is our intention that _____ percent of this group will _____ (goal) by (date) .

Using the above form, what would be one strategy statement for the Turkana as a result of the research that has been done there so far?

> We intend to evangelize the nomadic Turkana of Northern Kenya. Our approach will be to begin with one clan. A single missionary will attempt to establish a relationship with the clan chief and/or

2. One day the diviner was asked to take a spell which had been cast upon one member of the group and to cast it back on the one who had originally made it. The missionary suggested that it would be a much more loving thing to cast the spell completely away. After thinking this over the diviner agreed. This opened the way for further discussions on a new set of values based upon Jesus' intervention for mankind. The important thing to note here is that eventually the power of the Holy Spirit was described as meeting the everyday needs (handling spells) of the Turkana.

diviner. Once this is established the single missionary will be joined by a missionary couple (hopefully with two young children), and will live adjacent to the particular clan for a period of a year. During this time it will be our strategy to learn the customs of the Turkana and the needs of this particular clan and to share with them the power of Jesus Christ to meet their everyday needs. Of the 100 people within this clan we expect that 10 percent will move to +3, 75 percent will move to +2, 5 percent will move to −4 and 10 percent will move to −3. As people accept Christ, we will build a temporary shelter similar to the palm thatch temporary housing of the Turkana and will have this designated as a church.

We will share our strategy with the mission agencies involved, particularly the Africa Inland Church, and will ask that the missionaries living with this particular clan be allowed to stay isolated with them during this first year.

WHAT DOES THIS APPROACH EXCLUDE?

In the process of reviewing our strategy, some of the potential force for evangelism and possible means and methods will be discarded as inappropriate. For example, in Turkana, missionaries were not going to attempt to reach all of the other clans. Specifically, they were not going to attempt to reach the lakeshore dwellers who had abandoned their nomadic ways and had settled down to fishing. They were not planning to build a permanent church (the model of the Africa Inland Church). They were not going to use the tools of community development to attempt to better the life of the particularly Turkana clan (they might have brought a veterinarian to help with the many Turkana cattle). They were not going to attempt to bring the new Christians within the fellowship of the Africa Inland Church with its tradition of fixed church buildings.

In addition they were going to avoid being seen as those who came bringing a great deal from the outside. They were not going to build Western housing or supply themselves with Western food.

Now it does not follow that these were the right decisions. For instance, the missionaries might soon discover that they could not live on the local diet (camel milk and blood). But it is helpful, to both themselves and their fellow Christians in the area, to make these going-in statements.

The above example of strategy was for those attempting to reach the nomadic Turkana. What might be a strategy statement for those intending to begin with the lakeshore Turkama?

> We intend to evangelize all the Turkana. Our approach will be to establish a strong church among the lakeshore Turkana, a church with the responsibility of evangelizing their nomadic brothers and sisters. Six missionaries will establish a permanent base at Kalakol, will learn the language, and will establish a relationship by providing medical and material assistance to the sedentary Turkana. During this time the goal will be to learn the customs and culture of the Turkana so that a culturally appropriate method can be developed for Turkana Christians from the small AIC church to communicate the gospel. Of the five thousand people living permanently on the lakeshore we anticipate that in ten years there will be one hundred evangelists (+3), one thousand church members (+2) supporting these missionaries, and only fifty to one hundred people who have not moved to some knowledge of the gospel (−5) or beyond. We will share our strategy with others who are attempting to reach the Turkana, and will modify our strategy based upon their experience and ours.

The important thing about these strategies is that they are *statements of intent*. They help us narrow down what we will and will not do so that we can now get on with the business of deciding how to proceed.

IS THE STRATEGY APPROPRIATE?

After making a strategy statement, it is a good idea to go back and review the whole process that we have been through thus far. Remember, (again) we are still in the thinking process. There is plenty of time to change.

Does it appear that this strategy is compatible with our original understanding of our mission? Does this strategy fit our own capability as we understand it? (Review the organizational checklist on pp. 233–234 of chapter 17.) To the extent that it does not, it needs to be modified. Stating our approach to strategy is comparable to a stopping off place on the way to anticipating outcomes. It is an attempt to organize, in a clear and communicable way, what it is we want to accomplish.

CHAPTER 23

Assumptions

THE NEED

*U*p until this point in our analysis we have assumed that by asking some well-thought-through questions we will gain the kind of information needed to discover God's strategy for reaching a particular people. The difficulty with this approach is that every situation is different, and every people is unique. No matter how lengthy our list of questions, there will always be others which need to be added for a particular strategy.

Another way to uncover the shades and nuances of the situation and our relationship to it is to discover our *underlying assumptions* about what we are doing. Everyone works and thinks out of his or her own context, his or her own bias. In the same way that few of us are aware of our own culture, few of us are aware of all of the presuppositions and assumptions we make about life. It is only when we question our assumptions or our underlying motives in taking a certain approach that some of these hidden factors are discovered. They need to be discovered because they are important.

Listing our assumptions often uncovers *hidden agendas*. Just as everyone has his or her own personal set of biases, so we all have our own agendas, those things that we want to see happen. Often we are unaware of what they are. For example, one person's hidden agenda in wanting to reach a people may be to further the overall goals of the organization. Another person's hidden agenda may include a personal role for himself or herself. None of these is bad in itself; however, if we do not understand that they are there, we can often end up having the wrong motivations.

Listing our assumptions helps us to discover *missing steps or needs.* We may realize that we have been assuming that someone else will be responsible for a particular role when in fact no one else is planning to take that step.

Listing our assumptions helps us to clear up any *misconceptions* we might have about our situation. One person may have an entirely different view of the future, for example. He or she may believe that the economic situation in the country in which we are planning to work is going to continue at an even pace, while someone else may be thinking that this same economy will experience a great deterioration in the coming years. This difference of viewpoint will result in a different set of plans.

Listing our assumptions helps us to *communicate more effectively,* to let everyone know what we are expecting to happen and what we hope to gain from it all. When we recognize that we have different assumptions about ourselves or the world, it permits us to state our differences and to move ahead to common ground. For example, if one listed the underlying assumptions about evangelism held by a Roman Catholic and an evangelical Protestant, one might discover that both would carry out the same type of evangelization. In a local fellowship, however, these assumptions about the Church would be different and thus important.

We need to know our assumptions about ourselves, our organization, our church or mission, the country within which we will be working, and the world in which we live.

ASSUMPTIONS ABOUT YOURSELF

What is your understanding of the problem? Why do you believe this is so? How did you learn about it? How accurate is your information? Is this the common understanding; are there others who will think as you do? Is this common understanding the correct understanding? Why do you believe that you are *capable* of understanding the problem?

Perhaps you are not. Perhaps you only see part of it. We are reminded of a large sign over the doorway of a major aerospace firm: "If you can smile in the face of the situation, you just don't understand the situation."

What are your gifts and capabilities? For the most part, they are to understand, to plan, to solve, to act, to communicate, and to evaluate. Do you understand why these gifts and capabilities are needed to reach this particular people?

What is your role? We will discuss this later at some length. Why do you believe that you are the one to carry out this particular role, whether it be planning, directing, acting, or evangelizing?

What ability do you have to bring about change? After all, that is our goal—to bring about change, to bring people from darkness into light. Part of this process of change is to convince others of the claims of Christ. What are you assuming about your ability to bring about change in yourself?

How are you perceived as a person? Who do *you* say you are? Who do *others* say you are? What is your role as perceived by others in the situation, for instance, by others in the organization?

What is your perception about what your organization will allow you to do? Have they allowed others to do this same kind of thing? What do they forbid? Why? What evidence do you have that the answers to these questions are so? What is your experience with this organization?

Do you have the courage to carry out this task? Leadership can be lonely. Do you have the courage to be misunderstood? To be wrong? To fail? To sacrifice? It does not take a lot of courage to face a known situation. Courage is most needed when we recognize that there is a high possibility that we will not succeed.[1]

Do you have the right to move forward with this task? What are your other commitments; to your family, friends, to the organization? Many people love a new challenge primarily because it relieves them of the responsibility of dealing with an old and difficult challenge.

Why do you want this to happen? What needs do you have that will be met by this program? What are your present personal goals? Where do you picture yourself ten or fifteen years from now? What is it you really enjoy doing?

1. For additional reading on this subject, see Rollo May, *The Courage to Create* (1975).

ASSUMPTIONS ABOUT THE ORGANIZATION

What are the organization's purposes? Why does it exist? Is it doing the same thing today that it was doing originally? Does it demonstrate that it really believes in its purpose? Does the organization assume it is carrying out its purpose when, in actuality, it is not?

What are the organization's goals? A goal is a measurable future event that the organization plans to make a past event. Are the goals of the organization clearly stated? Have the goals been communicated and understood? Are these goals owned by particular people within the organization? Are they the generally accepted goals? Are they actually process rather than accomplishment goals? For example, an organization may have a process goal of publishing 100,000 gospel tracts. Its goal of accomplishment would be what it expected those tracts to do for the Kingdom.

Is the organization willing to change? Is there any evidence of this from its past history? Is the organization in the process of changing now? How rapidly is it changing? What ability do you perceive it has to change? Has the organization settled down to a point where it is more interested in efficiency (how well things are done) rather than effectiveness (what it gets done)?

What is the organization's mode of operation? How does it go about doing things? What is it that it can or cannot do as related to this particular project?

Does the organization have the ability to carry out the plan and support it? Does it have people, resources, spiritual strength, and community spirit?

What are the relationships within the organization? Who is in charge? Is there a strong and formal organization that has a great deal to say about the operation of the organization? Are the relationships within the organization apparent to the organization? Is the organization chart at least 75 percent accurate?

ASSUMPTIONS ABOUT OTHER CHURCHES AND MISSIONS

There will normally be other churches and mission agencies as well as other individual Christians with whom you will and should relate in order to reach a particular people.

How much cooperation can you expect? What do these other organizations think about you and your organization? How do they perceive your motives? Do they have the ability to do the things that they have committed themselves to?

Are other organizations willing to allow this to happen? Will they oppose it, stay neutral, or cooperate?

Do other organizations or churches desire to see change? Are they content with the present situation? Is there discontent?

What is your view of these other Christian organizations? For example, do you view them as "separated brethren" or sub-Christian?

Does your organization have common goals with other organizations? Are the organizations moving toward opposite goals?

What is the other organization or church's self-understanding? Do they consider themselves *the national* church? Do they see themselves as part of a larger body or as separated from a larger body?

What is the other organization's view of mission? Is mission something which results in the planting of a church? Do they believe that the church should grow and can grow? Is this view of mission held by all of the people in this organization?

ASSUMPTIONS ABOUT THE COUNTRY IN WHICH YOU WORK

What is the national stance towards religion? What laws exist about religious organizations? What freedom will you have to preach? What freedom does the church have to reach out to others?

Does the government have active plans regarding the people you are trying to reach? Do they see them as a people in the same way you do? Do they have plans for helping or hindering this particular people?

What is the role of modernization in this country? Is the government planning to see the country developed? If so, how rapidly and in what direction? Do they plan to nationalize any of the industries? Do they plan to nationalize the Church? How successful do you think they are going to be?

What legal restrictions will the government put on the type of approach you are planning to use?

What is the political situation inside the country? Is it stable? Will it change? Are there factions in the country? Rebellious groups?

What is the status of justice and liberty within the country? Is this an authoritarian regime? Will you ethically be able to operate within this type of political structure?

What is the future of the economy in the country? What impact will this have on your ability to support yourself or your organization? Are there any restrictions on financial exchange? Are the material resources needed to carry out your task available in the country?

ASSUMPTIONS ABOUT THE WORLD

It may seem rather grandiose to try to put down one's assumptions about the world, but because we do it so seldom, it can sometimes be quite surprising to see what our view of the world is, particularly our view of the future.

What will be the future of the world's economy? Will it be such that it will be able to support our type of endeavor?

How does the world in general perceive our ministry? For example, many people would feel that evangelism which ignores the physical condition of the people is fundamentally wrong.

WHAT NOW?

We are always in tension between how much time we should take in thinking and planning as compared to how much time we should take in attempting that which we believe God wants us to do. But one of the ways that God has of teaching us is through the experiences of our history and the history of others.

After you have reviewed the questions about assumptions and have added your own, you will discover that some are very appropriate, while others have no bearing on what you are doing. But, for those which are appropriate, what do the answers tell you about your strategy statement? Do you still feel comfortable with your goals for movement along the Engel scale? Are the people that you propose for the force for evangelism still appropriate? Are the means and methods best as far as you can tell?

Finally, restate your strategy and move ahead into the next section—anticipated outcomes. What is it that you expect God to do as a result of this strategy?

QUESTIONS

Planning the Strategy

1. What will be your grand strategy for reaching a particular people?
2. What will be your mid-range strategy for reaching a particular people?
3. What will be your short-range strategy?
4. What will your strategy exclude?
5. What will it not do?
6. How does your strategy change your force for evangelism?
7. How does your strategy change the means and methods to be used?

Assumptions

1. Why is it important that we state our assumptions about our task?
2. What assumptions do we need to uncover about ourselves? (See questions on p. 325.)
3. What assumptions do we need to uncover about our organization? (See questions on p. 326.)
4. What assumptions do we need to discover about other churches or missions? (See questions on p. 327.)
5. What assumptions do we need to discover about the country in which we are working? (See questions on pp. 327–328.)
6. What assumptions do we need to discover about the world? (See questions on p. 328.)

STEP 6

ANTICIPATED OUTCOMES

Considerations

Movement Toward Christ

The Resulting Church

Ready for Results

Changes in Yourself

Questions

CONSIDERATIONS

1. We expect great things to happen when the gospel is proclaimed because we ourselves have experienced the power of the Kingdom of God and know what it can do to transform human life.

2. Conversion is more properly thought of as a process than a single event. We experience conversion throughout our life as we continue putting off the old and putting on the new.

3. When we anticipate outcomes, we are not, and should not be, limited to the threshold events of decisions, baptisms, and membership.

4. It is very much a matter of faith when we say such and such will happen. God controls the future. Our control of it is much less than we think. However, we can state what we believe God wants at this moment and then make new statements of faith as the future reveals itself.

5. We cannot project a detailed blueprint for the resulting church. But we can use methods that will give local Christians the freedom to decide what that blueprint will look like.

6. The model of the church which we live is the one most likely to be adopted by a people.

7. One of the perpetual tensions in cross-cultural evangelism is the imperative to bring into being a community of the people of God that is both culturally and biblically authentic.

8. The ultimate goal for evangelization is the creation of communities which will participate in evangelization.

9. The questions we ask to clarify the future are more important than the answers.

10. Stewardship of the gospel includes a stewardship of results.

11. The easiest way to avoid accountability for results is to confuse means with ends.

12. Most churches and missions report their results in terms of how much activity has taken place rather than how much has been accomplished.

13. If we are not fair and honest with ourselves about results, if we seek a selective evidence of positive results in order to make ourselves and our supporters feel better, we will never discover the information we need to become more effective servants of the Lord.

14. One of the major changes that takes place when a people is evangelized is a change in the evangelist.

CHAPTER 24

Movement Toward Christ

INTRODUCTION

See how patient a farmer is as he waits for his land to produce precious crops. He waits patiently for the autumn and spring rains. James 5:7

The farmer who has done the hard work should have the first share in the harvest. II Timothy 2:6

*E*very farmer has a crop in mind after the seed is sown. This anticipation includes not simply the increase over the seed sown but what to do with the harvest. Will it be sold? Who might buy it? What will be done if the rains are late or a disease or pest infests the growing crop? The farmer keeps an eye on the weather, the market, and the labor force. At different times more workers will be needed and certain skills will be in demand. The farmer responds to the various events as they unfold—all with an eye on the harvest.

Like the farmer, the evangelist sows the seed of the word of God with the hope that God will bring an increase. Selecting methods that are suited to the particular mission, and putting laborers into the field to do the work are done with the intention that the seed will take root and young Christians will enter Christ's Kingdom. We aim at the establishment of a community of the people of God. If we believe that God will accomplish his work, then we must prepare to do something with the results of our labor.

We cannot control all the results or events that have an important impact on the resulting church. But we can anticipate what might happen and be ready for a drought as well as an abundant rain that brings a large harvest. If we do not anticipate the outcomes of our approach, we will not be ready to train new Christians, or we might not be ready for the persecution that develops in opposition to new Christians. Forewarned is forearmed! To anticipate the future stretches our experience and imagination. Without anticipation, our strategy is blind and becomes no more than a cynical rationalization after the fact. It takes courage and faith to step into the future and say, "This is what I think will happen. . . . "

MOVEMENT TOWARD CHRIST

To have faith means to expect that God will do great things in and through his people. God *is* reconciling people with himself through Christ and we *are* participating in that word of reconciliation. Throughout virtually every corner of our world, people are discovering how they can draw near to God as they commit their lives into his hands. This is not a day when we can poison our attitude with pessimism. Large numbers of people become Christians every year. In 1980, there will be more than 3.2 million new converts in Africa (based on Barrett, 1969). In Latin America, the Protestant evangelical movement was adding approximately five thousand new churches every year at the end of the 1960s (Read et al., 1969, p. 326).

Part of our pessimism in the West is due to secularism, materialism, and totalitarianism in the Church. While the faith of millions of Western Christians is decaying into a powerful secularism, the faith of millions more is gladly yielding to Jesus Christ in places like Assam, Kerala, New Guinea, Uganda, South Korea, and Hong Kong.

As we proclaim the message of the Good News in the power of the Spirit, we must believe that God can provide the increase. Little faith will see little results. With William Carey we must "Attempt great things for God; expect great things from God" (Neill, 1964, p. 262). We do not believe in this way because of a false illusion of "possibility thinking" or the autohypnotic spell of positive thinking. We believe because it is part of our identity as those who have experienced the power of the Kingdom of God. We know that that power can transform human life. But we are not lulled into thinking that the best methodology and keenest cultural sensitivity will overcome the struggle that continues in the hearts of all humankind. We agree with the Willowbank report:

> Messengers of the gospel who have proved in their own experience that it is 'the power of God for salvation' (Rom. 1:16) rightly expect it to be so in the experience of others also. We confess that sometimes, just as a Gentile centurion's faith put to shame the unbelief of Israel in Jesus' day (Matt. 8:10), so today the believing expectancy of Christians in other cultures sometimes shows up the missionary's lack of faith. So we remind ourselves of God's promises through Abraham's posterity to bless all the families of the earth and through the gospel to save those who believe (Gen. 12:1–4; I Cor. 1:21). It is on the basis of these and many other promises that we remind all messengers of the gospel, including ourselves, to look to God to save people and to build his church.
>
> At the same time, we do not forget our Lord's warnings of opposition and suffering. Human hearts are hard. People do not always embrace the gospel, even when the communication is blameless in technique and the communicator in character. Our Lord himself was fully at home in the culture in which he preached, yet he and his message were despised and rejected. . . .   (Lausanne Committee, 1978b, p. 15)

THE MEANING OF CONVERSION

Conversion is one of the words that captures the nature of what the Good News demands (Laubach et al., 1975; Bertram, 1971). While it has come to have some negative connotations in the modern world, it is still a word that is central to a Christian understanding of evangelism (Stott, 1975, chapter 5; Green, 1970, chapter 6). It refers to the response desired on the part of one presented with the gospel: to change the direction of one's thinking and life, to abandon the old way of life and take up a new life; to return home to one's Maker and Redeemer. To convert is to experience an inner transformation. It is a turning away from sin and idols and a turning to God by faith through Jesus Christ.

Conversion refers to the events which take place in the human experience as God's Spirit brings about the new birth, regenerating the sinner who is dead in trespasses and sin. As such it takes many phenomenolog-ical forms—from a sudden dramatic crisis experience (such as Paul's conversion experience on the road to Damascus) to the more subtle but equally profound change that occurs over a long period in the experi-ence of a person who is raised by Christian parents. Even the issue that precipitates a crisis of change differs. For one it may be a power en-counter between the gospel and the old system of gods (Tippett, 1967, chapter 7). For another it might be a vague sense of malaise and aim-lessness in life, or the disintegration of personal and family life because of drugs and alcohol, or a dramatic healing. The occasions of conver-sion are extremely diverse, but they all lead to the same process by which human life is turned toward Christ.

In assessing the meaning of conversion in the light of its outcomes we anticipate that there are a number of important dimensions within which we must guide our thinking. We will sketch only an outline of some of the more important considerations.[1]

1. By its very nature conversion is a change that reaches to the deepest roots of human life. It is described as a re-creation, a resurrec-tion from the dead, a transfer from the kingdom of darkness into the Kingdom of light. We are described as those who have been "crucified with Christ" (Gal. 2:20). We cannot demean the essence of conversion by reducing it to "cheap grace," or a matter of character improvement by a process of self-discipline. Conversion is something which draws its dynamic from the act of the Holy Spirit convicting and renewing the sinner.

2. Conversion should not be thought of as an event but as a continu-ing process. It is an ever present reality which we continue to experience as we put off the old and put on the new. Conversion may be described as sanctification. It will take years to bring many areas of life under the Lordship of Christ. Because we never stop repenting or turning to God in faith through Christ, we never stop experiencing conversion. It is a life-long process, yet we shall never know the fullest meaning of conver-sion until we see Christ coming in his glory.

3. Though conversion is personal, it is never solely individualistic. The conversion of an individual always has an impact on others, espe-cially family and friends. Studies from many societies indicate how faith is often transmitted along the network of kinship and communal sol-

1. Much of this is based on the *Willowbank Report—Gospel and Culture* (Lausanne Committee, 1978b, pp. 19–22).

idarities. Further, conversion is often communal. One thinks of Cornelius and his household (Acts 10–11), or the Philippian jailor and his family (Acts 16:31–34) as examples of what the Church Growth movement has called "multi-individual, mutually interdependent conversion" (McGavran, 1970, p. 302; Tippett, 1971). People often make a commitment to Christ in solidarity with other family, clan, or community members. Finally, conversion goes beyond the individual level because its essential dynamic touches the structures and institutions of those societies where Christians become "light" and "salt" (Mt. 5:13–16). The transformation of socio-cultural realities, while not an automatic result of individual conversion, is rooted in the dynamic created by the converting power of the Kingdom of God. Brazil is a case study of the socio-cultural change implicit in conversion (Willems, 1967, esp. Part V).

4. The essence of conversion is a change in "religious" allegiance (Kraft, 1979, chapter 17). The governing principle of life is changed from some human idolatry to a loyalty to Jesus Christ. This cannot be identified with some particular form or issue. It is easy for the evangelist or Christian community to associate conversion with a particular set of issues which are part of the experience of the evangelist. This can be done only insofar as that form or issue touches the governing principle of life of a particular people and is being used by the Holy Spirit to bring about conversion. This is a delicate matter since the freedom of the Spirit is at stake. We cannot predict or bind the Spirit to a particular way of bringing about a change of allegiance. The importance of conversion is that a human life is being bound solely to Jesus Christ. A specific list of issues or ethical matters which seem important to the evangelist cannot be made more important than the question of allegiance. Without the transfer of *allegiance,* conformity to or rejection of some set of particular forms thought to be indispensable signs of conversion will simply create bad faith and outward reformation without inner transformation.

5. Conversion, however, is not isolated from the forms and meanings which govern a people's life. Most fundamentally, conversion affects the world view of a people and produces change at the very heart of a people's cultural inheritance. The principles by which all of life is organized and ordered are not left untouched by conversion. While an integrated Christian world view may take many years to mature, the first changes in world view are visible at the beginning of the process of conversion. Without a change in world view, the conversion process cannot be sustained nor can it produce dynamic changes.

6. Conversion also affects the standards and behavior which govern our relationships. It does this by giving us a new power to obey the demands of the gospel—to love one another (as our social traditions, even apart from Christian revelation, have taught us), to give fair measure in our dealings with one another, to respect human life, and so on (Dye, 1976; Lewis, 1947). It also introduces us to new sources for standards of behavior found in the Bible and our experience with God. These stand in judgment over our socially inherited standards. They not only fulfill our social aspirations, but correct them and give us new direction for living. Yet they do not do this so as to de-culturize us. Conversion re-makes, but it does not unmake.

7. Conversion does not necessarily divorce us from our kinsfolk, though it may be that the opposition to Christian commitment is so strong that, like it or not, the new Christian finds himself or herself in painful conflict with family. Conversion means that one is spiritually distinct, not socially segregated, and every effort should be made to remain a loyal, respected member of one's community and family network. Conversion not only brings about a separation from the evil that is in the world but adds a new commitment to the world which demonstrates the love of Christ through witness and service.

Hence, in pressing toward the goal of seeing a people converted to Christ, we anticipate a transforming experience for the people who are personally involved with Christ and become part of his Kingdom. We also anticipate the formation of a community of the people of God whose life-style will increasingly witness to the presence of the Holy Spirit, making the Lordship of Christ real in every area of life, from the most basic issue of inner allegiance to the outward customs that govern the way people relate to one another in very mundane, "this-worldly" affairs.

THE STARTING POINT

Movement toward Christ is a relative matter. Progress is dependent in part upon where one begins (C. Kraft, 1979, pp. 239–245). Peoples begin with a variety of differences in terms of their understanding of the Good News, customs and cultural ideals, and receptivity to the message of Christian faith. We suggested that the evangelization process involves moving a people toward an eventual confrontation with Jesus Christ. At one level this means dealing with what they understand or know about the Christian faith. At another level, evangelization deals with attitudes that make a people more or less positive toward the notion of a change in their religious allegiance. At still another level, it implies a behavioral change ("fruits that befit repentance"), especially in those areas where the Holy Spirit is already convicting them of sin. Finally, it means the formation of new relationships, which refers partly to new relationships in a community of faith based on a shared allegiance to Jesus Christ, and partly to transformed relationships with old friends and family members. In each of these areas, the movement toward Christ is anchored in the socio-cultural milieu. The form it takes, the speed with which it moves, and the way in which it is implemented are all culturally relative and not easily judged by an outsider. The Holy Spirit has many surprises when he moves into a new people and begins a new community of faith!

We might recall our categories for understanding a people: the meaning system (language, hermeneutic, world view, and symbols), the need context (aspirations, values, ideals, and fears), and the cultural practices and institutions (customs, social structures, and institutions). If we were to put these in a diagram, they would dramatize the various types of movement which happen as a result of the multi-leveled impact of the gospel. Evangelization attempts to move a people in several dimensions simultaneously, the net result of which increases or decreases receptivity or resistance to the Kingdom of God. In Figure 24-1, we would be trying to move a people downward into the right, front, bottom quadrant:

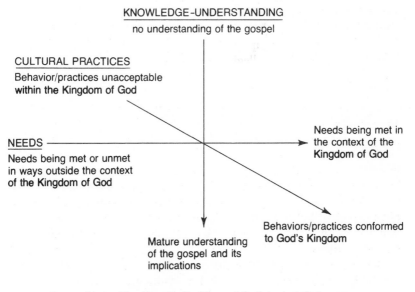

Figure 24-1   The People Profile and Anticipated Outcomes

As we engage in the ministry of the Church, our purpose is to move people toward an increasingly clear realization of how their deepest needs are met by God within the context of his Kingdom, an ever increasing understanding of the revelation of the gospel, and a continuing transformation of cultural practices and institutions toward Christlikeness. To the extent that a people comes to see that God meets their needs, that the gospel is a sensible, reasonable understanding of God and this world, and that new ways of behaving and living in God's Kingdom are better than their present ways, to that extent they will respond positively to evangelization. Thus, the joint effect of these dimensions increases or decreases responsiveness to the gospel and the community that presents it.

Individuals and families within a people will be located at different starting points in these dimensions. Depending upon where they begin, we will anticipate different changes. A nominal Christian group (such as a middle-class, well-to-do Catholic professional suburb of Quito, Ecuador) will already have a good deal of knowledge about Christian faith and generally will have favorable attitudes about it. Their actual pattern of living, however, will be guided largely by a Western, materialistic ethic. Movement toward Christ on their part must be seen in quite a different manner from that of a Thai Buddhist fishing village which has never had a single Christian living in its midst. They begin with a vastly different level of understanding and knowledge, with needs and customs that have developed with little direct contact with the Christian tradition. For them movement toward Christ will mean a different set of consequences and changes, even though both of these groups will begin their journey outside the Kingdom of God. It may even be easier to see progress toward faith among the Thai fishers than among the middle-class nominal Christians.

We start where people actually are, not where we would like them to be. The purpose of evangelization is to engender those changes which will help them move forward toward Christ with the eventual goal of having a culturally authentic, valid opportunity to submit to the claims of Christ. We start where people are because we believe this is the way grace works (God started where we were, even when we were hostile enemies of his). But we do not stop at this point. We need to ask about the outcomes of our strategy for each of these three dimensions: To what extent will people come to see Christian faith and Christians as concerned about and able to help in the struggle to meet those needs? How will we know that people are beginning to relate their real needs to the Kingdom? To what extent will evangelism meet people at the point of their current knowledge and carry them further in their apprehension of the gospel? How will this strategy dramatize the connection between the gospel and their current customs and institutions? Will they sense the gospel as an "enemy" of their culture or something which will fulfill their culture?

THE ULTIMATE OBJECTIVE

Ultimately we are looking for the establishment of a community of the people of God who are an integral part of the evangelization process in their own context, and who will carry that process out until the end of this age. It is admittedly difficult to decide when or whether such a state has been reached. We can look for some estimate in those who are professing Christians, those who are "practicing" Christians, and those who are actively engaged in the evangelism of their own ieople. Each of these will tell us something about the establishment of this community. While we can talk about movement toward Christ, we need also to talk about some of the critical points in that movement where we see people entering the Kingdom of God, and where we then see them moving on to an effective ministry as they utilize the gifts with which God has equipped them.

When a person or a people wants to become Christian, what changes or indications do we look for as proof that an authentic, valid commitment to Christ has occurred? Churches and missions have debated this at great length and there is no easy, single answer. But it is a question that must be squarely faced in terms of the results we look for when we engage in evangelization.

Think again of the three dimensions: How much understanding and knowledge must a person or a family have in order to commit themselves to Christ? How much must they understand in order to be baptized and brought into the fellowship of believers? Must they feel a sense of guilt or a specific sin which needs to be forgiven? Or can they merely sense that Christ can bless them and that they need that blessing? What specific need context or sins must they see as part of the transaction that takes place when they decide to follow Christ? What behaviors or customs will the potential convert be asked to repudiate in order to become a genuine Christian? Will the potential convert be asked to leave some part of his or her past life as an indication that the decision is authentic? All of these questions must be answered if we are to be able to point to the results which indicate that our evangelism is achieving its purpose.

These are not questions which can be taken for granted or simply derived from the past accepted practices of many "evangelists." What for one group is a valid commitment to Christ, is to another only the first vague venturings of a people toward Christ whom they only dimly (if at all) understand. What appears to one church a hopelessly legalistic attitude in the Church, may to another church be raised to the position of the critical point where a person either moves into faith or turns back to the world. How do we know (humanly speaking) when a person or family has become part of the Christian family?

The question of the community into which new Christians are brought will be discussed at length in the next chapter. Since it is in some senses the ultimate goal of evangelization in terms of earthly results, it warrants a careful examination, beyond the limits of this chapter.

DETOURS AND OBSTACLES

Part of the problem of defining the outcomes which we seek and expect lies in the very freedom of the Christian. We have no "supra-cultural" abstract definition of Christian faith that can be utilized for measuring every manifestation of Christian faith and community. We have an authoritative Word, the Bible, which must be interpreted and understood within every context into which the gospel enters. But church history shows us the complexity and variety of ways in which earnest and careful students of the Scripture have understood that Word. Not all these understandings have equal legitimacy. Some depart very markedly from even the most central themes of revelation. Because of this, a great variety of Christian expression has developed, a variety that is accepted as legitimate by most Christians even when they may not personally feel comfortable with other alternatives. To see charismatic Pentecostals sitting in common worship with black-robed Coptic bishops and Baptists is to witness part of the diversity which coexists within the Christian body. There is no such thing as a supra-cultural disembodied Christianity.

In reckoning with that dynamic center to which we give common witness, Christians have recognized that certain contextualizations of the gospel contradict the very nature and meaning of the Kingdom of God. The line between a gospel which has been successfully expressed in indigenous idioms and socio-cultural patterns, and a gospel which has undergone a process of syncretism is difficult to draw in borderline cases. The early Church examined how to formulate the doctrines of the Trinity and of the person of Christ. Orthodoxy became an important issue because Christians are those who *believe*. Orthopraxis has become an equally dominant issue in our day as Christians have tried to discern how to live in the modern, international, interdependent structures which have grown up with the technological revolution of the past century. Christians are those who *act* and *relate* and therefore the limits of acceptable practice are also issues that concern the Church.

We have to recognize the possibility that some of the outcomes of our evangelism may foster movements that are *simultaneously* toward Christ and toward the world (Yamamori and Taber, 1975). Syncretism is not an isolated issue which we can dismiss as an aberration that occurs only in exotic places as the result of inept evangelism by aliens. A great deal has been written on the problem of "Christo-paganism" in Latin America and other parts of the world. It is a term which characterizes the outcome of the inadequate "christianization" of indigenous populations of Latin America by force. Jesus, Mary, and the Saints were all taken on as the indigene professed faith. But they were made part of a larger complex of ritual and mythology that fundamentally transformed the meanings of the central concepts of the gospel. Instead of the Lord of the universe, Jesus became one of a panoply of saints and spirits, earth lords and devils, ancestral souls and magical rites. This Christo-paganism continues to influence a great deal of Catholicism in Central and South America with the tacit awareness of the church hierarchy, and indicates that evangelization there is only partially successful.

In many of our churches in Europe and America there is another syncretistic form of contextualized Christianity which might well be called "Christo-Westernism." It is an amalgam of basic values such as the "American way of life" (Herzberg, 1966; Berger, 1961), business-oriented, highly technological methodologies, and philosophies such as "possibility" or "positive" thinking (Meyers, 1965), which not only give a distinctive character to Western Christianity but at times displace crucial elements of authentic faith. This has often been carried overseas on the wings of well-meaning missions, only to reproduce itself in a bastardized "Christo-Westernism" which appears even more inadequate and static than its parent. A variation of this might be "Christo-denominationalism" where elements of denominational tradition have come to be more important than the dynamic word of God. Here the westernism is of a particular nature. Specific strata of a denominational history have become encrusted on the gospel and made part of the essential definition of movement toward Christ. Even Paul contended with a party faction within a church that made "Christ" their distinctive leader (I Cor. 1:12). Combined with an exclusivism and harshness toward other Christians, it becomes an ecclesiastical form of worldliness.

Part of the anticipation which we must bring to an evaluation of the effectiveness of our proposed strategies is a healthy awareness of the potential for our strategies to fall into traps, to get sidetracked by some version of "Christo-_____" (you fill in the blank). In other words, to confuse style for substance. Christ cannot be made the leader of some human program, the new avant-garde revolutionary of the right or the left, the cipher whose meaning can be filled in by the latest human fad. Christ is Lord of all, and only movement toward an authentic Christ can fulfill the purposes of evangelization.

GOALS FOR EVANGELIZATION

Having said all this, we must return to the very practical concern of specifying what kinds of outcomes we will accept and look for to indicate movement toward Christ. Given our understanding of the central core of Christian faith and practice, of how we believe God will work within the people we are evangelizing in a way that is indigenous to their culture, and the potential our strategy might have for producing some type of syncretism, we need to state what we believe will happen as the result of our actions in obedience to the great commission.

We must remember that we are not thinking of the movement toward Christ as a single step. There are proximate, intermediate steps which lead to that goal as well as to the goal of a church equipped and active in propagating the gospel. The people profile which we have been utilizing throughout the book suggests the various points at which we need to have a statement of outcomes: We have illustrated this in Figure 24-2. We are not limited in our measurement of movement toward Christ by the traditional threshold events such as decision for Christ, baptism, or formal incorporation into a local congregation. Each of the points along the scale can be used as a measurement that we are making progress in the eventual confrontation with Jesus Christ.

This profile reminds us that we can monitor three types of outcomes: the changes that are taking place in *knowledge* of the gospel, the changes in *attitude,* and finally, the *rate of change.* What we expect to happen will have profound influence on the plans we make. One can

Figure 24-2   Anticipated Outcomes

THE PEOPLE PROFILE			YOUR RESPONSE			ANTICIPATED OUTCOMES
DECISION POINT	ATTITUDE + 0 −	RATE OF CHANGE	FORCE FOR EVANGELIZATION	MEANS AND METHODS		
NO AWARENESS −7						
AWARENESS −6						
SOME KNOWLEDGE −5						
KNOWLEDGE −4						
IMPLICATIONS SEEN −3						
PERSONAL NEED −2						
CONFRONTATION −1						
CONVERSION						
RE-EVALUATION +1						
INCORPORATION +2						
PROPAGATION +3						

imagine the difference in plans and action of the two evangelists whom
Al Krass describes:

> One catechist I met told me: "I went to a certain place to preach
> for the first time last Sunday. Many people repented. I am now
> preparing them for baptism." He expected an immediate and total
> response.
>   A priest I knew was quite different. He had been preaching in
> several villages for a number of years. I asked him whether he felt
> the people were ready to become Christians. "Oh no," he replied.
> "I don't suppose they ever will. We just go out to let them know
> what the Christian faith is all about. Maybe some of their children
> who go to school will become Christian, but we don't really expect
> we can convert the fathers." (1974, p. 87)

In chapter 31 we will develop in more detail the way in which our
expectations of results influence our setting of goals and the importance
of making faith statements. We are interested in discovering what the
will of God is for evangelization—not simply in discovering his will for
personal matters such as vocation or whom we ought to marry. Rather
we are interested in discovering what his will is in the sense of what he
wants *accomplished* by us in this generation. We must act responsibly
and authentically even when we are not sure of what to do or what the
exact results will be. We must trust God to bring about the miracle of
people seeing Jesus and desiring to put their trust in him. Even when we
have done our best, we still have a keen sense that we are unworthy
servants who do no more than what they have been commanded.

Yet we cannot allow such a statement to justify sloppy methods, lazy
habits, and inexcusable actions that take no regard for easily anticipated consequences. One can imagine a new version of the parable of
the pounds (Mt. 25:14–30; Lk. 19:11–27) in which the modern stew-
ard of the treasures of God says: "Lord, I invested your pound and left
the results to God. Unfortunately, he did not do a very good job of
taking care of your pound. The stock market fell and all that you gave
me was lost!" To leave the results with God can be irresponsible if it
justifies failure due to poor strategy or inadequate attitudes toward the
body of Christ. There are results which we can anticipate, results which
we can even control.

God expects us by faith to decide what we are to be and do, and what
we believe the outcomes of our lives and actions ought to be. We are
stewards (I Cor. 4:1, 2), and we are required to be faithful to our master. Faithfulness is more than simply putting in time or working hard at

commendable activities. There is more than enough "good missionary work." Faithfulness is a matter of doing what the master requires, of accomplishing the task we set to do. What counted in the parable of the pounds was not good intentions or long hours of work, but the gain made from the resources received.

Measurable, carefully specified outcomes are important because they are one way in which we more firmly establish our faith. By not stating outcomes we have little basis for evaluating whether we are making progress toward our goals, toward fulfilling the mission which we believe God has given us. Measurable outcomes keep us from getting stuck on means and never reaching our goals. We have no way of guaranteeing the future. But we can state what we believe God wants at this moment, and then make new statements of faith as the future reveals itself to us.

The farmer is able to point to barns which are full of hay, silos which are filled with the fruits of the harvest, and storage bins which bear the yield from his fields. Like the farmer, we need to anticipate what might happen as God blesses and as we enter into the struggle against the principalities and powers for the allegiance of the hearts of people. Just as we can prepare for trouble ("Sensible people will see trouble coming and avoid it, but an unthinking person will walk right into it and regret it later," Prov. 22:3), so we can also believe God will bring about a harvest of joy.

CHAPTER 25

The Resulting Church

We are not interested simply in people making "decisions" for Christ. We are in the business of seeing the power of Christ change people into new communities that in turn carry the Good News to others within their group and ultimately to other unreached peoples. The end goal of evangelism is a vital, dynamic, witnessing church. What that church will look like—how it will worship, how it will show its love for one another and the world, how it will express the power of God in its midst—has an important influence on what our evangelistic methods ought to be. Often it is the model of the church which we live that is the one most likely to be adopted by the resulting church.

Any approach to evangelization that does not deal with the reality of the Church is deficient. Evangelization is a process which grows out of the nature of the Church as a redeemed community of people who have been made stewards of the grace of God. While it may not be true that there is no salvation outside the Church, there is no salvation that is unrelated to the Church. Those who share the Good News and those who embrace it are members of one body, fellow participants in a wider solidarity of people who share the same life and Lord.

As we conclude this discussion on the anticipated outcomes of our evangelization we are faced squarely with the question of the church that will be formed by the Holy Spirit. It would be easy to argue that the question of the Church should be addressed directly after our analysis of the people; after all, the *goal* of evangelization is a church. Unfortunately, it is impossible for anyone to stand outside a culture and anticipate with any degree of accuracy the form that the church should take. As we will discuss in considerable length in the balance of this chapter, all too often we have fallen into the error of assuming that we *did* know what the church will be like. Again we will see that questions are more important than answers. There are broad and general questions that can be asked about the nature and form of the church that is to be planted from outside the society. As we move into that society, there are more specific questions that God can use to keep us from imposing cultural forms on the new church.

THE CHURCH AS THE AGENT AND RESULT OF EVANGELISM

The Church is the agent and result of evangelism (Snyder, 1977, p. 103). Evangelism sparks church growth, and evangelism takes place as a result of the vital life of the church. Churches are the active agents of the Kingdom of God through which God is calling his people to live and serve in the world after the pattern of their Lord.

The Church is an agent of the Kingdom in terms of what it *is:* a messianic community, existing in love, exercising the gifts of the Spirit, serving God as a royal priesthood, and participating in the power of the age to come. It demonstrates a unique quality of life which attracts those who seek more out of life than what they have found through purely human, this-worldly endeavors. It demonstrates and displays the sacrificial community that acts as the pillar and foundation of the truth. It is a light set on a hill that cannot be hidden.

Is is also an agent of the Kingdom in terms of what it *does:* it touches the world through its evangelism, calling all to repentance and faith, through its prophetic ministry, giving witness to the judgment of God on all injustice and human structures that serve to alienate us from God and one another, and through its diaconate, extending loving care and service to the poor, the helpless, and others in need. Whether by evangelism, prophecy, or service, the Church acts on behalf of and motivated by the reality of the presence of the Kingdom of God. Insofar as the Church is what it ought to be and does what it ought to do, it leads to the confrontation with the powers of evil, to the conversion of those who have been prepared by the Holy Spirit, and to the formation of new congregations of people who have found refuge and release in the message and ministry of that Church.

New Christians need the support and nurture of other Christians. In some cases this will simply be a process of assimilation and incorporation into existing congregations. In others it will mean the development of completely new fellowships. In either case we will have to be concerned with the authenticity and adequacy of those congregations for carrying out the task of assimilating and nurturing these new Christians.

THE CHURCH IN THE FREEDOM OF THE SPIRIT

Part of our problem in figuring out the dimensions of the resulting church for a particular people is that we do not know what the Spirit might be pleased to do among them. Often the error of cross-cultural church-planting efforts has been the attempt to reproduce the home church, with its forms and structures, in the new environment: Anglican bishops and surplices in central Uganda, Southern Baptist "amens" in the jungles of Kalimantan, Wednesday evening prayer meetings in a farming village in Bangladesh. If we knew the outline of the resulting church, our task of selecting methods and undertaking a strategy would be much simpler than it is.

As it is, we often impose our Western church models onto a new situation instead of following its unique logic. Many non-Western churches have adopted the pattern of Western, full-time, seminary-educated, paid clergy for leadership. It simply is not possible to turn into pastors all those graduating from all types of Christian leadership training Bible colleges and seminaries. Even if we did, they would not cover a fraction of the new congregations that are springing up. Theological Education by Extension is an effort to meet this problem. But it is a problem which is largely the result of outsider decisions about leadership within peoples of different cultures (Braun, 1971; Read, et al., 1971, chapter 22).

One of the reasons we so easily export models of church life and organization is that we do not have a strong awareness that the Church is the creation of the Spirit of God. The Bible sees the Church primarily in charismatic terms rather than in institutional or organizational categories. It exists by means of the grace which the Spirit imparts, built up through the gifts of the various members of the body of Christ, and structured in terms of an intertwining network of loving relationships that give form to the community of the saints. The Church is a living organism and cannot be confused with or reduced to organizational forms. Nor can we do a very good job of predicting what those organizational forms ought to be among a people. In some ways the best we can do is project what the Church will *not* be like. What it will be like will be the result of the leading of the Spirit among the natural leaders of the new church and cannot be authentically imposed by outside evangelists and church planters. But we can follow methods that will foster the process by which those leaders emerge and find the freedom to develop their own forms.

One of the problems faced by faith mission agencies that have drawn their members from many denominations is that they had no mechanism for thinking through an appropriate expression of the church. Often each missionary did what was good in his or her own eyes.

EXAMPLE VS. MANDATE
IN THE NEW TESTAMENT CHURCH

We begin with the freedom of the Spirit in the Church because the most common error has been to allow the "accidents" of organization, institution, and tradition to become more important and characteristic of the churches we have planted than the true "essentials" which alone give it authenticity. We have even confused what is exemplary in the New Testament with what is mandatory, thinking that our task is to attempt to structure all churches according to a New Testament blueprint for the Church. As Michael Harper has written:

> If the New Testament is our blueprint for ministry in the Church, all one can say is that it is a strange blueprint. There is a certain haphazardness about the appointments to office in the New Testament which only makes sense if you view them as the *ad hoc* prompting of the Holy Spirit, amidst the most taxing of circumstances. The Church was having to make adjustments all the time. It was growing rapidly and spreading widely. It was crossing all kinds of racial, social and cultural frontiers. It was often under fire from its enemies. It had to make, at times, radical adjustments, to rapidly changing situations. This was to go on for many years beyond the first century when the New Testament was being written. . . .
> The New Testament writers . . . are more concerned with "life"

than with defining too closely how the Church should be governed and who should do what. For instance, those who attempt to find the origins of the order of deacons in Acts 6 have a hard time proving it. Here is an *ad hoc* situation, and the Church responding sensibly to it. To establish the order of deacons here is to read back into scripture what was not there originally. In any case, Stephen very soon began to behave like an apostle (no doubt because the Holy Spirit led him to), and he lost his life as a result. Another of the seven, Philip, was soon fulfilling the function of an evangelist, while someone probably filled in for him in his role of looking after the widows. We see no stereotype here, but flexibility to the movings of the Holy Spirit. (1978, pp. 24–25)

What we understand as ecclesiastical titles in the New Testament, which correspond to our own church organizational titles, were in the early Church designations of functions and ministries. They were not rooted in formal bureaucratic organizations which were run according to standardized manuals of church order or constitutions listing job descriptions. There was no "professional clerical" class who met a given set of educational and ecclesiastical tests. When we read our own traditions back into the New Testament and then try to insist that it is the mandatory pattern for all churches, we err in two directions. First, we do not properly understand the function of the New Testament. It does not intend to give a detailed chart for deducing church structure. Rather, it gives us an example of what the early Christians did to meet the pressures of their day in order to continue with the business of communicating the Good News through all corners of their world. Second, we do not properly understand the difference between our churches and those of the New Testament. We cannot go back to the first century. We live in a different time and must discover for our generation what the Spirit will creatively give us to solve our problems (for further elaboration of this see Harper, 1977; Snyder, 1975, 1977; Brunner, 1953).

VARIETY AS THE NORM FOR CHURCHES

The Church as a community of the Spirit exists in freedom because it lives in the presence of the Lord (II Cor. 3:17). The same flexibility, fluidity, adaptability, and growth seen in the New Testament ought to be present among our churches. We cannot confuse things that have the same labels as those found in the New Testament as necessarily having the same reality. When is a church a *church?* When it has the proper hierarchy of offices—prophets, teachers, evangelists, bishops, deacons, elders? Are Sun Myung Moon's Unification Church and the Christian Science Church New Testament churches? Without the operation and power of the Spirit, there is no church.

Nor is something a church because it ordains "qualified" candidates to an organized clergy. It is not a matter of title, structure, or legal definition but rather the gift of the Spirit that forms a community in many different structures and through them creates the Kingdom of God on earth. All the other matters of time, place, frequency and structure of gathering for meetings, dress, architecture, organization for ministry are conventions, the legitimacy and authenticity of which have little to do with any church that has existed in space and time. Rather they are all subject to the freedom of the Spirit and the imperative of the church to be the community of the Spirit.

All this is not to say that formal organization is the enemy of the Spirit or that structure is illegitimate. To suppose that would be to misunderstand the point we are trying to make. Life has to have form to sustain itself and to effect change in the environment. This is no less true for the life of the Spirit in the church. Structure is inevitable, but it is also no more than a tool or channel of indispensable functions, functions which may be carried out in widely variant ways. "Particular structures will be legitimate or illegitimate depending not only on what they are intended to accomplish, but on their function—what they actually do accomplish" (Snyder, 1977, p. 139).

All forms of animal life must fulfill certain indispensable functions in order to continue their existence: they must be nourished, find ways to reproduce and raise their young, defend themselves against their natural enemies, and adjust to environmental changes. The diversity in these common functions is enormous. To contrast the fish, the birds, the mammals, and the insects with one another on any of these functions is to discover the amazing creativity of God.

So too, the Church is in a wide variety of cultural worlds, worlds with radically different social structures, linguistic categories for labeling the world, and tempos. If we think of them as different "ecological" niches into which the Church is introduced, within which the life of the Spirit will operate to produce a uniquely distinctive form of Christian community, we can get some idea of the freedom which characterizes the results of an authentic encounter of the gospel with the peoples of differing cultures. The Church must have the same functions that are found in other peoples. But the structures and forms which are developed to do so may be quite different from those to which we are most accustomed.

Historically, the Church has not been the friend of freedom. In most eras the Church has enhanced its power, has increased its control over the affairs and diversity of Christian life, and has formulated more precise sets of norms and laws by which to govern everyday life as well as church life. When it has carried the gospel overseas, the Church assumed that its standardized forms and patterns of life would be adopted by those who responded to the gospel. There would be a "Southern Baptist Church" of Nairobi, Kenya, or Jayapura, Irian Jaya, recognizable in many of its formal features as the offspring of the mission efforts of the Southern Baptist Convention in the United States or an American Lutheran Church, a Free Methodist denomination, or Reformed Church. Denominational and cultural distortions were part of the standardized, pre-formed package of expected results that were carried over (along with the standardized methodologies).

The impact of this lack of freedom is seen in the eight thousand Independent Church movements in Africa as well as independent churches in virtually every corner of the globe. All these movements seek to find a cultural authenticity and freedom not found in their parent bodies. The lack of freedom is also seen in movements that have sputtered along, only reluctantly yielding transfer of authority from the parent church or mission to the young church, and requiring leadership to assimilate Western, bureaucratic models. Church constitutions, books of order, and decision-making patterns have all been exported with the assumption that they would be adopted and utilized by the emerging churches. This is now being repeated as Third World missions begin cross-cultural evangelism (see Krass, 1974, pp. 20–21).

What is at stake is the question of the tension between the form and freedom of the Church. When does it have the structure and form to serve as a community that can carry forth its mission, minister to its members, and reproduce itself in the next generation? When does that form threaten the freedom that is essential for the community to adapt to changing times and cultures? Every mission and church must answer these questions.[1]

1. Francis Schaeffer, *The Church at the End of the 20th Century* (InterVarsity Press, 1970) illustrates the virtues and vices of this procedure. Schaeffer attempts to specify what he sees as universal and permanent as forms to structure the freedom of the church. The result (not surprisingly) seems very "reformed." He argues for eight norms and a general philosophical approach: (1) Local congregations are to exist, made up of Christians. (2) They are to meet together

Again they are matters that cannot be defined in an abstract way, apart from a given ecclesiastical tradition or theological commitment. The dictates of the situation as the gospel enters it will set a distinctive agenda.

MODELS FOR THE RESULTING CHURCH

Attempts have been made to develop models or paradigms for developing criteria that could serve as goals or guidelines in planting churches. We have to go beyond ideas of what conversion might mean for the individual, whether alone or in a family network, and begin to set out at least the main parameters of the type of community we are seeking as the result of our evangelism. Contemporary literature basically discusses three images of the Church: the "three-self" church, the dynamic equivalence church, and the contextualized church.

1. The "three-self" church

During the nineteenth century, Henry Venn of the Church Missionary Society and Rufus Anderson of the American Board of Commissioners for Foreign Missions articulated ideas that have come to be known as the "three-self" formula (Warren, 1971; Beaver, 1967, 1979; Verkuyl, 1978, pp. 184–188). Churches that were "self-governing," "self-supporting," and "self-propagating" were stressed as a corrective to the dangers of dependence and paternalism which were evident and all too easily a part of cross-cultural evangelization. Rufus Anderson urged that the aim of missions be:

---

in a special way on the first day of the week. (3) There are to be church officers (elders) who have responsibility for the local churches. (4) There are to be deacons responsible for the material needs of the church. (5) The church is to take discipline seriously. (6) There are to be specific qualifications for elders and deacons. (7) There is a place for form (church organization) on a wider basis than the local church. (8) The two sacraments of baptism and the Lord's Supper are to be practiced. (9) Anything the New Testament does not command in regard to church form is a freedom to be exercised under the leadership of the Holy Spirit for that particular time and place (pp. 59–67). This list is shorter and more generalized than most. But it still retains a very denominationally and culturally influenced reading of Scripture. Howard Snyder, *The Problem of Wineskins: Church Structure in a Technological Age* (InterVarsity, 1975) argues for only three essential elements: (1) Leadership through gifts. (2) Fellowship experienced in a small group setting. (3) Worship and community expressed in a large-group gathering (pp. 162–168).

(1) The conversion of lost men,
(2) organizing them into churches,
(3) giving these churches a competent native ministry, and
(4) conducting them to the stage of independence and (in most cases) of self-propagation (Beaver, 1979, p. 95).

Churches that resulted from missions were (and are) often tied to the supporting home church, financially dependent, inhibited in the development of native leadership, forced into patterns of organization that were non-indigenous, and unable to stand authentically within their own social context.

Roland Allen's *Missionary Methods: St. Paul's or Ours?* (1962) is a classic statement of the importance and value of the "three-self" model of the resulting church. Because of his writings and the common problems that faced missions overseas, the "three-self" formula probably became the most broadly shared perspective for defining criteria for success in church planting. This has been particularly true since World War II and the ensuing movements of national self-determination. As broad parts of the Third World achieved their independence and nationalism grew, it was only natural for many churches and agencies to turn to "indigenous" church principles as a mode of operation which would maximize the independence of the younger churches and reduce some of the tensions.

But the "three-self" formula has been criticized for several reasons. First, it has become a "catch phrase" without any common meaning, repeated by virtually everyone engaged in cross-cultural evangelism and church planting. It has become a smokescreen for continued practices that create and foster dependence. It is applied to widely variant church situations and for that reason has little concrete meaning.

Perhaps most fundamentally, the "three-self" formula has been confused with "indigeneity." When it has become possible for a church to be "self-governing," it often has neither broken the ties of dependence on the founding church nor become rooted in indigenous patterns of leadership. This is because the devolution of former controlling relationships leaves the Western agency or missionary in control of desired monies and in a position to "pull strings." Also the leadership of the church may have been installed on the basis that they have been adequately indoctrinated in the Western way of doing things. Their leadership is simply a native imitation of Western leadership. However, the reception of funds from outside the bounds of a local church is not a criterion that necessarily renders it "non-indigenous." Even the

Jerusalem church in its poverty received gifts from the Gentile churches of the Roman world (Acts 20–21). It did not make it less indigenous simply because it was not "self-supporting":

> If the church makes its own decisions, without outside interference, as to how its funds shall be used, and does so on the basis of economic patterns natural to it in its own cultural setting, this church may be considered indigenous, even if funds are provided by an outside source. (Smalley, 1967, p. 149)

The problem with the "three-self" formula is that it does not stipulate the quality of indigeneity and has too often been understood in terms of Western individualism and independence rather than being rooted in the indigenous patterns of the new church's culture.

A third criticism of the formula has been that it is applicable only in certain situations. It works best, claims McGavran, where many are converted quickly (McGavran, 1970, p. 345). Where resistant populations or slowly growing churches exist, it is often impossible to adhere to the three-self formula and continue to maintain a witness. There simply may not be churches large enough to provide the basis to implement these principles or to expect them to finance auxiliary or supporting structures such as hospitals or schools.

Furthermore, from the perspective of evangelization the three-selfs do not invariably lead to increased rates of church growth and evangelistic outreach. Factually speaking, one can point to great churches which grew up on the basis of paid pastors and evangelists who were managed within a structure run by foreign missionaries. It is true that over time they have moved toward an indigeneity which has included the three-selfs, but they were not originated nor expanded by them.

2. The dynamic equivalence church

For these reasons and others there has been a move toward more adequate and carefully developed models for "indigenous" churches.[2]

2. Indigenous churches have been defined in various ways. We are leaving it without a careful definition because it is a complicated concept which would take a great deal of careful discussion. Here are some representative definitions: William Smalley: "It is a group of believers who live out their life, including their socialized Christian activity, in the patterns of the local society, and for whom any transformation of that society comes out of their felt needs under the guidance of the Holy Spirit" (1967, p. 150). Daniel C. Hardin: "An indigenous church is a church in which God, Christ, and the Holy Spirit, in contact with

One model is that of the "dynamic equivalence" church (C. Kraft, 1973, 1979a, chapter 16; 1979b). It is based on the analogy of translation which attempts to produce the meanings of the Bible in a new language so they have the same dynamically equivalent impact that they had when God originally conveyed them. *Today's English Version, The New English Bible,* and *Phillips' New Testament* are "dynamic equivalence" translations. Such a translation contrasts with the traditional "literal" translations (now called "formal correspondence" translations) such as the *American Standard Version,* the *New American Standard Version,* and the *Revised Standard Version.* In a formal correspondence translation the validity of the work is evaluated on how close the forms approximate the source language (e.g., if the source language employs a Greek word meaning "bowels" then the receptor language should use a word that also means "bowels" without trying to translate or interpret the figurative meaning that might lie behind that word as in Phil. 1:8; 2:1).

In contrast the dynamic translation is concerned not with an equivalency of forms but with the response of the hearer. It changes and recombines the linguistic forms (e.g., by translating "bowels" as "liver" or by the literal meaning of a word such as "kindness" depending on what is most meaningful to the receptor language). It is evaluated on the closeness of the response and understanding of the receptor to what occurred in the original situation.

> A "dynamic equivalence church," then, is the kind of church that produces the same kind of impact on its own society as the early church produced upon the original hearers. In that equivalence the younger church will have need of leadership, organization, education, worship, buildings, behavioral standards, means of expressing Christian love and concern to unconverted people. A dynamically equivalent church will employ familiar, meaningful, indigenous forms, adapting and infilling them with Christian content. (C. Kraft, 1973, p. 49)

---

people of a particular cultural setting, give rise to a Christian body that is outwardly and uniquely molded by that culture over a fixed framework of fundamental scriptural doctrine" (1978, p. 184). Alan Tippett: "When the indigenous people of a community think of the Lord as their own, not a foreign Christ; when they do things as unto the Lord meeting the cultural needs around them, worshipping in patterns they understand; when their congregations function in participation in a body, which is structurally indigenous; then you have an indigenous Church" (1969, p. 136).

This model suggests that we ought to transcend the way new churches have been made to imitate the forms of the churches or missions that originated them by focusing on the impact or functions which a church is to have in its own distinct context. However different the forms of liturgy, leadership, education, witnessing, and serving the community may be from our own, if they are similar in impact to those of the New Testament, we can feel certain that we are viewing an indigenous church, living in the power of the Spirit. Whether it even conforms to the three-self formula is irrelevant if it possesses indigenous forms for Christ, and conveys them to the surrounding society.

The advantage of this model over the three-self formula is patent. It is self-anchoring in both the culture of the developing church and the culture of the New Testament. It does not assume that there are some specific forms (such as a particular order of ecclesiastical government or liturgy) by which one can identify an authentic church that is growing within its culture in faithfulness to God. It also provides healthy leverage for dissatisfaction when one faces a weak and insipid three-self church that is propagating itself solely on the basis of biological or transfer growth. Like the New Testament Church, the dynamically equivalent church grows by the conversion of non-Christians.

There are, however, several reservations with this model. It can be utilized only when there is an understanding of the biblically recommended functions of the people of God in the New Testament. This is no easy issue to settle, as anyone who has studied the matter can attest. For one thing, we are not told about many of the "impacts" or functions which the early Church had within its society. Furthermore, it is clear (from the example of the Corinthian church) that the New Testament churches functioned in inadequate and at times sinful ways—the dynamic equivalences of which we would be very unhappy to reproduce.

Additionally, there is the serious issue of the differences between societal contexts. The Church today has to function in ways completely different from and unanticipated by any of the forms or functions of the New Testament Church. A good example of this might be the way the Church (and the Old Testament people of God) functioned in relationship to capital-formation and interest-bearing notes. Usury was viewed as sinful and for many centuries the Christian Church opposed the use of interest-bearing notes. Yet in the modern, bourgeois, capitalist world, it would be disastrous for the Church to oppose the use of such notes. The same could be said for the approach the Church took toward the institution of slavery in the first century. It was fundamentally passive, attempting only to transform relationships and attitudes within the structure. There was virtually nothing it could do to extinguish the institution at that point of history. But today we would not argue that the Church be passive toward the institution and only work to change relationships and attitudes within it.

The early Church also grew in a responsive setting with particular socio-historical dimensions that were quite different from other contexts. One wonders whether the Church can have equivalent response or impact where it has become the dominant state religion (as compared with the New Testament Church which was a minority movement of enthusiastic-charismatic congregations in urban areas of the Roman world). What of a small church in a resistant setting where people are becoming Christians one by one over long stretches of years? Can the Church indeed function in an equivalent fashion?

Even this model can become a cipher, whose critical dimensions are filled in by the particular traditions of a denomination or cultural expression of Christian faith held by the evangelizing agent. Ambiguity is a vacuum into which people find an almost compelling necessity to pour their own values and conclusions, be they good or bad. If this attempted advance on the model of an "indigenous" church as "three-self" is to succeed, it will have to spell out in more detail the nature of its assumptions about the functions of the New Testament Church for which we will seek dynamic equivalences in the churches that spring up as a result of our evangelization.

3. *The contextualized church*

We should also mention the more recent discussions which center on the concept of "contextualization" (see issues of the journal *Gospel in Context;* Taber, 1978; Hesselgrave, 1978b, pp. 71–127). Much of the literature discussing "liberation theology" is relevant here as well, since it is seeking a theology of the church as contextualized within Latin America and other regions where social-political-economic oppression is an acute reality.

This discussion attempts not so much to develop a model of a church which can be considered both culturally and biblically authentic as to analyze the processes by which the gospel is particularized for a specific people and setting, thus allowing the development of a contextualized church. While the discussion is focused on questions of communication, it reaches out and encompasses matters of church structure, liturgy, cultural adjustment in ethics, and so forth. It too is an attempt to

transcend some of the ambiguities and inadequacies of traditional formulations and uses of "indigenization" as a term for summing up what
we look for in an authentic evangelism program as well as an authentic
church. Charles Taber (1979, pp. 144–146) has summarized what he
sees as the distinctive advances in "contextualization" as over against
the traditional uses of "indigenization":

1. Whereas indigenization stressed communication and appropriate
cultural adaptation, contextualization incorporates that emphasis and
adds a concern with social, political, and economic questions. It recognizes that response to the gospel is conditioned by more than "culture"
in the narrow sense but also by wealth, food conditions, and inner
psychic senses of security and insecurity.

2. Indigenization tended to see culture in a static fashion. Contextualization moves to a more flexible concept that incorporates an
awareness of the changeableness of culture and is aware of the broad
secular process of culture transformation.

3. Indigenization developed largely out of experiences with small
communities which were isolated. We now face a globally interrelated
world which has impact on all the various societies and groups of the
earth. Missions must face the global system and be aware of how it, as
well as the peoples it addresses, are interpenetrated by this global system.

4. Indigenization usually was concerned with the process that was
happening "out there" on the mission field. Contextualization desires
to focus attention not only on the way in which the gospel is "indi-
genized" in the evangelist's culture, but also with the syncretism that
plagues his or her church as well. It asserts more clearly that demonic
qualities infiltrate *all* cultures, not just those of the people being
evangelized. The Western church is plagued by syncretism, not just the
churches which it has had a part in planting.

5. Indigenization was simplistic in that it viewed the gospel as "the
same" for all contexts. It dealt superficially with the way in which its
expression would have to be different. Contextualization argues that
what is universal in the gospel is less easily isolated and exists more
remotely from the surface level of verbal and symbolic expression than
has been previously acknowledged.

6. Indigenization was fundamentally concerned with the local
church and denominational structures and how they could be "indi-
genized." Seldom did it question the indigeneity of hospitals and

schools or whether the concept behind these supporting institutions was itself sound. As a result, extremely Western patterns and leadership were retained in these institutions alongside an ideology of indigenization even when the church was nationalized.

> Contextualization, then, is an attempt to capitalize on the achievements of indigenization, to correct its errors and biases, and fill in its gaps. It is the effort to understand and take seriously the specific context of each human group and person on its own terms and in all its dimensions—cultural, religious, social, political, economic—and to discern what the gospel says to people in that context. (Taber, 1979, p. 146)

To generalize this, we would say that it is the attempt to discern not only what is the gospel for a specific people in a given context, but also what the church must be as it responds to the commands and promises of God within its particular context. A church living under a totalitarian regime in a situation of affluence and secularism will be different from a rural church living in the midst of poverty in a relatively free, democratic context. Each will have different obstacles placed in its way of understanding the gospel and responding to it authentically. Each will have a unique constellation of meanings which it will have to incorporate in its life if it is to manifest the Kingdom of God among its own people. To reduce this to the "three-self" formula would be to confuse the issue by gross simplification of what is involved in contextualizing the gospel. Nor can the "dynamic equivalence" model provide the guidance that is necessary since it is predicated on a functional imitation of a first-century contextualized expression of the Kingdom of God, an imitation that may or may not be helpful or valid depending upon the new context in which there is an attempt to establish a locally appropriate, locally revolutionary representation of the Kingdom of God.

CRITERIA FOR THE RESULTING CHURCH

By what criteria, then, do we evaluate the resulting church or the church into which new converts will be integrated? We believe the church exists in the dialectic or tension between what it understands the voice of the Spirit to be saying to the church universal and what it sees as the particularization of that Word to its unique context. In anticipating outcomes in terms of the resulting church, we ask a number of questions:

1. What kind of biblical, worshipping fellowship would most likely attract other members of this same group?

2. What would be the means by which it worshipped?

3. How would it develop means for showing concern for fellow Christians?

4. How would it demonstrate its concern for the world and for the broader human issues that face the communities and kinship groups within which it lives?

5. Who would lead the church? How would leadership be identified and equipped? What criteria ought to govern the development and identification of leadership for the church?

6. What means might it employ in witnessing to non-Christians?

These questions are not easily answered, and they will change as the church itself grows in maturity and size. For those who come from faith mission backgrounds with a variety of church traditions, such questions are more difficult to respond to. In some ways denominational missions have had an easier time since they carried to the field a stronger image of what the resulting church should look like and thus could integrate that notion into their plans and the development of methods. Of course it must be said that the image they carried was often not very applicable to the indigenous context and was produced in the resulting church only by a long process of reeducating the native Christians.

For each of these questions we will need to remember the dialectic that exists between the gospel that is changing culture and the necessity for the church to be culturally authentic:

1. The church must be biblically authentic in that it will face the whole counsel of God and attempt to obey "all things" Jesus commands his disciples. Yet it must equally attempt to be culturally authentic, offering worship in forms in keeping with the indigenous culture, governing itself by modes that suit its local customs, proclaiming a gospel that has been "substantively particularized" to its unique context (Hesselgrave, 1978c, pp. 135–139), nurturing and caring for one another in ways that fulfill ideal cultural norms as well as the norms of the Bible. In short, while it incarnates the imperatives of the Bible to be the people of God, it will worship, fellowship, nurture Christians, and witness in ways that will make it attractive and culturally authentic within its own society.

2. The church will be a leaven within its society, confronting and changing that which is demonic and sinful, possessing for Christ that

which is positive and good, commending itself by works of righteousness and justice as an authentic expression of the Kingdom of God. The
church thus not only "clothes" itself in the garb of its host culture but
also "re-tailors" the cloth to bring out a new and even more beautiful
pattern. Contextualization, indigenization, "dynamic equivalence," or
whatever term one might use, involves not only a movement toward
utilizing culture but also a confrontation with it where it is ultimately
incompatible with the gospel. The church has a prophetic ministry as
well as a ministry of healing and compassion.

3. The church will be an evangelizing agent within its context. It will
assume major (though not exclusive) responsibility for the evangelization of its own people and will move toward a global responsibility in
completing the evangelization of our generation. In general (though
there are exceptions), churches often move through a period of dependence on the original sending mission, a reacting independence where
they attempt to establish their own identity, and then a subsequent
more mature interdependence. Evangelization as a mature church anticipates the development of forms and mechanisms by which committed communities will be formed within the resulting church which
will become mission-sending bodies themselves (as we now see in the
Third World mission agencies in Asia, Africa, and Latin America).
When somewhere between 10 to 20 percent of a people have become
practicing Christians, the period of independence and interdependence
ought to appear. As a rule of thumb it will have the potential for
continuing and completing the evangelization of its own people and the
base for forming mission to other peoples. But this is no more than a
rule of thumb. The percentage may be much lower as is the case with
many churches who are now in a phase of mature interdependence.

REALISM IN EXPECTATIONS
FOR THE RESULTING CHURCH

What we have been discussing are idealized models which attempt to
set forth specific elements as though they were achievable and ac-
tualized within history. We have had enough experience with actual
congregations and churches to know that we have discussed ideals that
are only approximated. Even the churches of the New Testament are
not presented to us as "finished" products, paragons of the full range of
God's desires. They, too, faced problems in distinguishing heresy from
orthodoxy, syncretism from a contextualized gospel, license from lib-

erty in behavior. There were disputes, schism, factionalism. They made wrong decisions. In short they resemble us in embodying the same afflictions that infect our contemporary efforts at producing communities of the people of God.

They too had a vision of the Kingdom of God that motivated the continued growth and effort to see more and more of God's will being done on earth as it is in heaven. Paul's letters were written as he tried to help churches change into more loving, caring, maturing, evangelizing communities. The vision of an ideal model for church community is no different from the ideal models of individual conversion which we construct from the New Testament materials. We are aware that past church models will only approximate the models we have built, but they are no less valuable for that reason. They still give us guidelines for the changes and continued actions we will take in order to move in a direction which is pleasing to God.

We must also be realistic about these idealized models as an essential part of our anticipated outcomes. Given a specific people with their context, an evangelizing agency with its limitations, a given set of methods arranged into a unique approach, we can expect that certain results invariably will fall short of the ideal which is pleasing to God. People are converted only partially, with mixed motivations. Communities of Christians grow up which only partially incarnate the revolutionary Kingdom of God in their society. We continue to work toward total conversion and toward dynamic communities of people who live in peace and love. Our expectations must be matched by the concrete limitations and humility that is a part of every human endeavor, even those that flow out of the mighty working of the Spirit. But they must never lose the sense of "not yet," the sense that there is more that God wants to do and will do as we move forward in evangelization.

Here as in conversion, we must realize that the starting point is not the place where God stops. He is willing and pleased to start with us wherever we might be, and then move us through a process of growth and change that will transform us more into the image of Christ. The same is true for a community of the people of God. God is more willing than we are to start with groups who, in their relationships and actions, do not meet his standards. God will transform a church into a community which will more and more reflect the image of his Kingdom. When we evaluate the resulting church or the church into which we expect new converts to be integrated, we must see it from two different perspectives: as a church which accepts a people as and where they are out of love and forgiveness, *and* as a church which sees a people's inadequacies in the light of the goal toward which God will move them as they are transformed by faith. How "adequate" the church must be before we consent to new converts becoming a part of it as opposed to establishing new (and also inadequate) churches, is a question that cannot be answered in abstract or generalized terms. The church must be adequate enough to nurture new Christians to be the people of God in this locality, and to worship and serve the Lord in an acceptable manner. What constitutes "enough" can be gauged only by individual cases.

THE MISSION OF THE CHURCH

We must come full circle in discussing the resulting church. So far, this book has not discussed the full range of the mission of the Church. This is evident in things like the people profile (see p. 157), which has its consummation in people who are propagators of the gospel. We do not mean to imply that this is the ultimate criteria for judging the resulting church or gauging the maturity of a Christian. There ought also to be those whose maturity leads them into counseling, working for social justice, teaching and ministering from the Bible, or heading large organizations. Evangelism is not the only activity that characterizes the movement of a person or people toward Christ.

To speak of the resulting church with a focus on its "self-propagating" quality is to view it from only one viewpoint, however important and significant that viewpoint might be. Still, our ultimate objective in *evangelization* is a community of people who are able and are actively engaged in completing the evangelization of their own people.

We must reiterate, lest we be misunderstood, that the mission of the Church is larger than evangelization even as the Kingdom of God is larger than the Church. Yet mission does not exist apart from or without evangelization anymore than the Kingdom of God in this age can be described apart from or separated from the body of Christ. We anticipate that the establishment of a church will see the development of a wide range of relationships and activities that will go far beyond evangelization in the narrow sense. Because it will be the Kingdom of God breaking in and becoming present, there will be evangelism—and much more!

CHAPTER 26

Ready for Results

*B*y this time it ought to be clear that the outcomes we look for cannot be captured by a standardized list of desirable results. The *standardized* solution attempts to deal with the problem of what to do by providing a prescription for action that can be learned outside the situation to which it is to be applied. It comes with a set methodology, a set of pre-packaged roles, and a standardized scenario for outcomes. It already knows what the results should look like and imposes that image of the future onto its mode of action. The results too often are disastrous, with conversions that require cultural dislocation, decision patterns that ignore traditional patterns of decision-making, church organization that mimics the sending hierarchy, and leadership development that replicates the Western, seminary-educated, full-time ministry. The true logic of the infinitely diverse contexts of the various peoples is ignored, and the results can be seen on all continents of the globe.

UNIVERSAL QUESTIONS, UNIQUE ANSWERS

Questions that clarify the future are always more important than the answers. *The questions are universal while the answers are always unique to the situation.* We can have a fairly clear idea what our purposes are, the direction in which we are heading, and the broad shape of "things to come." But the details, the "here and now" that we anticipate, are matters that are intimately tied up with the concrete details of the changing situation in which we evangelize, the force for evangelism, the people being evangelized, the adequacy of our assumptions, the effectiveness of our methods, and so on.

We can look for the eventual conversion of a people and the development of a church and have some idea of where the process is in terms of the people profile. We can have some broad ideas about the qualities which should characterize a community of the people of God who live in the Spirit and give local expression to the Kingdom of God. But we cannot specify what conversion will look like and how it will be registered apart from the details of a unique context with its own logic. Nor can we specify the details of what an authentic community of the people of God will look like in a concrete sense apart from a knowledge of the actual socio-historical dynamics of the societies within which the community will exist.

Attempts to devise such standardized portraits inevitably shipwreck on the shoals of several unchangeable facts. The more generalized and abstract a formulation of results, the less it applies to any concrete historical situation. Thus the more successful we are in devising a universally true statement of results, the less help it will be in guiding our action. The very act of universalizing empties statements of their content.

Further, an examination of statements which have specific content *and* which claim to be universal in application shows that they are invariably guilty of cultural confusion. What is specific in their content turns out to be culturally limited. They are only sets of forms which someone has mistakenly supposed could be grafted on to all the cultural roots from which the Church must draw sustenance. To carry out programs with such statements would be to plant an irrelevant and alien form of Christian faith, to restrict the freedom of the Spirit to develop a new and creative expression, and to set the stage for a syncretism which will draw its inspiration in part from the attempted imposition of imported cultural expressions.

This is seen in almost every church service in the Muslim world (and many other cultural domains as well). The structure and nature of the model which missions or foreign evangelists used to develop worship forms was fairly standardized. Expecting Muslim converts to adopt it was to expect them to engage in distasteful behavior. By anticipating a different set of forms as the outcome of evangelism, a new day may dawn for Muslim evangelization. For example, Phil Parshall writes of a new experiment in Bangladesh:

—Muslim linguistic forms have been used in place of the more traditional Hindu-Christian vocabulary of the church.

—A facility for washing prior to prayer is provided just outside the worship center.

—Believers remove their shoes and sit on the floor during prayer times.

—Wooden stands are used as Bible holders similar to the ones used for the Koran in the Mosque.

—Prayer is offered with uplifted hands and often with eyes open in Islamic fashion.

—Chanting of the attributes of God, the Lord's Prayer, and personal testimony are performed with great zeal.

—Embracing is done in brotherly Muslim style.

—No particular emphasis is placed on Sunday, for the Muslim considers Friday the holiest day of the week.

—Fasting is encouraged, but it is clearly explained that the thirty-day fast as practiced in Islam does not lead to merit or acceptance with God.

—In the early stage the missionary takes the role of teacher, but within a short time a convert begins to assume this responsibility.

—The name "Christian" is avoided. It is replaced by "Followers of Isa" (Jesus), which has less negative connotation to Muslim society.

—Organization of churches is proposed along autonomous lines much like the loose-knit administrative structures of the mosque.

—Total financial responsibility for church expenses, workers, and buildings is that of the community of believers. From the beginning, no foreign assistance is allowed.

—Development of a homogeneous Muslim convert church. A Hindu, Animist, or "traditional Christian" would be most welcome to worship in the church, but they would be expected to adopt the practices of the convert believers.

—There is no option of flight for the converts. They are expected to remain in their society and maintain a discreet witness to their family and neighbors, which will add to the body of Christ . . . .

—Spiritual dynamics are emphasized. Fasting, prayer, and study of the Word of God are absolute prerequisites of a healthy church. (1979, p. 31)

Such an expectation about the resulting church is effective and of real value simply because it specifies what the church will be like. But it is by no means a definition of outcomes that could be transferred to other than similar Muslim contexts. Parts of it are specific only to Bangladesh and Pakistan where much of the traditional Christian community has a Hindu background. What were the results of the changed expectation in Bangladesh?

> In the past four years, over seventy-five Muslims in Bangladesh have become believers. This is almost insignificant when measured against a population of 70 million Muslims. It is important, however, to realize that this probably exceeds the total number of Muslims converted in Bangladesh during the past fifty years. (Parshall, 1979, p. 31)

Because the specification of results for particularized situations is idiosyncratic, we are not able to set forth a general checklist or programmed pattern of what ought to be in a statement of expected outcomes. But we want at least to point out some perspectives which we ought to bring to the endeavor in order to get leverage on the future.

FOUR TYPES OF POSSIBLE OUTCOMES

Very simply, we can say there are four types or classes of outcomes that may or may not have important effects on our strategies for evangelization.[1] They can be arranged in a diagram where one axis is whether or not we had actually anticipated the result and the other axis is whether or not we consider the outcome to be desirable and included in our plan for evangelization. Putting these two axes together produces the diagram in Figure 26-1 which we will use to classify results.

1. *Anticipated positive outcomes* are what we usually call *goals*. They are outcomes which we intend, which we pray for, and toward

---

1. We are not going to attempt to solve the very practical and theoretical problem that all of our actions produce an infinite number of results. When we examine any concrete event from an objective viewpoint, we find that it has an infinite number of characteristics from which we make a selection. We abstract some parts of the totality of the event or situation because they have significance to our goals and values. We are assuming the abstraction process and will not try to draw the relationship that necessarily exists between our goals and world view and what we choose as important results for the evangelization process.

Outcome

Positive   Negative

	Positive	Negative
Anticipated	1	2
Unanticipated	3	4

Figure 26-1   Classification of Anticipated Outcomes

which our efforts and behavior are directed. Because they are such a fundamental part of every plan for evangelism, they have a separate identity on the strategy cycle. We will spend a good bit of time discussing the nature of goals and how we go about setting them, writing them into a plan, and communicating them with other Christians. They are discussed under Step 8, "Planning." It is at this point that our models of outcomes for conversion and for the establishing of a community serving Christ intersects most directly. We anticipate that God will bless and bring about some of the events and happenings that will move a people toward Christ. They are crucial in shaping the action we take.

2. *Anticipated negative outcomes* are what we consider undesirable. They have a negative effect on our overall mission. We usually call these *problems* (Dayton, 1971). Oftentimes we can anticipate problems if we have a good knowledge of the various elements we are making a part of the evangelization process within a given people. Here we think of a variety of outcomes with which we would be unhappy, but with foresight can take action to correct. Some examples:

—A study of campaign evangelism indicates that the vast majority have a "follow-up" gap. Of the many who come forward in a crusade meeting to register a "decision" for Christ, only a small percentage (some as low as 3 percent) can ever be objectively traced to later participation in a local congregation of believers. Anticipating this, one can either abandon the method or revise it in ways that will enhance its true contribution with a broader process of evangelization. An example of this might be the "Rosario Plan" for evangelism that makes the crusade only a part of a year-long attempt to establish "daughter" churches and help the local churches into a growth mode prior to the evangelist's crusade. Studies indicate that nearly 60–70 percent of the people making decisions wind up in churches as a result of this redesign of the crusade.

—A radio station in Africa surveyed its listening audience and discovered that only a miniscule percentage of its potential audience ever listened to the station. It was also discovered that people preferred music and programming that was more African and secular than the American music and programming which was broadcasted. Many of the programs had been recorded in the United States and rebroadcast on the station. The station decided to use more live programs produced in Africa which utilized more African and pop music, and to include more programming on "secular" subjects. There was no plan to lessen the evangelistic goals or emphasis of the radio station. After the new programming was instituted the listenership zoomed from about 2 percent of the audience to 40 percent! The results were beyond what they had hoped. But within a short period of time several missionaries left the station, complaining that it it had become "worldly." An ensuing struggle within the mission community resulted in the cancellation of the new programming (the old was reinstated, and listenership once again declined). Not anticipating a rising level of disagreement among fellow missionaries over the suitability of the new programming eventually led to its demise in spite of its superior ability to achieve goals for a larger audience. Had it been anticipated several steps could have been taken which would have alleviated the tensions and neutralized this negative effect.

—Studies indicate that a large percentage of people in schools and prisons who receive Bibles through "indiscriminate" distribution programs, throw their Bibles away without reading them.

> Bibles were given to every inmate in a large United States prison. A few days later it was discovered that 90 percent of these found their way into trash cans, thus causing the unnecessary expenditure of more than $250,000 when this program was prematurely spread to other prisons. (Engel, 1977, p. 14)

This is not a difficult result to envision or even to discover. Having become aware of this negative result, the method can be modified so that Bibles are distributed through a program that ensures that people have access to a Bible when they want to read it.

Such a list can be extended indefinitely. Evangelization has numerous "side-effects" which we can anticipate—it might lead to increased persecution and pressures on Christians (as have the large Muslim conversions in Indonesia). It can turn large numbers of people against Christian faith ("I tried that when I was younger—and it didn't do any good") while only winning a few. It can create the impression that Christian faith is only for the young and educated and thus effectively exclude the older leaders (as has the "school" method in Africa in many cases). If any plan is to be put into action, it is essential to anticipate not only the obstacles that stand in its way, but also its negative side-effects. Only then can decisions be made as to whether those side-effects can be "handled" and neutralized or whether the approach will have to be given up in favor of one with less negative results.

3. *Unanticipated positive outcomes* are pleasant surprises, though sometimes they create rather ambivalent feeling. When a plan succeeds far beyond our wildest dreams, it often creates a whole new situation which necessitates a complete rethinking of what we are doing. In Irian Jaya no one was expecting the rapid conversions to Christ among the highland Dani. After a relatively short time of preaching, vast numbers of people came by clans and tribes to burn their fetishes and commit themselves to Christ. Missions which were anticipating a long, slow haul against paganism were suddenly moved from a situation where less than 1 percent professed faith to a situation where 60–70 percent had become Christians in one or two months! Now the problem was what to do with all these new Christians—how to disciple them, increase their understanding, and prepare them for baptism.

Of course not all unanticipated positive outcomes swamp a plan. It may be that fellow Christians who we thought might be hostile to our plan and thus a problem, simply changed their minds and joined us, strengthening what we are doing and making it more possible for us to achieve our goals. Imagine how the Christians felt in Palestine when Saul became a Christian and an ally instead of an enemy! It was a completely unanticipated event and created a new impetus, but it did not necessitate a whole new plan for evangelizing the eastern parts of the Roman world.

In an ideal world we would get to the point where we could anticipate all the results of the actions which we and our agencies take. But we do not live in such a world and we are not as perspicacious as we would like to be. Yet we can, through experience and research (of the kind Jim Engel has so well advocated), come to have realistic and practical expectations about the results of given lines of action. One of the purposes of planning is to reduce the number and importance of type 3 and 4 outcomes to our mission and its achievement.

4. *Unanticipated negative outcomes* are headaches, *unpleasant surprises*. They are the kind of problems that can take 80 percent of our time and activity that we had meant to give to more productive and important matters. Because they are unanticipated, we have no way of preparing ourselves or the church to handle them. They have to be coped with as and when they occur, however inconvenient they may be. To find ourselves fighting fires rather than giving ourselves to more important actions is a thoroughly frustrating experience (even when we learn through it). As Proverbs 22:3 says: "Sensible people will see trouble coming and avoid it, but an unthinking person will walk right into it and regret it later."

One can immediately ask, "If 80 percent of our outcomes are going to be negative unanticipated ones, what's the sense in doing any planning?" Two observations are helpful: First, most of life *is* failure. We do fail more often than we succeed. Let us not be so overcome with the success that we come to believe that most of life is controllable. It is not. Second, the many successes (anticipated or unanticipated positive outcomes) we do have indicate that a serious attempt to reduce negative outcomes and increase the positive is fruitful.

We approach these systematically through the planning cycle and through a period of growth as we learn how systems of humans interact and react in a given socio-historical context. We can reduce unanticipated negative outcomes by paying more attention to possible outcomes. We cannot control the future, but we need not be surprised by it (Kahn and Wiener, 1967). At this level we have to do better than a pietistic response that denies both the reality of "negative" results (all that comes our way is there by God's design and must be seen only or exclusively as a positive event) or their ultimate negativity even when they eventually are taken up by God and transformed into some good (as the cruel and unjust death of Christ). We must be ready for such unanticipated problems and be confident that, with God's help, we will find a solution.

We should assume that all four types of results will be part of our programs, and we should be ready to capitalize on the outcomes that actually occur. We will have to think through what it is we are looking for and have means for evaluating the results of our program. This has not been a uniform characteristic of evangelization in the past (much to our chagrin). A lack of concern for results is becoming less and less justifiable in our present state of knowledge and capability. If we are good stewards of the gospel, we must be good stewards of results as well.

WAYS WE HIDE FROM OUTCOMES

Knowledge of outcomes is not always sought. There are a number of "dodges" which are practiced with various levels of skill in the evangelistic world. For some reason people often do not want to know the results of their efforts. They seem afraid to face the truth in an objective way. It might be so devastating that they will be unable to continue functioning in activities which they obviously find rewarding and significant. It does not seem to matter that this objective feedback might enable them to become even more effective. It does not seem to matter that they might discover an even more fruitful area where God wants their talents. Humans obscure the present by denying the past and thus prevent the very changes that could transform them into something better. Some of the ways we keep ourselves from being ready for the results of our efforts include the following. (See more on this in chapter 31, "Goals for Evangelization.")

1. *Measuring activity instead of outcomes.* Probably the most common way of avoiding results is to confuse means with ends. Missions and churches often report results in terms of the activity which took place: so many tracts given out, so many meetings held, so many hours of broadcasting in so many languages, so many Bibles distributed, so many patients treated. The evaluation of their agency hinges not on *what has been accomplished* but on *how much activity* has taken place. The activities become an end in themselves and people forget the purpose of those activities. What comes to be important is that the meeting was held as scheduled and that the stadium was full, not what it accomplished in making disciples or whether it made any difference in the life of the Church. We have all seen how a bureaucracy, founded for one purpose, outgrows that purpose and continues to exist mainly to keep the bureaucrats employed. The means come to displace the ends.

Of course means are very important. They enable us to effect change in our world. But we cannot measure results simply by recounting how carefully or often we utilized the means. It is like the little boy who was given five pennies to get gum from a gum-ball machine. When he came back empty-handed, he dutifully said he had put each penny in carefully and had pulled the handle the whole way, but had not been tall enough to see that the machine was empty! In evangelization it is important to recount our use of means, but we also have to look and see how many "gum-balls" we have as a result of those procedures.

2. *Justifying activities by unknown results.* The second most common way to avoid results is to appeal that "only God knows how many people have come to faith as a result of this great endeavor." We seem to have a perverse presumption that God will bless whatever we do so long as we are zealously and sincerely seeking to bring people to Christ. So we often do not try to determine whether he is indeed blessing our endeavor or whether there might be a much more effective way of going about the same task. It is hard to put the question of results to an organization that is in the full swing of ministry. But when we "leave the results to God," we better be sure we are leaving him something that is pleasing and not a great witness to our impatient stupidity! We may not always be able to trace the lines of influence and impact of a ministry God has given to us, but there are tools and means available to discover the impact of much of what we do. How can we consider ourselves good stewards if we refuse to discover how we are doing? Instead of doing the works of God, we may be deceiving ourselves and others and simply perpetuating failure in blissful ignorance.

3. *Obscuring the results by propaganda.* Many of us are in organizations and churches that have to engage in fund-raising to support their ministries. One of the deadliest enemies of strategy is the power of the myths that are generated by public relations activities. Once we have sold a public on the viability of certain means, there is a great deal of pressure to come up with results that look good.

Our approaches have gone beyond being simply methods and have become "movements" and "causes." Evaluation and the measurement of results have been obscured because the ideology attached to each said they should be effective. That effectiveness has been demonstrated by appeals to testimonials (pastors who said a certain movement was the greatest thing to happen in Guatemala, or a selection of accounts of those who were converted), statistics (4,000 prayer groups meeting, 11,356 telephone calls made), and results that were not clear indications of goal achievement (24,867 prayed to receive Christ). Only later when more objective criteria have been used to measure the results has it become apparent that the promise and the propaganda have been better than the results. We recall with a sense of wonder a letter we received early in the ministry of MARC. The head of a well-known Christian agency wanted us to do some research that would prove conclusively that the medium this agency was using was "ten times more effective than so-and-so." When we asked if he was interested in an unbiased survey that would ascertain what indeed was happening, he responded that he was only interested in proof that what they were doing was the best.

Propaganda buttressed with selective evidence of positive results lulls us into thinking we are reaching out in an effective way when we are not. It deceives us and our supporters and keeps us from attempting some alternative strategy that would reach the unreached. Christian radio and television stations are riddled with propaganda that justifies their support and continuation on the basis of their "witness" to non-Christians when it is easily demonstrable that mostly Christians listen to these programs. Who are we kidding?

One of the side-effects of this propaganda is that various means become sacred. It becomes impossible either to assess fairly the effects (a set of evaluation techniques is developed that is biased toward producing positive evaluations which can be cranked back into the fund-raising machine) or to change them in the light of more objective measurements of results. More and more unreality enters the system as the agency or organization attempts to remain "faithful" to the original vision and strategy. The method becomes less and less effective as time goes on, but it is not discontinued because it has gained a life all its own, with a constituency that is committed to supporting it.

Another effect of this "sacralizing" is the tendency toward a "messianic" complex. The methodology, having met all the tests of experience and "results," is advertised as a "key" for evangelizing the world. People come to confuse their own understanding of God's strategy at a given point in history with God's strategy. So the strategy and its methods are exported all over the world with a disastrous inability to predict the true dimensions of results as it touches down in any given context.

OUTCOMES AND THE STRATEGY CYCLE

Anticipated outcomes of our approach need to be fed back into the strategy cycle. We have to expect effects on the various components that make up the system of evangelization of which we are an integral part. Normally we think of the outcomes of evangelism in terms of the two major things we stressed in chapters 21 and 22: the movement toward Christ that we hope will eventuate in conversion, and the establishment of contextualized communities of the people of God who will themselves become significant parts of the evangelization process. But we also have to turn the focus of our attention to other matters suggested by the strategy cycle:

1. *The force for evangelism* is itself touched by the events of evangelism. The change agents in any program aiming at change are changed themselves by the actions and relationships which are part and parcel of the process. We need to anticipate how they will change in the process as well as how they need to change if they are to become more effective in their task. (See the next chapter.)

—Once the evangelists begin implementing the strategy, will they be able to sustain it? Will they have the cross-cultural sensitivity necessary to penetrate the differences and touch the heart of a system? What will they learn as a by-product of carrying out the strategy?

—How will they react to various types of outcomes in light of their ultimate goal? Will they be discouraged by slow response? Swamped by large response? Will positive results alleviate any latent doubts about the legitimacy or wisdom of the methods?

2. *The people to be evangelized.* How will those who do not turn to Christ feel about those who do? Will the effects of asking for decisions that separate a person from his or her family turn the community against Christian faith? What capability is there of reversing bad effects among those who have not yet been brought into the Church?

3. *Strategy.* Given the effects which are anticipated as a result of carrying out a proposed approach, can we still consider our approach valid? Do the positive anticipated outcomes outweigh the negative? Can the negative be neutralized? If not, what needs to be modified so that the outcomes can hopefully be more positive?

4. *Resources.* If these results are known by those who are providing the source of monies, equipment, and personnel, will they continue to support the evangelism? Are there results which are positive within the people being evangelized but which may not be understood (or even liked) by the supporting constituency? How can the results be interpreted with integrity so they can understand them? Should we look for alternative sources of support?

FAILING ON PAPER

By now many readers will feel overwhelmed and frustrated. There are so many considerations that one is tempted to throw up one's hands and abandon the task or withdraw from responsibility and say, "I'll do the best I can, and leave it up to the Lord!"

We believe the task of cross-cultural evangelism is one of the most difficult tasks or callings in the world. It is so difficult that in chapter 18 we compare the preparation needed as being greater than that required for the medical profession. But it is also a glorious task, and the fact that a handful of men and women have been used by God to turn the world upside down is an indication that we are empowered to be channels of change in the world.

All these considerations, questions, and plans are at once part of our education and training, and at the same time our preparation to be used by God to reach a particular people. Up until now we have been discussing all the things we can consider and do *before* we begin the test. It is our belief that it is much better to fail on paper than to fail in practice! If the hours of study, discussion, planning, research, and prayer increase the probability that an entire people will be swept into the Kingdom, is not every hour well invested? We believe it is.

These are all *beginning* considerations. Only after we have moved into a situation will we know whether the steps we have planned are appropriate. "You may make your plans, but God directs your steps" (Prov. 16:9).

CHAPTER 27

Changes in Yourself

*H*ow easy it is for us to stand outside the problem that we are describing. Too often we forget in our planning that we too will change with time. Indeed, we must change. Growing in grace needs to be accompanied by growth in wisdom and Christian maturity. In chapter 18 we discussed the need to see each missionary as a growing and developing person on what might best be described as a career path. The first termer and the veteran of twenty years are two different people. But the veteran was once a beginner. He or she became something different in the process of carrying out or attempting to carry out the missionary task.

In this brief chapter we will attempt to highlight the importance of anticipating changes in both the individual and the organization, and planning for these changes as part of our anticipated outcomes.

KNOWLEDGE, ATTITUDE, BEHAVIOR, AND RELATIONSHIPS

Every individual in any organization enters any situation with a certain knowledge, attitude, behavior, and relationships. As we move through history each of these changes to a greater or lesser degree. At the basis of all formal education is the idea that it is possible to change these four dimensions of life in a planned and predetermined way.

Logic says that relationships are based upon behaviors (how we act toward one another), behaviors, in turn, are dependent upon our attitudes (we act out our feelings and our perceptions of the world), and our attitudes can be changed by changing our knowledge ("For as he thinketh in his heart so he is," Prov 27:7a). In practice the relationship of these four is much more complex and much more inter-dependent. The theory of cognitive dissonance puts forth the view that any time our behavior and our beliefs are at odds with one another, we will either have to change our belief or change our behavior or become schizophrenic. There is a great deal of evidence that people can also change the way they think by the way they act, either voluntarily or involuntarily. But regardless of the interconnection between the four, it is useful to see that these are four different ways of describing a situation or an individual, and they can aid us in understanding changes that will be brought about in ourselves or our organization.

Some of these are self-evident. For example, when we go to evangelize a particular people, we obviously go to establish a relationship with them. In order to establish this particular relationship we know that we will have to act in a certain way. We will have to have cultural understanding. Their perception of our actions must be such that they believe we are people of good will.

Knowing *how* we should act and acting that way is the most difficult of all human endeavors. We cry out with the apostle Paul:

> So I find this law at work: When I want to do good, evil is right there with me. For in my inner being I delight in God's law; but I see another law at work in the members of my body, waging war against the law of my mind and making me a prisoner of the law of sin at work within my members. What a wretched [person] I am! Who will rescue me from this body of death? Thanks be to God— through Jesus Christ our Lord! (Rom. 7:21–25)

Somehow if we are going to behave correctly, our attitudes have to reinforce our behaviors. It is true that love is not thought but action. It is equally true that people often are able to see through righteous actions that are not really generated by an attitude of love. So in order to minister to a given people we must have a positive attitude about what we are going to do, an attitude which is motivated by the Holy Spirit, an attitude that sees this people as being equal before God and highly prized by him.

The door to changing our attitudes is knowledge. We may stand outside of a particular people group and observe their behaviors and be repulsed by them. The Turkana people we described in chapter 22 have a diet of camel and goat milk mixed with blood from their animals. Because of their environment they seldom have any opportunity to bathe. The men wear a mud-packed hairdress which is redone every six months. All of these cultural practices may be repulsive to us, and because of them we may quickly view the Turkana as less than human.[1] But if one can come to know the Turkana and to understand their values, then it is much easier to change one's *attitudes* about the Turkana. The Turkana place a very high value on friendship. Indeed, the Turkana value things only as they belong to friends (compare that value system with the Western one which appears to value people on the basis of what they own!).

In Figure 27-1 we have reproduced the Engel Scale and put it alongside the four categories of knowledge, attitude, behavior, and relationships. This is an important way to think about yourself and your organization. We have noted two columns for the profile—present and planned. Let us assume that you have done enough research to describe this people's present movement toward Christ on the Engel/Søgaard Scale. Put that down under "present." From your strategy you should have developed a goal of where you expect this group to be in the future as the result of your efforts and the efforts of others. Describe that under "planned." Comparing these two will immediately help you understand the change that will be needed in the people you are attempting to reach. Now what will have to be the changes in *you?* What knowledge will you need? What attitudes will you have to hold? What behaviors will be required; in other words, how will you have to act? Finally, if you are going to become a part of this people's life, what relationships will have to be established, both with them and with others working with you?

CHANGES IN YOURSELF

This book is about the effort to change relationships in the world, to bring people who are outside of Christ into a relationship with him. In order for this to happen numbers of men and women throughout the

1. This is not just a Western problem. Members of other people groups within Kenya have this view of the Turkana.

Figure 27-1 The People Profile: Present and Future Plans

THE PEOPLE PROFILE		PRESENT				PLANNED			
DECISION POINT		% 25 50 75	ATTITUDE + 0 −	RATE OF CHANGE	KNOWL- EDGE	ATTITUDE	BEHAVIOR	RELATION- SHIPS	
NO AWARENESS	−7								
AWARENESS	−6								
SOME KNOWLEDGE	−5								
KNOWLEDGE	−4								
IMPLICATIONS SEEN	−3								
PERSONAL NEED	−2								
CONFRONTATION	−1								
CONVERSION									
RE-EVALUATION	+1								
INCORPORATION	+2								
PROPAGATION	+3								

world will have to act out the role of cross-cultural missionary effectively. They will have to change their behavior in some way. In order for this behavior to be changed new attitudes will have to be adopted. People must begin to perceive and experience the world in new and different ways. They must begin to believe that world evangelization is possible and that reaching one particular unreached people is in itself a glorious task. This book attempts to present knowledge in such a way that attitudes will be changed, behaviors will be changed, and relationships will be changed! In one sense you are a different person as a result of having read these pages. At the very minimum you have read a book that you have not read before. At the very maximum this book may be motivating you to take action. The knowledge which you have discovered in this book has changed your attitudes.

As you look forward to further service for Christ as part of a cross-cultural evangelistic effort, your first step is to see where you fit in the overall task and within any organizations of which you might be a part. We will discuss the analysis of this at greater length in chapter 29. The best way to discover what God wants you to do with your life is, we believe, to imagine what you will be doing ten to fifteen years in the future. Where will you be working? Within the context of this discussion on reaching unreached people, such an effort will help you to see what role you hope to be playing in the task of world evangelization. To give an illustration, let us assume that right now you are a missionary who has graduated from college, has had one year of post-graduate work, and has had five years of experience in another culture. Let us further assume that you are dissatisfied with both your own personal impact upon the world and the way that the Church is trying to reach a particular people group. You have thought through in your own mind, or with others, what you think might be God's strategy to reach a particular people. You see yourself as part of that strategy. But you need to see yourself not only as what you will be doing this year and next, but what you will be doing ten years from now. If the anticipated outcomes that you believe God desires actually come to pass, what effect will they have on you? Hopefully, you will be even further qualified to continue reaching this particular people, or reaching another people, or to guide others in reaching a people.

Now looking at a profile of a particular people with whom you might be involved—the way they are now and what you hope they might be in ten years—what knowledge will you need to acquire either formally or informally to be a part of this? What attitude changes will you have to have? These might be both attitudes that you can imagine you have now and attitudes which may develop as a result of additional study. For example, you might be highly motivated to take one step, but at the moment you might not have the motivation to move on to further steps.

How will you have to act, to behave, to play your role effectively in each of these different situations? The most effective leaders, as well as the most effective missionaries, are those who are able to change their style of behavior depending upon the situation they are in. Perhaps you are a person who seems to have only one style of operating, a style which you can see is not going to be effective in every situation.[2]

Finally, what will be the relationships that you will have? First, there are the relationships within your own organization. Ten years from now will you be in a different role than the one you are in now? Will you be in a position of leadership? What does this tell you about the knowledge you will have to have at that time? What does it suggest about the learning experiences that you will have to have? What will be the relationships you will have with new people? If you are going to be the on-the-ground missionary in this particular strategy, what relationships will you have to develop with the people, with other Christians who are already there, with governments, and so forth?

The point is that *you* are one of the outcomes of this strategy! You cannot be a part of it and remain untouched by it. Understanding how you may change will be of great benefit to you in thinking through God's strategy for reaching this particular people.

CHANGES IN YOUR ORGANIZATION

In chapter 30 we discuss bringing about change within organizations. Here we need only point out that the above discussion about changes in the individual also applies to an even greater extent to the organization. Many organizations want to succeed. Indeed, many young organizations assume that they will succeed. They dream about the day when they will have reached a particular plateau in terms of effectiveness, income, or outreach. Often, however, organizations do not plan to succeed in that they just do not realize that if they do succeed they will be different from the way they are now. They will not only have to act differently, they will have to think differently. Styles of management which are very appropriate for an organization of three to four people usually will not work very well for an organization of a hundred or more. (See Bassett, 1966.)

2. For further discussion about leadership we recommend Glenn Bassett (1966).

Again turning to the people profile, both for the present and the one that you hope to have ten years from now, what does this tell you about the organization?

The knowledge within an organization is the sum total of the knowledge of all the people within it, plus the knowledge that is embedded in policies and procedures. An organization which has taken the time and the effort to record its history in such a way that it can build upon its successes and failures has a tremendous advantage. Ten years from now what kind of knowledge will your organization have? It will be not only the knowledge of abstract ideas but also the knowledge of experience.

If your organization is effective in carrying out its plan for reaching this particular people, what will be the organization's attitude, both about itself and about the task that it has undertaken? Attitude can be summed up under such phrases as *esprit de corps,* self-awareness, self-confidence, vision, faith, and courage. These are expressed in many ways. How are they expressed now? How do you imagine that they will be expressed ten years from now?

BEHAVIORS FOR THE ORGANIZATION, MANY LEVELS

We call formalized, routine behaviors *procedures.* They are the standard ways we do things. How the organization will act in a particular situation is usually based on the organization's *policies.* Procedures and policies describe what the organization will do in the future in the face of a given situation. What are the organization's policies and procedures now? How will they change as a result of the organization accomplishing what it set out to do?

An organization has many relationships. They are generally divided into internal and external. An organization's internal relationships are described by the behaviors of its staff toward one another. An organization's external relationships are much more diffuse. Right now your organization has a set of relationships, some of which are formally defined and others which are only understood. For example, a mission organization may be formally related to a mission association, or it may be part of a national council within a country. It also has a whole set of variously defined relationships with others. It has, as a result of its policy and/or its statement of faith, certain groups of people which it automatically includes or excludes. For example, some mission agencies will cooperate only with those who hold the same doctrinal distinctives, while others will work alongside any who claim Jesus as Lord, and still others will not work with non-Christians.

If this people that we are attempting to reach is actually reached, what will be the result in terms of the organization's relationships, both internally and externally?

THERE MUST BE CHANGE

Change is what we are about. We need to change this world into a world more pleasing to God. All planned change starts with people. Let us begin.

QUESTIONS

Movement Toward Christ

1. If the approach we have chosen is successful, what do we expect will happen? What will God do?

2. How will we know it has happened so we can build on the results?

3. How do we know when a person has become a Christian? What changes or indications do we look for as "signs" of conversion to Christ?

4. Should we anticipate problems with syncretism as a result of our approach? If so, what do we need to do to correct or change our approach?

5. What changes do we expect in the "people profile," and at what steps on the scale?

The Resulting Church

1. Who decides what the church should be like in a specific context? What process is involved in indigenous decisions being made about the nature and forms of the life of the church?

2. How do we protect new churches from the "imperialism" of the churches and missions that originate it, and from replicating the structures of these churches however non-indigenous they might be?

3. For this particular people, what can we say about the nature of the fellowship that needs to develop? (See p. 365 for more specific questions.)

Ready for Results

1. What problems or difficulties can be anticipated with the use of the methods and approach we have chosen? What can be done to neutralize or reverse those outcomes?

2. What results or outcomes are crucial for understanding how much we are accomplishing with all the activity and spending of resources? How do we protect ourselves and our organizations from looking for only the positive results?

3. What impact do these anticipated results have on our overall approach? Is it still valid? Do we have to revise our ideas about the force for evangelism? The means and methods?

4. What changes will have to be made in us as individuals and in our organization? Knowledge? Attitude? Behaviors? Relationships?

Changes in Yourself

1. If you were going to attempt to reach the people you have been describing, what changes would have to come about in yourself?

2. What role do you see yourself playing in reaching this particular people?

3. How would your organization have to change in order to reach this particular people?

STEP 7

YOUR ROLE

Considerations

Who Are You?

Where Do You Fit?

Bringing About Change

Questions

CONSIDERATIONS

1. Different people play different roles.
2. Different roles are needed for the missionary task. Too often this fact is not recognized.
3. Just because we have thought about reaching a people does not mean that we are the ones whom God is calling to reach them.
4. Ecclesiology can never be separated from methodology.
5. The most difficult change we may have to bring about is change in ourselves.
6. Everyone resists change.
7. Change only takes place when there is discontent.
8. Organizations tend toward stability and thus toward bureaucracy.
9. Change takes time.
10. Changing ourselves and changing our organizations is the only way to change the world.

CHAPTER 28

Who Are You?

INTRODUCTION

*W*e have looked at almost all the elements of the planning process. One more remains. It is one we too often omit: ourselves. In our experience of working with veteran missionaries and experienced national leaders as they sought to plan for the future of their organization and to attempt new things for God, we have been struck time and again by this missing dimension. The planner cannot stand outside the system he or she is planning (Churchman, 1968), nor can the planner assume that his or her organization stands outside the process. Planning for others always includes planning for ourselves. When we are seeking to bring about change in others, we quickly discover that we must also change.

It takes time to be introspective, either individually or organizationally, but it is well worth it. That is why we have added this step in the planning process.

In this chapter we will become somewhat philosophical and discuss the individual (you) in terms of roles. We hope that this will contribute not only to your understanding of yourself, but also to your understanding of how other people "work." In chapter 29 we will discuss where you (and your organization) fit. Should you lead the effort you are considering? Should you play a minor role? Should you have additional training in order to accept greater responsibility? Would it be best for you to pass on what you have discovered to others? What will the future bring? Will you play the same role five years from now? Because our experience has also shown that many outstanding plans fail because of the inability of the individual to bring about change within *his or her own organization,* chapter 30 will present some ideas on both the problem and the solution.

WHO ARE YOU?

Tachai is a Chinese collective farm located in the difficult area of Shansi province. The soil is infertile and the weather unpredictable. Hard times have been common in the past. From 1874 to 1876 there was virtually no rain. No help came. In this province alone ten million people died.

Farming in Tachai is serious business. It means life or death for the eighty families that make up the collective. Land is so precious that they expend one million hours of labor just to add three acres of land. With care and planning the yield of their land has increased seven-fold in thirty years. While things do not always go smoothly, everyone has a place, an important role to play. A great deal of work is simply hard labor—weeding the fields, planting the seeds, hauling water for the plants, harvesting, and separating chaff from grain. But farming is also more than labor in the fields: mechanics are needed to repair machinery, brick and stone masons are needed to build housing and the walls that retain the soil on the steep hillsides, carpenters are needed to build new farm implements and furniture, bookkeepers are needed to care for the sale of the crop and the distribution of rewards, and administrators are needed to coordinate and oversee the collective. Clothing has to be made, baskets woven, children cared for and trained, shoes repaired, and animals treated when they are sick. It takes a wide range of skills and roles to make a collective farm work.

The Henry farm of Missouri Gulch is situated in a hilly, semi-arid area just north of Pendleton, Oregon. Fifteen hundred acres, half of which can be planted each year, are spread through eight different fields. The soil is fertile and yields forty bushels per acre of hard red winter wheat in good years. Most of the time there are only five people living on the farm: the owner's family and one hired hand. With

$350,000 worth of machinery and three people working, the farm will produce over 28,000 bushels of wheat a year, not to speak of the cattle, chickens, and vegetables. The owner has a master's degree in agriculture, watches the dynamics of a volatile futures market, can discuss the chemical makeup of various fertilizers and pesticides, drives and repairs all the latest tractors and combines, and serves as an extension teacher, training other farmers in the latest techniques of farm management.

The roles that people play in farming are quite diverse. They include not only the "jack-of-all-trades" who does most of the direct soil preparation, planting, weeding, and harvesting, but also the veterinarian who heals sick animals, the executive who runs the farm cooperative which provides storage for the crops, loans of money, the latest seed, the hired hand who is good at overhauling diesel engines in tractors, the seed researcher who is searching for a higher yielding species, the Secretary of Agriculture who determines political policy that affects the market and production potential of the farms, and so on.

The apostle Paul recognized that different roles would be played in the ministry of evangelism: "Each one of us does the work which the Lord gave him to do: I planted the seed, Apollos watered the plant, but it was God who made the plant grow ... we are partners working together for God, and you are God's field" (I Cor. 3:5, 6, 9). Evangelization demands an enormous range of interests and skills beyond the simple, direct personal witness that every Christian can give to his or her faith. The various methodologies all presume a variety of skills and activities whether it be electronic engineering to maintain radio equipment or linguistics to reduce unwritten languages to written form.

Christians bring different competencies and interests to the task of world evangelization. Those who can speak with the tongues of angels, those who can befriend even the unfriendliest, those who can research evangelism and write learned tomes, those who can train others in personal witnessing—all are part of a mosaic of roles which the Spirit is able to put together into a beautiful picture. We need to know what God has gifted us to be and do and where we fit in with others he has called to reach the same people. We are a body that is intended to function properly with a harmony that the Spirit produces, releasing each of us to make his or her distinctive contribution to the health and activity of the whole.

This step focuses on the questions that concern role definition. We will raise the issue of role more broadly than simply what an individual might be and do, and will examine also what an organization or a church might be and do. There are great things to be done for God. We need to find where we can pitch in and become part of the great harvest in our generation.

Paul's question, "What shall I do, Lord?" (Acts 22:10), has been reechoed by Christians through the centuries. This book attempts to describe a process by which we can become much more deliberate and self-conscious about discovering what God would have done so that a people might be given a valid opportunity to receive Christ. To a large measure we are attempting to shift the attention from ourselves to the people who need to be reached. Our premise is that we should respond to their needs out of love and not simply impose our solutions on them willy-nilly. But we must also ask some personal questions: What has all this to do with *me?* Where do I fit into the picture of need which has been drawn for this particular people? What ought to be my role in the evangelization of this unique part of the world?

It is at this point that the danger of short-circuiting the whole process arises most acutely. We might be like the owner of the highly mechanized, sophisticated wheat ranch in Oregon, who has been asked to become a part of the Tachai collective in Shansi, China. Her first and most natural inclination would be to attempt to introduce Western machinery, fertilizers, and technology into a context where it makes little sense and would have little benefit. That is because she knows farming in terms of her own background and experience, an experience with many valuable insights and techniques. But this experience is of little use to agriculture based on hard labor with a different set of ecological conditions.

Our first reaction in a new situation is to fall back on the roles we have grown accustomed to playing, to attempt to apply the solutions that worked in the past. We forget that the present has its own logic, that the methods we use and the roles we play must grow out of this context and be devised in the light of the needs, meanings, and social customs of the people we serve. Only if we keep our goals in focus and continually remind ourselves of the context in which they must be accomplished can we discern what it is we ought to do, might be able to do, or even ought *not* to do.

Our Western training and education is heavily biased toward the assumption that there are universally applicable strategies and methods. Seminaries and Bible colleges do not teach us how to solve problems, how to create new approaches, or how to learn new roles. Rather we are taught how to communicate in a more or less accepted form in church services through a particular homiletical style, usually mono-logical expository preaching. Apprenticeships in churches, field edu-cation, and special workshops are organized around these standard solutions.[1] We are theoretically taught how to function acceptably in the traditional roles of the professional clergy of the West.

Even with all the specialized training we receive it is apparent that such an approach does not work very well even when those skills and approaches are applied in the same culture in which they were taught, much less among people of a different culture. Our seminary graduates almost universally find themselves ill-prepared to perform their roles of ministering to laypeople. The theology they have learned does not fit the questions laypeople ask. The actual context in which they have to work has a particular constellation of people problems which they cannot handle on the basis of abstract principles of counseling. A great deal of the actual learning of ministry skills and roles is done "on the job" rather than through the traditional, abstract, formal classroom situa-tion.

When we move into other cultural situations, the inadequacies of our role models show up even more starkly, though we are often blind to this inadequacy. We export educational models based on the Western seminary with its formal classroom and abstract-truth approach to training. We develop professional standards for the ministry which are predicated on approximating the standards used by the home churches in the West. We assume that progress is to be measured by the degree to which roles develop in the receiving culture that approximate our own.

It has been our experience that the missionary enterprise is often hindered because men and women and organizations with goodwill and good intentions assumed that these two attributes were sufficient im-petus to move them into a cross-cultural evangelistic situation. This assumption must be challenged. The question of where we fit, our role, is of such importance that we have chosen to make it a major step in the mission strategy cycle.

In the balance of this chapter we will discuss roles from a sociological and psychological viewpoint. In the following chapter we will outline a procedure for ascertaining the role of the individual or the organization in reaching a particular people.

---

1. Even the Lausanne Congress of 1974 had many papers dealing with either standard solutions (methodologies) or with searches for standard solutions for particular classes of people such as "college students" or "rural people."

WHAT ARE ROLES?

All the world's a stage,
And all the men and women merely players:
They have their exits and their entrances;
And one man in his time plays many parts. . . . [2]

The "parts" we play in life are often prearranged for us. We are "child" then "student" then "young adult," and then "husband" or "wife," "father" or "mother." We play a number of other roles: scout, soccer goalie, president of the debating team, treasurer of the PTA, accountant, Sunday School teacher, salesperson, patient in a hospital, customer, physicist, broadcaster, journalist, waiter, cook, and so on. We have some idea of the kind of behavior to expect from a person wanting to undertake any of these roles.

Not all roles can be so easily identified. Think of the "clown" of the party or the "scapegoat" in a social group. These are informal roles. Other informal roles such as the "Judas" or the "seductress" refer to recognizable patterns of behavior in people.

Defining what role is might seem a simple matter, and in some ways it is since we all play certain roles. But it is also true that as we try to think more carefully and deeply about roles and how they operate, we discover that they are more complicated than we thought. We will describe roles in a very simple fashion and only highlight some of the important dimensions which are especially significant for cross-cultural evangelization.

"Role" is one way of describing the regularities which we observe in interpersonal behavior. Each of us has relationships to other people that shape our behavior in very particular and regular ways. Many of these come in reciprocal pairs: mother-daughter, salesperson-customer, driver-passenger, doctor-patient, defensive guard-offensive guard, teacher-student, uncle-nephew, husband-wife, criminal-victim. In each of these cases there are some very general, regular ways in which we expect the partners to behave toward one another. These regular ways of behaving are very important to people. One of the quickest ways to create a disturbance and upset people is to start playing a different role from the one they are expecting. Next time you see your doctor, ask him to take his clothes off so you can examine him! Or try to tell your parents that it is their bedtime.

2. William Shakespeare, *As You Like It*, act 2, scene 7, lines 139–142.

Each of these categories of people is collectively recognized. We call them "positions." A position refers to a socially defined location in a social structure or network of relationships. For example, in a family the father, mother, daughter, son, grandparent, uncle, aunt, and various in-laws are all "positions." Each of these "positions" has a role associated with it. We define a role as the enactment of prescribed behaviors which are collectively associated with a given position. There are certain obligations which are part of a person's position: a doctor is supposed to be able to analyze various symptoms, diagnose the cause, and prescribe a cure or treatment. A patient is supposed to listen to the advice of the doctor and follow his or her directions. A referee monitors the observance and violations of the rules as a game is being played and does not grab the basketball and slam-dunk it for the team he or she wants to win.

These are all very simple and very obvious matters, but they have profound ramifications especially in cross-cultural situations. Each society develops a somewhat different social structure, with positions and roles unlike our own. Consider the position of "doctor" in our own society. What happens when it is transported to another social context?

India, for example, has a healer's or a doctor's role. In fact, certain parts of India distinguish four classes of healers. One could thus reason that a Western doctor as a healer would readily fit into one or other of these four kinds of healer slots, but this need not be so. Consider the features of the four healer slots:

1. *Saint.* He asks no questions, charges no fee, and cures by prayer. He is very highly respected as a religious person.

2. *Doctor.* He knows everything about the human body so he need ask no questions to diagnose a patient's problem. He charges a high fee, but he guarantees his results—no cure, no fee. He is a highly respected person of much secular knowledge.

3. *Shaman.* He asks no questions but divines the cause of the illness. He makes small charges for his services, but gives little guarantee. His cures usually are highly visible rituals. He rates much lower in the scale of community respect.

4. *Quack.* He is the lowest level doctor with minimal knowledge, so he must ask all kinds of questions while he hunts for the disease and its cause. He often uses bought medicines since he usually is incapable of preparing his own. He charges only small fees, but collects in advance and gives no guarantee of results. His status is very low.

It is easy to see that the missionary doctor emits mostly the cues of a quack. (Loewen, 1976a, p. 220)

This simple example demonstrates some of the issues that are involved in the role a person plays in a given socio-historical context. We need to spell out some of the dynamics that are involved in roles:

Social structures differ. This means that cultures have different positions and roles for people to occupy, that societies permit different people to occupy those roles, and that they view the suitability of various social arrangements in different ways than we do. This difference is not a matter of right or wrong as such, though the meanings and practices associated with a given social structure might be highly objectionable (e.g. racism), and therefore need to be changed (Abrecht and Smalley, 1959, pp. 140–144). The many social structures which we observe are varying ways of organizing group behavior into regularized patterns for accomplishing tasks and helping people cooperate with each other. Many Western societies have a political organization known as democracy with a prime minister or president in the top political position. But Christians must not argue that a society with a monarchy (as ancient Israel) is morally wrong. Monarchy and democracy are merely different. We cannot transfer ourselves and skills from one social context to the other and necessarily expect the new context to have positions with appropriate roles into which we can fit with only minimal change on our part. We have learned roles for positions that fit one social structure. They may not fit a new one.

Role expectations, rights, and obligations vary. There is no simple equivalence between cultures in the types of behavior that are expected from people who play the "same" roles we have in our society. We are well aware of this at the linguistic level. We cannot find any single word to translate what "koinonia" (fellowship, community, participation) or "sarx" (body, flesh, the principle of evil that controls human behavior, etc.) means. Greek words are not equivalent to English words. The same is true for roles. In Japan, for example, the "sensei" or teacher does many of the same things an American teacher might do: gives instructions about the subject, answers questions, disciplines unruly or disruptive behavior, administers and grades exams. But there is much more:

> The Japanese teacher does not make a sharp distinction between specific classroom duties and a general responsibility for his pupils. . . . School teachers are expected to be available during vacations, and the school principal has the right to require them to

report for work at any time. Even during summer vacation, a teacher will be expected to come to school at least two or three times to evaluate the progress of children's play activities.

The teacher to some extent is held responsible even for the safety and behavior of a child outside school . . . the school does have a responsibility for inculcating basic moral virtues. . . . The teacher sends memos to parents, particularly at vacation times, outlining the procedures the parents should follow to insure that their child has a healthful vacation and listing places considered inadvisable for the child to visit. (Vogel, 1963, pp. 58–59 and Singleton, 1967)

There is nothing in "teaching" as a position that can settle a question as to whether the more diffuse and intimate involvement in the life of the students which the Japanese teacher takes is right or wrong as compared with the American role definition. What we would view as an invasion of privacy and illegitmate attempt to control outside or "family" matters is viewed as expected behavior by the Japanese teacher.

Role performance is evaluated according to *indigenous standards.* Our best intentions in an unknown situation can easily go awry. That is because our behavior is being evaluated by standards and role expectations quite different from our own. Until we learn what those standards are and how they are applied to our behavior we will continue to be mystified by the "absurd" responses that people give us, and by the "strange" people to whom they give the highest degrees of respect and honor.

Outsiders are assimilated to positions already provided for in the indigenous social structure, if at all possible. Some of these are "insider" roles, roles which are customarily performed by people who are native to the society, and others are "outsider" roles, such as merchant, foreign agent, or even missionary. Any such situation is primed for both opportunity (since an outsider can often act in novel ways that sets off dynamic change in a society) and danger (since the outsider can be completely misunderstood). Misunderstandings are often patterned after the following general sequence:

1. The outsider is assimilated to a particular indigenous position. This happens without his or her explicit awareness or knowledge of the range of rights and obligations that are part of that role.

2. The insider makes demands and looks for expected behaviors which are unknown or even inappropriate to the outsider.

3. The outsider feels that the "strange" demands are unfair or inappropriate and resists them in order to retain a sense of "integrity" based

on the outsider's own cultural expectations for a person holding such a role.

4. The insider's expectations are not fulfilled. The outsider does not behave as expected, violates important obligations, and shows that he or she is hypocritical and not caring—obviously not a person of integrity and worth.

As in his own culture, the outsider in an alien setting is given prerogatives according to the role to which he or she has been assigned. What behavior is expected and what rights are accorded (in terms of what can be asked, legitimately known, done, and expected in terms of respect) are consistent with the native interpretation of that position.

Building trust and credibility is largely a matter of performing the roles indigenously assigned and tacitly accepted by the outsider. This means an understanding of the indigenous role system and the options available and expected of the outsider is a key for maximizing the goals of mission. Much distrust is rooted in the contradictory cues outsiders give off. On the one hand they play the role of "religious expert" or "teacher" or "godly person." On the other, their behavior betrays (according to native role expectations) that they are anything but servants of God. Loewen writes of this problem in Southeast Asia where he characterizes the conflict between indigenous expectations and the actual way they perceive the missionary:

—Holy men wear one dirty, yellow robe.
—Missionaries have a wardrobe of stylish clothes.
—Holy men have a begging bowl and beg for a living.
—Missionaries have bank accounts and endless foreign income.
—Holy men are celibate.
—Missionaries indulge in sex. (If you doubt it, just count the number of missionary women in relation to men on any mission station.)
—Holy men are totally dedicated to the gods.
—Missionaries say so too, but they have cars and go on furlough.
(Loewen, 1976a, p. 221)

As should be apparent, the question of role is not a simple one. As in our own culture, many of our roles in alien settings are not ones which we choose but rather which are assigned to us by the host society. We have little choice in the matter. But we can come to understand and appreciate the difference between our own system and the one in which we are now trying to be a part. We can also consciously work to keep ourselves from being assimilated to roles which will restrict our credibility or ability to act in ways that will further evangelization. The lesson of missions in nineteenth-century China[3] or that of the imperialistic, superior missionary of the past must be heeded. We cannot be so foolish as to think that a whole society will change to suit our ideas of roles. Nor can we claim special rights and privileges within our host societies simply because we are ambassadors for Christ. To the best of our ability and with a good deal of hard cultural work, we must discover roles which will enable us to develop relationships in our new setting.

PERSONAL ROLE DEFINITION

How we come to assume a particular role is not simply a function of a larger social group imposing a certain definition upon us. Even though we have to admit that our behavior is channeled and our alternatives are limited by the inventory of roles which a society has developed, we must still admit that personal factors are very important. Who we are as persons will influence both the roles which society assigns to us and the skill and "style" by which we play that role.

How people come to see themselves as suited to engage in certain roles is a very complicated matter. We know that the availability of role models from whom a person can learn is an important element in a person deciding that something is what they would like to be and do. But so is that x-factor: motivation. Special aptitudes show up early in some people. Parents and teachers encourage the development of only a selected range of traits and habits which they see as desirable. Somehow it all fits together in a complex way to form the person who decides to acquire and express certain skills. Having done so, a social group will

3. Paul A. Cohen, *China and Christianity* (1963), ably chronicles the cultural disasters growing out of the assimilation of the missionary to the mandarin or literati status in China. Coming in as teachers of a new philosophy, they found themselves in competition with the traditional literati of China with their Confucian philosophy. Inevitably, this role alienated the most respected and powerful part of Chinese society and brought about a powerful anti-foreign movement (exacerbated by the missionary's tendency to get out of trouble by appealing over the heads of local officials to the extra-territorial rights of the foreigner). The Boxer rebellion of 1900 had deep roots in the hostility of the Chinese literati to the "Christian literati foreigners" and their resort to the superior power of their home country intervention. From Africa see Harris Mobley, *The Ghanaians' Image of a Missionary* (1970).

allow them to play certain roles and will evaluate the success with which they perform their obligations.

We also know that the Spirit gives "gifts" (*charismata*), special attributes which Paul tells us every member of the body of Christ possesses. Without these gifts, the Church does not have the ability to achieve the results it seeks. We have no idea of why one gift is given to one member and not to another. All we are given is the assurance that God does it so that all the various gifts necessary for the total life and ministry of the Church are potentially available.

When a person discovers that he or she is gifted by the Spirit in a particular direction, it influences his or her role definition. How a person discerns his or her particular gifts is a very personal matter. It involves sincere prayer and experience and interaction with fellow believers who will give feedback that will either confirm or discourage the adoption of a certain role. Further, we cannot say that gift identification is a one-time-for-all experience. Gifts may vary over the lifetime of an individual so that one or another emerges at a different stage in life. Also it seems that some gifts (such as teaching, wisdom, pastoring) do not descend in full bloom, but are developed through years of experience. They grow and mature as they are exercised. We grow in the grace of gifts of the Spirit just as we grow in the fruits of the Spirit.

We are not writing a book on how to discover one's spiritual gifts or how they relate to personality and natural abilities. There are other books and resources that provide that information.[4] The issue of discovering a self-identity that leads to basic vocational and role choices is a broad one which involves more than gifts.[5] Yet the question of role for the Christian must always involve coming to terms with gifts within the body of Christ. In answering the question of who we are and what we ought to do, we must keep several general principles in mind as Paul articulated them in I Corinthians 12:4–7:

> There are different kinds of spiritual gifts, but the same Spirit gives them. There are different ways of serving, but the same Lord is served. There are different abilities to perform service but the same God gives ability to everyone for their particular service. The Spirit's presence is shown in some way in each person for the good of all.

First, Paul tells us that people will be doing different things. There is no single gift that is adequate for all the needs of the body of Christ.

4. See C. Peter Wagner, 1979.
5. See Dayton and Engstrom, 1976 and Bolles, 1976.

Second, there is an underlying unity or harmony because in every case it is the same Lord who is at work in giving ability, gifts, particular services. We are able to recognize the way in which God is fitting us together to do his work in spite of very different ways of doing things even with the "same" gifts.

Third, there is no single uniformity in the ways in which a gift or service is carried out. There are different ways of serving the Lord. Two people may have the same gift of "evangelism," but have radically different ways of expressing and carrying out that gift with equally fruitful results. This should not serve as the occasion for controversy and suspicion, but rather for praise to the one Spirit who makes it all work together for his glory. It may well be that for each people group with its distinctive culture and characteristic temperament there is a distinctive way in which a gift must be carried out for it to be effective. The aggressive, public, mass evangelism of the Western world (as exemplified by Billy Graham or Luis Palau) might be completely inappropriate among a Muslim people. There a more interpersonal, quiet, face-to-face evangelism would be most effective.

Fourth, there are different levels of ability with which people can express their gift and service. Some are able to bring in a harvest of twentyfold, others a hundredfold. But the differences in ability are given by God and are an expression of his presence, not something that can be pridefully displayed.

Fifth, Paul speaks of particular service. While there are a number of implications in this concept, we believe one of them has to do with the calling to a particular people (as Paul was called to evangelize the Gentiles, while Peter and the twelve apostles were specially called to the Jews). The gifts, the way of serving, the ability needed, all vary according to the people who are to be brought to the confession that Jesus is Lord! Cross-cultural evangelism is a very demanding and difficult type of service to render to the Lord and requires particular gifts, abilities, and ways of serving. We cannot assume a priori that a person who is a successful evangelist, counselor, administrator, pastor in one cultural setting, among one people, will also be effective in a different cultural setting among another people.

The question of personal role definition has to be faced within the context of a particular service and a given fellowship of believers (with their diversity of gifts and ways of serving the Lord). In the light of what we have set forth as the particular ministry needs of the people we are concerned to evangelize, what role ought we to play? If we bring to bear all we know about ourselves—our gifts, the faith we have in God for this situation, our experience, the skills and training we have acquired, our personality and interests, the opinions of others about our strengths and weaknesses, our relationship to our family, organization, local church—we are able to answer such a question. Are we the logical people to carry out the approach, utilizing the methodology we believe is essential for moving a people toward Christ?

OUR PRIMARY ROLE IDENTIFICATION

We talked earlier about world view as the central component of culture. All the other elements in a cultural system are connected to the world view. Permanent, significant change in a culture must touch this area for it to be effective. In a similar way, each person comes to have a primary role identification that most completely and deeply answers the question: who are you? It is rooted in the maleness and femaleness of the individual as well as the age, status, occupation, and life situation. When we examine people from a role-perspective, we discover that there normally are one or two roles they play that are most important to them in forming their sense of personal identity. All the other roles they play are done in relationship to or in harmony with their primary role identification. When most people are asked who they are, they respond with their name. If they have to give a second answer, they will usually respond with some important or primary role identification: I am a tennis professional, a feminist, a theologian, a housewife, a fundamentalist. Primary role identification thus refers to that role which a person plays which gives special meaning to his or her life. People who do not have a strong primary role identification usually sense anomie and malaise. Their life does not have the zest of someone who has found a niche or a cause to which to give themselves.

As evangelists and as Christians we need to identify our primary role identifications. Whatever they are, they will influence the way we play any of our other roles. Certainly one of them, or the indispensable modifier of our primary role identification, ought to be "Christian," whether it be Christian businessperson, Christian athlete, or Christian executive. The fruits of the Spirit are the transformative factor in all role enactment or performance undertaken by the Christian.

Consequently, though the form or the way these fruits are expressed may vary depending on the culture, the Christian who becomes a healer, a patron or patient, a merchant or teacher, will carry out those roles in a qualitatively different way from those whose primary role identification is not Christian. Because of the way in which Jesus carried out his primary role identification as the Messiah, we have a model by which to gauge our own performance. We will know a renunciation of self and an identification with those to whom God has called us that transcends the natural selfishness of our human condition. In some ways, the way we carry out our roles in love and humility may have far more effect in communicating the meaning of the gospel than the precision and skill with which we learn and meet the obligations of a new role in an alien culture. As the Willowbank Report indicates, we will know a renunciation of status (because we come not to dominate but to serve), a renunciation of independence (recognizing that we are part of an interdependent body), and a renunciation of immunity from the hurts and temptations of the people we live with and serve.[6] Just as Jesus renounced his prerogatives and became a servant, so we too evangelize in humility and love, identifying ourselves with the people we serve as we declare to them that the Kingdom of God has come.

Ultimately, the answer to our question of role is answered by Jesus Christ in his incarnation and death. We are those who belong to the crucified and risen Savior who has demonstrated how to live in all roles of life. In the midst of all our cultural sensitivity we must also have a deep and spiritual centering of our being that brings a qualitatively new dynamic to the way we live out all roles.

6. *Lausanne Occasional Paper #2:* "The Willowbank Report" (LCWE, 1978).

CHAPTER 29

Where Do You Fit?

*T*hat you have been thinking about reaching a particular people should not automatically lead you to the conclusion that you are the one to reach the people. It could be that God wants you to do nothing more than think and pray! In the previous chapter we discussed role definition. Here we will attempt to see how the individual and/or organization fits into the task at hand.

DIFFERENT TYPES OF INVOLVEMENT

There are many different ways that we can individually or organizationally be involved with a particular people. They range from rejecting any further interaction with this people to moving ahead to undertake the complete evangelization of the people. Later on in this chapter we will discuss some important questions that we need to face in analyzing where we fit. But first let us point out these different degrees of involvement.

First, we could decide to do nothing more than pray. An examination of the total context, as discussed below, might show us that we are just not the individual and/or agency to be directly involved with this particular people.

Second, we could use what we have learned through this study to discover another people, another situation into which we think we might fit much better. We need to remind ourselves continually that attempting a study such as the one proposed by this book is an integral part of the total process of mission. There are two ways to gain "experience." The first involves attempting something and discovering what happens. The second attempts to analyze on paper and/or orally through discussion what might happen if we took a particular approach. Often the second is far superior to the first.

Third, we can respond to our analysis thus far by passing on what we have discovered. Perhaps we have concluded that another agency or another church would be far more suited to reaching this particular people. Contacting them and explaining why we think this is so and what we have discovered may make a major contribution toward reaching the people.

Fourth, we may conclude that we can only move ahead if others are willing to cooperate with us, even perhaps to take the lead in the effort. This might lead us to call a conference of other agencies or churches and to discuss with them how together we might best reach this particular people.

Fifth, we may conclude that we really do not know enough to decide whether we are the ones to be involved. Our decision therefore may be to do more research before making any decision.

Sixth, we might conclude that we know of no one who is presently qualified, including ourselves, but we believe that if our organization obtained more training or did more research, we could become qualified. Consequently, we might decide to begin a new training and research program.

Seventh, we may recognize that our organization is qualified because of its past experience and understanding, but that it needs additional people or resources in order to go further. Our next step might therefore be an attempt to bring others into the organization.

Eighth, we may see ourselves as playing just one part in the overall task. We may conclude that our role is to be the planners, or perhaps we are to be the initiators. We may see ourselves as team members with others or as just fund-raisers. Finally, we may see that we could be bridge builders, that we could bring together others who, as a team, could do the job.

Ninth, we could conclude that ours is the agency to take on the total task, that we have the capability and should go to work to do whatever is needed to plan, to gather resources, and to attempt to evangelize this people.

REVIEWING THE MODEL

In Figure 29-1 (see p. 414 below) we again show the Engel/Søgaard Scale, including the rate of change. We have shown profiles for three different peoples. In People A we have the vast majority of the people with only awareness or some knowledge of Christianity, but as far as we can tell, a favorable attitude toward Christianity. There is a small church. It would appear that someone with good cross-cultural experience and ability to cooperate with the existing church would be best able to reach this particular group.

In People B we have a situation where although there is a sizeable church, it is stagnant, and those who do know about Christianity are indifferent toward it. Here an organization with good experience in strengthening local churches and in helping them to set up their own mission agency might be very effective. If this particular group was in an urban setting, then an organization which had good skills in doing urban mass evangelism would be particularly effective.

In People C we have a very difficult situation, perhaps a Muslim country. Here the people have no real knowledge of the gospel, and the awareness that they do have is very negative. This situation calls for an agency which is able to be extremely sensitive to the cross-cultural situation and to find ways of moving these people from a negative to a positive attitude before attempting to move them further along.

What these illustrations show us is that different people are needed in different settings. They also show us that if we were going to attempt to undertake the total evangelization of a people who were presently grouped around −6 on the Engel Scale, then we must have a considerable number of different skills and be able to play a number of different roles. Early in the process of evangelization we must be skilled at bringing people to a favorable awareness, and we must culturally sensitive to the type of communication and church that will eventually come forth. Later on we will have to concentrate on strengthening the church and helping it to stand on its own feet. Often this total task can be best carried out by *different* agencies.

To give an extremely idealized example which will hopefully communicate the point, the most effective team effort might be one in which different missionary teams moved in and out of the situation at different times. The first team might be used to bring the people to a favorable awareness, the second one might be used to demonstrate the power of the gospel, the third group might be used to bring the people to a point of confrontation and into initial fellowship. The fourth group might be used to build and strengthen that fellowship. A reason for suggesting

Figure 29-1 Three People Profiles

DECISION POINT	PEOPLE A			PEOPLE B			PEOPLE C		
	% 25 50 75	ATTITUDE + 0 −	RATE OF CHANGE	% 25 50 75	ATTITUDE + 0 −	RATE OF CHANGE	% 25 50 75	ATTITUDE + 0 −	RATE OF CHANGE
NO AWARENESS −7	▮								
AWARENESS −6	▮	X	1% year	▪	X	0	▮	X	0
SOME KNOWLEDGE −5	▪			▮	X	0	▮	X	0
KNOWLEDGE −4									
IMPLICATIONS SEEN −3									
PERSONAL NEED −2									
CONFRONTATION −1									
CONVERSION									
RE-EVALUATION +1				▮	X	0			
INCORPORATION +2	▪ .2%	X							
PROPAGATION +3									

414

this idealized model is that too often the new church becomes overly dependent upon the missionaries that helped to bring it into being. In many cases the only way in which it can become independent is for those particular missionaries to withdraw. Often the reason given for not withdrawing is the obvious fact that the local church still needs help. By replacing the initial team with a different one, this particular problem can sometimes be overcome.

QUESTION OTHERS' SUCCESS

It is helpful to discover what other kinds of organizations have been effective either in the situation that we plan to enter or in one similar to it. After a period of time every mission and church seems to have a distinctive identity. This is partly due to the distinctively gifted people who influence and shape the organization. Depending upon its reputation, influence and connections, people, and the resources it can mobilize, each organization has its own profile of competence. It has a repertoire of ministries and ministry styles which enables it to do some things very effectively and others not at all.

In thinking about saturation evangelism, one would turn very quickly to the Latin America Mission or the Sudan Interior Mission for help. Just as Pelé is synonymous with soccer and Bjorn Borg with tennis, so their histories of involvement with In-Depth Evangelism and New Life for All make them "experts" in the particular strategies that aim at mobilizing all believers in continuous witness. The same is true for Bible translation (Wycliffe, Lutheran Bible Translators, UBS, etc.).

QUESTIONS ABOUT YOURSELF

Each of us (as well as our organizations) lives and works within a given tradition of Christian faith. Most of us do so out of a mixture of personal conviction (we really believe the distinctives are important and can be supported from Scripture) and compromise (we aren't entirely happy with all of the elements or emphases in our tradition). Ecclesiastical traditions permit more or less freedom in personal religious lifestyle, ecclesiastical cooperation with other traditions, doctrinal definitions and formulations, liturgy, style of ministry, and selection of methods. Part of understanding ourselves has to do with coming to terms with the tradition in which we live and to which our organization belongs. These have a profound influence on the models of philosophy of ministry we find compatible with our understanding of what we think needs to be done.

When evaluating our own and the strategies of others, we can never separate the ecclesiastical profile from methodology. How a potential convert perceives the gospel depends, in part, upon how he or she perceives the church, what kinds of life-style changes it advocates, and how it expresses its faith and love. We have to face the reality that the variety of religious styles (from rather restrained, highly educated, liturgical emphases to more emotional, simple, non-liturgical) that have developed in the history of the Church are not due simply to theological issues, but are also due to cultural and social class differences of the average members of the churches. The Pentecostal churches, with an emphasis on ministry of the laity, healing, miracles, and the gifts of the Spirit will inevitably take a different role in evangelization from non-charismatic Presbyterians with seminary graduation requirements for all their ordained evangelists.

We must admit that the particular ecclesiastical tradition from which we come may not necessarily be the best for evangelizing a given people. It is always a bit of a shock to a self-confident American evangelical from an independent church tradition to discover the powerfully effective and spiritually dynamic Anglican Church of Uganda. The Presbyterians are dominant in Korean church growth and life, but in Latin American countries, Presbyterians have largely stopped growing at the very time Pentecostals have been experiencing enormous success and growth. The Baptists and Methodists are the largest churches in the United States of America and have been the most successful denominations in evangelizing frontier peoples in America. But compared to the Anglicans or the Africa Inland Church, they are not doing well in Kenya. Different traditions seem to meet with varying success among the various peoples of the world. We cannot overlook the fact that the particular ecclesiastical style and expression of Christian faith have a profound effect upon the success of a mission to a given people.

If we are able to admit these things to ourselves (and not take the narrow position that there is only one legitimate expression of faith, namely ours), then we must ask whether or not our tradition is the most suited to the people we will be evangelizing. We may decide that the most effective avenue to the consciousness of a people is ministry that combines clear preaching of the gospel (using native analogies and concepts) with faith healing. In the society in question there might be many traditional healers with a great deal of concern for health and sickness.

As people come into the church, church leaders might inaugurate a corps of Christian healers, laying hands on those who, after prayer and fasting, feel God is calling them to such a ministry. They would then develop a new set of Christian substitutes for the traditional healer's rituals and paraphernalia and provide a ministry of compassion for the sick. But what do we do if our denomination or mission agency takes a stand against "faith healing," denying that such a gift exists for today?

Another people we are attempting to evangelize may feel that simultaneous praying in tongues, which is part of our tradition, is confusing or disgusting. Their own cultural tradition may lead them to view such behavior as bizarre and only for the mentally disturbed. A formal, staid approach to worship may impress them more deeply. What role should we take if our ecclesiastical tradition does not permit the freedom to explore alternative ways of incarnating a Christian life and worship style? Do we doggedly insist that these people be taught how to worship and to conform to an expression of faith exported from a Swedish immigrant community in America?

We find ourselves in tension here. We are part of a community that is somewhat ethnocentric. It demands that we reproduce a Baptist, Presbyterian, Independent, or Anglican church. Yet we may also realize that the freedom of the Spirit might seek a different adaptation to this people and thus achieve a more authentic, indigenous Christian movement. On the one hand, we are caught by our loyalty and unity with our church tradition. On the other, we want to give priority to those who need to be evangelized and their right to develop their own ecclesiastical forms. Part of our deciding where we fit will depend upon the compromises we can and must make with our own ecclesiastical traditions. This is why the discussion on the resulting church (chapter 25) is so important.

Second, we need to ask about our own experience. Have we ever evangelized a people like this before? If we do not have the experience, do we believe that we can gain it? It is important to understand that because we have been effective in one situation does not mean that we will be effective in another. One way of understanding this further would be to make profiles of all of the situations within which we have been successful. First we should attempt to describe the people as they were when we first began our ministry among them. Then we should attempt to plot the various steps they went through to become what they are today. With this information we can compare the particular people that we are now considering reaching with those that we have had success with in the past.

As an aside here, it is important to ask the question, "Do we still have the experience?" Often the experience that our organization had fifteen or twenty years ago is now lost. What has actually happened is that the organization has changed. We have noted a number of mission agencies who started out as pioneer mission works and have now converted over to being church-supporting organizations.

Third, we need to ask about our own resources. Do we have the management capability, the people, and the resources, particularly finances, to carry out what needs to be done to reach this particular people? A negative response to these questions does not automatically rule us out. However, it does face us with the fact that there is going to be more to it than just getting on with the task.

Fourth, we need to ask about our organizational structure. We may see that reaching a particular people is going to require a different type of structure than we have had in the past. For example, we might discover, as did Overseas Crusades in the mid-1970s, that we needed to send out teams of people, rather than individual couples. If we have had no experience in sending a team, this may cause us to rethink our organizational structure.

Fifth, we need to question our ability to communicate what we are about to undertake with our present or future constituency. What is our reputation with them? How will they view our attempts to reach this particular group? It could well be that we have been led by the Spirit to attempt a very innovative and new approach. For example, perhaps we have never attempted to combine community development with our evangelistic efforts. If we now launch a major effort of community development as a means of meeting the spiritual and physical needs of this particular people, will we be viewed by our constituency as truly preaching the gospel?

Sixth, do we have the vision to reach this particular people? In chapter 30 we discuss the problems of bringing about change within an organization. In order to change we have to be discontent with the status quo. We need a high and holy vision of what we could and should be as opposed to what we are. Does this vision exist within the organization?

Seventh, do we have the faith to believe that this is what God wants us to do and that this people can be reached? We are not talking about blind faith. We are talking about the kind of faith which understands all of the dangers, all the possibilities of failure, all of the things that can go wrong and *still* believes that this is the way forward.

Eighth, do we have the courage to move forward? Vision, faith, and courage are all closely related, but does the *organization* have the courage, does it have within its experience and history that "can do" feeling that if God is calling it will respond?

WHERE DO YOU FIT?

The important thing, as we have mentioned time and again, is to ask questions. Step 7 is a major step in your own self-understanding in really closing the gap between the theory and reality. If, after having reviewed all of the possibilities, you now believe that you should move forward, you are ready to begin the planning process of Step 8.

CHAPTER 30

Bringing About Change

*T*his is a book about how to reach unreached peoples, how to cross cultural barriers to bring the gospel of Christ to a people who do not know him. In the broadest sense, we are talking about how to bring about change in others. But the Christian missionary does not stand outside the system of which he or she is a part. Neither does the Christian mission agency. We enter into life with the people. In order for someone else to change *we* need to change.

We need to change because the situation will change. The future will be different from the present. Circumstances will not be as we describe them now no matter how good our forecasting or research. Means, methods, and approaches that worked five or ten years ago need to be modified. Policies and procedures that enabled us to work out our ministry in the world in the previous decade seldom fit the decade in which we are presently living.

We need to change in order to be effective cross-cultural evangelists. We have to change in order to learn a language. We have to change in order to be inculturated within a different society. Our organization has to change in order to be able to relate to any new church which will come about.

Change is difficult. All organizations tend toward stability. As we find "more efficient" ways of doing things, these become codified into policies and procedures. As time passes, they become "the way we do things around here." We are comfortable with them. They give us a greater feeling of control over the future and over our organization.

CHANGE ONLY TAKES PLACE
WHEN THERE IS DISCONTENT

Change only takes place when there is discontent. This is an important idea, both for us and (as we will discuss below) for those we are trying to reach. If we as individuals or as an organization are satisfied with ourselves and the world that we face, we will have no reason to change.

There are two kinds of discontent, positive discontent and negative discontent. Positive (or holy) discontent can be brought about in many ways. We can receive a new vision from the Lord as to how we should be, the world should be, or Christ's Church should be, and, as a result, we can become discontented with what we are doing now. This new vision spurs us on to do new things which require us to change.

We can become discontented in a positive way because we have a new perspective on the world or how we might go about things. As we grow and mature, both as individuals and as organizations, our perspective on life and the world changes. Life appears to be a series of hills, plateaus, and valleys. When we reach the mountain top of a new success, we often see that across the valley there lies another opportunity. This new perspective can cause us to want to change, to make ourselves different, to make the world different.

And then there is negative discontent. It also can be brought about by many things. A failure to reach one's goals or to meet one's perceived needs brings about discontent. We feel the weight of failure, the weight of a goal not reached. We conclude that the way we went about things or the goals we had were wrong. We become discontented with them. We see the need to change. We can become dissatisfied with our relationships, both personal and organizational. For reasons that we may not even understand, we are no longer satisfied with our day-to-day interaction. We feel as if something is missing.

We can be discontented and dissatisfied with the means and methods that we are using. We may see that others are doing a better job or using what appear to be more effective methods. We may be getting inappropriate response from those with whom we are working. We may sense that we are not moving rapidly enough to bring about the change that we would like to bring about in the world.

We may discover as we attempt to carry out what we perceived was God's calling for us, that God really has something else in mind. The Holy Spirit stirs in our hearts, telling us that we could do better in another situation.

THE REASONS FOR CHANGE ARE UNIVERSAL

It is important for us to see that since what we are about as evangelists is to bring about change, all we have discussed about changing others is applicable to ourselves. This is an important idea. It has been our experience that both missionaries and mission agencies seldom have this type of introspection. We are continually surprised how often those who are well skilled in the social sciences, those who have been effective in bringing about change in others, seldom see that the same rules, the same understanding applies to them. And yet at the same time, we are not surprised. As we examine our own lives and our own hearts we see how difficult it is for *us* to see the beam in our own eye.

The process of bringing about change in ourselves follows the same sequence that we have followed throughout this book:

—Discover who needs to change.

—Discover where the felt need is. Where is the area of discontent?

—Analyze who is most able to communicate the need for a new approach. Who are the opinion-makers? Who are the innovators?

—Discover what means and methods we would use to bring about change in the same way that we would select means and methods of evangelism.

—Lay out an overall approach as to how we will go about it.

—Anticipate outcomes, paint a picture of the ideal future.

WHO NEEDS TO CHANGE?

In Step 7 we are trying to see that we need to be a part of the total system that we are attempting to describe. If, after analyzing our overall approach which is based upon the steps that have preceded it, we believe that we are ideally suited to carry out this particular mission, then there is no need to change. But this is seldom the case. In almost every situation there will be people who need to be changed by the training,

organizational structures that need to be changed by reordering, individuals who need to be replaced by others, or new people that need to
be brought into the organization.

DISCOVER THEIR FELT NEEDS

Organizations have a life of their own. As we play out our roles
within an organization, we are really working in a sub-culture, a special
social system. In one sense, we all have our own personal agendas, our
own personal goals. Hopefully we see ourselves as related to other
Christians and their goals. But each one of us is a universe to himself or
herself. Those who are doing the thinking about planning to reach an
unreached people need to ask themselves about their own felt needs and
the felt needs of others in the organization. One may have a felt need to
be greatly used of the Lord. Another may have a felt need to see the
organization more accurately reflect the community that is described in
I Corinthians 12. Some may have more selfish motives because of fear
or sin "which doth so easily beset us." What are the felt needs of these
people? For it is only as we attempt to understand people's felt needs
and their present areas of discontent that we can move ahead to give
them a new vision of what God might do through and with them.

WHO ARE THE CHANGE AGENTS?

In every social system there are opinion-makers, change agents, innovators. Who within the group or the organization will most likely
help to move the needed change forward?

In a book with the rather worldly title of *The Art of Getting Your
Own Sweet Way*, Philip Crosby (1972) presents what he calls Situation
Analysis. Crosby points out that in almost every human situation one of
the barriers to success is people's opinions. He points out that we need
to ask, "What does that head think now?" and "What does that head
need to think in order for this situation to be resolved favorably?"
There is wisdom in these questions, wisdom that we ignore at our own
peril. In the same way that the gospel will only move forward if there
are those whom the Holy Spirit uses as innovators and change agents
within a culture, so the change needed within an organization will not
happen unless these same opinion-makers and innovators are present.
Who are they? How do we reach them?

MEANS AND METHODS

There are means and methods that will either bring about discontent, if it is not already there, or means and methods that will help to change or to meet the apparent discontent.

When a preacher addresses a congregation, his or her purpose is often to bring about holy discontent. The Holy Spirit might use this preaching to inspire people to a new vision of what they might become, and to make them discontented with their present situation. We sometimes call this a challenge. A challenge can be brought about not only by preaching but by people who show us a new understanding of what God would have us do. The very act of discovering an unreached people can be used by the Holy Spirit to bring about holy discontent. One of the major means and methods that we can use is to describe the world as God sees it—as unreached people—and then to sketch out as best we can how God might have that world reached. Plans that show that something is *possible* have a way of bringing about discontent. Once we see that we could be something greater than we are, we become discontented with what we are.

There is a great deal of literature on means and methods. We recommend Lyle Schaller's *The Change Agent* (1972). Ed Dayton and Ted Engstrom have addressed this question in depth in their book *Strategy for Leadership* (1979). The homework we do here will have high payoff in the long run.

Everything we have discussed above has been in the thinking stage. One can think about these things without ever sharing them with anyone else. One can even make this kind of analysis on paper. But eventually we will need to crystallize our thoughts and questions into an overall approach, an overall plan on how we will bring about change in our organization.

ANTICIPATE OUTCOMES

The reason for discussing change was our desire that our organization or we should be different from the way we are now. In the book *Strategy for Living*, Dayton and Engstrom (1976) describe the approach of painting an ideal picture of how the future might be, of looking ahead ten years in the future and trying to imagine what God would have us do at that time. What are the ideal purposes for your organization? What goals would be needed to support those purposes? What type of organization should you have in order to have this happen? In chapter 14 we discussed organizational structures. What kind of structure should you have?

All the ideas form a circle. It is almost impossible to think of them independently of one another. Now that we have anticipated outcomes, it is useful to go back and ask again whether the first five things we went through were useful and to again make an overall plan as to how we should bring about change.

AXIOMS FOR THE CHANGE AGENT

A great deal has been discussed about change within organizations and societies. We need to be aware of how much has been done, both positively and negatively, in this area. In their book *Social Intervention,* Hornstein et al. (1971) have compiled the work of a large number of people who have looked at this whole question. The titles of their six parts are instructive: "Individual Change Strategies of Social Intervention," "Techno-Structural Strategies for Social Intervention," "Data Base Strategies for Social Intervention," "Organization Development: Cultural Change of the Strategy for Social Intervention," "Violence and Coercion as Strategies for Social Intervention," and "Non-Violence and Direct Action as Strategies of Social Intervention." There are many other texts which can be useful to you. We have listed below some axioms for the change agent, particularly for those working within Western culture and attempting to bring about change in their own organization. These are based upon our own experience.

Look for needs

One of the axioms of management is, "Find out what a person wants and make a deal with him." If you can meet a desire that I have, then I will be willing to think positively about some of the desires that you have. What does it mean to make a deal with someone? A deal is something from which both parties hopefully profit. Find allies whose needs *you* can meet.

Take a long-range view

It is much easier to plan your way backwards from an ideal future than it is to analyze how to get out or change the situation we are in now. Try to picture the kind of organization you would like to have five or ten years from now in order to meet what you believe are the goals toward which God has called you. Use these to find discrepancies in the present organization.

Take your time

Most of us greatly overestimate what we can do in one year and greatly underestimate what we can do in five or ten. People in organizations do not change quickly. If you are a recognized change agent or a leader in your organization, you will discover that one of the ways forward is to allow your followers to push you.

Involve as many people as possible

There is an old saying that "Good goals are my goals and bad goals are your goals." Most of us are interested in the things that we have planned. We all have a great deal of difficulty in following someone else's agenda. As we will note below, we cannot necessarily involve everyone all at once. But we need to involve an ever-growing circle of people in bringing about change. The ideal situation is when everyone in the organization feels that he or she has participated in whatever changes are needed.

Be open to new ideas

None of us has all the wisdom we need. What we perceive to be the ideal could very well be improved with others' ideas. As Christians we have a unique gift: each one of us is indwelt and empowered by the Holy Spirit. We should not be surprised that that same Holy Spirit brings ideas to the minds and hearts of others which are just as potent as our own. To put it another way, the *Christian* change agent needs to be willing to submit himself or herself to the same type of process that is being expected of others.

Break it down into steps

Do not try to do everything at once. Reduce the changes that need to be taken to bite-size and chewable pieces.

Use examples

Rather than try to change everything at once, maybe you need to try to change just one part and use this as a kind of pilot project. For example, if the organization has not been involved in recent years in reaching a particular unreached people, it may be that your attempt to reach one unreached people could be used as a model or an example for the whole organization. By involving the rest of the members of the organization in this "experiment," they can become owners as well as observers of the experiment. To the extent that it succeeds, they can participate in the success. To the extent that it fails or does not appear to do what it set out to do, they do not have to be directly involved. "After all, it was only an experiment."

Build on success

What is it that your organization does well? (All of this, of course, bears on the whole question of what role your organization should play.) Do not ask the question, "How can we get rid of this bad thing we are doing?" Rather ask the question, "How can we use the success that God has given us in this area to broaden ourselves in his service?"

Affirm progress

We all need to be told that we are moving in a positive direction. If we have set about on an experiment or a pilot project, if we are in the business of trying to change our organization, we need to communicate to people that progress is being made.

Uncover the future slowly

You may have a dream for what your organization could be doing ten years from now. However, the insight you have gained over a period of many years of thinking and studying cannot be easily communicated within a very short time. You need to assess how much of the vision people will accept as their own. Do not push ahead with the next step until the first one has been accepted by an adequate number of innovators. Bringing about change is identical to the discussions we have had on the Engel/Søgaard Scale. At this moment there are many people in your organization who are unaware that any change needs to take place. In order to make a decision to accept the new order of things, they have to go through the same steps that we described in a group making a decision for Christ.

Expect to be led by the Holy Spirit

It amazes us how often we act as though we do not believe that the Holy Spirit will lead. Expect the Holy Spirit to lead in your thinking, planning, and discussions. Especially expect the Holy Spirit to operate in the lives of others. They too will have ideas. Expect the Holy Spirit to lead us together as a *body*. Expect the Holy Spirit to operate in those who are "less honorable" in the organization as in those who are "more honorable" (I Cor. 12).

QUESTIONS

Who Are You?

1. What is the difference between roles and positions?
2. In what way does our training and education bias our roles and the way we act them out?
3. What is a role?
4. How does a social structure influence roles?
5. What is your opinion about the relationship between roles and gifts of the Spirit?
6. What is your primary role identification?

Where Do You Fit?

1. What action should you take as a result of what you have studied so far?
2. What action should your organization take as a result of what you have studied so far?
3. In light of the larger context (see chapter 14), can you fit into this situation? In light of the political context, the economic context, the social context?
4. Is your ecclesiastical tradition acceptable to the church that is already there?
5. Will your ecclesiastical tradition fit the culture of the people?
6. What has been the experience of others in the same situation? What

does that tell you about yourself? Do you have the experience to carry out this task?

7. Do you have the resources to carry out this task?

8. Do you have the necessary organizational structure?

9. Do you have the ability to communicate this undertaking to your constituency?

10. Do you have the vision to reach this particular people?

11. Do you have the faith to believe that this is what God wants you to do?

12. Do you have the courage to move forward?

Bringing About Change

1. In what way will your organization have to change in order to carry out this task?

2. Who are the change agents within your organization? Are you one?

3. How much time do you have to bring about the desirable change?

4. What other people will have to be involved in bringing about this change?

5. How can you break down the necessary change into a number of different steps?

STEP 8

PLANNING

Considerations

Goals for Evangelization

Plans for Evangelization

Questions

CONSIDERATIONS

1. If you do not care where you are going, any road will get you there.

2. If one draws the bull's-eye after the bullet is fired, then anyone can hit the target.

3. What we are doing is not as important as what we get done.

4. Most people have not decided what it is God wants them to accomplish in measurable terms.

5. Measurable goals have awesome power to change us.

6. Clear goals attract clear plans.

7. No one can forecast the future. To state a goal or to make a plan is to make a statement of faith.

8. Good goals are our goals, and bad goals are your goals.

9. Planning for people is extremely difficult.

CHAPTER 31

Goals for Evangelization

I f you do not care where you are going, any road will get you there. If one draws the bull's-eye after one has fired the bullet, then anyone can hit the target.

What we are doing is not as important as what we get done.

These three simple sentences focus in on one of the major problems of many Christian endeavors: the failure to set measurable goals for the future. In this section we will attempt to define the differences between purposes and goals and will lay out some procedures as to how goals for missions can be written and how to think about them. The statement of purpose, followed by a statement of measurable goals, should always be the beginning point of any planning. In this chapter we will focus on goals, and in the following chapter we will discuss what we mean by planning and how we go about it.

THE DIFFERENCE BETWEEN PURPOSES AND GOALS

We need high and noble purposes. You and your organization need to have an ultimate purpose in life. The first answer to the Shorter Catechism sums it up well: "The chief end of man is to give glory to God and enjoy him forever." For members of the body of Christ, this is a high and noble purpose.

But one may then want to ask *how* one gives glory to God. We might answer that we give glory to God when we worship him, when we are his witnesses, when we care for one another, and when we express Christ's love to all of humanity. These four purposes support the highest purpose of giving glory to God. Thus we might say that the purpose of our mission is to proclaim God's love among people who do not know him. Although this is a well-understood and acceptable purpose for us, it is very difficult to express what *actions* we will take as a result of this purpose. It is our contention that while high and holy purposes give us an aim for an ideal future, they need to be supported by measurable goals.

Unfortunately, the English language has many different words that may mean the same thing. For example, what we define as a purpose others might call an aim or an objective, or even a goal. What we call a goal, others might call a step, an objective, or even a task. We define a *purpose* as an aim or a description of why we are doing what we are doing. We define a *goal* as a measurable and (in the mind of the person setting it) accomplishable future event. It is measurable both in terms of time (when it will become a past event) and by performance (how we will know it has happened). "To have a worshipping church of twenty-five people among the Chinese refugees from Vietnam in France by the end of this year" is a clear-cut goal, while "to share Christ with the refugees from Vietnam" is a very fuzzy purpose.

Since goals lie in the future, they are statements of faith. James reminds us:

> Now listen, you who say, "Today or tomorrow we will go to this or that city, spend a year there, carry on business and make money." Why, you do not even know what will happen tomorrow. What is your life? You are a mist that appears for a little while and then vanishes. Instead, you ought to say, "If it is the Lord's will, we will live and do this or that." (Jas. 4:13–15)

The Bible is full of people who made such statements of faith. Nehemiah asked the king if he might go and rebuild the walls of Jerusalem, and in his mind he pictured the way the world should be, the way God wanted it to be. He had the faith to believe that given the adequate resources, God would use him to rebuild those walls.

Paul had the goal to move on past Rome to Spain:

> But now that there is no more place for me to work in these regions, and since I have been longing for many years to see you, I

plan to do so when I go to Spain. I hope to visit you while passing through and to have you assist me on my journey there, after I have enjoyed your company for a while. (Rom. 15:23, 24)

Neither Nehemiah nor Paul knew whether he would accomplish his goal. But by stating it clearly they were making statements of faith about what God would have them do. This explains why our definition of evangelism on p. 80 needed three parts. The aim and purpose are *intentional.* The goal is *measurable.* Without a measurable goal we are at sea without a compass.

THE AWESOME POWER OF GOALS

Purposes can inspire us, but goals have the power to push us forward. The Holy Spirit uses a clear picture, a clear statement of faith, of what could and should be to push us on. The world understands this well. Dr. Ari Kiev (1973) of the Cornell Medical Center writes:

> With goals, people can overcome confusion and conflict over incompatible values, contradictory desires and frustrated relationships with friends and relatives, all of which often result from the absence of rational life strategy.
>
> Observing the lives of people who have mastered adversity, I have repeatedly noted that they have established goals and, irrespective of obstacles, sought with all their effort to achieve them. From the moment they fixed an objective in their mind and decided to concentrate all their energies on a specific goal, they began to surmount the most difficult odds.

And Paul understood it well:

> Not that I have already obtained all this, or have already been made perfect, but I press on to take hold of that for which Christ Jesus took hold of me. Brothers, I do not consider myself yet to have taken hold of it. But one thing I do: Forgetting what is behind and straining toward what is ahead, I press on toward the goal to win the prize for which God has called me heavenward in Christ Jesus. (Phil. 3:12–14)

One of the best illustrations of the power of setting goals can be found in the Church Growth movement. The central core of all Church Growth theory is the idea of making growth projections, statements of faith about the future, and setting goals for the local church. Time and time again when local churches have set specific goals as to how their church is to grow during a specific period of time, these goals have had tremendous power to motivate the members of the congregation toward church growth.

We are beginning to see the same thing happen as mission agencies set goals for the number of specific unreached peoples that they are going to attempt to reach. By shifting the emphasis away from sending (a process activity) to reaching (a definable, measurable goal), the mission agencies are beginning to find new life and vitality.

THE RELATIONSHIP OF GOALS TO ONE ANOTHER

Since goals are future events, they are related to one another. There are higher goals and lower goals, greater goals and lesser goals. We have all kinds of language to describe the dependency of goals. We talk about primary goals, intermediate goals, or immediate goals. We discover this to be true in our personal life as well as in our organization.

For example, our personal goal might be to graduate from a university with a particular degree at a certain time. But before this "primary" goal can be recognized there are probably some "intermediate" goals that need to be fulfilled. For example, we have to have enough money to pay the tuition fees, and we have to meet residency as well as academic requirements. But even before these "intermediate" goals can be met there is a whole network of "immediate" goals that need to be fulfilled. We have to meet our nutritional and sleep requirements for each day. Also, the relationships we maintain with our families will greatly influence our ability to perform longer-range goals.

The same is true for organizations. Your organization may have a goal to plant a church of twenty-five people among the Chinese refugees from Vietnam in France by the end of the year. But before that can be implemented there will be other goals dealing with the number of people, the number of missionaries and resources involved, and so forth.

GOALS NEED TO BE OWNED

We said earlier that good goals are our goals and bad goals are your goals. Our point is that goals need to be owned by someone. A goal that does not have an advocate is an abstract idea. Whether it is a long-range goal or a short-range goal, whether it is a primary goal or an intermediate goal, each goal needs to be owned by someone. After all, goals can only have power over someone who believes that it is *his* or *her* goal. We will have more to say about this in the next chapter.

THE ADVANTAGE OF CLEAR GOALS

When goals are fuzzy or nonexistent, when an organization or an individual only has purposes in life, it is very difficult to keep the organization alive and in step with the times. Clear goals give us great advantages.

Clear goals strengthen communication

"Can two walk together unless they be agreed?" (Amos 3:3). When I tell you my goals you know the direction in which I am moving. You also know that I do not intend to move in some other direction.

Clear goals are basic to good planning

As we will see in the next chapter, all planning needs to begin with purposes and then immediately move to statements of goals or how we want the future to be. Without goals, we begin to plan for *process*. We get all wrapped up in the things that we are *doing*. Standing committees continually fall prey to this. The first question at the first meeting of the newly formed committee is, "What should we do this year?" The question should be, "What should we get *done* this year?"

Clear goals provide a basis for discussion and change

As we discussed earlier in the chapter about bringing about change in the organization, we need to point out where we going, what we want done. We cannot expect others to read our minds. We need to think and express ourselves before we act. It is only as we tell other people what we believe is the right way to go and express this concretely that they can adequately interact with us.

Clear goals help to show the direction of progress

Clear goals are like stopping off points on a journey, like intermediate cities on a map. Since we can tell when they have become a past event, we can know that we are moving past one and on to another. This gives both high motivation and a good sense of direction.

Clear goals strengthen and test our faith

Every goal, every statement about the future, *is* a statement of faith. The greater the goals, hopefully the greater our faith. As we see ourselves "fail" or "succeed" in reaching a goal, we can see the Holy Spirit operating in and directing our lives.

WHY ARE WE AFRAID OF GOALS?

It has been our observation that many Christians and many Christian organizations are afraid to set the type of specific and clear goals that we are discussing here. There are a number of reasons for this, some quite sound and others questionable. We are afraid of goals because we might fail. None of us likes to fail. And yet as we examine life, we often discover that most of life is "failure." To use a very American example, the batting average of the best baseball player in the world has never been better than 40 percent (batted .400). For every ten times he stood at the bat, he missed (failed) six times out of ten. And yet we recognize that this is a very good "batting average." We need to see that the advantage of clear goals far outweighs the discredit that might come when we do not reach those goals.

We are afraid of goals because we are afraid of being presumptuous. We are afraid that we might "be doing the work of the Holy Spirit." Here we see the major paradox of the Christian life. The Bible is very clear that God is completely sovereign, yet it is also completely clear that man is free. We cannot think of God being 50 percent sovereign and man being 50 percent free. We are faced with the paradox that both are completely true. God is completely sovereign and men and women are completely free. This is intellectual paradox, but faith and life demonstrate that both are true. When we set a goal, when we make a statement of faith about the future, we are exercising the freedom that God has given us, even as we trust that his will will be done.

We are afraid of goals because goal setting seems to be "secular." We are afraid of being caught up in the ways of the world. Much of this comes from our Western dualism. A great deal of Western Christianity focuses in on the propositional truth and misses the whole idea that thought and action are intimately entwined in the Bible. We think of goal setting and planning as being carried out by worldly organizations. We fail to see that this is God's world and it operates under God's laws. The law of gravity is one of God's laws. The "laws" of human relationships are God's laws. There are no sinful things, only sinful people.

WRITING CLEAR GOALS AND PURPOSES

All goals should be related to their purposes. One of the tests as to whether a goal is appropriate for an organization or an individual is the question, "Does this relate to our (my) purpose?" We need to begin by writing the over-arching purpose for which we believe we are called as an organization and then to keep writing out the supporting purposes for the organization. Once this key statement of purposes has been written, we need to get on to writing clear goals.

Well-written goals are stated in terms of end results rather than a process or an activity:

Good:

Ten missionary candidates successfully pass their oral evaluation by August 1.

Poor:

Ten missionary candidates begin their training on July 1.

Well-written goals should be achievable within a definite time. Poorly written goals are never fully achievable, or have no specific target date.

Good:

The church in Barrville has grown to sixteen members by July 1, 19__.

Poor:

There is a growing church in Barrville.

Well-written goals are definite as to what is expected, while poorly written goals are often ambiguous.

Good:

A three-thousand-word sermon is typed for delivery by June 15.

Poor:

A good sermon is preached.

Well-written goals are practical and feasible. Goals that are theoretical or idealistic should be avoided.

Good:

Twenty invitations are given to local civic leaders by March 15.

Poor:

> As many outstanding civic leaders as possible are invited to the meeting.

Well-written goals need to be precisely stated in terms of quantities where applicable.

Well-written goals also need to be limited to one goal or statement. Avoid writing two or more goals where only one is needed to explain what needs to happen (Dayton and Engstrom, 1979).

GOALS FOR PEOPLE

In the past most evangelistic and mission efforts have had only two types of accomplishable and measurable goals: either 1) the number of decisions or affirmations of faith made by people, or 2) the number of people who actually have joined a local fellowship. In recent years this second has been particularly effective in helping local congregations all over the world to make statements of faith about what they believe God would do with them and through them. The Church Growth movement has focused in on this particular measurement.

However, we can and should also write goals for each step of movement along the Engel/Søgaard Scale (see p. 215). In each case we want people to move with a positive attitude from one place to another. We therefore need to set goals either to bring about attitudinal changes or to bring about informational changes at an intellectual level, or both.

The difficulty of writing goals for attitudinal changes is that we have to make our own analysis based upon our assumptions as to what would constitute a change of attitude on the part of the people. Sometimes this is easy, and at other times it is very difficult. To illustrate, let us move through the scale. Suppose that there is a group at -7. As far as we know, they have absolutely no knowledge that Christianity even exists. Let us assume that this people was hostile to all outsiders. In this case we want to persuade them to accept us as Christians. Writing a measurable and hopefully accomplishable goal in this case would be quite simple:

> The chief of the _____ clan has extended an invitation for two missionaries to live with his family by August 1.

Accomplishing such a goal would be strong evidence that at least people were now ready to listen.

On the other hand, if the attitude toward outsiders was favorable, our goal to move people from -7 to -6 might be something like:

> The chief of the _____ clan tells the members of his sub-group that the four missionaries living in their midst worship a God called Jesus who they believe created the world.

We could write similar goals for moving people from −6 to −5. We could set up tests for intellectual knowledge, but we should also have some statements about what kind of attitude these people will display and how we will know they will display it.

The same thing is true for −4. However, let us remember that people have attained complete intellectual knowledge without having moved further.

As we discussed earlier, it is very difficult to assess whether people see the personal implications of the gospel in their lives (−3), and whether they see the gospel as meeting a need (−2), or even whether they truly have been challenged to receive Christ (−1). Here we have to set goals (statements of faith) that describe what we believe this people would *do* if they were going through these particular steps.

The same thing is true for the reevaluation of a decision (+1). Here we may not be able to evaluate what is going on in their minds. However, we can set some specific goals after they have made some type of overt affirmation of faith. As we have often noticed, this can be one of the most critical times in Christian growth of an individual or a group. A goal for us in this case might be fairly straightforward:

> Those making an affirmation of faith as a result of _____, are to complete the Christian brotherhood program in ten weeks.

Writing goals for +2 and +3 is also fairly straightforward. However, do not overlook the need to continue to reinforce positive attitudes at +2 and to set goals to move people on to +3. The end goal is to see a church equipped to evangelize its own people.

In all of the above discussion we are not saying that we should set specific goals for every people for every step of the Engel Scale. As we have discussed earlier in chapter 11, the way people actually encounter Jesus Christ may have no apparent relationship to the scale. The scale is only a tool to help us design appropriate strategies and to write good goals. We will better understand this as we move on to the next chapter in our discussion on planning.

For further insight on how to write good goals we would recommend the prize-winning book by Charles Hughes, *Goal Setting* (1965) and Ed Dayton's *God's Purpose/Man's Plans* (1971). Robert Mager's *Goal Analysis* (1972) is a small book that is helpful in setting clear-cut goals.

CHAPTER 32

Plans for Evangelization

*I*n many ways this chapter is the crux of this book. All the best intentions, all of the careful research, all of the hours of concerted prayer can easily shipwreck on rocks of the future. History is littered with the hulks of mission efforts that ran aground because planning was narrow, too limited, or altogether missing.

WHAT DO WE MEAN BY PLANNING?

The Alaskan Eskimos have a large number of words for "snow." The average European has difficulty imagining that there is more than one kind of snow. Unfortunately "planning" has suffered the same fate in many quarters. In the sense that planning is contemplating the future, everyone plans, even if one imagines that the future will be just like the past. But few missionaries ever had a course on planning as part of their missionary preparation. Consequently, when the word "planning" is mentioned, many of us immediately picture the blueprints or drawings that one puts together to build a building. Indeed, we often talk about "a blueprint for the future."

When one examines the phrase "a blueprint for the future," it seems rigid, with little room for flexibility. After all, when we think about blueprints for a new building, we certainly do not contemplate changing the design halfway through the construction. Unfortunately, we have taken this technological model and too easily applied it to human relationships. But there is something in us that rightfully is repelled by the idea of blueprints for people. Christ's Church is much grander than that. His Kingdom is not comprehensible by the human mind. No wonder we shy away from planning for *people*.

We need to disavow immediately this mechanistic view of planning. Planning should be thought of as a bridge between where we are now and the future that we believe God desires for us. It is true that planning usually includes a series of well-thought-out steps of how we will proceed in order to achieve our goal. What people often fail to see, however, is that plans for people need to be continually revised. We take the first step forward, look backward, look forward, and then replan if necessary.

Planning is an attempt, in the words of Herman Kahn (1976), to produce surprise-free futures, to anticipate as much as possible what the future is likely to hold and how we will respond to it.

David Ewing (1969) points out that all organizations overlook the *people* dimension of planning at their peril. It is likewise a mistake to attempt to transfer the type of planning that has been learned in the creation of *things* to the business of communicating the gospel. Still there is much that has been learned about planning that needs to be put to work by those seeking to reach the unreached. The literature on planning is voluminous. We will not attempt to repeat it here. Rather we will attempt to show why plans for evangelization are a key part of world evangelization and then point the reader to some of the more useful literature.

HOW DOES A CHRISTIAN THINK ABOUT PLANNING?

Any statement about the future is a statement of faith. Like goals, plans are statements about the future. Like goals, plans are statements of faith. This is a key idea. When we talk about what we are going to do in the future, we are essentially making our statement of faith before one another and before our Lord about what we believe he wants us to do. Understanding this idea about both goals and plans is extremely helpful, particularly as we attempt to bring others into the planning phase of evangelization.

PLANNING IS CORPORATE

As Christians we claim that we are part of a fellowship that can only be described as a body. We believe that in ways too mysterious for us to comprehend, we are all intimately interconnected with other Christians. We believe we are part of something that is greater than the sum of its parts. We believe that each member of the body of Christ is indwelt by his Holy Spirit. These statements have tremendous implications for planning. It is true that purposes and decisions can and should come from leadership. But if every Christian is led by the Spirit, we should expect that ideas will come from within the group as well as from its leadership. By planning together, by sharing our dreams and hopes for the future in concrete terms, we make it possible for the body to function smoothly.

Planning may be a gift function. Some people are skilled in visualizing the future. They can take what others see as disjointed and unconnected pieces and fit them together into a whole. People thus gifted are not necessarily the ones who have the vision of the future, nor are they necessarily the ones who can best execute plans.

In his helpful book, *Your Spiritual Gifts Can Help Your Church Grow*, Peter Wagner (1979) indicates that we have a lot to learn about spiritual gifts. He believes that the Bible does not give us a limited number of gifts. Certainly the gift of administration includes being able to relate or interrelate the many things that need to be done to accomplish any major endeavor.

Planning is necessary for good stewardship. If our resources are to be invested wisely, then we have to make wise decisions. It is impossible to make decisions for the future. We can only make decisions now which will *affect* the future.

Planning means taking risks. Planning is not the avoiding of risk, but rather the calculating of risk. Planning assumes an unknown future. It assumes that the problems we face will be unlike those we have faced in the past. For many people this is a new idea in history (see chapter 2). Proverbs assume that there will be a standard solution or answer to a particular problem. But proverbs fit all situations. For example, "A stitch in time saves nine," and "Haste makes waste." Both of these standard solutions are useful. Planning helps us to see where we can apply them.

BASIC PLANNING CONCEPTS

You will find much more help in such books as Ed Dayton's *God's Purpose/Man's Plans* (1971) and Engstrom and Dayton's *The Art of Management for Christian Leaders* (1976) and *Strategy for Leadership* (1979). Here we will only briefly review what has been covered in other places, and we will attempt to put it in a context that will be useful for our discussion on cross-cultural evangelization.

1. Describe the goal

Almost every goal requires a plan. The larger the goal, the more extensive the plan. As we will see, most plans are nothing more than a series or a string of sub-goals fitted together. But effective planning can succeed or fail right here. As we discussed in a previous chapter, fuzzy or inadequate goals lead only to fuzzy or inadequate plans.

Often there will be different goals for different phases of a program. To give an example, let us assume that we have described a particular people and discovered that there was no one in the group who did not know of the existence of Christianity (−7). Ninety percent were at −6 (aware of Christianity) on the Engel Scale, but most of these were negative toward Christianity. The remaining 10 percent were at −5 (some knowledge of the gospel), and, as best as we could tell, were neutral toward it. Given this situation one might forecast the following major phases of our attempt to reach them as follows (we have shown the hoped-for profile for each phase in Figure 32-1):

Phase 1 — Personal acceptance

Phase 2 — Acceptance of Christianity

Phase 3 — Needs met

Phase 4 — Teaching

Phase 5 — Confrontation

Phase 6 — Church growth

Phase 7 — Outreach

These phases, these preliminary plans, are our first attempt to find general purposes. For each of them we might go on to attempt a goal. For example:

1. Gain acceptance: Within two years group leaders A and B will identify missionary couples X and Y as their friends.

2. Acceptance of Christianity: Within three years 50 percent of the people within this unreached group would answer "Yes" to the question, "Are Christians good people?"

3. Needs met: Within five years this community will no longer be dependent upon truckers to buy their produce for resale.

Figure 32-1 Phases of Growth

PROGRAM PHASE

GOALS / PRIMARY GOALS	1	2	3	4	5	6	7	8
	Two years: Couples X & Y are friends of leaders A & B	Three years: 50% answer "Yes" to question "Are Christians good people?"	Five years: Community no longer dependent on truckers	Six years: 50% taking courses on basic Christianity	Seven years: Those completing course asked to receive Christ	Ten years: 2000 adult church members	Fifteen years: 5 full time evangelists	Eighteen years: Missionaries leave
No Awareness −7								
Awareness −6								
Some Knowledge −5								
Knowledge −4								
Implications Seen −3								
Personal Need −2								
Confrontation −1								
CONVERSION								
Re-evaluation +1								
Incorporation +2								
Propagation +3								
	100%	100%	100%	100%	100%	100%	100%	100%

447

4. Teaching: Within six years 10 percent of the people in this group, including 50 percent of their leaders, will be enrolled in basic courses in Christianity.

5. Confrontation: Within seven years those completing the teaching will be asked to accept Christ and become members of his Church.

6. Church growth: Within ten years church membership will have grown to two thousand adults.

7. Within fifteen years the new church will be supporting five full-time evangelists.

At first glance the attempt to plan ten to fifteen years into the future may seem absolutely hopeless. In many ways it is. But it does show our *intent*. It helps us to see where we are going. It helps us to see that what we are doing in Phases 1, 2, and 3 eventually will issue forth into something in the years ahead. Our timetable may run ahead or it may run behind. As we will see below, we must periodically re-examine the goals.

2. Describe the present situation

In addition to a description of the people we have reviewed so carefully in previous chapters, examination of what we call helping and hindering forces is very useful for planning. Psychologist Kurt Lewin (1935) initially proposed the idea of a force field analysis. Lewin pictured human situations as being the result of a balance between two forces, a force that might be driving them to a better situation, and a force that might be hindering them from reaching the better situation. Movement will occur when the helping force is increased or the hindering force is reduced.

For example, in the situation that we have given above we assumed that although 90 percent of the people were aware of Christianity, most were antagonistic toward it. This antagonism is a hindering force. The group has not seen any positive examples of Christians. Consequently, our first goal is to attempt to strengthen the helping forces by living out lives that are good examples to the people we want to reach.

This idea of helping and hindering forces is very useful as we try to write subgoals to meet our higher goal. Any time you need to change a situation, make a list of what you consider to be the helping forces and the hindering forces and choose the one that will be easiest to move.

3. Choose methods

We have described what the goal is. Now we have to decide what is the best way of reaching it. We need to remind ourselves that we will very seldom have a perfect fit between the human situation and a previous solution. We have to reinforce the idea that each situation is, to some degree, unique. Out of all we have learned and others have learned we need to discover new means and methods.

4. Lay out the sequence of events needed

Just selecting means and methods is not enough. We now need to decide what the sequence of events will be. Here is where some of the planning tools such as PERT (Program Evaluation Review Technique), flow charts, Gantt charts, and other devices described in literature are useful (see Dayton, 1971). The primary reason for making plans is to coordinate the work of many people. Demonstrating these plans graphically is an important tool for communication.

For example, in our first phase described above there are many things that have to be done. People have to be selected and trained, government permissions need to be obtained, the logistics of support need to be laid out, the means of raising funds have to be decided upon, and the means of evaluation and communication have to be described. Theoretically, each of these things could be carried out by a different individual or a group of individuals. When some of them begin will depend upon when others finish. If one of them fails, all may fail. In many ways it is like a relay race in which one person cannot begin until he or she has received the baton from someone else.

Each of the events can be thought of as a subgoal. That means that it needs to have a goal owner and a date when it will be accomplished, and that its relationship to other goals has to be shown. In Figure 32-2 (see p. 450 below) we have shown a fairly simple PERT chart for planning an evangelistic program. By following the diagram from left to right, the great interdependency of people and events immediately becomes apparent.

5. Calculate the resources needed

Resources include time, people, facilities, finance, and cooperation. Unfortunately too much planning *begins* here. It is true that we should not sit down to build the tower without first counting the cost, but it is

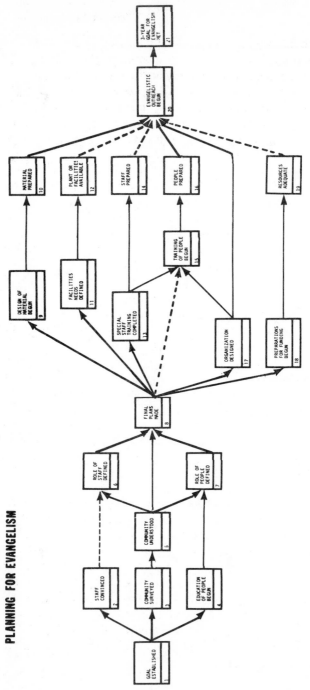

PLANNING FOR EVANGELISM

Figure 32-2 PERT Diagram

450

also true that we had better design the tower before we figure out that we cannot afford it. Often, as we mentioned above, one of our goals is to find the people or the money for the task.

A few hints are in order here. There are two ways to calculate time: 1) the elapsed or calendar time, or 2) people time or people hours. For example, the amount of time to obtain a visa may be one month. This is calendar time, and no amount of expenditure of energy on our part will speed up the process. However, the number of people needed to obtain a visa may be only four or five hours when one considers the actual work in filling out the visa forms and mailing them to the right place. Do not confuse these two different kinds of time.

In thinking about people there is a natural tendency to think that six different people should be assigned to six major goals. One of the advantages of the PERT technique is that it shows us not only how long it may take to reach a particular goal, but the interrelationship of goals. Often six goals can be shared by only two or three people, because the work needed for them can be carried out at different times.

Too often we equate good stewardship with the use of the poorest or least adequate facilities. The most valuable commodity we have is people. There is no replacement for trained and experienced people. We need to have the faith to believe that God wants us to use the best tools. If our methods call for one tool, the substitution of another means that we have changed our method. For example, suppose we have planned to produce some teaching materials using a small offset press which could be supplied with materials found inside the country in which we are working. The substitution of a mimeograph machine, with stencils that had to be sent from outside the country, might greatly hinder our whole plan.

Finances are the bugaboo of mission endeavors. The time to cut back on finances is *not* during the planning stage. We may ultimately have to change our plans because of lack of finances, but do not *plan* this out at the beginning! Honestly assess what you believe will be needed and then add 10 to 15 percent to cover contingencies.

We do not often think of *cooperation* as a resource. But often success or failure lies in the hands of others. We need to pay for some cooperation, as when we depend on someone to deliver needed supplies. Other cooperation, such as that needed from others working in the same area, needs to be worked for and maintained. Make sure you list all of the different organizations and individuals whose cooperation will be needed for the endeavor.

6. *Analyze resources*

When all of the resources needed are added up, when you have calculated the number of calendar days, the number of person hours, the facilities, finances, and cooperation needed, do your faith and plans match? If they do, you are ready to move ahead. If they do not, you need to seek alternate solutions. Do not be discouraged if your plans do not appear workable at first. It is far better to fail on paper than to fail in practice.

A simple plan form that we have used over and over is reproduced in Figure 32-3. Note that this form includes all of the ingredients we have discussed. It begins with a *purpose*. Related to this purpose is a *measurable goal*. This goal has a *date* when it will become a past event. A goal is supported by *plans* (each of which should in turn have a date associated with it). The plans are *owned* by individuals. Someone knows that he or she is responsible. Finally the *cost* has been calculated.

This form will seldom be large enough for most tasks. However, it does communicate in a fairly terse way all of the elements of effective planning.

THE DYNAMICS OF PLANNING

Plans need to be constantly revised. The further plans stretch into the future, the less likely they are to describe what will really happen. The example we gave above encompassed fifteen years. Phases 2, 3, 4, and beyond were our best estimate of what might happen. The future may be entirely different. It is in Phase 1 that we begin. Even as we move into Phase 1, we need continually to review and revise our plans. Certainly we need to review an overall plan for the future every year. The very dynamics of the planning process help us not only to communicate with one another, but also to attempt to understand what God is teaching us through our experience and the experience of others.

1. *Planning for people is extremely difficult*

What is more complex than the human mind! People are infinitely variable. The more people involved, the more complex their tasks. Do not let this discourage you. As we have mentioned earlier the questions are often more important than the answers. Planning is a system by which we attempt to raise questions.

GOAL NAME _____   GOAL NUMBER _____

PURPOSE For this reason: _____

_____

_____

_____

GOAL We plan to
accomplish this: _____

_____

_____

by this date: _____

We will know it
has happened
because: _____

_____

STEPS We plan to take
these steps: _____

_____

_____

_____

_____

_____

_____

PEOPLE These people
are responsible: _____

COST It will cost this
amount: _____

Figure 32-3 Organizational Planning Chart

In order to be effective, plans must be owned. The way plans become owned is by participation in the planning process. Dayton and Engstrom have discussed this at great length in their book *Strategy for Leadership* (1979). Much has been learned through group process and the ownership of plans.

2. *Plans are powerful tools for communication*

Look at the PERT diagram on Figure 32-2 (p. 450 above). Imagine that each one of the boxes or events on the diagram represents people. What the diagram would then show would be the relationship of people to one another. It immediately shows that what some people do is completely dependent on what other people do. Putting a picture like this in front of all the people who are involved shows them how they fit together and how important they are to one another.

3. *Plans are difficult to coordinate*

Too often one will discover that people in the field office and those in the home office will be planning the same thing from a different viewpoint. We need to share our plans. We need organizational strategy. Effective organizations *plan to plan*. For example, World Vision International began its planning for the year 1980 in December of 1978 when it asked each of its field leaders to make a ten-year forecast of what they believed God would have happen in their various ministries. This was reviewed at headquarters in late January 1979, and an overall analysis of what each field was saying was made and sent back to all fields. The fields were then asked to make a one-to-five-year forecast based upon their ten-year forecast and the headquarters' response. This one-to-five-year forecast was reviewed in May and compared with the forecasted income expected to be received by the home countries from their supporters. With this information in hand the fields were asked to present their detailed plans and budgets. These were approved as given or modified in August of 1979. In December of 1979, the process began again for the year 1981.

At first glance this seems like a great deal of work. It is! Planning takes time, but it is worth it. When we plan we make fewer mistakes. Many of our failures have occurred on paper rather than in practice. When we plan we allow the Holy Spirit to operate within each member of the body. By having a continual interchange of information as described by World Vision's 1980 planning process above, there is time for understanding to grow and for the Holy Spirit to be at work in the hearts and minds of all involved.

4. Planning gives us a better understanding of why we succeeded or failed

It is only when we have stated ahead of time what we intended to do that we can see when we have departed from it. Too often we only learn from our successes. "Failure" can be a great teacher.

5. Planning heightens the sense of community and the body of Christ

Our understanding of each other increases as each of us is given the opportunity to contribute ideas and understand the plans of others.

6. Planning takes time

Although planning does take time, our experience shows that in the end, effective planning will reduce the total amount of time and energy needed to reach the goal.

SHORT-RANGE PLANNING

Short-range planning, which is usually less than one year, is essentially problem solving. The "problem" is to reach a particular goal. All of the techniques of problem solving and decision making are important here. Part 4 of Ed Dayton's *God's Purpose/Man's Plans* (1971) discusses problem solving, using evangelism as an example.

Short-range planning should always be done within the context of long-range planning. A major weakness of many organizations is that they plan year by year without contemplating where they are going. This is all too easy for not-for-profit organizations whose incomes depend upon the future. However, not-for-profit organizations who have set high goals for four- or five-year financial campaigns have usually found excellent results. It is unfortunate that the faith needed to put a "$50 million challenge" in front of our constituency cannot be extended to the challenge reaching ten unreached people groups within five years! Too often we hear, "If we only had the money...." Our response would be, "If we only had the challenging goals!"

LONG-RANGE PLANNING

Long-range planning normally covers one to five years. Some call planning beyond five years "forecasting." Again, we suggest you turn to other literature for more insight into long-range planning. We do not believe that the techniques required for Christian organizations are essentially different from those required for non-Christian organizations. (We do believe that Christian organizations have a tremendous advantage: they know what the outcome will eventually be!) There are some things that should be inherent, however, in long-range planning:

1. A clear statement of purpose should be our beginning

Why are we in the ministry that we are in? What is our overall purpose? Starting with the idea of giving glory to God, we need to work backward as (described in the previous chapter) to define our purpose.

2. We need a clear understanding of our mission

What is it we are attempting to do? What is it we are *not* attempting to do? In terms of this book we are back to Step 1 in chapter 8. By defining what we are going to do we also help define what we are not going to do.

3. Forecasting is needed

What will the world be like that we will be working in? This is closely related to the assumptions discussed in chapter 23. The further we move into the future the less reliable our forecast becomes. But if we do not forecast what the future will be like, it is very difficult to know how we should begin.

4. Examine alternatives

There are many roads between now and the desired future. Which ones should and could we take? It is very helpful to consider a number of alternatives so that when one fails, another is at hand.

5. Select methods

Again you can see how the planning cycle used in this book is developing. Once we know the way we want to go, we need to think through how we will get there.

6. *Include evaluation*

This is the major failure of most plans. The reason we have an odometer on an automobile is to tell us whether we are going as far as we should. It is very difficult to install an odometer in an automobile not designed to have one. In the same manner, we need to include evaluation as we do our planning.

7. *Design the organization*

Too often this is the first step. As we described in our theory of organization in chapter 5, we believe that organization should follow the needs of the goals and plans, rather than the goals and plans following the organization. But there must be organization. There need to be those who are going to be responsible for the work. The work needs to be organized into some recognizable whole. Often the existing organization will fit the need. At other times the organization will have to be modified or completely changed in order to realize our long-range goals.

8. *Estimate cost*

One of the great values of long-range planning is that it gives us time to raise the money we need. It is unlikely that the details of our long-range plan will be more than 50 percent accurate at best. However, the overall cost of the plan may not be so far off. And having a plan will often help us raise the money we need.

9. *Long-range planning is repetitive*

This needs to be said over and over again. Planning has to be built into planning. It is the *process* of planning that is of the greatest value. The plans may change and they may be wrong, but what we learn in the planning process is of inestimable value.

PLANNING METHODS

There are many planning methods. Dayton and Engstrom's *Strategy for Leadership* offers some good insights. The important thing is to tailor the planning methods to the need. Avoid over-planning. If you are planning to build a building, then it is obvious that you need to do a great deal of detailed planning. Each window, each doorframe, each pipe needs to be specified. But as we have said above, buildings and people are two different things. The building will sit quietly and wait to be built. People will not. One can have a reasonably high degree of confidence that if adequate resources are available, the building that one plans now will rise three years from now looking very much as we planned. One can be equally sure that detailed plans for a group of people will seldom fit together three years in the future.

WHAT YOU WILL HAVE TO PLAN

All planning should begin with the ultimate goal, for example, "20 percent of the Turkana people become practicing Christians by January 1, 1990." As we discussed in a previous chapter, every goal can be thought of as being supported by a series of subgoals. We suggested that a program to reach a particular people could be broken down in phases with a goal for each phase. Each of these goals is dependent upon the one before it. It is not likely that the goal from phase 4 will be reached if the goals for phases 3 and 2 are not reached.

There is another dimension in organizational planning which is helpful to see. For each of those phases there will be the need for people, finance, facilities, relationships, and organization. In Figure 32-4 we have attempted to show this relationship by laying out the seven phases and goals of the program described earlier across the top of the chart and then listing down the side these five supporting areas of planning. Each of the phases will have to have subgoals for these five, as well as others that you will see. All of these are means to the end. But means, too, need to be planned.

PLANNING IS LIKE A PRAYER

Jesus often called his disciples to come apart and pray. He knew that they had to be drawn out of the "everydayness" of their ministry and the continual needs that met them at every turn. In that sense planning is very much like prayer. We need consciously to stop what we are doing and evaluate, re-think, and make new statements of faith about what we believe God would have us do.

Planning, like prayer, is hard work. They both need to be directed by the Holy Spirit, and both require an act of our will as we thoughtfully and purposefully consider what God is saying to us through his Spirit.

Figure 32-4 Program Phase

| GOALS | | PROGRAM PHASE | | | | | | | |
		1	2	3	4	5	6	7	8
PRIMARY GOALS		Two years: Couples X & Y are friends of leaders A & B	Three years: 50% answer "Yes" to question "Are Christians good people?"	Five years: Community no longer dependent on truckers	Six years: 50% taking courses on basic Christianity	Seven years: Those completing course asked to receive Christ	Ten years: 2000 adult church members	Fifteen years: 5 full time evangelists	Eighteen years: Missionaries leave
SUPPORT GOALS									
People Needed									
Finances Needed									
Facilities Needed									
Relationship Needs									
Organization Needed									

QUESTIONS

Goals for Evangelization

1. What are the differences between your organization's purposes and goals?
2. How do your organization's goals relate to its purposes?
3. Does your organization have well-defined goals?
4. In thinking about reaching a people, what is your statement of purpose? What are your goals?

Plans for Evangelization

1. Does your organization presently have a planning system?
2. Have you made specific plans to reach this particular people?
3. How are you planning to reach this people?
4. How do your plans fit into the long-range plans of the organization?

STEP 9

ACT

Considerations

Taking Action

Questions

CONSIDERATIONS

1. Thinking, planning, acting, and evaluating can never be separated from one another. They all go on at the same time.
2. The primary problem is not money; it is people and organizations. Every missionary team is unique and has its own unique needs.
3. Most mission organizations do not plan to succeed.
4. One thing you can always expect is the unexpected.

CHAPTER 33

Taking Action

As we discussed in the previous chapter, our ability to make detailed plans for the future is severely limited. The future is the one thing over which we have the least control. We cannot do all of our planning, stop, and then start acting out our plans. The moment we start to act, we have to start evaluating where our actions are not conforming to our plans and then make the necessary corrections.

If you think about it for a moment, this is true in all parts of life. For example, when an aircraft is coming in for a landing, the pilot is constantly measuring the sideways movement of the airplane that may be due to a crosswind and assessing whether the aircraft will eventually be lined up with the runway. The pilot is continually making course corrections. If, at the last moment, the plane cannot be lined up with the runway, the pilot aborts the approach and tries again.

It is important to see that this is the natural order of events. We should not be surprised that things do not turn out exactly as we planned. Rather, if we *anticipate* that things probably will be different than we imagined, then we are ready to make the necessary corrections and to replan as necessary.

The pilot *knows* that there is a possibility that a crosswind will blow the plane off course. The pilot also knows that sometimes those crosswinds will be so strong that another approach will have to be attempted rather than continue the landing. It is this knowledge and anticipation that things will be different that makes an effective pilot. It is this same kind of knowledge that makes an effective cross-cultural missionary.

Taking our ten-step circle and boiling it down to abstracts produces the diagram shown in Figure 33-1. The processes that we need to go through are: think, plan, act, evaluate, think, plan, act, evaluate, and so forth.

We need to do this both on a grand scale and on a small scale. For example, for each of the major phases described in the nine-phase plan in chapter 32, we need to evaluate what we have just done, think what this means for the future, make newer and more thorough plans, act on those plans, and then evaluate the result of our actions. The same thing is true on a much smaller scale. For example, the goal for the day may be to establish a relationship with a particular leader in the group we are trying to reach. We may have thought out our plan of approach after having considered all the alternatives and evaluating what others have done. At the end of our attempt to establish this relationship, we will want to evaluate the result, think about the meaning of this evaluation, and then plan again.

The purpose of this brief section is to put the necessary action into the context of planning and evaluating so that we can better understand the total process. There is extensive literature on the various aspects of cross-cultural communication. In recent years there have been many excellent books that deal with all aspects of the missionary vocation. For example, the process of communication has been discussed by Engel

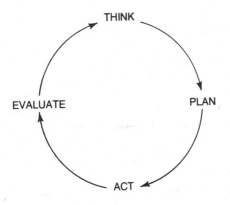

Figure 33-1   Think—Plan—Act—Evaluate

and Norton (1975), Engel (1977, 1979), Nida (1960), Hesselgrave (1978), Mayers (1974), and others. Missionary anthropology has been discussed by Luzbetak (1963), Loewen (1975), and C. Kraft (1979). Numerous works demonstrating examples of theory which have been implemented or uncovered are found in the Church Growth literature, notable among which are McGavran (1970, 1972, and 1959), Tippett (1970, 1973, and 1967), Read (1965), Holland (1974), Wagner (1973, 1971), and Smith (1978).

RESOURCES, MEANS, GOALS

When we plan, we begin with the goals, not resources. This should come last. After deciding on the goal, we then move on to the *how*, the means and the methods. After deciding what we believe are appropriate means and methods, we analyze what resources are necessary. The sequence is goals, means, resources (see Figure 34-1, p. 479 below). However, when we begin to act, the reverse is true. We must first start with the resources, use them to carry out our means and methods, and then hopefully realize our goals.

It is important to see that we have subgoals for these too. We have a goal for obtaining resources. We also have a goal for achieving means and methods. As we discussed in the previous chapter, these different events are actually a chain that is linked together. If one of the links fails, the entire enterprise is jeopardized. Therefore, the process of think, plan, act, evaluate, think, plan, act, evaluate applies at each of the steps of finding resources, supplying means, and reaching goals.

GATHERING RESOURCES

Almost always we begin with finances and people. In order to raise finances there has to be someone committed to raising finances. Traditionally in the faith mission system the person primarily responsible for raising the finances has been the person who is going to carry out the work, namely the missionary. Without discussing this at any length, we question this particular practice.[1] We recognize that it can be an excel-

1. A major aid to the present faith mission fund-raising system would be for the home board to raise major funds for projects. The missionaries would then have the funds they need, and the home board would have a percentage to carry out *its* task. Too often the home board has to raise funds for itself, a very uninspiring effort.

lent exercise in developing and strengthening faith, but we see little connection between the gifts and skills necessary to be a communicator of a need and the skills needed to be a communicator of the gospel in a cross-cultural situation. To use the medical analogy that we described in chapter 15, we suspect that there are not very many medical doctors who would make very good fund-raisers, particularly if they had to raise the funds for themselves. Another weakness is that the local church is too often given the impression that the major task is to "send a missionary overseas." There is little doubt that knowing a missionary personally, understanding his or her personality and needs, is very helpful when it comes to giving prayer and financial support. However, there are obviously many other ways that this personal interaction can be carried out without putting the missionary through a regimen that has as its *primary* task an appeal for funds.

The task of carrying the Good News to people who have hever heard is a glorious one. It is incomparable in its scope and potential impact. It is the task to which Christ has called his Church. Can it be that we are incapable of communicating such an effort to local churches? We think not. All over the Western world local churches have caught the vision and have felt the passion of taking the gospel to those who have never heard.

In the same way that it takes time and effort to communicate cross-culturally, so it takes time and effort to communicate what we are about. We live in a day when there is a growing criticism of "the cost of fund-raising." Rightfully so. There are too many instances of those who have been in the business of fund-raising for their own benefit rather than for the benefit of those they claim to be serving. But this is not the whole picture. If we send an improperly trained and/or supported missionary team to reach an unreached people, and if because of that inadequate support or training they spend four years and accomplish nothing, then the "cost of fund-raising" has been essentially 100 percent! We receive nothing for the funds invested. What is the true cost of fund-raising when a missionary spends nine to twelve months visiting churches for the purpose of raising support? We recognize, of course, that much more happens on such visits than just the simple matter of funds. But we do need to see that the costs of such visits are not insignificant.

Christian agencies which have attempted to raise funds on behalf of their staff rather than through their staff, have discovered that they can be quite successful when the cost of fund raising varies between 8 and 12 percent. When compared to the 25 to 35 percent that most secular agencies invest in fund raising, this is a commendable effort. It is heartbreaking to see Christians who claim that their Lord owns the cattle on a thousand hills acting as though God barely has a lease on one pasture.

The same discussion applies to local churches. Local churches need to spend a reasonable amount of the money collected from missions on missionary education. Whether we like it or not, we in the West live in a culture with a huge communication overload. Western advertising agencies spend thousands of dollars and person hours to design commercial spots for television. They study the culture in extreme depth. They probe every aspect of the "people group" (market) they are attempting to reach. They know exactly what kind of response they are anticipating as a result of their investment. Sometimes the advertising is designed just to keep a name in the back of our minds. Other times advertising is designed to make us feel good about the producer of the product. Other advertising is intended to provoke an immediate response from us—to pick up the telephone and call a particular number to obtain a service or a product (or even give a donation). Our streets and highways are cluttered with billboards. Our mailboxes are full of unsolicited advertisements. We view films on television or in the theater that cost millions of dollars to produce.

The local church cannot hope to compete with this level of communication, but it can recognize that the importance it gives to what is being communicated will be the importance associated with that communication. Important programs are ones which people are talking about, looking forward to. An *important* mission conference would be one that one had been looking forward to for four months. We ascribe importance to events on the basis of how well they had been planned and how well they have been executed. We do not expect to find Hollywood quality audio-visual presentations within our local church, but against the standards which have been set for the church, we interpret the importance of any presentation on the basis of how much *comparative* effort has gone into it.

All of this says that it is not only necessary but appropriate for the local church to invest time, energy, and money in communicating the needs of a broken and lost world. Is it wrong to think that a church should spend perhaps 5 percent of its missions budget on missionary education in communication? Would not such an effort both demonstrate the church's commitment to missions and produce responsive prayers, contributions, and commitments from the congregation?

THE RIGHT PEOPLE MIX

In chapter 18 we discussed our opinion about the need for different levels of missionaries in terms of training and experience. Missionary pioneers through the centuries have demonstrated that it is possible to get "on-the-job training," to move into a society with little knowledge of their culture or their language, and still be effective. However, history has also shown that those with experience and maturity are more likely to be effective leaders when faced with unknown circumstances.

Good planning includes planning for the kind of people needed for the mission. If the plans change, then the people need to change. For example, if the only people available to move into a pioneer area have little or no field experience, then we should revise our plans to include "on-the-job training." We should assume that the first three or four years of their involvement should include quiet observation, learning, and adaptation.

It does not sound very glamorous for an agency to spend two to three years and employ four to six people to "do research." It is often difficult to maintain the motivation of the missionaries and those who are involved in supporting the project. But to move ahead without such determined training and results will bring far from glamorous results. In chapter 32 we discussed the idea of moving a people from a field after a given phase of a project was completed. If we are going to reach unreached people, we often will need mature veterans to lead the group. The idea that one is committed to a particular field for life sounds noble on paper, but in practice it is less effective than moving a person who has had a great deal of experience in one area into another. This will, of course, require the learning of a new language. But hopefully the mature missionary's experience in understanding a culture will not only ease the requirement to learn the language, but will make that person much more effective as a missionary.

In most pioneer situations utilizing a missionary team of both mature and less experienced missionaries is the most effective way to go. Such a mix requires that there be a clear understanding of lines of authority. There needs to be an understanding of how the group is to be organized and what is to be delegated. There need to be regular times of evaluation, as we will discuss in the next chapter. Whenever possible this team should train together. This training should start before they move into the field. The study of the people to be reached, the rethinking of plans, the discussion of contingencies, analysis of the life-style that will be led, the way that the missionary team will demonstrate itself as being part of Christ's body—all will need to be thought and talked about by those who are actually going.

The lines of communication between this team and the support base need to be clearly understood. Communicating across thousands of miles is difficult. Once the team plunges into the business of getting on with the task, it becomes emotionally separated from those who are "back home." There is a natural tendency to let communications slide because of the need "to get on with the work." This needs to be resisted. The great value of outside leadership is that someone can look objectively at what the team is doing. It is here that monthly evaluation and review of goals is extremely useful.

Here again we need to return to the question of the expenditure of funds. Most mission agencies are loath to build up large numbers of home personnel. They view such personnel as "overhead," and in many ways, as a necessary evil. They view with alarm organizations which have a large number of bureaucrats. However, mission agencies would do well to examine the practices of those who live in the world of commerce and whose only real goal may be profit. One could assume that such a company would do its very best to eliminate all extraneous people, to keep its cost as low as possible. Yet, when one examines profit-making companies that are in businesses similar to Christian agencies, one finds a large number of people involved in support. Just as most modern armies find that it takes three or four people on the home front to support one person in the field, so do these profit-making companies find that in order to be effective in the field, they have to give good support. Missions, too, are in business for profit. Our profit is profit for the Lord. Our profit is the coming of the Kingdom. The question, as we will discuss in the next chapter, is not: Did we spend too much on overhead or have too many people at home? but: Did we accomplish what God wanted us to accomplish?

APPLYING MEANS AND METHODS

The task of mission is the task of the whole Church. Specific people groups need specific members of Christ's body assigned to reach them. But the mysterious link between the different parts of the body remains. We are not a group of individuals, each one doing his or her own thing. In some cases the support base will be minimal. But even as Paul carried out a tentmaking ministry, supporting himself with his own hands as he preached, there were certainly those in Antioch who remembered him in prayer, not to mention those in the churches that he had planted! A similar situation exists with an organization such as the Missionary Fellowship Prayer Band in India. Here people who were constrained to pray for other cultures within their country eventually were constrained to go to other cultures. They are supported by those who are continuing to pray for them in their home state. Certainly prayer support is part of "means and methods."

When there are larger distances to travel, and/or the people to be reached are more remote, then means and methods have to be applied all along the line. Means and methods are needed to keep in communication with those who are involved in financial and prayer support. Means and methods are needed to insure that the necessary logistics are maintained for those in the field. Means and methods are needed to insure that ancillary services, such as medical care, are provided. Finally specific means and methods are needed by the missionary team to communicate the gospel within an unreached people group.

In the same way that the needs of a particular people will be unique, so will the needs of a particular missionary team be unique. Western mission agencies tend to develop policies and procedures which will be uniform for all fields. We question the wisdom of such uniformity. Uniformity *does* often lead to reduced expense, but uniformity can also increase the eventual cost to the particular missionary team. In the book *The Homeless Mind,* Peter Berger, et al. (1973) point out that bureaucracy is one of the unforeseen outcomes of democracy. Democracy implies that everyone is equal. But if everyone is equal, no one is special. Organizations which are designed to deal with people as though everyone is equal soon begin to treat people as though no one is special. Since everyone is to be treated equally, since no one is to be given any special attention, the bureaucracy begins to think of itself as the thing of primary importance. In the end the bureaucracy operates like a machine, and people are relegated to a product. This desire to be treated equally or "fairly" is in constant tension with the specialties that we all have. We have no neat solutions to the dilemma. We would only suggest that for each unreached people, we need to think back and see what means and methods need to be applied to the entire mission organization so we can do the best we can to meet the specific need.

A word needs to be said here about becoming too comfortable in a foreign land. A few paragraphs above we made a strong plea for adequate support for the effort going on in the field. Many missions appear to be operating on a shoestring budget. Yet, paradoxically there are missionary compounds and institutions all over the world that apparently exist only for the benefit of the people running the institutions. Thus we now find schools that were originally intended to educate missionaries' children in the field with as many as three-quarters of their students coming from non-missionary families. When one considers the large number of "missionaries" needed to support such institutions, as well as the investment in plant and property, one can often discover that it would be cheaper to fly the children to a school in the home country.

The reason that most of these institutions exist is that the mission and the missionaries did not *plan* to succeed (this is about the fourth time we have noted this!). They did not set a deadline for when the job could be done and they could withdraw. If these missionary bases were in countries where there were still numbers of unreached people, and if one discovered that the missionaries being supported by these institutions were indeed attempting to reach these unreached people, then it would not be difficult to modify this criticism. However, often the very presence of the institution strengthens the "settled-downness" of the entire missionary community. We need to give adequate support, but we need to plan to end that support.

COURSE CORRECTION—REPLANNING

Think, plan, act, evaluate, think, plan, act, evaluate. Once we begin to act, it is often very difficult to stop to evaluate. This is particularly true if we believe we are succeeding. If we are succeeding because we are following the plan we originally made, then we are probably all right. But often we are succeeding in carrying out actions which we did not originally plan. As we move forward in the joy of success, it is easy to forget that what we are doing now is part of a much larger whole.

We need to stop occasionally and see whether what we are doing fits into our total plan. In the previous chapter we talked about the need for continuous replanning. Even in the slow-moving pace of many Third World cultures, setting some time aside weekly to review what actually has been done during the week and thinking ahead as to what will be done next week is of vital importance. A monthly written review, even if it is written only to ourselves, is the kind of disciplined exercise which will help us understand how we are moving. Planning takes time. If we face a situation which is so dramatically different from the one we anticipated that an entirely new plan is required, then it behooves us to take the weeks and even the months that might be necessary to think through a new plan.

The kind of evaluation we will discuss in the next chapter is never comfortable. It is not a pleasant feeling to discover that we are not doing as well as we anticipated or that the reason we are succeeding is due much more to some external circumstances than to our own efforts. In general, missionaries are very much like school teachers. They do not like to evaluate one another. Consequently, many annual or semi-annual field meetings of missionary staffs within a country are times of sharing blessings and recounting *activities*. They are seldom times of evaluation. What a difference it might make if a group of missionaries shared with each other what they hoped God was going to do with them in the coming year and then returned a year later to compare what actually did happen and to discuss together what they might do to reach their goals!

To identify change, we have to compare what we are doing with what we intended to do. When change does come, whether it be for the good or for the bad, we need to estimate what impact it will have and how we will have to change our ability to do what we plan to do in the future.

Consequently we learn to expect the unexpected. Planning and reevaluating help us learn from our experience. The necessity to change plans does not indicate failure. If we believe that God is leading, then we need to ask, "How can we take this unexpected event and use it to maximum advantage?"

It is only in attempting to act that we can gain experience. Planning helps us to anticipate the different kinds of futures we may face, but our skill in handling the unexpected and the wisdom that comes from experience can be gained only after we act.

QUESTIONS

Taking Action

1. Is your organization's primary concern with raising money or reaching people?
2. Does your organization have a long-range planning system that includes definable goals?
3. Does your organization have built into it the necessary communication system to inform people?
4. Does your organization have the right mix of people for the task it is attempting?
5. Does your organization usually do its homework?
6. Do you have good lines of communication between those in the field and those at the home base?
7. Does your organization normally have a plan to *leave* a field?

STEP 10

EVALUATION

Considerations

Evaluation

Questions

CONSIDERATIONS

1. Evaluation only takes place when we *plan* to evaluate.
2. Evaluation should begin with goals, not with resources.
3. The most difficult evaluation is personal evaluation.

CHAPTER 34

Evaluation

L ife is wondrously complex. If we have a major goal for a year, and if that goal is supported by fifty-two other goals, one for each week, and if that week is made up of individual goals for each day, we only begin to appreciate the complexity of life. The marvelous thing is that we not only survive, but we thrive in such a complex world!

As we close the circle, we come to an area to which most organizations have given the least attention: *evaluation* of whether we reached our goals, whether the way we went about it was appropriate, and whether we still believe the goals are worthy.

In order to solve any problem or to make any plan we have to draw on previous experience, the lessons history has taught us. In this sense we are always evaluating. We are making trade-offs between what seem to be good approaches and what seem to be poor ones. That is what experience is all about. However, we must not only see the "lessons of history" as one-time solutions. What history tells us is that things will probably not be the same in the future as they were in the past. And though our experience can be used to help us through the future, we also need to gain new experience from our immediate situation.

There is a natural tendency to think that what has worked in the past will be an appropriate course of action for the future. It is here that the organization can fall into the biggest trap. In many ways there is nothing quite so dangerous as success (Dayton and Engstrom, 1979). Because of our natural inclination toward standard solutions (interchangeable parts!) we easily believe that we have found *the* solution. The trouble is that the problem keeps changing! One friend of ours has described it as trying to paint a freight train while standing on another moving freight train. We have to keep moving and changing in order to stay abreast of our moving and changing world.

SET UP AN EVALUATION PROCEDURE

An evaluation procedure should be a natural part of the planning process, for the planning process should always include a review of purposes and goals. To review should mean to evaluate. This means that specific times should be set aside to evaluate performance and effectiveness. (A word of caution: we will *never* do everything we set out to do, nor will we do it in just the way we planned.) It is of paramount importance that we evaluate performance, not persons. The reason most people fear evaluation is that they view it as a mechanism to place blame.

As we discussed in the earlier chapter, evaluation needs to be continuous. However, in order to gain a greater understanding of how to carry out evaluation, it is useful to think of evaluating goals, evaluating means and methods, and evaluating our use of resources. Earlier we talked about the need in planning to start with goals, move on to means and methods, and plan for resources last. We noted that when one starts carrying out the work the opposite is true: we begin by finding the resources, then apply means and methods, and hopefully reach our goals. In evaluation we reverse the process. We start first with goals (Did we reach them?), then move on to means and methods (Did they work?), and last evaluate resources (What did we use?).

Figure 34-1 helps us to see how this works.

	PLANNING	ACTING	EVALUATING
GOALS	1 ↓	↑ 3	↘ 1
METHODS	2 ↓	↑ 2	↓ 2
RESOURCES	3 ↘	↗ 1	↓ 3

Figure 34-1 Planning, Acting, Evaluating

GOALS EVALUATION

The first question to ask is, "Did we reach the goal?" We may have come by a different route than we expected. We may have spent more or fewer resources than we anticipated, but did we reach the goal? Now it could be that we reached a different goal from the one we expected, and it could well be that we changed our definition of the goal as we moved through the replanning and evaluation process. Regardless of the outcome, there needs to be some time set aside to look back and see what God has been doing (and what Satan has been doing too!). What we are discussing here are not everyday or weekly goals, but rather overall goals. For example, in our discussion on planning we talked about the seven phases of reaching a particular people. Phase 1 had to do with a goal of demonstrating that we were acceptable within the group into which we had moved. The question before us at the end of Phase 1 is, Are we or are we not acceptable? It may be that the measure by which we know we are acceptable has changed. As we learned more about the culture of the group, we may have discovered that they have different ways of accepting newcomers than we had anticipated. Fine. Let us be careful that we do not change the measurement in order to prove to ourselves that we did what we set out to do.

If we met the goal we originally set, why did we meet it? This anticipates the questions that we will ask below about means and methods, but asking the question here is extremely useful. We may discover that we met the goal through a series of entirely unplanned circumstances. In chapter 22 we discuss the example of reaching the Turkana people of Northern Kenya. The young Kenyan who did this knew that he had to establish a relationship with a diviner within the group, and this was one of his goals. Quite unexpectedly the missionary met the wife of the diviner and befriended her, and she was so impressed that she introduced him in a positive way to her husband. Now in this case the missionary did not plan to reach the goal of becoming acceptable to the diviner in this particular way. But this is the way it happened. From such an example one can learn both the lesson of being ready to accept the unforeseen opportunities that God puts in our way, and also the lesson that there is usually a chain of relationships leading to the person that we want to come to know.

If we did not reach our goal, why did we not reach it? Was the goal unrealistic? Is there a possibility that we could still reach it if we gave it more time or more energy? Was the goal inappropriate? Did we abandon it? What can we learn because of not reaching the goal?

If we did reach the goal, did it have the desired result? As we have noted many times previously, all of our goals are linked together. The one in the future depends upon the one that we are attempting to meet now. Will the meeting of this goal lead us to a better opportunity? Or will it have a bad effect? Will it ultimately help us to realize our purposes? Were they really the goals we wanted? Have we learned something in the process of working them out that would cause us to restate them if we were to begin again? Are there some goals that should have been dropped? For example, perhaps there had been a goal to launch a new publication. This goal was part of a larger purpose which was to make this people feel positive about Christians and Christianity. Perhaps the goal has been reached, a new magazine has been launched, but now our evaluation tells us that for some reason it is not having the impact we anticipated. It is so easy to rejoice in the accomplishment of the goal that we forget *why* we originally wanted to reach the goal.

Finally, as we examine our success or failure to realize a goal, we need to ask what we can learn for the future as a result of this attempt. How can we share what we have learned with others? How can we utilize this approach or avoid it in the future?

EVALUATING MEANS AND METHODS

We have already asked the question: Did we meet the goal(s)? If we did meet it, did we use the means and methods that we said we would? Or did we have to find other means and methods? Why did the means or methods work or not work? Did it have something to do with us individually? Was it a question of outside circumstances being different than we anticipated?

Did we use the means and methods *when* we said we would? In other words, did we apply them in a timely manner?

Have we adapted our methods to the situation as we found it? As we developed new methods, what did we learn? What did we learn about the people we are trying to reach? What did we learn about ourselves? What did we learn about these particular procedures?

Did the means and methods produce some unexpected outcomes, goals that we had not planned for? If they did, were these goals good or bad?

Were the means and methods we used viewed as Christian and humane? As we look back on them how do we feel about them? Were they culturally sensitive? Did they properly portray the body of Christ?

What did our organization or agency think about the means and methods? Were they opposed to certain policies or procedures of the organization? Do these policies and procedures need to be reviewed in light of the effectiveness of our means and methods?

How did other Christians view our means and methods? We are often working side-by-side with Christians from other churches or other agencies. How did they see us? Did they feel that our means and methods honored our Savior?

Finally, and most importantly, how did these means and methods appear to the people we are trying to reach? Were we manipulative? Did we model means and methods that they could use, or were the means and methods foreign and Western? Did these means and methods leave this people more able to find their own selfhood within Christ, or did they become dependent upon outsiders?

EVALUATING RESOURCES

Missionaries and mission agencies in general have a great tendency to use whatever resources are at hand. There is always the feeling that there never are enough resources, and what we do have will be inadequate. At the other end of the scale we often do not attempt things because we do not think we have adequate resources. We need to evaluate resources, but only after we have evaluated goals, means, and methods.

Too often we do not view *time* as a major resource. It is. Did we use the amount of time we said we would, or more or less? Why? Remember, there are two types of time. There is elapsed time and people time. Did we use the *number of people* we said we would? To put it another way, did we use the number of people hours? Often we fail to see that *people's* time is money. There is a definite cost associated with every hour that someone serves in an organization. This is why it is correct to take the total income of an agency and divide it by the total number of people working for the agency. The result is the amount of money required for each person in that agency, on the average, to do his or her job. Thinking in these terms, what was the cost in terms of people? Did we expend more or less? If it was more or less, what happened that permitted us to spend less or required that we spend more?

What did your evaluation tell you about the *people* themselves? Hopefully, all of the goals were related to someone's accountability.

Did you discover new strengths or weaknesses? What have you learned about the personal goals of the individuals? Were they really motivated by what they did? From such questions you can hopefully gain some insight about future assignment or the need to relieve some people of their present tasks.

Turning specifically to money, did we use *the amount of money* we said we would? More? Less? Why? One of the worst possible answers is, "Because we couldn't raise the funds." Remember, our plans were based upon a given amount of resources. If we could not raise the funds, we should have changed the plans, and thus the goals. Finally, what did your evaluation tell you about your *organization?* Did you form some new organization subsets, such as a task force, that should be continued? Are there some formerly excellent organizational components that should be disbanded?

Overall, was our expenditure of resources good stewardship? If we had to do it again would we believe that this investment of time and people and money was a good use of God's gifts?

EVALUATION AS A PROCESS

We cannot overemphasize the need to see this kind of evaluation as a built-in process. Too often single-minded people are also narrow-minded. They glory in "looking to neither the left nor to the right." But life is not like that. To the left or the right may be better opportunities that God wants us to seize. The purpose of evaluating is not to demean or control people. We are evaluating *work.* Evaluation should be both the beginning and the ending of every Christian endeavor.

POSTERIORITIES

This leads to the idea of posteriorities, deciding what you are *not* going to do next year. Organizations are like an alligator whose tail keeps growing. We keep adding on new organizational components, goals, procedures and seldom drop any of the old ones. As a consequence the tail soon gets so large that we can hardly move ahead.

What we need is a calculated yearly decision on what part of the organization we are going to disband, what goals we are going to set aside for the coming year.

MEANS OF EVALUATION

Thus far we have discussed the why and the what of evaluation without saying too much about the how.

Evaluation should be planned

We not only have to decide *when* we will evaluate and what we will evaluate, but the *measurement* of evaluation. This measurement is often called a *standard*. Sometimes this measurement will be the same as the goal. For example, if our purpose was to have two significant leaders within a group develop a positive attitude toward us, then our specific goal might be that we would be invited to their home to share a meal three times by such-and-such a date. In this case the measurement and the goal would be the same. At other times the measurement may not be clearly stated within the goal. For example, we might have a goal to move 10 percent of a group from −6 to −5. The measurement of the goal might be that so many people give a particular answer when asked a question about the gospel. This leads to the next point.

Means and measurements should be designed

Sometimes this is quite difficult. It is all too easy to assume that we have an understanding that 10 percent of the people have moved from −6 to −5. It may be quite difficult to design a culturally acceptable way of measuring whether this has actually happened. But by designing this measurement early, we can often discover ways of measurement that are closed to us once the project has begun.

Report against goals and milestones

One of the most effective ways of evaluating is to write regular reports to ourselves and others as to how many of our goals and milestones have been reached. Reporting in itself causes us to stop and evaluate.

Self-evaluation

This is one of the hardest disciplines to acquire, but one of the most profitable ones to master. To have regular personal times of evaluating one's performance and activities against one's intentions is extremely valuable.

Joint evaluation

We discussed earlier the idea of missionaries joining together to evaluate each other's individual and common goals. This is a very powerful tool. Once the initial reticence of sharing one's failures is over, times of evaluation can be great spiritual events. How can we pray for one another effectively if we do not understand each other's needs?

Regular planning and forecasting

Our ten-step cycle shows that evaluation should lead to a re-thinking of our mission and planning. By setting up an annual planning cycle which includes a five- to ten-year forecast, we have an excellent vehicle for evaluation. When we compare what we now believe will happen in the next five to ten years with what we stated one year ago, we gain very good insight into successes and failures.

PERSONAL PERFORMANCE EVALUATION

The Bible has a great deal to say about not judging one another. But that is not the question before us. We are dealing with organizations, and particularly Christian organizations, be they local churches or other forms of Christian ministry. We are not to judge persons, but we have to evaluate *work*. The effort of the organization is the sum of its parts.

Each of us needs appreciation and affirmation. We need to be appreciated for our effort, as well as for what we have accomplished. But true appreciation is based upon a true understanding of both the difficulty of the task and what was expected. Intuitively we all know this. A friendly smile and a pat on the back are always welcome, but they become meaningless if we do not believe that the person really understands what we are affirming. We need to believe that someone knows what we are doing and how well we are doing. We need to know that what we are doing is important. We need to have our performance evaluated.

Only in this way can we help people grow, not only in their technical performance but in their relationships to one another. The ultimate purpose is that the organization may perform better. But at the same time the organization has a *responsibility* toward the individual. It is never easy to hear that we have performed poorly, but all growth is painful.

Effective evaluation must begin on an agreement between the subordinate and the superior as to what the subordinate is to do and the parameters within which this is to be done. This is basic. But there are two steps beyond this: the subordinate and the superior must also agree on how they are both going *to know* when and how something has been done, and they must agree on how they will *measure* this performance. There is a difference between knowing that something has been done and knowing how it will be measured. For example, most position descriptions do not include the criteria by which the work of the position will be measured, and the standards that must be met in order to demonstrate that these criteria have been fulfilled.

HOW TO EVALUATE

A *job description or a position description is a must*

If your organization does not now have a formal procedure for providing a description of each position or job, then make a rough outline of what should be included, and ask each person to write one for your review (Engstrom and Dayton, 1976).

Goals

Although a job description usually gives the purpose, responsibility, and tasks of a job, often it will not include the specific goals that are to be accomplished, goals that are owned by this position and therefore the person holding the position. The next step is to define with the person the goals of the position. Goals tell us that purposes are being realized. This is not an easy task, particularly if the organization does not have an integrated planning procedure. But do the best you can (Mager, 1972).

Standards

Each of the goals should have a standard of performance, the specifics of how the goal is to be measured. What specific work is to be carried out?

Negotiation

The superior and subordinate should then jointly agree on both the standards and the time by which these standards will be met. Since a quarterly evaluation, or at least a semi-yearly evaluation, is a must, it is helpful to relate the standards to the evaluation time. This type of negotiating will not only clarify a person's understanding of the job, it will greatly strengthen the superior's understanding of the subordinate. It also lays the foundation for subsequent evaluation and informs the subordinate that the organization is concerned and interested in that person and his or her performance.

Appraisal is part of a much larger system of getting things done. Most books cover it as a subsection. An excellent book that handles this and many other aspects of the leadership task is *Human Relations Administration*, 4th Edition, by Robert Dubin (1974).

CLOSING THE CIRCLE

So we end, and so we begin again. For those already involved in the task of cross-cultural evangelization, evaluation should probably be a beginning point. We need to understand who we are. We need to understand our history. We need to face up to our successes and failures. All of this will lead us to a new understanding of the mission to which God has called us. The process that we have described at length in this book is not an easy one. It is more difficult to carry out than it is to explain. It is hard to change and give up ways of doing things that we understand. It is hard to begin again. It is much more comfortable to assume that the future will be like the past, and that if we just keep doing what we are doing, only perhaps a little better, then this will honor God. But of all of the peoples of the world, Christians should be the most ready for change. Our past is forgiven, our future is secure. If God be for us, who can be against us?

QUESTIONS

Evaluation

1. Do you have *goals* for evaluation?
2. Do you have a way of evaluating your means and methods?
3. Do you have a way of evaluating the effectiveness of the money that you are spending?
4. What are you doing now that you ought to stop this year?
5. How do you evaluate yourself against what you are doing? What should you do about it?

POSTSCRIPT

*W*e have attempted in these pages to lead you through a *planning* process. Planning has to do with what is yet to be. Planning has to do with the future. Planning for the Christian has to do with faith. Each of us has some perception of the way we believe God wants us to be and the way he wants the world to be. Both the Church and the world are flawed. As we seek to understand what it means to be conformed to the image of Christ, we assume that we have some idea, some picture of what that would mean some time in the future. As Christians we are continually faced with the questions of what God wants us to be and what he wants us to do.

At a base level we know that what we do flows forth from what we are. We realize that we, too, need to be changed. We have argued that this applies equally to the local church and to the "healthy" arm of the Church which we in the West call "missions." Organizations are *organic*. They are made up of *people*. As the people live and move and have their being, so does the resulting organization. Organizations are *responses* to a situation. They should never become an end in themselves.

Thus people and organizations are in process. We are moving toward what we have yet to become. In the West the process is accelerating, not through our choice, but almost in spite of it. The winds of change are at gale force. What is needed is a navigation plan that not only sees us through the storm, but takes advantage of the winds of change and the tides of time to move us in a Spirit-led direction.

We believe that the ten-step model we have presented is such a navigation device. Every organization, like every ship, needs a navigator. Navigators need to be trained. Some learn through experience, but experience alone is not enough to navigate through unknown waters. The passage through the waters below is *universally* based on the position of the stars above. It takes training to read the times and the tides. The model we have presented is both a training and operational tool.

There are other, simpler models. In other places (Dayton, 1979) we have reduced this model to only five steps:

1. What people does God want us to reach?
2. What is this people like?
3. Who should reach them?
4. How should they be reached?
5. What will be the result of reaching them?

You may find another set that better fits your situation. The important thing is not the exact order, nor the exact phrasing of the questions. The important thing is that we *ask* the questions before we begin, as we begin, while we are working, and as we conclude.

We have tried to list our reasons for the questions under the *Considerations* that introduce each step. We have tried to present useful *Questions* at the end of each step. In many ways what is sandwiched in between is a justification of both the considerations and the questions.

We welcome suggestions and criticism. We too are in process. We would only ask that what we have presented be placed within the context of *getting on with the task*. The question is not how well we know something but what difference it makes. We hope this book makes a difference in that part of the world to which God has called you.

APPENDIX

Unreached Peoples Questionnaire

FINDING THE UNREACHED: YOU CAN HELP!

You can help locate unreached people groups

You are part of a worldwide network of concerned Christians. There are millions upon millions of people in the world who have had little or no contact with the gospel of Jesus Christ. Because of this, we are asking you to help the Church locate and identify these peoples so it can reach them.

Within each country there are distinct and unique groups of people who may be unreached. This questionnaire is designed to help you describe such groups so that Christians everywhere may pray and consider how these groups might be reached with the gospel. This information will be continuously compiled and made available to the Church and her mission agencies. It appears each year in an annual directory, *Unreached Peoples*, produced by David C. Cook.

There are many different groups of people in the world. How varied they are! Consequently, this questionnaire may not always ask the best questions for understanding a particular people. The questions have been asked in a way that will give comparative information to as large a number of Christians as possible. Where you feel another form of question would better suit your situation, please feel free to comment.

What is a "people group"?

A people group is a part of a society that has some basic characteristics in common that cause it to feel a sense of oneness, and set it apart from other groups. It may be unified by language, religion, economic status, occupation, ethnic origin, geographic location, or social position. For example, a distinct group based on ethnic, language and geographic characteristics might be the Quechua of Bolivia; a sociological group might be the urban university and college students of Colombia, or the urban industrial workers of France. It is important to see that groups may share a common way of life and sense of oneness because of social, occupational or economic characteristics, as well as because of language or ethnic origin. Therefore, whenever possible, *describe the smallest number of persons who make up a distinct group;* that is, don't say that all persons in a region or province are a group, rather describe the specific subgroups within that region or province.

Who are the "unreached and unevangelized people"?

Christians have different definitions of the terms "unreached" or "unevangelized." For the purposes of this worldwide effort, we describe an unreached or unevangelized people as a people who has not received or responded to the gospel. This unresponsiveness may be due to lack of opportunity, to lack of understanding, or because the people has not received enough information about the gospel message in its own language through the eyes of its own culture so that it can truly respond to Christ.

We consider a people "unreached" when less than 20 percent of the members of the group are *practicing* Christians, that is, are active members of the Christian community. By "Christian" we mean adherents (church members, families and followers) of the historic Christian communions; Protestant, Anglican, Roman Catholic, Orthodox and such independent groups as may claim the Bible as the basis of faith and Jesus Christ as Lord and Savior. A group less than 20 percent Christian may yet need Christians from outside the group to help with the evangelism task.

How you can provide information

The attached questionnaire has two parts. If you only have information for the first part, send that in now.

Please fill in one questionnaire for *each* people group with which you are familiar. Do not put several groups on one questionnaire. (If you need more questionnaires, ask for extra copies or photocopy this one, or typewrite the questions you are answering on a separate sheet of paper.) We realize that one person may not have all the answers to these questions. Just answer what you can. PLEASE DO NOT WAIT UNTIL YOU HAVE ALL THE INFORMATION REQUESTED ON THIS QUESTIONNAIRE. SEND WHAT YOU HAVE. Other people may provide information that you do not have. Thank you for your help!

When you have completed this questionnaire, please return it to:

Unreached Peoples Program Director
c/o MARC, 919 W. Huntington Drive, Monrovia, CA 91016 U.S.A.

SURVEY QUESTIONNAIRE FOR UNEVANGELIZED AND UNREACHED PEOPLES

Do you see a group of people who are unreached or unevangelized? Identify them! As the Lord spoke to Ezekiel of old, so He speaks to us today. "Son of man, What do you see"?

Answers to the questions on these two pages will provide the minimum information needed to list this people group in the *Unreached Peoples* annual.

After you have read the directions, type or print your answers so they can be easily read. It is unlikely that you will have all the information requested. Do the best you can. What information you are lacking others may supply. If your information is a best guess or estimate, merely place an "E" after it. Send in what you have as soon as possible. Please ignore the small numbers next to the answers. They help others prepare your answers for the *Unreached Peoples* annual.

1. Name of the group or people: _____

2. Alternate name(s) or spelling: _____

3. Country where located: _____

4. Approximate size of the group in this country: _____

5. Vernacular or common language: _____

6. Lingua franca or trade language: _____

7. Name of religious groups found among this people:

CHRISTIAN GROUPS:	% who are adherents of this religion	% who practice this religion
Protestant	_____ %	_____ %
Roman Catholic	_____ %	_____ %
Eastern Orthodox	_____ %	_____ %
Other Christian: _____ (name)	_____ %	_____ %
NON-CHRISTIAN GROUPS OR SECULARISM:		
_____	_____ %	_____ %
_____	_____ %	_____ %
_____	_____ %	_____ %
_____	_____ %	_____ %
TOTAL FOR ALL GROUPS:	100 %	

8. In your opinion, what is the attitude of this people toward Christianity?

(01)☐ Strongly favorable   (02)☐ Somewhat favorable   (03)☐ Indifferent   (04)☐ Somewhat opposed   (05)☐ Strongly opposed

9. Questionnaire completed by:

Name: _____   Date: _____

Organization: _____

Address: _____

_____

10. Who else might be able to provide information about this people?

Name   Organization (if any)   Address

_____

_____

_____

11. If you are aware of any publications describing this people, please give title and author.

_____

12. What other information do you have that could help others to understand this people better? What do you feel would help in evangelizing them? *(Use additional sheet if necessary.)*

13. Are you also sending in pages 3 and 4? ☐ Yes   ☐ No

Please send whatever information you have immediately. Do not wait until you have every answer.

Mail to:

Unreached Peoples Program Director
c/o MARC, 919 W. Huntington Drive, Monrovia, CA 91016 USA

Name of people group described_____ Your name _____ Date ___

If you have any more information about this people group, please complete the following two pages as best you can. If not, please send in pages one and two now. If you can obtain more information later, send it in as soon as possible.

PEOPLE DISTINCTIVES—What makes them different? Why are they a people group?

14. A number of different things contribute to create a distinctive people or group, one that in some way shares a common way of life, *sees* itself as a particular group having an affinity toward one another, and differs to some extent from other groups or peoples. What would you say makes the people you are describing distinctive? Check the appropriate box of as many of the following descriptions as *are important* in making this people distinctive. Use the following scale: "High" importance, "Medium" importance, "Low" importance. For example, if you thought that the fact that they had a common political loyalty was of medium importance in unifying and making a group distinctive, you would place an "X" in the middle box under "Medium".

Importance   Importance

High Medium Low   *High Medium Low*

(01)□ □ □ Same language   (10)□ □ □ Common residential area
(02)□ □ □ Common political loyalty   (11)□ □ □ Similar social class or caste
(03)□ □ □ Similar occupation   (12)□ □ □ Similar economic status
(04)□ □ □ Racial or ethnic similarity (13)□ □ □ Shared hobby or special interest
(05)□ □ □ Shared religious customs   (14)□ □ □ Discrimination from other groups
(06)□ □ □ Common kinship ties   (15)□ □ □ Unique health situation
(07)□ □ □ Strong sense of unity   (16)□ □ □ Distinctive legal status
(08)□ □ □ Similar education level   (17)□ □ □ Similar age
(09)□ □ □ Other(s) _____   (18)□ □ □ Common significant problems
          (please write in)

15. How rapidly would you say the lifestyle of this people is changing? (check one)

(01)□Very   (02)□ Slow   (03)□ Moderate   (04)□ Rapid   (05)□ Very
   Slow   Change   Change   Change   Rapid
   Change   Change

PEOPLE LANGUAGES—What do they speak?

Please list the various languages used by the members of this people:

LANGUAGE TYPE	Primary name(s) of their language(s)	Approximate % who *speak* this language	Approximate % of people over 15 years of age who *read* this language
16. Vernacular or common language:	_____	_____ %	_____ %
17. Lingua franca or trade language:	_____	_____ %	_____ %
18. Language used for instruction in schools:	_____	_____ %	_____ %
19. Language suitable for presentation of the gospel:	_____	_____ %	_____ %

20. If there is Christian witness at present, what language(s) is being used? _____

21. Place an "x" in the boxes that indicate the status of Scripture translation *in the language you consider most suitable for communicating the gospel* (question 19):

	CURRENT STATUS			AVAILABLE		
	Not available	In process	Completed	In oral form	In print	On cassette or records
(POR)New Testament portions	□	□	□	□	□	□
(NT)Complete New Testament	□	□	□	□	□	□
(OT)Complete Old Testament	□	□	□	□	□	□

22. Of the <u>Christians</u> present among this people, what percent *over 15 years of age can* and *do read any language?*
    _____ %

52479C

CHRISTIAN WITNESS TO THIS PEOPLE—Who is trying to reach them?

23. If there are Christian churches or missions (national or foreign) now active *within the area or region where this people is concentrated*, please give the following information:

    (If there are none, check here: ☐)

CHURCH OR MISSION Name of church, denomination	YEAR Year work began in this area	MEMBERS Approximate number of full members from this people	ADHERENTS Approximate number of adherents (community including children)	WORKERS Approximate numbers of trained pastors and evangelists from this people
_____	_____	_____	_____	_____
_____	_____	_____	_____	_____
_____	_____	_____	_____	_____

24. What is the growth rate of the total Christian community among this people group?

    (01)☐ Rapid growth　　(02)☐ Slow growth　　(03)☐ Stable　　(04)☐ Slow decline　　(05)☐ Rapid decline

25. In your opinion, what is the attitude of this people to religious change of any kind?

    (01)☐ Very open　　(02)☐ Somewhat open　　(03)☐ Indifferent　　(04)☐ Somewhat closed　　(05)☐ Very closed

26. In your opinion, what is the attitude of this people toward Christianity?

    (01)☐ Strongly favorable　　(02)☐ Somewhat favorable　　(03)☐ Indifferent　　(04)☐ Somewhat opposed　　(05)☐ Strongly opposed

27. Most people move through a series of more or less well-defined stages in their attitude toward Christianity. Parts of a people group will be further along than other parts. Here are ten categories that attempt to show this progression. However, locating people in some of these categories can be difficult, so to make things simpler some categories are combined in the questions that follow.

    In your estimation, what percentage of this people can be described as those who: (These percentages are exclusive. Do not include people more than once. Your total should add up to 100%.)

    Have no awareness of Christianity . . . . _____ %

    Have awareness of the existence of Christianity . . . . _____ %

    Have some knowledge of the gospel . . . . _____ %

    Understand the message of the gospel . . . . _____ %

    See the personal implications of the gospel . . . . ⎫

    Recognize a personal need that the gospel can meet . . . . ⎬ _____ %

    Are being challenged to receive Christ . . . . ⎭

    Have decided for Christ, but are not incorporated into a fellowship
    (may be evaluating their decision) . . . . _____ %

    Are incorporated into a fellowship of Christians . . . . _____ %

    Are active propagators of the gospel . . . . _____ %

    TOTAL　　100 %

28. On the whole, how accurate is the information you have given us?

    (V)☐ Very accurate　　(F)☐ Fairly accurate　　(E)☐ Good estimate　　(G)☐ Mainly guesses

29. Are you willing to have your name publically associated with this information?

    ☐ No　☐ Yes　☐ Yes, with qualifications: _____

BIBLIOGRAPHY

ABRECHT, Paul and SMALLEY, William
  1959 "The Moral Implications of Social Structure," *Practical Anthropology*, Vol. 6, No. 3, pp. 140–144.
ACCAD, Fouad
  1976 "The Qur'an: A Bridge to Christian Faith," *Missiology*, Vol. 4, No. 3 (July 1976), pp. 331–342.
AHRENS, Theodor
  1977 "Concepts of Power in a Melanesian and Biblical Perspective," *Missiology*, Vol. 5, No. 2 (April 1977), pp. 431–442.
ALLEN, Louis A.
  1973 *Professional Management*, New York, McGraw-Hill.
ALLEN, Roland
  1962 *Missionary Methods: St. Paul's or Ours?*, Grand Rapids, Wm. B. Eerdmans Publishing Co.
ANDERSEN, Wilhelm
  1955 *Towards a Theology of Mission*, London, SCM Press.
  1961 "Further Toward a Theology of Mission," (from *The Theology of Christian Mission*, by Gerald Anderson) Nashville, Abingdon Press.
ANDERSON, Gerald
  1961 *The Theology of Christian Mission*, Nashville, Abingdon Press.

ARRINGTON, Leonard J. and BITTON, Davis
1979   *The Mormon Experience,* New York, Alfred A. Knopf.
BABBIE, Earl
1975   *The Practice of Social Research,* Belmont, Wadsworth.
BARRETT, David
1968   *Schism and Renewal in Africa,* Nairobi, Oxford.
1969   "The Expansion of Christianity in Africa in the Twentieth Century," *Church Growth Bulletin,* Vol. 5, No. 5 (May 1969), pp. 362–366.
1979   "In Defense of Mono-ethnic Churches," *Church Growth Bulletin,* ed. James Montgomery, May 1979, p. 276.
1980   *The World Christian Encyclopedia,* Nairobi, Oxford.
BASSETT, Glenn A.
1966   *Management Styles in Transition,* New York, American Management Association.
BEACH, H. P. and FAHS, C. H., eds.
1925   *World Missionary Atlas,* New York, Institute of Social and Religious Research.
BEAVER, R. Pierce
1967   *To Advance the Gospel: Selections from the Writings of Rufus Anderson,* Grand Rapids, Wm. B. Eerdmans Publishing Co.
1973   *The Gospel and Frontier Peoples,* Pasadena, William Carey Library.
1979   "The Legacy of Rufus Anderson," *Occasional Bulletin,* Vol. 3, No. 3 (July 1979), pp. 94–97.
BECKER, V.
1976   "Gospel, Evangelize, Evangelist," (*Dictionary of New Testament Theology,* Colin Brown, ed., pp. 107–115) Grand Rapids, Zondervan.
BEHM, Johannes
1964   "*glōssa heteroglōssa,*" (*Theological Dictionary of the New Testament,* G. Kittel, ed., Vol. 1, pp. 719–727) Grand Rapids, Wm. B. Eerdmans Publishing Co.
BELL, Daniel, ed.
1968   *Toward the Year 2000,* Boston, Houghton Mifflin Company.
BENKO, Stephen and O'ROURKE, John J., et al. (eds.)
1971   *Catacombs and the Colosseum,* Valley Forge, Judson Press.
BERGER, Peter L.
1961   *The Noise of Solemn Assemblies,* New York, Doubleday.
1974   *Pyramids of Sacrifice,* New York, Basic Books.

BERGER, Peter L., et al.
1973   *The Homeless Mind,* New York, Vintage Books.
BERKOUWER, Gerrit C.
1976   *The Church,* Grand Rapids, Wm. B. Eerdmans Publishing Co.
BERTRAM, Georg
1971   *"strephō,"* (*Theological Dictionary of the New Testament,* G. Friedrich, ed., Vol. 7, pp. 714–729) Grand Rapids, Wm. B. Eerdmans Publishing Co.
BEYERHAUS, Peter
1971   *Missions—Which Way?,* Grand Rapids, Zondervan.
1972   *Shaken Foundations: Building Mission Theology,* Grand Rapids, Zondervan.
BIERSTEDT, Robert
1970   *The Social Order,* Third Edition, New York, McGraw-Hill Book Co.
BIETENHARD, H.
1976   "People...," (*Dictionary of New Testament Theology,* Vol. 2, Colin Brown, ed., pp. 788–805) Grand Rapids, Zondervan.
BODLEY, John H.
1975   *Victims of Progress,* Menlo Park, Benjamin-Cummings Publishing Co.
BOLLES, Richard N.
1976   *What Color Is Your Parachute?* (Revised), Berkeley, Ten Speed Press.
BOWEN, Elenore S.
1964   *Return to Laughter,* Garden City, Natural History Pub.
BOWLES, Gordon
1978   *The People of Asia,* New York, Charles Scribner's Sons.
BRAATEN, Carl E.
1977   *The Flaming Center,* Philadelphia, Fortress Press.
BRADSHAW, Malcolm
1969   *Church Growth Through Evangelism-in-Depth,* Pasadena, William Carey Library.
BRAUN, Neil
1971   *Laity Mobilized: Reflections on Church Growth in Japan and Other Lands,* Grand Rapids, Wm. B. Eerdmans Publishing Co.
BREWSTER, E. Thomas and BREWSTER, Elizabeth S.
1976   *Language Acquisition Made Practical,* Colorado Springs, Lingua House.

BRIGHT, John
1953   *The Kingdom of God,* Nashville, Abingdon.
BRUCE, F. F.
1977   *The Defense of the Gospel in the New Testament,* Revised Edition, Grand Rapids, Wm. B. Eerdmans Publishing Co.
BRUNNER, Emil
1953   *The Misunderstanding of the Church,* Philadelphia, Westminster Press.
BÜCHSEL, Friedrich
1964   *"genea,"* (*Theological Dictionary of the New Testament,* G. Kittel, ed., Vol. 1, pp. 662–665) Grand Rapids, Wm. B. Eerdmans Publishing Co.
CANSDALE, George
1970   *All the Animals of the Bible Lands,* Grand Rapids, Zondervan.
CAREY, William
1961   *An Enquiry Into the Obligations of Christians to Use Means for the Conversion of the Heathen,* New Facsimile Edition, London, The Carey Kingsgate Press, Limited.
CHO, Ki Sun Joseph
1975   "Rural Evangelism in Asia," (*Let the Earth Hear His Voice,* J. D. Douglas, ed., pp. 624–633) Minneapolis, World Wide Publications.
CHUA, Wee Hian
1975   "Evangelization of Whole Families," (*Let the Earth Hear His Voice,* J. D. Douglas, ed., pp. 968–976) Minneapolis, World Wide Publications.
CLARK, Dennis E.
1971   *The Third World and Mission,* Waco, Word.
CLARK, Stephen B.
1972   *Building Christian Communities: Strategy for Renewing the Church,* Notre Dame, Ave Maria Press.
COHEN, Paul A.
1963   *China and Christianity,* Cambridge, Harvard.
COLEMAN, Robert E.
1963   *The Master Plan of Evangelism,* Old Tappan, Revell.
CONN, Harvie
1976   *Theological Perspectives on Church Growth,* Philadelphia, Presbyterian and Reformed Publishing Co.
COOK, Harold R.
1971   *Historic Patterns of Church Growth,* Chicago, Moody Press.

CORWIN, Charles
1978   "Japanese Bonsai or/and California Redwood," *Missiology,* Vo. 6, No. 3 (July 1978), pp. 297–310.

COSTAS, Orlando
1974   *The Church and Its Mission,* Wheaton, Tyndale.
1975   "Depth in Evangelism—An Interpretation of 'In-Depth Evangelism' Around the World," (*Let the Earth Hear His Voice,* J. D. Douglas, ed., pp. 675–697), Minneapolis, World Wide Publications.
1977   "Missiology in Contemporary Latin America: A Survey," *Missiology,* Vol. 5, No. 1 (January 1977), pp. 89–114.

COWAN, Marion
1962   "A Christian Movement in Mexico," *Practical Anthropology,* Vol. 9, No. 5 (Sept.–Oct. 1962), pp. 193–204.

CROSBY, Philip
1972   *The Art of Getting Your Own Sweet Way,* New York, McGraw-Hill.

DALE, Ernest
1967   *Organization,* New York, American Management Association.

DALE, Kenneth J.
1975   *Circle of Harmony,* Pasadena, William Carey Library.

DANEEL, M. L.
1971   *Old and New in Southern Shona Independent Churches,* Hawthorne, Mouton Publications.

DAVIS, Raymond H.
1978   "Church Growth and Cultural Change in Turkana," Fuller Theological Seminary, unpublished thesis.

DAYTON, Edward R.
1971   *God's Purpose/Man's Plans,* Monrovia, MARC.
1977   "Current Trends in North American Protestant Ministries Overseas," *Occasional Bulletin,* Vol. 1, No. 2.
1978a   *Planning Strategies for Evangelism: A Workbook,* Sixth Edition, Monrovia, MARC.
1978b   *Resources for Christian Leaders,* Second Edition, Monrovia, MARC.
1979   *That Everyone May Hear,* Monrovia, MARC.

DAYTON, Edward R. and ENGSTROM, Ted W.
1976   *Strategy for Living,* Glendale, Regal.
1979   *Strategy for Leadership,* Old Tappan, Revell.

DAYTON, Edward R., ed.
1976   *Mission Handbook: North American Protestant Ministries Overseas*, 11th Edition, Monrovia, MARC.
DeRIDDER, Richard R.
1971   *Discipling the Nations: A Biblical Basis for Missions*, Grand Rapids, Baker Book House.
DERWACTER, Frederich M.
1930   *Preparing the Way for Paul*, New York, Macmillan.
DICKSON, David
1974   *The Politics of Alternative Technology*, New York, Universe Books.
DOUGLAS, J. D., ed.
1975   *Let the Earth Hear His Voice*, Minneapolis, World Wide Publishers.
DuBOSE, Francias M.
1978   *How Churches Grow in an Urban World*, Nashville, Broadman Press.
DUNN, James D. G.
1977   *Unity and Diversity in the New Testament*, Philadelphia, Westminster Press.
DYE, T. Wayne
1976   "Toward a Cross-cultural Definition of Sin," *Missiology*, Vol. 4, No. 1, pp. 26–41.
EDWARDS, Christopher
1979   *Crazy for God*, Englewood Cliffs, Prentice-Hall.
ELKINS, Phil
1974   *Church-Sponsored Missions*, Austin, Firm Foundation Press.
ELLUL, Jacques
1964   *The Technological Society*, New York, Alfred A. Knopf.
1965   *Propaganda*, New York, Random House.
1967   *The Political Illusion*, New York, Alfred A. Knopf.
1976   *The Ethics of Freedom*, Grand Rapids, Wm. B. Eerdmans Publishing Co.
ENGEL, James F.
1977   *How Can I Get Them to Listen?* Grand Rapids, Zondervan.
1979   *Contemporary Christian Communications*, Nashville, Thomas Nelson Publishers.
ENGEL, James F. and NORTON, Wilbert
1975   *What's Gone Wrong With the Harvest?*, Grand Rapids, Zondervan.

ENGEL, James F., et al.
1973   *Consumer Behavior*, 2nd Edition, New York, Holt, Rinehart and Winston.
ENGSTROM, Ted W.
1976   *The Making of a Christian Leader*, Grand Rapids, Zondervan.
ENGSTROM, Ted W. and DAYTON, Edward R.
1976   *The Art of Management for Christian Leaders*, Waco, Word.
1979   *The Christian Executive*, Waco, Word.
ERIKSON, Erik H.
1968   *Identity, Youth and Crisis*, New York, W. W. Norton.
EVANS-PRITCHARD, E. E.
1973   *Peoples of the Earth*, 20 volumes, Danbury Press.
EWING, David
1969   *The Human Side of Planning*, New York, Macmillan.
FISHER, Ron
1978   "Why Don't We Have More Church Planting Missionaries?" *Evangelical Mission Quarterly*, Vol. 14, No. 4 (October 1978).
FORRESTER, Jay W.
1969   *Urban Dynamics*, Cambridge, MIT Press.
FOWLER, J. Andrew
1977   "Towards Wholeness in Ministry Among the Iban," *Missiology*, Vol. 5, No. 3 (July 1977), pp. 275–284.
FRASER, David A.
1979   "An 'Engel Scale' for Muslim Work?" (*The Gospel and Islam*, Don McCurry, ed., pp. 164–181) Monrovia, MARC.
FREILICH, Morris, ed.
1977   *Marginal Natives at Work: Anthropologists in the Field*, New York, Halsted Press.
FRIEDRICH, Gerhard
1964   *"euangelizomai,"* (*Theological Dictionary of the New Testament*, G. Kittel, ed., Vol. 2, pp. 707–737) Grand Rapids, Wm. B. Eerdmans Publishing Co.
1965   *"kērux,"* (*Theological Dictionary of the New Testament*, G. Kittel, ed., Vol. 3, pp. 683–718) Grand Rapids, Wm. B. Eerdmans Publishing Co.
GAGER, John G.
1975   *Kingdom and Community: The Social World of Early Christianity*, Englewood Cliffs, Prentice-Hall.

GARDNER, John W.
1961   *Excellence,* New York, Harper & Row.
1964   *Self-Renewal,* New York, Harper & Row.
GERBER, Vergil
1973   *A Manual for Evangelism/Church Growth,* Pasadena,
       William Carey Library.
GRANT, Michael
1960   *The World of Rome,* New York, New American Library.
GRANT, Robert
1977   *Early Christianity and Society,* New York, Harper & Row.
GREEN, Michael
1970   *Evangelism in the Early Church,* Grand Rapids, Wm. B.
       Eerdmans Publishing Co.
1975   "Methods and Strategy in the Evangelism of the Early
       Church," (*Let the Earth Hear His Voice,* J. D. Douglas, ed.,
       pp. 165–172) Minneapolis, World Wide Publishers.
GRIMES, Barbara
1979   *Ethnologue,* Dallas, Summer Institute of Linguistics.
GRUNDMANN, Walter
1964   *"dēmos,"* (*Theological Dictionary of the New Testament,*
       G. Kittel, ed., Volume 2, pp. 63–65) Grand Rapids, Wm. B.
       Eerdmans Publishing Co.
GULLIVER, P. H.
1951   "A Preliminary Survey of the Turkana," South Africa, Uni-
       versity of Cape Town.
HAHN, Ferdinand
1965   *Mission in the New Testament,* Naperville, Alec R. Allenson.
HALL, Edward T.
1959   *The Silent Language,* New York, Doubleday.
1966   *The Hidden Dimension,* New York, Doubleday.
1977   *Beyond Culture,* New York, Doubleday.
HARDIN, Daniel C.
1978   *Mission: A Practical Approach to Church Sponsored Mission
       Work,* Pasadena, William Carey Library.
HARNACK, Adolf von
1972   *The Mission and Expansion of Christianity in the First Three
       Centuries,* Magnolia, Peter Smith Publishing.
HARPER, M.
1977   *Let My People Grow,* Plainfield, Logos.

HENGEL, Martin
1974a *Judaism and Hellenism,* 2 volumes, Philadelphia, Fortress Press.
1974b *Property and Riches in the Early Church,* Philadelphia, Fortress Press.
HERBERG, Will
1960 *Protestant, Catholic, Jew,* New York, Doubleday.
HERZBERG, Frederick
1966 *Work and the Nature of Man,* New York, Thomas Y. Crowell Company.
HESSELGRAVE, David J.
1978a *Dynamic Religious Movements,* Grand Rapids, Baker Book House.
1978b *Theology and Mission,* Grand Rapids, Baker Book House.
1978c *Communicating Christ Cross-culturally,* Grand Rapids, Zondervan.
HIEBERT, Paul G.
1976 *Cultural Anthropology,* Philadelphia, J. B. Lippincott.
HILE, Pat
1977 "Communicating the Gospel in Terms of Felt Needs," *Missiology,* Vol. 5, No. 4 (October 1977), pp. 499–506.
HILLMAN, Eugene
1975 *Polygamy Reconsidered,* Maryknoll, Orbis Books.
HOCKING, William E.
1932 *Re-thinking Missions,* New York, Harper and Row.
1940 *Living Religions and a World Faith,* New York, Macmillan.
HODGES, Melvin L.
1973 *A Guide to Church Planting,* Chicago, Moody Press.
HOEKENDIJK, J. C.
1950 "A Call to Evangelism," Reprinted in McGavran, *The Conciliar-Evangelical Debate,* William Carey, 1977, pp. 41–55.
HOFFMAN, George
1975 "The Social Responsibilities of Evangelization," (*Let the Earth Hear His Voice,* J. D. Douglas, ed., pp. 698–712) Minneapolis, World Wide Publications.
HOLLAND, Clifton L.
1974 *The Religious Dimension in Hispanic Los Angeles,* Pasadena, William Carey Library.
HORNSTEIN, Harvey A., et al.
1971 *Social Intervention,* New York, The Free Press.

HOWELLS, William
  1948   *The Heathens: Primitive Man and His Religions,* New York, Doubleday.
HUGHES, Charles
  1965   *Goal Setting,* New York, American Management Association.
HWANG, Bernard
  1977   "Ancestor Cult Today," *Missiology,* Vol. 5, No. 3 (July 1977), pp. 339–365.
HYDE, Douglas
  1966   *Dedication and Leadership,* Notre Dame, University of Notre Dame Press.
INTERCRISTO
  1978   *Directory of Christian Work Opportunities,* Seattle, Intercristo (semi-annual).
INTERCHURCH WORLD MOVEMENT OF NORTH AMERICA
  1920   *World Survey, American Volume,* New York, Interchurch Press.
JANIS, Irving and MANN, Leon
  1977   *Decision Making,* New York, Free Press.
JEREMIAS, Joachim
  1969   *Jerusalem in the Time of Jesus,* Philadelphia, Fortress Press.
JUDGE, E. A.
  1960   *The Social Patterns of the Christian Groups in the First Century,* Wheaton, Tyndale.
JUDSON, David J. C.
  1975   "Evangelism Among the Blind, Deaf and Handicapped," (*Let the Earth Hear His Voice,* J. D. Douglas, ed., pp. 776–789) Minneapolis, World Wide Publications.
JUNKER, Buford H.
  1960   *Field Work: An Introduction to the Social Sciences,* Chicago, University of Chicago Press.
KAHN, Herman
  1964   *Thinking About the Unthinkable,* New York, Avon Books.
KAHN, Herman and WIENER, Anthony J.
  1967   *The Year 2000,* New York, Macmillan.
KASDORF, Hans
  1978   "Luther's Bible: A Dynamic Equivalence Translation and Germanizing Force," *Missiology,* Vol. 6, No. 2 (April 1978), pp. 213–234.

KELLEY, Dean M.
1972 *Why Conservative Churches Are Growing,* New York, Harper & Row.
KELLY, David C.
1978 "Cross-cultural Communication and Ethics," *Missiology,* Vol. 6, No. 3 (July 1978), pp. 311–322.
KENNEDY, D. James
1973 *Evangelism Explosion,* Wheaton, Tyndale.
KHAIR-ULLAH, Frank S.
1976 "Linguistic Hang-ups in Communicating with Muslims," *Missiology,* Vol. 4, No. 3 (July 1976), pp. 301–316.
1979 "The Role of Local Churches in God's Redemptive Plan for the Muslim World," (*The Gospel and Islam,* Don McCurry, ed.) Monrovia, MARC.
KIEV, Ari
1973 *A Strategy for Daily Living,* New York, Free Press.
KRAEMER, Hendrik
1938 *The Christian Message in a Non-Christian World,* Grand Rapids, Kregel.
1956 *Religion and the Christian Faith,* Luke House, Farnham Rd., Gilford, Surrey, Lutterworth.
KRAFT, Charles H.
1973 "Dynamic Equivalence Churches," *Missiology,* Vol. 1, No. 1 (January 1973), pp. 39–57.
1976 "Cultural Concomitants of Higi Conversion: Early Period," *Missiology,* Vol. 4, No. 4 (October 1976), pp. 431–442.
1979a *Christianity in Culture,* Maryknoll, Orbis Books.
1979b "Dynamic Equivalent Churches in Muslim Society," (*The Gospel and Culture,* Don McCurry, ed., pp. 114–128) Monrovia, MARC.
KRAFT, Marguerite G.
1978 *Worldview and Communication of the Gospel,* Pasadena, William Carey Library.
KRASS, Alfred C.
1969 "A Case Study in Effective Evangelism," *Church Growth Bulletin,* Donald McGavran, ed., Vols. 1–5, pp. 244–250, Pasadena, William Carey Library.
1974 *Go . . . And Make Disciples,* Naperville, Alex R. Allenson.
1978 *Five Lanterns at Sundown: Evangelism in a Chastened Mood,* Grand Rapids, Wm. B. Eerdmans Publishing Co.

KÜMMEL, Werner G.
 1973   *The Theology of the New Testament*, Nashville, Abingdon.
KÜNG, Hans
 1967   *The Church*, New York, Doubleday (Reprint 1976).
LADD, George E.
 1964   *Jesus and the Kingdom*, Waco, Word.
 1974   *A Theology of the New Testament*, Grand Rapids, Wm. B.
         Eerdmans Publishing Co.
LARSON, Donald N. and SMALLEY, William
 1972   *Becoming Bilingual*, Pasadena, William Carey Library.
LASCH, Christopher
 1979   *The Culture of Narcissism*, New York, W. W. Norton.
LAUBACH, F., et al.
 1975   "Conversion, Penitence, Repentance, Proselyte," (*Dictionary
         of New Testament Theology*, Vol. 1, Colin Brown, ed., pp.
         353–362) Grand Rapids, Zondervan.
LAUSANNE COMMITTEE FOR WORLD EVANGELIZATION
 1978a *The Pasadena Consultation—Homogeneous Units*, Wheaton,
         LCWE.
 1978b *The Willowbank Report—The Gospel and Culture*, Whea-
         ton, LCWE.
LeBAR, Frank M.
 1964   *Ethnic Groups of Mainland Southeast Asia*, Snyder, Human
         Relations Area File.
 1972   *Ethnic Groups of Insular Southeast Asia*, Snyder, Human
         Relations Area File.
LEVINSON, Harry
 1967   *The Exceptional Executive*, Cambridge, Harvard University
         Press.
LEWIN, Kurt
 1935   *Dynamic Theory of Personality*, New York, McGraw.
LEWIS, C. S.
 1947   *The Abolition of Man*, New York, Macmillan (Reprint
         1962).
LIAO, David
 1972   *The Unresponsive: Resistant or Neglected?*, Chicago, Moody
         Press.
LIEFIELD, Walter L.
 1978   "Theology of Church Growth," (*Theology and Mission*,
         David J. Hesselgrave, ed., pp. 173–187) Grand Rapids, Baker
         Book House.

LOEWEN, Jacob A.

1975 *Culture and Human Values: Christian Intervention in Anthropological Perspective,* Pasadena, William Carey Library.

1976a "Roles: Relating to an Alien Social Structure," *Missiology,* Vol. 4, No. 2 (April 1976), pp. 217–242.

1976b "Mission Churches, Independent Churches, and Felt Needs in Africa," *Missiology,* Vol. 4, No. 4 (October 1976), pp. 405, 425.

LOFLAND, John

1977 *Doomsday Cult,* Enlarged Edition, New York, Irvington Publications.

LONG, Norman

1977 *An Introduction to the Sociology of Rural Development,* Boulder, Westview Press.

LUZBETAK, Louis J.

1963 *The Church and Cultures,* William Carey Library, Pasadena, Divine Word Publications.

MAGER, Robert F.

1972 *Goal Analysis,* Belmont, Lear Siegler, Inc./Fearon Publishers.

MALHERBE, Abraham J.

1977 *Social Aspects of Early Christianity,* Baton Rouge, Louisiana State University Press.

MALINOWSKI, Bronislaw

1954 *Magic, Science, and Religion,* New York, Doubleday.

MALONEY, Clarence

1974 *The Peoples of South Asia,* New York, Holt, Rinehart and Winston.

MANDELBAUM, David G.

1970 *Society in India,* 2 volumes, Berkeley, University of California Press.

MARC (Missions Advanced Research and Communication Center)

1978 *To Reach the Unreached,* Monrovia, MARC.

1979a *World Christianity: Middle East,* Monrovia, MARC.

1979b *World Christianity: East Asia,* Monrovia, MARC.

1979c *You Can So Get There from Here,* Monrovia, MARC.

1980 *World Christianity: Southern Asia,* Monrovia, MARC.

MASLOW, Abraham

1970 *Motivation and Personality,* Second Edition, New York, Harper & Row.

MAURER, Christian

1974 "*phulē,*" (*Theological Dictionary of the New Testament,* G.

Friedrich, ed., Vol. 9, pp. 245–250) Grand Rapids, Wm. B. Eerdmans Publishing Co.

MAY, Rollo
1975   *The Courage to Create,* New York, Bantam.

MAYBERRY-LEWIS, David
1968   *The Savage and the Innocent,* Scranton, Beacon Press.

MAYERS, Marvin K.
1974   *Christianity Confronts Culture,* Grand Rapids, Zondervan.

McCULLOUGH, W. S.
1962   "Fish," (*Interpreter's Dictionary of the Bible,* George Buttrick, ed., Vol. 2, pp. 272–273) Nashville, Abingdon.

McCURRY, Don
1974   *The Gospel and Islam,* Monrovia, MARC.

McFARLAND, H. Neil
1967   *The Rush Hour of the Gods,* New York, Macmillan.

McGAVRAN, Donald
1955   *Bridges of God,* New York, Friendship Press.
1959   *How Churches Grow,* New York, Friendship Press.
1970   *Understanding Church Growth,* Grand Rapids, Wm. B. Eerdmans Publishing Co.
1974   *The Clash Between Christianity and Cultures,* Grand Rapids, Baker Book House.
1979   *Ethnic Realities and the Church,* Pasadena, William Carey Library.

McGAVRAN, Donald and ARN, Win
1973   *How to Grow a Church,* Glendale, Regal.

McGAVRAN, Donald, ed.
1977   *The Conciliar-Evangelical Debate: The Crucial Documents 1964–1976,* Pasadena, William Carey Library.

McLOUGHLIN, William
1959   *Modern Revivalism,* New York, Ronald Press.

McNEE, Peter
1976   *Crucial Issues in Bangladesh,* Pasadena, William Carey Library.

MEADOWS, D. H. and MEADOWS, D. L.
1974   *Limits to Growth,* New York, Universe.

MELLIS, Charles J.
1977   *Committed Communities,* Pasadena, William Carey Library.

MEYER, Donald
1965   *The Positive Thinkers,* New York, Doubleday.

MEYER, Rudolf
1967 "*ochlos,*" (*Theological Dictionary of the New Testament,* G. Friedrich, ed., Vol. 5, pp. 582–590) Grand Rapids, Wm. B. Eerdmans Publishing Co.
MILLER, Donald G.
1957 *The Nature and Mission of the Church,* Atlanta, John Knox Press.
MINEAR, Paul
1960 *Images of the Church in the New Testament,* Philadelphia, Westminster.
1977 "The Vocation of the Church: Some Exegetical Clues,"*Missiology,* Vol. 5, No. 1 (January 1977), pp. 13–37.
MISSIONARY RESEARCH LIBRARY
1960 *Occasional Bulletin*
MOBLEY, Harris
1970 *The Ghanaians' Image of a Missionary,* Long Island City, E. J. Brill.
MOUNCE, Robert H.
1960 "Gospel," (*Baker's Dictionary of Theology,* Everett F. Harrison, ed., pp. 254–257) Grand Rapids, Baker Book House.
MURDOCK, George P.
1959 *Africa,* New York, McGraw-Hill.
MURDOCK, George P., et al.
1971 *Outline of Cultural Materials,* Fourth Revision, Fort Meyers, Florida, Human Relations Area File.
MURPHREE, Marshall
1969 *Christianity and the Shona,* Atlantic Highlands, Humanities Press.
MURPHY, Edward F.
1975 *Spiritual Gifts and the Great Commission,* Pasadena, William Carey Library.
NEILL, Stephen
1964 *A History of Christian Missions,* New York, Penguin Books.
NELSON, Marlin L.
1976a *The How and Why of Third World Missions,* Pasadena, William Carey Library.
1976b *Readings in Third World Missions,* Pasadena, William Carey Library.
NEVIUS, John
1958 *Planting and Development of Missionary Churches,* Phil-

lipsburg, Presbyterian and Reformed Publishing.
NEWBIGIN, Lesslie
1978   *The Open Secret: Sketches for a Missionary Theology,* Grand
Rapids, Wm. B. Eerdmans Publishing Co.
NIDA, Eugene A.
1957   *Learning a Foreign Language,* New York, Friendship Press.
1960   *Message and Mission,* Pasadena, William Carey Library.
1964   *Toward a Science of Translating,* Long Island City, E. J. Brill.
1979a   "Why Are Foreigners So Queer? A Socio-Anthropological
Approach to Cultural Pluralism," paper presented to the
American Society of Missiology, June 16, 1979.
1979b   "The Other Message," *Occasional Bulletin,* Vol. 3, No. 3
(July 1979), pp. 110–112.
NIDA, Eugene A. and TABER, Charles
1974   *The Theory and Practice of Translation,* Long Island City,
E. J. Brill.
NOCK, Arthur D.
1964   *Early Gentile Christianity,* New York, Harper & Row.
O'CONNOR, Elizabeth
1968   *Journey Inward, Journey Outward,* New York, Harper &
Row.
O'DEA, Thomas F.
1957   *The Mormons,* Chicago, University of Chicago Press.
ORTLUND, Raymond C.
1974   *Lord, Make My Life a Miracle,* Glendale, Regal.
PACKARD, Vance
1957   *The Hidden Persuaders,* New York, David MacKay Co.
PADILLA, C. René
1976   *The New Face of Evangelicalism,* Downers Grove, InterVarsity.
PALMER, Donald C.
1974   *Explosion of People Evangelism,* Chicago, Moody Press.
PARSHALL, Phil
1979   "Evangelizing Muslims: Are There Ways?" *Christianity Today,* Vol. 23, No. 7 (January 5, 1979), pp. 28–29, 31.
PAUL VI, Pope
1976   *On Evangelization in the Modern World,* Washington, D.C.,
United States Catholic Conference.
PETERS, George
1970   *Saturation Evangelism,* Grand Rapids, Zondervan.
1972   *A Biblical Theology of Missions,* Chicago, Moody Press.

1975 "Contemporary Practices of Evangelism," (*Let the Earth Hear His Voice*, J. D. Douglas, ed., pp. 199-207) Minneapolis, World Wide Publications.

PICKETT, J. W.
1933 *Christian Mass Movements in India*, Lucknow Publishing House.

PICKETT, J. W., et al.
1973 *Church Growth and Group Conversion*, Fifth Edition, Pasadena, William Carey Library.

PONSI, Frank
1978 "Contemporary Concepts of Missions," *Missiology*, Vol. 6, No. 2 (April 1978), pp. 134-153.

POWDERMAKER, Hortense
1967 *Stranger and Friend: The Way of an Anthropologist*, New York, Norton.

PRICE, Frank and ORR, Clara E.
1960 *Occasional Bulletin*, November 23, 1960, New York, Missionary Research Library.

QUEBEDEAUX, Richard
1978 *The Worldly Evangelicals*, New York, Harper & Row.

RABINOW, Paul
1977 *Reflections on Fieldwork in Morocco*, Berkeley, University of California Press.

RANDALL, Max W.
1970 *Profile for Victory: New Proposals for Missions in Zambia*, Pasadena, William Carey Library.

READ, William
1965 *New Patterns of Church Growth in Brazil*, Grand Rapids, Wm. B. Eerdmans Publishing Co.

READ, William and INESON, Frank
1973 *Brazil 1980*, Monrovia, MARC.

READ, William R., MONTERROSO, V. M., and JOHNSON, H. A.
1969 *Latin American Church Growth*, Grand Rapids, Wm. B. Eerdmans Publishing Co.

RICHARDSON, Don
1974 *Peace Child*, Glendale, Regal.

RIDDERBOS, Herman
1975 *Paul: An Outline of His Theology*, Grand Rapids, Wm. B. Eerdmans Publishing Co.

ROBERTS, W. Dayton
1967 *Revolution in Evangelism*, Chicago, Moody.

514   *Bibliography*

1971   *Strachan of Costa Rica,* Grand Rapids, Wm. B. Eerdmans Publishing Co.

ROGERS, Everett M.

1962   *Diffusion of Innovation,* New York, The Free Press.

ROGERS, Everett M. and SHOEMAKER, F. Floyd

1971   *Communication of Innovations: A Cross-cultural Approach,* New York, Free Press.

ROSTOVTZEFF, M.

1957   *The Social and Economic History of the Roman Empire,* Second Edition, Revised by P. M. Fraser, 2 volumes, London, Oxford.

ROYAL ANTHROPOLOGICAL INSTITUTE

1951   *Notes and Queries on Anthropology,* 1971 Reprint, Boston, Routledge & Kegan.

SAFRAI, S. and STERN, M.

1974   *The Jewish People in the First Century,* Vol. 1, Philadelphia, Fortress.

1976   *The Jewish People in the First Century,* Vol. 2, Philadelphia, Fortress.

SCHAEFFER, Francis

1970   *The Church at the End of the 20th Century,* Downers Grove, InterVarsity.

SCHALLER, Lyle

1972   *The Change Agent,* Nashville, Abingdon.

SCHLETTE, H. R.

1963   *Toward a Theology of Religions,* New York, Herder.

SCHMIDT, KARL L.

1964a   *"diaspora," (Theological Dictionary of the New Testament,* G. Kittel, ed., Vol. 2, pp. 98–104) Grand Rapids, Wm. B. Eerdmans Publishing Co.

1964b   *"ethnos, ethnikos," (Theological Dictionary of the New Testament,* G. Kittel, ed., Vol. 2, pp. 364–372) Grand Rapids, Wm. B. Eerdmans Publishing Co.

SCHNEIDER, Louis and DORNBUSCH, Sanford

1958   *Popular Religion: Inspirational Books in America,* Chicago, University of Chicago.

SCHRENK, Gottlob

1967   *"patria," (Theological Dictionary of the New Testament,* G. Friedrich, ed., Vol. 5, pp. 1015–1022) Grand Rapids, Wm. B. Eerdmans Publishing Co.

SCHURER, Emil
1973 *The History of the Jewish People in the Age of Jesus Christ,* Revised and Edited by G. Vermes and F. Millar, Vol. 1, Naperville, Allenson.

SCHWARTZBERG, G.
1977 *Atlas of India,* Chicago, University of Chicago.

SEATON, Ronald and SEATON, Edith
1976 *Here's How: Health Education by Extension,* Pasadena, William Carey Library.

SHENK, Wilbert R., ed.
1973 *The Challenge of Church Growth,* Scottdale, Herald Press.

SHERWIN-WHITE, A. N.
1963 *Roman Society and Roman Law in the New Testament,* London, Oxford.

SHEWMAKER, Stan
1970 *Tonga Christianity,* Pasadena, William Carey Library.

SIDER, Ronald J.
1977 *Rich Christians in an Age of Hunger,* Downers Grove, Inter-Varsity.

SINGLETON, John
1967 *Nichu: A Japanese School,* New York, Holt, Rinehart and Winston.

SKIVINGTON, Bob
1978 *Mission to Mindanao,* Box 1594, Manila, Conservative Baptist Publications; also available through Church Growth Book Club, Pasadena, California.

SMALLEY, William
1967 *Readings in Missionary Anthropology,* Practical Anthropology, New Canaan, Connecticut.
1979 *Readings in Missionary Anthropology II,* Pasadena, William Carey Library.

SMELSER, Neil J.
1962 *Theory of Collective Behavior,* New York, Free Press.

SMITH, James
1976 *Without Crossing Barriers,* Pasadena, Fuller Theological Seminary, School of World Mission, unpublished thesis.

SMITH, W. Douglas, Jr.
1978 *Toward Continuous Mission,* Pasadena, William Carey Library.

SNYDER, Howard
  1975   *The Problem of Wineskins: Church Structure in a Technological Society,* Downers Grove, InterVarsity.
  1977   *Community of the King,* Downers Grove, InterVarsity.
SØGAARD, Viggo
  1975   *Everything You Need to Know for a Cassette Ministry,* Minneapolis, Bethany Fellowship Press.
SOPER, Edmund D.
  1943   *The Philosophy of the Christian World Mission,* Nashville, Abingdon-Cokesbury.
SPINDLER, George D.
  1970   *Being an Anthropologist: Fieldwork in Eleven Cultures,* New York, Holt, Rinehart and Winston.
STENNING, D. J.
  1964   "Salvation in Ankole," (*African Systems of Thought,* M. Fortes, et al., eds.) London, Oxford.
STEWART, James C.
  1971   *American Cultural Patterns: A Cross-Cultural Perspective,* Intercultural Network, Inc., 906 N. Spring Ave., La Grange Park, Illinois 60525.
STOESZ, Edgar
  1972   *Beyond Good Intentions,* Newton, United Printing, Inc.
STOTT, John R. W.
  1967   *Basic Introduction to the New Testament,* Grand Rapids, Wm. B. Eerdmans Publishing Co.
  1975   "The Biblical Basis of Evangelism," (*Let the Earth Hear His Voice,* J. D. Douglas, ed., pp. 65–78) Minneapolis, World Wide Publications.
  1976   *Christian Mission in the Modern World,* Downers Grove, InterVarsity.
STRATHMANN, H.
  1967   "*laos,*" (*Theological Dictionary of the New Testament,* G. Kittel, ed., Vol. 4, pp. 29–57) Grand Rapids, Wm. B. Eerdmans Publishing Co.
SUBBAMMA, B. V.
  1970   *New Patterns for Discipling Hindus,* Pasadena, William Carey Library.
SUNDKLER, Bengt
  1961   *Bantu Prophets,* Second Edition, London, Oxford Press.
  1965   *The World of Mission,* Luke House, Farnham Rd., Gilford, Surrey, Lutterworth Press.

SWANK, Gerald O.
1977 *Frontier Peoples of Central Nigeria and a Strategy for Outreach,* Pasadena, William Carey Library.
SWANSON, Allen J.
1971 *Taiwan: Mainline vs. Independent Church Growth,* Pasadena, William Carey Library.
TABER, Charles
1973 "Evangelizing the Unreached Peoples," (*Gospel and Frontier Peoples,* R. Pierce Beaver, ed., pp. 118-135) Pasadena, William Carey Library.
1978 "The Limits of Indigenization in Theology," *Missiology,* Vol. 6, No. 1 (January 1978), pp. 53-79.
1979 "Contextualization: Indigenization and/or Transformation," (*The Gospel and Islam,* Don McCurry, ed., pp. 143-154) Monrovia, MARC.
THEISSEN, G.
1977 *Sociology of Early Palestinian Christianity,* Philadelphia, Fortress.
THOMAS, Winburn T.
1959 *Protestant Beginnings in Japan,* Rutland, Charles E. Tuttle.
TILLICH, Paul
1963 *Christianity and the Encounter of the World Religions,* New York Columbia University Press.
TIPPETT, Alan
1967 *Verdict Theology,* Lincoln Christian College.
1971 *People Movements in Southern Polynesia,* Chicago, Moody Press.
1977 "Conversion as a Dynamic Process in Christian Mission," *Missiology,* Vol. 5, No. 2 (April 1977), pp. 203-221.
TOCH, Hans
1965 *The Social Psychology of Social Movements,* Indianapolis, Bobbs-Merrill.
TOFFLER, Alvin
1970 *Future Shock,* New York, Random House.
TRIANDIS, Harry C.
1971 *Attitude and Attitude Change,* New York, John Wiley & Sons.
TRUEBLOOD, Elton
1961 *The Company of the Committed,* New York, Harper & Row.
TUGGY, A. L.
1974 "Philippine Inglestani CHRISTI," Pasadena, Fuller Theologi-

cal Seminary, unpublished thesis.

TUGGY, A. L. and TOLIVER, R.
1972   *Seeing the Church in the Philippines,* Robesenia, Pennsylvania, O.M.F.

TURNER, Harold W.
1967   *African Independent Church,* 2 volumes, London, Oxford Press.

VANDER WERFF, Lyle L.
1977   *Christian Mission to Muslims,* Pasadena, William Carey Library.

VERKUYL, Johannes
1978   *Contemporary Missiology,* Grand Rapids, Wm. B. Eerdmans Publishing Co.

VICEDOM, George
1965   *The Mission of God,* St. Louis, Concordia.

VOELKEL, Janvier
1971   *The Eternal Revolutionary: Evangelical Ministry to the University Student in Latin America,* Fuller Theological Seminary, School of World Mission, Pasadena, unpublished thesis.

VOGEL, Ezra
1963   *Japan's New Middle Class,* Berkeley, University of California Press.

VOGT, Evon
1969   *Handbook of Middle American Indians: Ethnology,* Vols. 7 and 8, Austin, University of Texas Press.

WAGNER, C. Peter
1971   *Frontiers in Missionary Strategy,* Chicago, Moody Press.
1973   *Stop the World, I Want to Get On,* Glendale, Regal
1978   *Our Kind of People,* Atlanta, John Knox Press.
1979   *Your Spiritual Gifts Can Help Your Church Grow,* Glendale, Regal.

WAGNER, C. Peter and DAYTON, Edward R.
1978   *Unreached Peoples '79,* Elgin, David C. Cook.
1979   *Unreached Peoples '80,* Elgin, David C. Cook.

WARREN, Max
1971   *To Apply the Gospel: Selections from the Writings of Henry Venn,* Grand Rapids, Wm. B. Eerdmans Publishing Co.

WATSON, David
1976   *I Believe in Evangelism,* Grand Rapids, Wm. B. Eerdmans Publishing Co.

WAX, Rosalie H.
1971 *Doing Fieldwork: Warnings & Advice,* Chicago, University of Chicago.
WEBBER, Robert
1978 *Common Roots,* Grand Rapids, Zondervan.
WEBER, Max
1968 *Economy and Society,* 3 volumes, Berkeley, University of California.
WEEKES, Richard
1978 *Muslim Peoples,* Westport, Greenwood Press.
WHEELER, Alwyne
1975 *Fishes of the World,* New York, Macmillan.
WHITE, Hugh V.
1937 *A Theology for Christian Mission,* Willett, Clark and Company.
WILLEMS, Emilio
1967 *Followers of the New Faith,* Nashville, Vanderbilt University Press.
WILLIAMS, Thomas R.
1967 *Field Methods in the Study of Culture,* New York, Holt, Rinehart and Winston.
WILLIAMSON, John, et al.
1977 *The Research Craft,* New York, Little, Brown and Co.
WILSON, Samuel, ed.
1980 *Mission Handbook: North American Protestant Ministries Overseas,* 12th Edition, Monrovia, MARC.
WINTER, Ralph D.
1978 *The Unfinished Task,* Pasadena, William Carey Library.
WONDERLY, William
1968 *Bible Translations for Popular Use,* New York, American Bible Society.
WONG, James, et al.
1973 *Missions From the Third World,* Singapore, Church Growth Study Centre.
YAKER, Henri, et al.
1971 *The Future of Time,* Garden City, Anchor Books, Doubleday.
YAMAMORI, Tetsunao
1974 *Church Growth in Japan,* Pasadena, William Carey Library.
1977 "Toward the Symbiotic Ministry: God's Mandate for the Church Today," *Missiology,* Vol. 5, No. 3 (July 1977), pp. 265–274.

YAMAMORI, Tetsunao and TABER, Charles
1975   *Christopaganism or Indigenous Christianity?*, Pasadena, William Carey Library.

GENERAL INDEX

521

INDEX TO BIBLE QUOTATIONS